D0918870

JUNGIAN
LITERARY
CRITICISM,
1920-1980:

AN ANNOTATED, CRITICAL
BIBLIOGRAPHY OF WORKS IN ENGLISH
(WITH A SELECTION OF
TITLES AFTER 1980)

by

JOS VAN MEURS
with
JOHN KIDD

The Scarecrow Press, Inc.
Metuchen, N.J., & London
1988

PN
98
.P75
M48
1988

Library of Congress Cataloging-in-Publication Data

Meurs, Jos van, 1925–
    Jungian literary criticism, 1920–1980.

    Bibliography: p.
    Includes index.
    1. Psychology and literature--Bibliography.
2. Psychoanalysis and literature--Bibliography.
3. Jung, C. G. (Carl Gustav), 1875–1961--Criticism
and interpretation--Bibliography. 4. Criticism--
20th century--Bibliography. I. Kidd, John (John Edward)
II. Title.
Z6514.P78M48 1988 [PN98.P75] 016.82'09'353 88-18276
ISBN 0-8108-2160-5

For NETTIE

for everything

To create a little flower is the labour of ages.

William Blake,
The Marriage of Heaven and Hell.

I promise nothing complete; because any human thing
supposed to be complete must for that very reason
infallibly be faulty.

Herman Melville, *Moby-Dick.*

ACKNOWLEDGMENTS

First of all I wish to thank Nettie, my wife, for her unfailing support and partnership in the ups and downs of the many years of Jungian labor; for sharing the excitements of book-searching in dusty stacks as well as the dull work of endless xeroxing; and for mastering the personal computer and remaining cheerfully critical while doing all the typing and correcting.

The material for this bibliography could never have been collected without the efficiency of the American library system and the well-furnished open stacks of the university libraries in which I was fortunate enough to be able to do most of the research during our several visits to the United States. I gratefully remember the ready assistance given by the staff of the reference rooms in McHenry Library of the University of California at Santa Cruz and of Alderman Library at the University of Virginia, Charlottesville. Special thanks for answering queries must go to Jane Greenspan of the Public Library of New York, to Doris Albrecht, the librarian of the C.G. Jung Institute of New York, and to bibliographer Wanda Wawro of Cornell University. In Switzerland the stacks of the C.G. Jung Institute at Küsnacht were explored and in England the libraries of London University and Cambridge University, while John Costello let me inspect the collection of the Analytical Psychology Club of London.

John Kidd's cooperation and his share in the reseach for this book are acknowledged in the introduction. My wife and I value the friendship and help he gave us during our stays in America.

By undertaking to write a number of annotations, Karen Shostak gave practical support at a time when it was much needed, which makes me especially grateful for her contribution to this book.

At my home university in Groningen I profited much from the ever friendly encouragement of Professors David Wilkinson and Walter Schönau, and from their painstaking critical scrutiny of all I wrote. My colleagues in the English department kindly shared in the work by taking over my teaching duties during the sabbatical leave I spent as a visiting scholar at the University of Virginia. The Dutch Jung Society was revived at an opportune moment in 1983 for me to establish valuable contacts and be stimulated by discussions with friends in study groups and at conferences.

And lastly, this book would never have reached its final printed form without the time, expertise and patience generously bestowed upon our typing efforts by Marc Dupuis of the computer department in the Groningen Faculty of Letters.

An earlier version of the "Survey of Jungian Literary Criticism in English" was read as a paper at the Hofstra University Jung Conference in November 1986 and will appear in the volume *C.G. Jung and the Humanities: Towards a Hermeneutics of Culture*, to be published in 1989 by Princeton University Press.

J.C.v.M.
Groningen, April 1988.

CONTENTS

ABBREVIATIONS

q.v., qq.v.   see entry in bibliography

*   a star before an author's name in the bibliography indicates good or excellent criticism

DAI   *Dissertation Abstracts International*

ELH   *ELH: Journal of English Literary History*

PMLA   *Publications of the Modern Language Association of America*

INTRODUCTION

Aims and scope.

This book aims at offering a complete bibliography of all secondary works (books and articles, critical and scholarly), written in English, that apply the psychology of C.G. Jung to the interpretation of literary texts, written in English. The first Jungian literary criticism appears around 1920. The inventory is as complete as I could make it for the period 1920 through 1980. For the years after 1980 the search could no longer be exhaustive, but it seemed unreasonable not to include the material already found, especially as regards books, and therefore a selection of titles published since 1980 has been included, with brief annotations.

The bibliography is restricted to literary texts and criticism in English, partly because these are my own subjects of study, partly because by far the greater part of Jungian literary criticism has been done in this field, and for the obvious reason that it would have needed a team of scholars to cover other languages for an annotated bibliography. To illustrate the kind of limitation this implies, I have inconsistently included Aniela Jaffé's classics of Jungian interpretation of German texts by E.T.A. Hoffmann and Hermann Broch, of which the latter essay was translated into English.

As regards literary texts I have drawn the line at fairy tales, but have included an article by Karen Rowe on "Feminism and Fairy Tales" (1979) that provides an excellent bibliography of Jungian publications on fairy tales. Interpretations of Bible stories have not been included either, though it is a field in which a good deal of Jungian work has been done.

The criterion for inclusion has been that the critic should have made substantial use of notions directly derived from Jung's psychology, or of Jungian ideas as developed by Jung's disciples Erich Neumann, Joseph Campbell, and James Hillman. Not included are specimens of archetypal or myth criticism of a more general kind, nor studies based on Northrop Frye's theories about literary archetypes (see the section on Frye in my survey, and the entries on Frye and Wheelwright in the bibliography).

For Freudian literary criticism there exist various surveys (see Hoffman, Morrison), introductions (see Kaplan, Mollinger), and bibliographies (see Kiell, Natoli). Jungian literary criticism has so far been only very incompletely covered in some bibliographies of larger fields (see Duncan, Kiell, Natoli, Vincie), and there has been no attempt at a survey. Judging from what was published before 1970 a complete inventory of the field of specific Jungian literary criticism seemed a fairly limited job, and in 1979 an annotated and criticial bibliography was projected. When it was gradually discovered how much had been published in the United States and Canada during the 1970s, and how many Jungian dissertations had been written in the later seventies, the bibliography turned into a much larger undertaking than was foreseen.

Research and collaboration.

The most obvious place to start the library research seemed the Kristine Mann Library of the C.G. Jung Institute in New York, one of the largest collections of Jungian books in the world. When in the fall of 1979 I wrote to the librarian, Doris Albrecht, she replied that by a happy synchronicity that same week she had received a similar request from a young American scholar, John Kidd, of the University of California at Santa Cruz. Our joint interests made us decide to pool our findings and work together on a comprehensive bibliography.

John Kidd and I met in Zurich during 1980 when he was a Rotary International Fellow at the C.G. Jung Institute. We collaborated in my library research in California in the summer of 1981 and during my sabbatical semester in 1985 at the University of Virginia, where he is on the Faculty. His cooperation was most important for me in the early years of library research, and the first 250 annotations I wrote greatly profited from his critical comments and expert editing. Within the period of work on this book he developed into a James Joyce expert. The research on his edition of *Ulysses* took up progressively more of his attention and energy. As a result his part became severely restricted. Still, he gathered many entries in this book and forwarded from America scores of photocopied articles unavailable in the Netherlands. The writing of this book has been my work. In the final stages another American, Karen Shostak, then studying in the Department of English at the University of Groningen, gave welcome assistance by summarizing sixty articles. All annotations written by Karen Shostak and the dozen by John Kidd have been initialed.

Format of bibliographical entries.

Except for a very few titles we could not get hold of, all critical texts before 1981 were read and annotated. All items are provided with brief summaries of contents that indicate the Jungian aspects. If no critical assessment is given, the book or article was considered average competent Jungian criticism. But critical evaluations have been appended to what appeared to me particularly perceptive or particularly inept Jungian criticism. Stars (*) precede the names of authors who have written outstanding Jungian books or articles. In short pieces my appraisal is often given by means of a discriminating adjective at the beginning; in longer annotations the assessment is set out, briefly reasoned, in one or two separate paragraphs at the end. As a rule, but not always, the length of the annotation corresponds to the importance of the Jungian book or article.

As a matter of principle the critic's own words and key phrases have frequently been cited in order to give an impression of his or her style and argumentation. Always in my annotations I have aimed at liveliness and readability in the hope of encouraging the reader to browse and explore.

Literary dissertations that make substantial use of Jungian theories have been included without summaries, since the authors' abstracts are available in *Dissertation Abstracts International*. For easy reference the details about volume and page number given in the *Comprehensive Dissertation Index* have been added so that the abstracts may be directly looked up in the volumes of *DAI*.

Critical standards.

This bibliography is not only designed as a complete inventory of its field, but through its critical annotations also attempts to be a guide to what over the years has been achieved in Jungian literary criticism. Working my way through so many Jungian interpretations, I have naturally felt the need to discriminate. By starring what I consider excellent Jungian interpretations I hope to have made a useful pre-selection for the interested reader.

In the body of each annotation the main argument and the Jungian aspects of any literary interpretation are abstracted as objectively as possible. I am aware that even a brief summary may in its wording already betray a subjective slant, and that explicit judgment in literary and psychological matters is by definition subjective. Since I do not want to preclude critical debate, it is only fair that I attempt to indicate briefly my critical assumptions so that the reader may know what to expect and how to judge my judgments.

My first criterion is the depth and breadth of the critic's reading and understanding of Jung. Though I am not a psychologist, ten years of intensive reading of Jung's works and of Jungian literary criticism have given me the confidence to praise and to find fault.

Secondly, I presume to judge the quality of the critic's application of Jungian psychology to the literary text and the measure of literary elucidation resulting from the interpretation. Is it little more than an attaching of archetypal labels to texts, or is the Jungian parallel used to shed light on themes and symbols, the motivations of characters and author, or on the whole structure of meanings in a text?

This involves, thirdly, my estimate of the critic's sensitiveness to the complexity of the literary work. Any psychological interpretation worth its salt as literary criticism, even if it is intent on bringing out only one aspect of a literary text, must be alive to the density and the multileveled unity of the work of art as a whole.

Lastly, as a teacher of literature, my critical position is a practical literary one. Psychological theory should assist the literary reading of a text's human contents. Jungian notions are useful as analogues. The archetypes, the individuation process or dream theory should never be imposed upon the text, which must in the first place be grasped in its intricate literary coherence of content and form. I am less interested in literary theories than in adequate practical criticism, adequacy being measured against my own sense of the "felt life" evoked in the text, its expression of "vivid truths about human nature and emotion."[1] My critical views have been particularly influenced by the later New Criticism of, for instance, Brooks and Warren. If my point of view must be classified theoretically, I suppose it belongs in the hermeneutical corner. The New-Critical emphasis on the autonomy of the text was too extreme a reaction against the biographical-historical school, but we may accept its restatement of Coleridge's view that the literary work of art is an organic unity of structure and meaning organized through words, images and symbols around one or more central themes. Though there is never "one right interpretation," I believe that sensitive and intelligent readers (that is, Samuel Johnson's "common readers") may arrive with a degree of completeness at the "most probable meaning" of a literary text, if they let themselves be guided by the view that "a text brings with it the hermeneutics by which it can be interpreted."[2]

If some of my critiques of what I consider poor Jungian studies seem rather severe, I hope the purpose of this book warrants the outspokenness. The inventory of so much Jungian literary criticism written over the past sixty-odd years shows clearly that, if sensitively, flexibly and cautiously used, Jungian psychological theory may stimulate illuminating literary interpretations. On the other hand, precisely because great literature is in large measure the result of an author's individual, often very subtle, intuitive psychological insights, the unsubtle and rigid application of preconceived psychological notions and schemes will result in particularly ill-judged or distorted readings of literary texts.

To maintain a measure of critical balance, a number of forthright general critiques of the Jungian approach have also been included (see Burke, Crews, D.W. Harding, Hoffman, Kaplan).

For representative samples of my own critical practice I refer the reader to my evaluations of studies of major writers: for instance, the books on Melville by Baird, Edinger, Murray, and Pops; on Shakespeare by Aronson, Goddard, Kirsch, Maitra, Scott, and Vyvyan; on Blake by Digby, Gallant, and Singer; or the books on T.S. Eliot by Drew, and on Emily Dickinson by Ward.

It is hoped that my criticisms throughout will at least be found to be consistent, and, what is more, that the undertaking may be of value to students of literature, Jung scholars, and all interested readers.

Bibliographical sources.

The principal bibliographical sources used are listed below:

Vincie, Joseph F. and M. Rathbauer-Vincie. *C.G. Jung and Analytical Psychology: A Comprehensive Bibliography*. New York: Garland, 1977. Has a limited number of items relevant to literature and psychology, because only psychological journals were covered.

Catalog of the Kristine Mann Library of the Analytical Psychology Club of New York. 2 vols. Boston, Mass.: G.K. Hall, 1978. Contains much early material, but is an unsystematic collection.

Kiell, Norman, ed. *Psychoanalysis, Psychology, and Literature: A Bibliography*. 2 vols. Second edition. Metuchen, N.J.: Scarecrow Press, 1982. The standard bibliography with about 20.000 unannotated entries. Wide coverage with Freudian emphasis. The Jungian entries are incomplete. In my bibliography there are 766 titles dated before 1980 (Kiell's final year), of which 315 are in Kiell.

Duncan, Joseph E. (q.v.) "Archetypal Criticism in English, 1946-1980." *Bulletin of Bibliography* 40:4 (1983) 206-230. Contains 329 titles, of which 146 also occur in my bibliography. The other titles are not specifically Jungian, but generally archetypal or mythical.

Natoli, Joseph and Frederick L. Rusch. (q.v.) *Psychocriticism: An Annotated Bibliography*. Westport, Conn.: Greenwood Press, 1984. Gives very brief indications of the contents of articles and books dealing with the "literature and psychology relation" in the period 1969-1982. Covers all schools of psychology. Of the 1435 entries 121 Jungian titles deal with literature in English.

Morrison, Claudia. (q.v.) *Freud and the Critic: The Early Use of Depth Psychology*. Chapel Hill: University of North Carolina Press, 1968. Also covers Jungian criticism till 1927.

Holland, Norman. (q.v.) *Psychoanalysis and Shakespeare*. New York: McGraw-Hill, 1966.

Wilbern, David. "A Bibliography of Psychoanalytic and Psychological Writings on Shakespeare: 1964-1978." In *Representing Shakespeare: New Psychoanalytic Essays*. Eds. Murray M. Schwartz and Coppélia Kahn. Baltimore: Johns Hopkins University Press, 1980. 264-288. Continues where Norman Holland left off. Indexes Jung.

Abstracts of English Studies. The yearly volumes of this series index Jung since 1963.

American Literary Scholarship. Yearly volumes index Jung since 1966.

Arts and Humanities Citation Index. Checked for the years 1976 through 1980. Causes a lot of unproductive work, for many of the articles listed under Jung cite him only in passing.

MLA International Bibliography. Jung in the index since 1981.

The Year's Work in English Studies. Yearly volumes index Jung since 1966.

Comprehensive Dissertation Index. Indexes Jung and various archetypal keywords, and refers to authors' abstracts in *Dissertation Abstracts International*.

Further important sources have been the standard bibliographies of individual authors if they index Jung, and especially the many written communications from scholars in America, Canada and Australia in reply to my requests for further infomation about their publications.

Comprehensiveness and further research.

In a bibliographical venture of this scope completeness is the ideal, and at the same time only a devout wish. It is hoped that we have cast our nets sufficiently wide for only a few Jungian fish that swam out before 1980 to have escaped us. All the same it will be appreciated if scholars report any omissions to the author at the English Department, Faculty of Letters, University of Groningen, The Netherlands. Please give full bibliographical details. Information about books and articles after 1980 that make substantial use of Jung will also be welcome. Perhaps at some future date it will be possible to publish a supplement to this bibliography.

The selective entries for the years 1981 through 1987 cover all the Jungian books and some important articles indexed in *American Literary Scholarship* (checked through 1984), *The Year's Work in English Studies* (through 1985), *Abstracts of English Studies* (through 1986), *MLA International Bibliography* (through 1985), and *Dissertation Abstracts International* (through 1987).

To my knowledge there are few books in English on the theory of literature, or on psychology and literature, that deal at any length with the Jungian approach. Attempts by the literary scholars Bettina Knapp (1984) and Clifton Snider (1984) (qq.v.) to write general introductions to Jungian literary criticism have not been successful. The most useful brief treatments are Willeford's article (q.v.) on Jung for the *Encyclopedia of World Literature in the 20th Century* (1975), Natoli's survey (q.v.) of "Archetypal and Psychological Criticism" in *Magill's Critical Survey of Poetry* (1982), and Radford and Wilson's 1982 essay "Some Phases of the Jungian Moon: Jung's Influence on Modern Literature" (q.v.). No doubt the very best introduction to Jungian criticism will be the reading of some of the fine books and articles singled out in this bibliography.

Finally, I hope that this bibliography will enable the interested reader to discover how much imaginative and illuminating work has been done in the field of Jungian literary criticism.

Notes:
1. E. D. Hirsch, Jr., *The Aims of Interpretation* (Chicago: Chicago University Press, 1976) 157.
2. James Hillman, *Archetypal Psychology: A Brief Account* (Dallas: Spring Publications, 1983) 9.

A SURVEY OF JUNGIAN LITERARY CRITICISM
IN ENGLISH

Jungian literary criticism begins with Jung himself. The first extended application of Jung's psychology to the interpretation of a literary text is to be found in his book *Psychology of the Unconscious* (first German version, 1912).[1] In this book, which marks Jung's break with Freud and gives us the first formulation of his own archetypal psychology, there is a long discussion of mythical motifs in Longfellow's narrative poem *Hiawatha*. The events of the hero's life, which include a miraculous birth and battle with a sea-monster, are viewed as symbolizing the transformation of his life force in a development towards greater consciousness that Jung later called the process of individuation. After the publication of the English translation of this book in 1916 Jung began to acquire a wider readership in the English-speaking world. Among creative writers who in these early years were influenced by Jung are Jack London, Eugene O'Neill and D.H. Lawrence. In 1917, the last year of his life, Jack London wrote some very Jungian short stories.[2] And, although it does not show directly in his work, Lawrence, in a letter written in 1918,[3] tells his correspondent that he was impressed by "the Jung book." Eugene O'Neill was strongly influenced by Freudian psychology, but he also wrote some plays that bear witness to his reading of Jung.[4]

Around 1920 we also find the first tentative applications of Jung's psychology to literature and art in essays by some literary critics and in a study by the English philosopher John Thorburn, *Art and the Unconscious* (1925). It is Jung himself, however, who is the first to theorize about the relation between analytical psychology and literature in two lectures delivered in 1922 and 1930.[5] The impact of great art, Jung claims, is due to the artist's tapping of archetypal images. "Whoever speaks in primordial images speaks with a thousand voices," as he puts it rhetorically.

Jung distinguishes between two forms of art: on the one hand psychological or personalistic art that expresses the personal psychology of the author, consciously developed; on the other hand visionary art that is symbolical and archetypal. Goethe, Dante and Melville are mentioned as striking examples of archetypal art. Jung never wrote a full psychological analysis of a literary work, as Freud did of the story *Gradiva* by the German novelist Wilhelm Jensen, but in 1932 he wrote a long essay on James Joyce's *Ulysses*.[6] This is a personal effusion rather than an analysis of the novel. Jung frankly confesses that the book bores and irritates him, though he values it as a perfect expression of the futility and squalor of modern life.

After these first beginnings in Jung's writings, it took a surprisingly long time for Jungian literary criticism to develop. The English critic Herbert Read commented on Jung in several essays written in the 1920s, but although he knew Jung personally and later lectured at Eranos conferences, he makes only occasional reference to Jung in his criticism. The two pioneering works in Jungian literary criticism were published by two English women, Maud Bodkin and Elizabeth Drew, in 1934 and 1947. Neither book had any real critical follow-up. It is only in the 1960s, and then for different reasons, that Jungian literary criticism begins to catch on.

Maud Bodkin, in some articles published in the 1920s, was the first to begin a more systematic investigation into the relevance of the new psychology of the unconscious for art criticism. This resulted in her book *Archetypal Patterns in Poetry* (1934), which for many years remained the only extensive Jungian literary study. Her aim was to test Jung's hypothesis that the emotional significance of great works of art is due to the "stirring in the reader's mind of unconcious forces or archetypes." She discusses her own responses and those of some well-known critics to archetypal patterns such as rebirth, heaven-hell, devil, hero and God in great European writers like Homer, Virgil, Dante, Shakespeare, Milton, Goethe and T.S. Eliot. Bodkin's book is rich and sensitive, full of suggestive insights that might have been taken up and developed by other critics. But her study actually seems to have had very little immediate influence. One of the reasons for this neglect is no doubt that her frankly subjective method clashed with the current movement towards objective methods in literary studies. Bodkin's laudable attempt to base her psychological analysis of poetry on a full awareness of "the emotional and intuitive experience communicated" aimed at appreciating poetic suggestiveness rather than at abstraction and scientific exactness. I suspect, moreover, that the academic world was shy of an amateur student of literature who was neither a professional psychologist nor a professional literary scholar, and, equally bad, who made eclectic use of Freud, Jung and other psychologists.

In spite of the lack of interest in the scholarly world, Jungian literary criticism slowly began to gain ground after the Second World War, much more so in America than in England and on the continent of Europe. If we look at England first, we notice that little psychological criticism was written there, although the

Analytical Psychology Club in London flourished and some Jungian analysts ventured into the literary field. In the lecture series of the Guild of Pastoral Psychology in London, for instance, analysts regularly turned for their popularization of Jungian notions to examples from myth and literature, but we find very few extended literary studies. In the universities there seems to have been hardly any reactions to Jung. However, in the best English tradition, there are some idiosyncratic amateurs who wrote interesting Jungian books, perhaps after they had profited from personal analysis. The literary application of Jung is related to enthusiastic pleas for Jungian depth psychology and personal individuation as the best answers to the need for psychological progress in a divided and chaotic post-war world. Examples include Percival Martin's book *Experiment in Depth* (1955), which studies common themes in the work of the historian Toynbee, the poet T.S. Eliot, and Jung; and David Streatfeild's lengthy archetypal analysis of the best-selling hard-boiled police novel *No Orchids for Miss Blandish* by James Hadley Chase (Streatfeild, 1959).

Among the literary scholars interested in Jung there is the well-known poet-scholar Kathleen Raine, who in her early work was considerably influenced by Jung. Her studies of the background of William Blake's work led her to investigate, however, the hermetic, occult and Neo-Platonic traditions that influenced both Blake and Jung, rather than apply Jungian psychology to the interpretation of Blake's poetry. One of the few university teachers who acknowledged Jung's influence was Graham Hough, professor of English literature at Cambridge, who lectured at the Zurich Jung Institute and at Eranos conferences.

No doubt the scarcity of Jungian literary criticism in Europe is due to the general dismissal of Jung by the academic world. One reason for this is to be found in some remarks Jung made in the early 1930s about Jewish psychology and the Aryan unconscious, as well as in his chairmanship of the International Society for Psychotherapy throughout the thirties. These are considered political slips which many still hold against him.[7] Another reason is that academic theorists are often offended by the intuitive and mythic character of Jung's thinking, with the result that Jung is kept out of most university courses in psychology, with the occasional exception of a professor who has developed a personal interest in Jung.

In America before and after the war the situation was rather different. The Jungian archetypes found a greater response in the United States than in Europe. For one thing, I suppose, simply because more Americans had the money to have themselves analyzed by Jung; for another, because of the greater flexibility and openness of the American university system compared with the more rigid academic traditions in Europe.

Among the first generation of those who had personal analysis with Jung and who went back to the United States to become analysts themselves, there were several who attempted psychological interpretations of literature. These pioneers of the Jungian movement were mostly women. Of these, Esther Harding was the first to write on the poetry of T.S. Eliot in her 1935 book *Women's Mysteries*. After the war she published an article on Rider Haggard's novel *She* (one of Jung's own pet examples of anima description) and she wrote a book on Bunyan's *Pilgrim's Progress*. Among the men who discovered Jung and wrote on literature, the best-known are James Kirsch on Shakespeare, Joseph Henderson on T.S. Eliot and, later, Edward Edinger on Melville. Analysts naturally tend to look at literature through psychologically colored spectacles with the result that their interpretations are often more Jungian than literary. Perhaps the best literary discussions written by an analyst that I have come across are Joseph Henderson's essays on T.S. Eliot's poetry.

If we turn to the literary scholars and teachers in America who made use of Jung, we reach the second landmark in Jungian literary criticism, the study by Elizabeth Drew of Eliot's work called *T.S. Eliot: The Design of His Poetry* (1949). It was her book that sent me off on my own Jungian quest. Her excellent discussion of Eliot's work aroused my curiosity about the psychological theory she cautiously and tactfully applies, and about the surprising fact that in Eliot scholarship Drew gets very little notice. The book still seems to me a model for an analysis that does not reduce the work of art to something else, but that provides really illuminating, sensitive and sensible interpretation. At the same time it is an example of what is possibly the most fruitful way in which Jung's psychology can be applied to literature. Drew traces parallels between the symbols and patterns in Eliot's poetry as it develops over the years, and the progression of dream symbols and mythical archetypes Jung discovered in the individuation process.

As happened with Maud Bodkin's book in the 1930s, Elizabeth Drew's excellent Jungian study had no immediate follow-up in the 1950s. In the therapeutic field the Jungian school was establishing itself in various parts of the States, notably in New York and California.[8] And the Bollingen Foundation in New York supported for many years Jungian and archetypal studies that spread the knowledge of Jung's psychology and of related fields of mythology, Eastern religion and art by means of its splendid series of Bollingen publications. All this provides the groundwork, but in the

1950s we still only find an occasional article of Jungian literary criticism.

It should be emphasized that the Jungian literary criticism I am discussing must be distinguished from other types of "myth criticism" or "archetypal criticism" with which it is often grouped. After 1945 "myth" became for a time a very popular, though often confusing term in literary analysis. The impact of Frazer's great comparative studies of the world's folklore, magic and rituals in *The Golden Bough* (rev. ed. 1911), and, to a lesser extent, of Jung's combination of psychology and myth in his *Psychology of the Unconscious* (1912) is clear in the work of literary critics like Richard Chase (*Quest for Myth*, 1949), Francis Fergusson (*The Idea of a Theatre*, 1949), Philip Wheelwright (*The Burning Fountain*, 1954), and the influential "archetypalist" Northrop Frye (*Anatomy of Criticism*, 1957). Their studies of the recurrence of mythic formulas and archetypes apply to plot patterns, genres and literary conventions, rather than to the psychology of character. Northrop Frye acknowledged the influence of Jung on his theory of literary myths and he borrowed the term "archetype" from him. But symbols, myths and archetypes are for Frye strictly literary concepts. He means by an archetype "a typical or recurring image ... the symbol which connects one poem with another and thereby helps to unify and integrate our literary experience."[9]

The criticism collected in this bibliography uses "archetype" in the specific sense of Jung's depth psychology as a structuring element in the human psyche. Jungian literary criticism studies the psychological aspects of the characters and their relations, as well as the mythical and archetypal symbols of literary works in themselves and as expressions of the author's "inclusive" psyche. It applies the theories of Carl Jung and the extensions of Jung's ideas in the works of his most influential followers Erich Neumann (*The Origins and History of Consciousness*, 1949, and *The Great Mother*, 1955), Joseph Campbell (*The Hero with a Thousand Faces*, 1949, and *The Masks of God*, 4 vols, 1959-1968), and James Hillman (*Re-Visioning Psychology*, 1975, *The Dream and the Underworld*, 1979, and *Healing Fiction*, 1983).

The great stimulus for the more wide-spread study of Jung and for the literary application of his ideas came in the 1960s with the counterculture of the younger generation that, for a variety of reasons, started a radical questioning of the effects and the foundations of our rational, scientific thinking and our technological society. It was not only the political disasters of those years that made the need for cultural self-criticism so strongly felt. Among all the cultural, social and political factors that contributed to the rise of the counterculture, alongside the general interest in myth, in feminine-oriented psychology and non-Western religions, Jung's psychology became a popular subject for study. Though archetypes and the individuation process will seldom have featured in official American university courses, Jung must have been widely read by the students of the arts and humanities. For, in the 1960s, articles begin to appear in university periodicals, while in the 1970s we begin to have the first of many doctoral dissertations that apply Jung. These were followed in the late seventies and early eighties by monographs that view the totality of an author's work from a Jungian perspective. We already have several Jungian studies of Shakespeare, and two each of Blake, Melville and Doris Lessing. There is a pleasant and witty book on Tolkien and a brilliant study of the writer of horror fiction H.P. Lovecraft. Furthermore, there are Jungian books on, among others, Bunyan, Keats, the Brontë sisters, Lawrence, Yeats, Forster, Norman Mailer, Charles Olson, the Australian novelist Patrick White and the Canadian Robertson Davies, book-length studies of more than 20 authors, and no doubt more will follow.

This growing interest in Jung may be illustrated from a count of the American dissertations that apply Jung's psychology. The *Comprehensive Dissertation Index*, section Humanities, lists some 340 dissertations written between 1955 and 1982 that make substantial use of Jung.[10] There are occasional Jungian dissertations before 1960, an average of about 5 per year in the sixties; the yearly totals swell in the early seventies to about 20 per year, and in the peak years of 1977, 1978 and 1979, mount to 31, 33 and 35 respectively. In the early eighties the figure falls below 20 again.

Another way in which Jungian concepts have made their mark in colleges and universities is in the appearance since 1970 of a number of anthologies for literary survey and writing courses in which the texts are arranged to illustrate the major archetypes. Most notable among these are two anthologies edited by Harold Schechter and Jonna Gormely Semeiks. One is a sourcebook for a writing course, called *Patterns in Popular Culture* (1980), a most attractive collection of a variety of pieces ranging from classical myths and epics, fairy tales, poems and prose to pop songs and comic strips, with stimulating commentary and questions. The whole book makes an excellent popular introduction to the world of Jungian archetypes. Equally good is the anthology published in 1983 by the same authors, *Discoveries: 50 Stories of the Quest*, in which the stories are arranged according to the stages of Joseph Campbell's hero quest to give an idea of the individuation process.

Jungian criticism works well with literature that has strong symbolical and mythical elements. That is why nineteenth century romanticism has been a fruitful subject. If the reviews by specialists in the annual surveys of the bibliographical series *American Literary Scholarship*, together with my own impressions, are anything to go by, it can certainly be argued that a number of studies written in recent years from Jungian perspectives have made real contributions to the interpretation of the work of Poe, Emerson, Whitman, Dickinson, Hawthorne and Melville. It is a development that has several notable aspects. One of these is that, however brief the tradition still is, Jungian criticism of the American romantics is cumulative. Martin Bickman's excellent book *The Unsounded Centre: Jungian Studies in American Romanticism* (1980, revised edition with new title 1988) summarizes and extends work done by a number of critics in the preceding decade. In his chapter on Poe, for instance, Bickman acknowledges essays written in the 1970s by four different critics who treated Poe from the frameworks of Jung and Neumann. One of these critics, with the beautifully romantic name of Barton Levi St. Armand, opened up new approaches to Poe when he related Poe's known interest in hermeticism and alchemy to interpretations of some of the stories as journeys towards a stage in which psychological opposites are reconciled. Bickman himself used Jung's and Neumann's Anima theories to explore the feminine elements in Poe's work and to argue that the theme of psychic dissolution in many of Poe's stories includes a complementary vision of psychic expansion. The theory of the psychologically contrasexual is also applied to other writers when Bickman discusses the imagery of widening consciousness and the theme of psychic growth in the poetry of Emily Dickinson and Walt Whitman. And Bickman is not the only critic who has made good use of Jung in a book-length study of the American romantics. In 1975 the poet-critic Albert Gelpi published a very fine study of the five major poets of American Romanticism: Taylor, Emerson, Poe, Whitman and Dickinson. Although Gelpi does not write from an exclusively Jungian point of view, the bias is Jungian. He sees a poem especially as the poet's effort to integrate the conscious and unconscious aspects of his psyche, and Gelpi's sensitive readings of the poems find fruitful support in the archetypal psychology, not only of Jung, but also of his followers Neumann, von Franz and Hillman.

It stands to reason that the most mythical and symbolical of American authors, Herman Melville, has also been the subject of numerous Jungian interpretations. There are some 20 titles of books and articles on my cards. Comparing four book-length Jungian studies of Melville may give an instructive picture of the insights to be derived from, as well as the limitations inherent in, the psychological approach. At the time of the *Moby-Dick* centenaries in 1951, the Harvard psychologist Henry Murray wrote a brilliant essay in which, drawing on both Freud and Jung, and freely linking up his interpretation of the novel with conjectures about the author's personal psychic development, he offered a reading that pertinently unites psychoanalytical, archetypal, religious and socio-cultural viewpoints. Ahab is seen as the embodiment of the satanic Antichrist who captains the forces of the Id in their rebellion against the white whale, symbol of the repressing Superego of New England conscience. At the same time, viewed archetypally, Captain Ahab is the protagonist of the great Goddess of oriental and primitive religions, the feminine principle dismissed by the Biblical mythmakers and the whole Hebraic-Christian and, particularly, the American Calvinist tradition. Melville, as a true poet, was "of the Devil's party," and fully aware that he had written what he called in his letter to Hawthorne "a wicked book." Henry Murray established his reputation as a Melville critic with his hundred-page introduction to the 1949 edition of Melville's novel *Pierre*, in which he gives an uncommonly thorough and perceptive analysis of the psychological complexities of Melville's wildly uneven novel.

The other fine Jungian study of Melville is James Baird's *Ishmael* (1956). Baird sees Melville as an essentially religious artist who, on the basis of his experiences of primitive life in Polynesia, created in his books new symbols for man's relationship to God to replace the Christian symbols impoverished by what he calls "the cultural failure of Protestantism." Of the six archetypal symbols Baird distinguishes, the most striking is, of course, that of the white whale, the mythic "chaos-dragon," Melville's supreme symbol of life and death, and of the ambiguity of the unknowable God.

Compared to the scope and the subtlety of Murray's and Baird's interpretations, the later Jungian books on Melville are disappointing because they tend to reduce the complexities of Melville's art too much to the psychological schemata. This criticism holds, I think, for the expansive book *The Melville Archetype* (1970) by the literary critic Martin Pops, who examines the symbolism in Melville's work "as a quest for the Sacred," and also for the concentrated study of *Moby-Dick* (1975) by the Jungian analyst Edward Edinger. However penetrating some of Edinger's insights may be, his overall interpretation of Ahab's voyage as an ongoing individuation process leads to distortions of both psychological meanings and literary effects.

It is important to keep in mind the limitations of all psychological literary criticism. Depth psychology, whether Freudian, Jungian or post-Freudian and post-Jungian, works with a unifying and simplifying scheme to explain and analyze the intricate workings of the psyche. Literature, it can be argued, and certainly great literature, tries to grasp and embody in words the concrete complexity of human experience. The critic who uses his psychological notions to bring out aspects of this complexity may provide insights, the critic who imposes his psychological scheme on the literary text will in all likelihood limit and distort.

It is obvious that some kinds of literature lend themselves better to the Jungian approach than others. Jung's archetypes and individuation process find their analogues especially in literature and other art forms of a symbolical and mythical character, in which images and events function to a greater or lesser extent as symbols. Although there are several Jungian books and some forty articles attempting archetypal interpretations of Shakespeare's plays, most of them are very disappointing. I suspect that, with the exception of *A Midsummer Night's Dream* and *The Tempest*, the psychological realism, the moral reference of themes and images, and the complex interrelations between characters and situations make Shakespeare's plays a form of literature for which interpretation through Jungian symbolism is less immediately relevant. On the other hand Jungian concepts can be applied very fruitfully to the interpretation of the strong symbolist and mythical elements in many 19th- and 20th-century writings, from the symbolic density of T.S. Eliot's poetry to the mythological simplicity of Rider Haggard's romances, Superman cartoons and Star Wars films.

What has already been achieved in Jungian criticism of some 20th-century authors is well expounded in an article written in 1982 by two Canadian scholars, F.L. Radford and R.R. Wilson, who write on Jung's influence in modern literature. They argue that characterization in modern novels, without necessarily being subtler than that in 19th century fiction, clearly incorporates important elements from the concepts of unconscious motivation developed by Freud and Jung. Building on a considerable number of earlier Jungian studies of D.H. Lawrence, Patrick White and Robertson Davies, Radford and Wilson show how the acquaintance of these authors with the theories of Jung lends archetypal significance to the characters in Lawrence's *Women in Love*, as well as in several of White's novels, and how it informs the patterning of the novels of Robertson Davies, who is in a direct line of descent from the Jung-influenced German novelists Hermann Hesse and Thomas Mann.

Surveying the whole field of Jungian literary criticism written in English, we find that, besides a good deal of disappointing stuff, a great many stimulating articles and books have been written during the past 25 years, and that a surprising variety of authors from the past and present have already been studied from a Jungian perspective. The boom in Jungian literary studies of the seventies may be over. Yet a working knowledge of Jungian and Freudian psychology will no doubt in future be part of any good critic's equipment, and I expect that we may look forward to further competent Jungian studies, especially overviews in a Jungian light of an author's total achievement. To put it more strongly, much may be expected if we take into account (to give a few more examples) the quality of the excellent psychological commentary in Theodora Ward's book on Emily Dickinson (1961) and Allegra Stewart's study of Gertrude Stein (1967), two critics who unobtrusively included a Jungian perspective in their sensitive analyses of the works and the inner lives of their authors. It is worth noting that throughout the years women writers have done particularly well in this field. Among present-day literary scholars who write excellent Jungian criticism there are once more a good many women, like Evelyn Hinz, Lorelei Cederstrom, Nancy Bailey, and Stephanie Demetrakopoulos. Furthermore, feminist literary critics have contributed significantly to the debate about the need for revising and developing some of Jung's theories, notably his conception of the anima/animus archetype. For this, see the volume of essays *Feminist Archetypal Theory: Interdisciplinary Re-Visions of Jungian Thought*, eds. Estella Lauter and Carol Schreier Rupprecht (Knoxville: University of Tennessee Press, 1985), and also the annotations in my bibliography to articles by Annette Benert, Zephyra Porat, Annis Pratt, and Diane Sadoff.

A promising new development in the 1980s is the increasing use that critics have been making of James Hillman's "re-visioning" of Jung's psychology. With its emphasis on images as the "poetic basis of mind," Hillman's archetypal psychology has obvious relevance for literary interpretation. Ralph Maud's essay "Archetypal Depth Criticism and Melville" suggests how Melville may be viewed in the light of Hillman's "imaginal" psychology with its notions of depression and the need to confront death as necessary elements in human "soul-making." And Hillman's elaboration of Jung's technique of dream interpretation by "sticking to the image" has been used with interesting results in essays on Blake and Henry James by Mary Stewart and Carolyn Zonailo, and in the dissertation of Evans. L. Smith.

Among the most remarkable Jungian criticism of the 1980s is the work that has been done on Patrick White by the Australian critic David Tacey, who was profoundly influenced by Hillman. In his lucid study *Patrick White: Fiction and the Unconscious* (1988) Tacey argues that there is a radical discrepancy between the genuine unconscious symbolism in White's novels and the author's superimposed intellectual constructs and interpretations. This thesis is persuasively developed on the basis of what Tacey sees as the starting-point for archetypal criticism, the critic's complete imaginative receptivity to the symbolic material in the novels.

In conclusion, it may be said that Jungian literary criticism is mostly what has been termed "expressive criticism," which holds the view that literature expresses the conscious and unconscious mind and feelings of the author, and thereby, in Jungian archetypal view, thoughts and feelings of man and woman in general. This means that it is opposed to the more intellectual and abstract pursuits of recent linguistic, structural, post-structural and deconstructionist schools of criticism. Competent Jungian criticism will always belong to that more traditional type of literary analysis and interpretation which focuses on the human content of the texts. It will be a psychological criticism that tries to unravel further strands in the "imaginal" life of images, symbols and themes of literary works by using the insights and concepts of depth psychology and the analogies with dreams and myths.

Notes:

1. Later version retitled. For details see this bibliography under C.G. Jung, *Symbols of Transformation*.
2. In the collections *The Red One* (1918) and *On the Makaloa Mat* (1919). See James McClintock, *White Logic: Jack London's Short Stories* (1975).
3. Letter to Katherine Mansfield, 5 December 1918.
4. *The Emperor Jones* (1921) and *The Great God Brown* (1925). See Doris V. Falk, *Eugene O'Neill and the Tragic Tension* (1958).
5. See C.G. Jung, "On the Relation of Analytical Psychology to Poetry" (original German lecture, 1922) and "Psychology and Literature" (published in German, 1930), *Collected Works*, vol. 15. (q.v.)
6. C.G. Jung, "Ulysses: A Monologue" (published in German, 1932), *Collected Works*, vol. 15. (q.v.)
7. See for Jung's attitude to Nazism the balanced essay on "C.G. Jung and National Socialism" in Aniela Jaffé, *From the Life and Work of C.G. Jung* (London:Hodder and Stoughton, 1972) 78-98.
8. See Joseph Henderson's essay "Reflections on the History and Practice of Jungian Analysis" in the handbook *Jungian Analysis*, ed. Murray Stein (La Salle, Ill.: Open Court Publishing, 1982) 3-26.
9. Northrop Frye, *Anatomy of Criticism* (Princeton: Princeton University Press, 1957) 99.
10. Of these 340 dissertations about one half (163) are on literary subjects. The others are in psychology (77), education (61), religion (31), philosophy (9), and a few in fine arts and sociology.

BIBLIOGRAPHY

1. ABENHEIMER, Karl M. "On Narcissism: Including an Analysis of Shakespeare's *King Lear.*" *British Journal of Medical Psychology* 20:3 (1945) 322-329.

    Ideas of both Freud and Jung are used to develop a view of narcissism as a response to regressive longings and the desire to dominate mother substitutes. The accompanying self-aggressive tendencies may be overcome through positive self-expression and active introversion for the sake of self-realization. *King Lear* is "the greatest description of narcissism in literature." Lear's demands for unrestricted love and the power-craving of Goneril and Regan are equally narcissistic, while Cordelia's self-assertion and self-respect give the contrasting example of mental and moral health.

    Convincing psychological perspective of important aspects of Lear.

2. ABENHEIMER, Karl. M. "Shakespeare's *Tempest*: A Psychological Analysis." *Psychoanalytic Review* 33:4 (1946) 399-415.
    Rpt. in *The Design Within: Psychoanalytic Approaches to Shakespeare.* Ed. M.D. Faber. New York: Science House, 1970.

    The Tempest read as "a dramatic representation of Prospero's inflated loneliness and paranoid isolation." In terms of Jungian individuation with large admixture of Freudian ideas Prospero (and Shakespeare himself) are criticized for not reaching self-realization. In spite of his contact with the shadow (Caliban) and with anima figures (Miranda and Ariel) Prospero matures insufficiently and remains in the end much the same dominating father figure with a longing for absolute goodness and consequent suppression of his own negative side. His isolation is not really broken down.

    In ascribing to Shakespeare a psychologizing aim the allegorical and moral nature of the play is lost sight of, and we are given a lopsided view of Prospero's symbolic character.

3. ACKERMAN, Stephen J. "The Vocation of Pope's Eloisa." *Studies in English Literature* 19:3 (1979) 445-457.

    In the course of a discussion of the suitability of Pope's heroic couplet form to the expression of Eloisa's "often frantic passions" (in the poem "Eloisa to Abelard") a parallel is drawn between her maturing from carnal to angelic love and the individuation process.

4. ADAMS, Hazard. *Philosophy of the Literary Symbolic.* Tallahassee: University of Florida State, 1984. xiv,466 pp.

    Contains exposition of Jung's symbol theory.

5. ADAMS, Robert M. "The Devil and Dr. Jung." Chapter in *Ikon: John Milton and the Modern Critics.*" Ithaca, N.Y.: Cornell University Press, 1955. 35-59.

    A facetious tone and insufficient appreciation of the implications of Jung's concept of the archetype characterize this critique of "the treatment which John Milton has undergone at the hands of the Jungians." Though they can hardly be called Jungians, Arnold Stein in his book *Answerable Style* (1953) and C.S. Lewis in *A Preface to Paradise Lost* (1952) are criticized for using the adjective "archetypal" as little more than a vague label. The author takes issue with the view that Milton has pictured Satan as a tragic hero, expressed by Maud Bodkin (*Archetypal Patterns in Poetry*, 1934) and R.J. Zwi Werblowsky (*Lucifer and Prometheus*, 1952). "Archetypal influences deserve nothing more than a minor ancillary role in the discussion of literary works."

6. AITCHINSON, James. "The Limits of Experience: Edwin Muir's 'Ballad of the Soul'." *English* 24, No. 118 (1975) 10-15.

    The archetypal symbolism of Muir's dreamvision is explained as reflecting "the crucial stage in the dreamer's individuation process" - the soul's immersion in the sea of the unconscious, contests with monstrous and imprisoning forces, painful rebirth of the self into a state of cosmic peace. The poem is based on an important "waking dream" Muir had in 1919 during his analysis by the Jungian psychologist Maurice Nicoll.

7. ALBERT, Leonard. "Joyce and the New Psychology." (Ph.D. 1957 Columbia University) 337 pp. *DAI* 18/04 A p.1424.

8. ALEXANDER, John M. "Myth as an Organizing Principle for a Literary Curriculum." *CEA Critic* 41:3 (1979) 32-38.

    A plea for structuring college courses in literature around the study of myths and archetypes. Following Joseph Campbell's distinction of the four functions of "living myth" in *Myths to Live By* (1972), Alexander argues that through the mythic approach to imaginative literature the student may gain insight "into the structure of contemporary society and its relationship to the past," and into the universal patterns of his own maturation process.

9. ALLEN, James L. "The Road to Byzantium: Archetypal Criticism and Yeats." *Journal of Aesthetics and Art Criticism* 32:1 (1973) 53-64.

    A plea for applying Philip Wheelwright's non-Jungian conception of archetypes ("symbols that have an identical or similar meaning for mankind generally") to Yeats's work rather than the archetypal systems of Jung or Northrop Frye. It is argued that Frye's "analytical structures" are foreign to the shape of Yeats's imaginative thought. In spite of striking similarities between some of Jung's and Yeats's ideas the application of Jungian archetypes to Yeats has only created confusion and misunderstanding. This confusion has the following causes: Jung did not invent the term archetype; Yeats was not directly influenced by Jung; Jung rejected the concept of a Godhead, based his views on empirical confirmation, and his theories show too many vestiges of Freudian thought.

Allen's argumentation shows insufficient appreciation of the psychological character of all of Jung's notions.

10. ALLEN, John A., ed. *Hero's Way: Contemporary Poems in the Mythic Tradition.* Englewood Cliffs, N.J.: Prentice Hall, 1971. lii, 473.

A stimulating anthology of poems, mostly contemporary, thematically arranged "to correspond with the successive stages of the traditional Hero's Quest" as mapped out by Joseph Campbell. The reader and student of the poems is invited to assemble his own version of the quest journey and, along the road, "to learn a number of interesting things about himself as well as about poetry." There is useful comment and an annotated bibliography of books on myth and psychology.

11. ALPERT, Barry. "Dawson's Jungian Strategies." *Vort* 2:1 (1973) 41-42.

A brief note indicating how the characters in the fiction of Fielding Dawson may reflect an ongoing process of individuation in the author himself once he started reading Jung.

12. ANDERSON, Mary Castiglie. "Staging the Unconcious: Edward Albee's *Tiny Alice.*" *Renascence* 32:3 (1980) 178-192.

The dreamlike qualities of Albee's play (1965) warrant an archetypal interpretation that goes beyond the limited psychological view that lay brother Julian's desire for martyrdom springs from his repressed sex drive. On the symbolic level the other characters represent parts of Julian's own psyche. In his quest for self-discovery he relinquishes his loyalty to Mother Church and integrates vital aspects of his unconscious in encountering the anima qualities of Miss Alice. She is in turns protecting Good Mother, engulfing witchlike Terrible Mother, and Temptress testing the hero. In this mythical perspective Julian's death on a symbolic sacrificial altar becomes a modern rite of initiation suggesting spiritual rebirth.

This seems a pertinent psychological reading of Albee's enigmatic play, although the Jungian concepts are not always expertly handled.

13. ANDRIANO, Joseph D. "Our Ladies of Darkness: Jungian Readings of the Female Daimon in Gothic Fiction." (Ph.D. 1986 Washington State University) 283 pp. *DAI* 47/06 A p.2150. (Matthew Lewis, Irving, De Quincey, Poe, Stoker)

14. ANGHINNETTI, Paul W. "Alienation, Rebellion, and Myth: A Study of the Works of Nietzsche, Jung, Yeats, Camus, and Joyce". (Ph.D. 1969 Florida State University) 467 pp. *DAI* 30/05 A p.1974.

15. ANON. "Acta Interviews Robertson Davies." *Acta Victoriana* 2 (1973) 68-87.
    Davies describes Jung's influence on his thought (pp. 82-84).

16. ARENBERG, Carol Rakita. "The Double as an Initiation Rite: A Study of Chamisso, Hoffmann, Poe, and Dostoevsky." (Ph.D. 1979 Washington University) 227 pp. *DAI* 40/02 A p.834.

17. ARMENS, Sven. *Archetypes of the Family in Literature*. Seattle: University of Washington Press, 1966. xi,264 pp.
    This study examines the archetypal imagery of family relationships in plays by Aeschylus (*Oresteia* trilogy), Sophocles (*Oedipus* plays) and Shakespeare (*Hamlet, King Lear*). Following Jung, Neumann and Fromm, the conflicts in these plays are viewed as disruptions of a basic "Family Covenant", in which ideally there is integration of masculine and feminine elements - "patriarchal demands of the father and the nurturing care of the mother." Chief symbol of the former is the Sacred Fire on the altar of ancestor devotion, and of the latter the Physical Hearth round which the family groups itself "with bonds of mutual affection." The opposing claims of matriarchal tenderness and patriarchal authority underlie Agamemnon's dilemma in the sacrifice of his daughter. Orestes' guilt and suffering make possible the reunion of justice and love when the persecuting Furies are transformed into the gracious Eumenides. Similar oppositions between Good and Terrible Mothers, Tyrant Fathers and Questing Sons or Suffering Maidens are traced in the relations of Oedipus, Hamlet and Lear.
    There is much sensitive analysis of the "poetic communication" of key passages in the plays. The symbolism of the generalized scheme seems to fit quite well the starkness of the emotional relationships in the Greek plays, but its usefulness is more limited when applied to the motivational and situational complexity of

Shakespeare's characters. To see the transformation of Hamlet in the course of the play merely as "a process of degeneration," because in the end he fulfils the patriarchal demand for revenge, seems to misrepresent the Hamlet of act V. The reconciliation of Lear and Cordelia may be said to demonstrate the moral force of the principle of matriarchal love, but comparing Edgar with Oedipus results in the distortion of this suffering character into a "solar Warrior-Hero of the patriarchal orientation."

18.   ARNOLD, St. Georg Tucker, Jr. "The Raincloud and the Garden: Psychic Regression as Tragedy in Welty's 'A Curtain of Green'." *South Atlantic Bulletin* 44:1 (1979) 53-60.

Neumann's concept of "uroboric incest," the regressive retreat into unconsciousness, is applied to an archetypal reading of Eudora Welty's short story, in which after the tragic death of her husband Mrs. Larkin withdraws from society and seeks oblivion in mindless work in her wildly overgrown garden.

19.   ARONSON, Alex. *Psyche and Symbol in Shakespeare*. Bloomington: Indiana University Press, 1972. vi,343 pp.

The emphasis in this Jungian study of Shakespeare's dramatic work is "on psychic content rather than on character development." The attempts of "fragmentary ego-consciousness" to integrate the forces of the unconscious and the striving for self-knowledge on the road towards greater self-realization are seen as the main themes of both comedies and tragedies. Connecting links between the plays are found in the symbols "that the unconscious projects into nature or into man." Thus, the three parts of the book consider, first, the Shakespearian hero as *Ego* "in terms of the conscious mind only." Prevalent symbols are those of the mask (of kingly power), of appetite in all its shapes, of the shadow thrown by the hero's persona, and of the inner voice that tempts the hero into doing evil, and so "prepares the way toward individuation." Secondly, *Anima* elements indicate "the shift from the personal to the transpersonal." The "archetypes of integration or division" are traced in the anima-animus, Logos-Eros relations of lovers, of fathers and daughters or sons and mothers, while the Hecate figures embody the destructive maternal archetype. Thirdly, the *Self*, the archetype of wholeness and enlarged consciousness, is found in characters like Friar Francis in *Much Ado About Nothing*, Duke Vincentio in *Measure for Measure*, and Prospero in *The Tempest*. As wise old men and suffering healers they are related to the mythical figures of Prometheus, Orpheus and Asklepios. Examples for archetypal analysis are taken from many other plays, such as: Falstaff as Hal's and Iago as Othello's shadow; Isabella as

Angelo's inner voice; Lear who rediscovers his anima in Cordelia; Ophelia unable "to free her anima from her father's Logos"; Hamlet and Coriolanus "swallowed" by mother figures, "each invariably a projection of the son's unconscious"; the myth of the Hecate-like Great Mother applied to Gertrude, Lady Macbeth, and Goneril and Regan.

With a wealth of quotations from Jung and extensive parallels from a variety of myths Aronson eloquently develops his archetypal analysis. Valuable psychological insights result from his procedure. For instance, when several of Shakespeare's kings are shown to cling to their personas, when the villains in various plays are viewed as "embodiments of the tragic hero's unconscious," or when the mythical Demeter/Kore and Amor/Psyche parallels are pursued in discussing the Helena-Bertram and Hero-Claudio relationships in *All's Well That Ends Well* and *Much Ado about Nothing*.

More often, however, the Jungian interpretations seem wilful and the reader feels that Shakespeare's characters and themes are being dressed in ill-fitting psychological robes. Rather than providing literary illumination the analysis frequently uses the plays to prove Jungian theories, while the moral and psychological substance of Shakespeare's characters is lost sight of. This shows especially in confusing applications of Jung's rigid anima-animus polarity, as when the fathers of Rosalind, Viola and Portia are seen as fulfilling "a very real psychological need" in being the recipients of "their daughter's anima-projections long before the lover and prospective husband appeared on the stage." Equating Hamlet's mother and Lady Macbeth as examples of destructive mother archetypes seems to put too much weight on Gertrude, while the argument that it is the "very indistinctness" of the latter's character that turns her into "a symbolic representation of the power of the anima archetype" begs the critical question.

A few more examples of questionable interpretations must suffice. The appearances of the ghosts in *Julius Caesar, Macbeth* and *Hamlet* are lumped together as confrontations with the archetypal "invisible," as if these three different dramatizations of conscience and the unconscious are all the same. To say that Falstaff represents "an unacknowledged portion" of Hal's personality is simply to misread the play. And is "the murder, rooted in Macbeth's unconscious, only feebly resisted in a moment of clarity" and finally carried out in "obedience to blind fate"? Though seeing Iago as Othello's psychological shadow is helpful, statements like "Iago is the embodiment of a singularly repulsive form of trans-personal evil" and "Othello surrenders to an archetype of the collective unconscious" leave the reader feeling that Shakespeare's psychology is a good deal more penetrating than such applications of Jung. (See critique by Rosemary Gordon in *Journal of Analytical Psychology* 19:2 (1974) 215-216.)

20. ASALS, Frederick. *"Flannery O'Connor: The Imagination of Extremity."* Athens: University of Georgia Press, 1982. 288 pp.

An exploration of the central dualities in O'Connor's fiction. In two chapters the analysis makes explicit use of Jung.

21. *ASALS, Frederick. "The Mythic Dimension of Flannery O'Connor's 'Greenleaf.'" *Studies in Short Fiction* 5:3 (1968) 317-330.

A persuasive demonstration of the mythical level in O'Connor's story about a conflict over a stray bull between genteelly cramped Mrs. May, owner of a dairy farm, and her vulgarly vital tenants, the Greenleaf family. With quotations from Jung's *Symbols of Transformation* and from Church Fathers discussing Christ's marriage to the Cross, it is argued that the description of Mrs. May's death on the horns of the bull, together with many more of the story's oppositions and paradoxes, find meaningful parallels in Dionysian spring rites, Mithraic bull sacrifice, and the mythic death and marriage of the Crucifixion.

22. ASSAD, Thomas J. *Tennysonian Lyric: "Songs of the Deeper Kind" and* In Memoriam. New Orleans: Tulane University, 1983. 323 pp.

Application of Jung's psychological theory in a study of poetic structure, pattern and mood in Tennyson's lyric poetry.

23. *ATKINSON, Michael. "Robert Bly's *Sleepers Joining Hands*: Shadow and Self." *Iowa Review* 7:4 (1976) 135-153.

A demonstration of psychological patterns in a volume of poems expressive of the American experience in the 1960's, by "delineating the system of archetypes that coherently applies throughout the book, linking Biblical allusions to contemporary consciousness and connecting dream with myth." Many of the shorter poems deal with the repression of the shadow through personal inner denial and public outward oppression. Bly's poems are accompanied by an essay that sketches the profiles of the Great Mother and identifies the stages and personifications of the anima. The symbolism of the longer dream poems in the title sequence *Sleepers Joining Hands* (1973) involves conscious acceptance of the shadow and confrontation with the "Teeth Mother" (the Magna Mater in her negative, devouring aspect) during a mythic journey of integration. The questing protagonist discovers the light of the Self in his meeting with an old man who releases "the energy inside us."

Fine, imaginative exposition of the archetypal themes consciously incorporated by Bly as "an implicit and continuous parallelism to Jung's schema of dream imagery in the individuation process."

24. *ATKINSON, Michael. "Soul's Time and Transformations: *The Wife of Bath's Tale*." *Southern Review* (Australia) 13:2 (1980) 72-78.
     By exploring analogues in the tale itself the transformations and the development of the knight's anima are traced. How much the hero's ego-consciousness is initially divided from his anima/psyche is symbolized in his rape of the young woman. The king's/superego's radical punishment is shifted by the soulful queen and her ladies to the level of the collective. They impose a quest for feminine understanding throughout a year's circle of the seasons. On the extra day allowed, the knight, defeated in his intellectual approach, is led to the meeting with the dancing ladies on the edge of the forest (of the unconscious). Their miraculous change into the ugly lady is the prelude to the final transformation of hag into fair maiden, but only after the knight has accepted marriage to this ugly symbol of his neglected soul.
     Subtle analysis of Chaucer's tale as the symbolic expression of the knight's inner experiences.

25. AYCOCK, Linnea. "The Mother-Daughter Relationship in the *Children of Violence* Series." *Anonymous: A Journal for the Woman Writer* 1:1 (1974) 48-55.
     Aycock demonstrates that Doris Lessing's protagonist, Martha Quest, suffers from a mother complex as described by Jung. After trying several ineffectual forms of rebellion, Martha's "struggle to understand her mother forces her to explore her unconscious; through this struggle and exploration she evolves to a higher consciousness." K.S.

26. BAILEY, Edgar C., Jr. "Shadows in Earthsea: Le Guin's Use of a Jungian Archetype." *Extrapolation* 21:3 (1980) 254-261.
     Developing points from Ursula Le Guin's lecture on "The Child and the Shadow" (*Quarterly Journal of the Library of Congress*, q.v.), Bailey applies her discussion of the Jungian concept of the shadow to Le Guin's own fantasy novel for children *A Wizard of Earthsea* (1968). In sometimes explicitly Jungian terms this story tells how the young hero Ged in "his hazardous but necessary journey to maturity" is pursued by all kinds of shadows. Only when he realizes that he is fighting his own dark side, does Ged manage to "turn around and confront the shadow" and so gain knowledge of "his whole true self."

27. BAILEY, Nancy. "Fiction and the New Androgyne: Problems and Possibilities in *The Diviners*. Atlantis 4:1 (1978) 10-17.

The archetype of the androgyne is reappearing in our Western culture. An ideal psychological androgyny may be defined as the harmonious balance within an individual of masculine and feminine polarities, each having their own validity. How this concept may throw light on the process of artistic creation is illustrated from Margaret Laurence's novel *The Diviners* (1974). Its writer-protagonist Morag Gunn develops an inner state of wholeness through the symbolic progression of her inner self consistent with Jungian individuation. Managing to balance the opposites within her, yet "rest in the tension," she achieves a freedom from emotional dependence on others which at the same time brings a certain isolation. "Morag's ability to remain whole, loving and creative while still separate and alone is as remarkable as any of the male victories recorded in literature."

The possibilities of applying the concept of androgyny to the analysis of a fictional character are well indicated.

28. *BAILEY, Nancy. "Margaret Laurence, Carl Jung and the Manawaka Women." *Studies in Canadian Literature* 2:2 (1977) 306-321.

"Some of Jung's most penetrating intuitions are exemplified and illuminated" in Margaret Laurence's four Manawaka novels: *The Stone Angel* (1964), *A Jest of God* (1966), *The Fire-Dwellers* (1969), and *The Diviners* (1974). The quest for identity by the women protagonists progresses from the problems of the persona and the unadapted shadow in the early novels, "through increasing awareness and acceptance of the animus figure in *The Fire-Dwellers*, to the completed individuation of Morag Gunn in *The Diviners*." Although Laurence does not seem to have "any more than a lay knowledge or interest in Jung," her fiction is "spiritually akin to the psychologist," and "her work has the scope and the articulation of a complete cultural myth which lends itself appropriately to Jungian analysis."

The critic's searching analysis of the women's psychic struggles and of the archetypal symbols in the novels focuses on Morag's spiritual growth into the integrated personality who expresses her "divining gift" in the creativeness of her own novel-writing. Jung's individuation theory is applied with much insight, while a subtle argument is developed to show how Laurence seems to question and "go beyond Jung's ideas on female-male relations." The inadequacy of the animus figures in their lives causes the Manawaka women to find salvation "inside the self and outside the traditional and recognized societal patterns for the female." *The Diviners* may be "a pioneering novel" in suggesting that "a twentieth century understanding of self-fulfillment" for both men and women will have to be based in a different awareness of consciousness and social roles than the male-dominated European attitudes which conditioned Jung's views.

29.   *BAILEY, Nancy . "The Masculine Image in *Lives of Girls and Women*." *Canadian Literature* 80 (1979) 113-120.

The masculine image is of crucial significance in the protagonist's development as a woman and as an artist in Alice Munro's novel *Lives of Girls and Women* (1965). "Munro's view of the self and its relations to others shows remarkable similarities to Carl Jung's theory of individuation." All the men in Del Jordan's world lead stunted lives, because their often strong male personas hide week shadow sides through repression of the Eros qualities of relatedness, feeling and intuition. Since the women share the masculine image that is projected as the "real world", Del only begins to find her own creative identity when she learns that the "sterile Logos orientation" of her society's emphasis on action, ambition and distinctiveness entails a denial of her own Eros-relatedness. Ironically, it is the mentally disturbed Bobby Sheriff who, as psychologically androgynous figure and archetypal wise fool, stimulates the animus development in her that may lead to the integration and balance of feminine and masculine qualities.

There is much subtle psychological and literary analysis in this essay in support of the argument that the masculine portrets in this novel "are sound demonstrations of the way the female consciousness interacts with the male at different levels of being."

30.   BAILEY, Nancy. "The Recovery of Self in *The Stone Angel*." *Inscape* 14:2 (1978) 67-72.

Overwhelmed by resistance to her mother, Hagar, the central character of Margaret Laurence's novel *The Stone Angel* (1964) denies in herself the instinctive feminine qualities of feeling, intuition and relatedness, adapting her persona to the requirements of the negative masculinity dominating Manawaka society. Although she destroys her husband and son, it is paradoxically through recognizing "the feminine within," repressed but present in the male characters around her, that Hagar shortly before her death approaches "the freedom to be herself."

With the help of illuminating quotations from Jung's works, Hagar's progress towards psychological integration away from her false persona and restricting ego is very ably "traced in the novel's settings and in its secondary characters."

31.   *BAIRD, James. *Ishmael*. Baltimore: Johns Hopkins Press, 1956. xxviii,445 pp.
      Chapter "Puer Aeternus: The Figure of Innocence in Melville" rpt. in *Puer Papers*. Ed. Cynthia Giles. Irving, Texas: Spring Publications, 1979. 205-223.
      This study of "primitivism" and of Melville as "a religious artist" is firmly based on Jung's theory of archetypes. Baird develops the thesis that the "cultural failure" of Protestantism forced artists like Melville to replace the impoverished Christian symbols with "new symbols to describe the relationship of man to his God." The true "primitivist" is the author who derives his new symbolic idiom from direct contacts with the oriental cultures of the Pacific and of Asia. Baird sees Melville as the new symbol-maker who "in answer to the basic human need for sacrament" taps archetypes of primitive feeling and impresses these with the unique forms or "autotypes" of the artist's individual physical and emotive experiences. As one of the wandering Ishmaels among 19th century artist-travellers Melville on his Polynesian voyages absorbed the archetypal images and symbols of primitive life that contrast with the "civic barbarism" of Western materialism and religious orthodoxy.
      Baird discusses six "archetypes of transformation" or "avatars" (descents of the deity) in Melville's work. Most essential is the *puer aeternus*, incarnated in the physically perfect tattooed Polynesian, and in the innocent youth-outcast of Western society. Their ideal friendship or *tayo* shows in the fraternal love between Queequeg and Ishmael, and in the sacramental innocence of Melville's ultimate symbol, Billy Budd. In him Melville unites the trusting acceptance of Polynesian *tayo* with the image of an unorthodox Christ as the selfless innocent among men, not the suffering Christ on the cross. Other Melvillean symbols embody the multiple and contradictory nature of God in the paradox of the savage wise man (again Queequeg), in the polarities of light and dark contained in whiteness, in shadowy and erotic symbols (such as Fedallah), in the archetypal fusion of the Polynesian tree of life with the cross, and lastly, of course, in the white whale, "the most complex symbol in the history of American art." Moby-Dick is Melville's most striking "non-anthropomorphous God-symbol," mythic "chaos-dragon," Vishnu avatar in the form of Leviathan. In the fullness of Melville's "linked analogies," Moby-Dick "becomes the whole of man's religious history" and Melville's supreme symbol of life and death, of the ambiguity of the unknowable God.
      Baird's fine study explores in revealing detail how Melville's symbols of "religious sensibility" are rooted in "the archetypes of

primitive feeling" experienced during his brief immersion in the social and religious life of some Polynesian islands.

32. BAIRD, James. "Jungian Psychology in Criticism: Theoretical Problems." In *Literary Criticism and Psychology*. Yearbook of Comparative Criticism, vol. 7. Ed. Joseph Strelka. University Park: Pennsylvania State University Press, 1976. 3-30.

While hedging his statements with academic reservations, Baird reviews "that portion of Jungian theory that has exerted a force in modern criticism." Any critic examining the literature of the West since the end of the eighteenth century will recognize the reappearance of "paganism" and the poet-priest in the person of the Romantic artist who opens his imagination to the unconscious and seeks new symbols to replace "the waning power of traditional Christian symbols." Even if one is critical of Jung's "collective unconscious," the archaic and mythic forms of the "new" symbols prove the relevance of his theory of archetypes. Baird explains Jung's "primarily intuitive" notions of libido, the archetypes of the unconscious, the God-imago, and the reconciliation of opposites. He emphasizes that for Jung art is a basically visionary, spiritual experience and he refers to poems of Wordsworth, Whitman, Mallarmé and Stevens for his illustrations.

In his somewhat evasive essay Baird makes valuable points about the relevance and influence of Jung and about the essential subjectivity of all art criticism. When discussing some "modifications and rejections" of Jung by critics like Maud Bodkin, Joseph Wheelwright and Northrop Frye, he contends that "no purely Jungian criticism of literature has yet appeared." This present bibliography challenges that statement.

33. BAKER, Howard. "Wallace Stevens and Other Poets." *Southern Review* (Baton Rouge) 1:2 (1935) 373-396. Excerpted in *The Achievement of Wallace Stevens : A Critical Anthology*. Eds. Ashley Brown and Robert S. Haller. Philadelphia: Lippincott, 1963. 89-91.

In this omnibus review we find the earliest comments on correspondences between Stevens' impersonal "psychical symbols" and Jung's collective archetypes of human experience.

34. BALTENSPERGER, Peter. "Battles with the Trolls." *Canadian Literature* 71 (1976) 59-67.

Psychological growth to wholeness is the theme underlying the first five novels of Robertson Davies from *Tempest-Tost* (1951) to *The Manticore* (1972). The progressive development of the fictional characters reflects the author's own quest for fulfillment, self-realization and mystical experience. The protagonists are mentored towards greater self-knowledge by Magus figures in all novels, but it is the visionary revelations of the "transcendent Liesl" that enable Ramsay and Staunton in *Fifth Business* and *The Manticore* to attain fuller spiritual wisdom.

35. BANKS, Landrum and John S. Zil. "Misanthropy and Antisocial Behavior in Houyhnhnmland: Equine Symbolism in Book IV of Jonathan Swift's *Gulliver's Travels*." *Corrective and Social Psychiatry and Journal of Behavior Technology Methods and Therapy*. 26:1 (1980) 31-34.

The purely rational Houyhnhnms in Swift's *Gulliver's Travels* (1726) represent "a neurotic inversion of the Jungian archetype" of "the intuitive, impulsive, dynamic, and live-giving horse." As an individual rather than a universal symbol, they reveal much about Swift's own "stinted emotional life." The authors find examples of similar inversions in Freud's case history of "Little Hans" and in the boy who blinds six horses in Peter Shaffer's play *Equus* (1973).

36. BARNUM, Carol M. "Archetypal Patterns in the Fiction of John Fowles: Journey toward Wholeness." (Ph.D. 1978 Georgia State University) 247 pp. *DAI* 39/07 A p.4236.

37. BARRET, Jeannine Allison. "Frye and Jung: Mirrored Harmonies. A Jungian Explication of Northrop Frye's *Anatomy of Criticism*." (Ph.D. 1978 New York University) 494 pp. *DAI* 39/12 A p.7331.

38. BARRET, John W. "Lawrence Durrell's *The Black Book* and *The Alexandria Quartet*: Some Existential and Jungian Correspondences." (PH.D. 1978 University of Northern Colorado) 364 pp. *DAI* 39/08 A p.4952.

39. BARTLETT, Lee. "The Dionysian Vision of Jack Kerouac." In *The Beats: Essays in Criticism*. Ed. Lee Bartlett. Jefferson, N.C.: McFarland, 1981. 115-126.

With a brief definition of "symbol" and "sign" in the Jungian sense, Bartlett deftly integrates the psychological with the more narrowly literary-critical issues. With the Nietzschean contraries of Apollonian and Dionysian he studies the spontaneity of Kerouac's novels. Without trying to label stages of individuation in Kerouac's writings, Bartlett concludes that Kerouac chooses "the pulse of the jazz-man [...] to surrender himself to the womb of the collective unconscious, bodying forth the Dionysian ideal."

Bartlett's attitude is much indebted to William Everson's "Dionysus and the Beat Generation" (q.v.). J.K.

40.   BEATSON, Peter R. "An Approach to the Religious Content of the Novels of Patrick White." (Ph.D. 1974 University of Cambridge, England) Not in *DAI*.
      Became book *The Eye in the Mandala* (1976).

41.   BEATSON, Peter. *The Eye in the Mandala. Patrick White: A Vision of Man and God*. London: Paul Elek, 1976. xii,172 pp.
      The "non-rational elements" in White's novels relate his awareness of "a mystery of Being running through the material world" to the thinkers by whom he was influenced: Weil, Maritain and Marcel, Jung, Eliot and Buber. His novels "explore the implications of the descent of the soul into matter," the central theme of Western metaphysical thinking and so much of the world's mythology, which in our time "has been given a metapsychological reinterpretation by C.G. Jung."

42.   BEAUCHAMP, Gorman. "The Rite of Initiation in Faulkner's *The Bear*." *Arizona Quarterly* 28 (1972) 319-325.
      Ike's initiation in Faulkner's story (1942) is viewed as a formal ritual of death to the boy's prior life and of his spiritual rebirth as a man and hunter. Guided by an archetypal old man, Sam Fathers, Ike is granted his vision only after relinquishing his gun, compass and watch, symbols of his will over nature and of the restrictions of time and space. The initiation is complete when in a symbolic return to the womb he loses his conscious orientation in the labyrinth of the wood and then sees the bear, Old Ben, androgynous spirit god of the wilderness, who becomes both father and mother to the initiate.

43.   BEAUCHAMP, Gorman. "Wordsworth's Archetypal Resolution." *Concerning Poetry* 7:2 (1974) 13-19.
      In the poem "Resolution and Independence" Wordsworth describes his meeting with a lonely old man, who paces "about the weary moor continually" in search of leeches. The deep impression this leech gatherer makes is ascribed to his impact on the unconscious mind as an embodiment of the archetype of the wise old man, symbol of psychic wholeness that helps lift Wordsworth out of his depressive mood.
      Carefully argued analysis.

44.   BEEBE, John. "The Trickster in the Arts." *San Francisco Jung Institute Library Journal* 2:2 (1981) 22-54.
      Wide-ranging psychological discussion of the trickster theme in Western European and American literature. The ambiguity of Henry James's *The Turn of the Screw* and of Shakespeare's *Hamlet* is

analyzed in terms of disturbing reader/audience effects, trickster integration in the literary characters, and possible mid-life crises of the authors.

45.   BEEBE, Maurice. "The Artist as Hero." In *A Portrait of the Artist as a Young Man*, by James Joyce. Ed. Chester G. Anderson. New York: Viking, 1968. 340-357.
Excerpted from *Ivory Towers and Sacred Founts*. New York: New York University Press, 1964.
There is a genre of portrait-of-the-artist novels *Pierre*, *Lost Illusions*, *Sentimental Education*, *The Way of All Flesh*, *Sons and Lovers*, *Remembrance of Things Past*, *The Counterfeiters*, *Doctor Faustus*, and *A Portrait of the Artist as a Young Man*. Three themes interlock in these semi-autobiographies: the Divided Self, the Ivory Tower, and the Sacred Fount. For his exposition of the Divided Self, the only section of this work drawing on Jung, Beebe quotes at length Jung's *Modern Man in Search of a Soul*: "Every creative person is a duality or a synthesis of contradictory attitudes." Stephen Dedalus' "uncreated conscience of my race" corresponds to Jung's notion of the artist as an aspect of "collective man." J.K.

46.   BEGG, Ean C.M. "The Lord of the Rings and the Signs of Times." Guild Lecture No. 178. London: Guild of Pastoral Psychology, 1975. 23 pp.
While investigating "the archetypal background of our contemporary situation," Ean Begg finds symbols for its negative aspects (unlimited power drive and violence) and positive aspects (reintegration of the feminine principle) in one of the imaginative books that "made the greatest impression on the post-war generation." In Tolkien's *The Lord of the Rings* the Hobbits are remarkable for their "relative immunity to the power drive." One of the book's principal themes is the individuation process of ring-bearer Frodo, traced through the stages of his anima development in his relations with Goldberry, Arwen, and Galadriel. The "archetypal rage and frenzy" of Wotan (in European history so often to our cost negated and repressed) finds positive expression in the "ecstatic and mantic" qualities of Gandalf the Wizard, who may be seen as "a renewed and transformed image of the Wotan archetype and a sketch for the sort of saviour figure one might expect to inspire our new age."

47.   *BEGIEBING, Robert J. *Acts of Regeneration: Allegory and Archetype in the Works of Norman Mailer*. Columbia: University of Missouri Press, 1980. 209 pp.

Basing his discussion of archetypal patterns and images on Jung, Campbell and Neumann, Begiebing sets out to prove that Mailer's work, both fiction and nonfiction, should be read as "symbolic allegory." Mailer uses the archetypal quest as a form of social criticism in which the forces of "Life" (the natural, instinctive man) struggle with the "alliance of Death" (technology, commercialism and totalitarianism). He seeks a hero for our time who would embody the five qualities he feels are necessary for "heroic consciousness": metaphorical perception, divine energy, revolutionary consciousness, faith in the extraordinary individual and the "impulse to restore a 'wholeness' and balance to the self and society."

Barbary Shore (1951) establishes the pattern of Mailer's future work: the archetype of rebirth. *The Deer Park* (1955) is more explicit in being "a novel of attempted 'regressions' to the sources of one's being, a novel of the death of the old man and the birth of the new, and a novel of the transfer of spirit as the dynamic principle of life and as the power within to survive and defy the incursions of a fallen, deadening world." *An American Dream* (1965) is a "mythical Night Sea Journey to rebirth." *Why Are We in Vietnam?* (1967) ends in the triumph of Life over Death.

"Mailer's nonfiction period provides the writer with the opportunity not only to try to become the artist-hero he found absent in his time, but to become, through a cathartic process of self-assertion, the objective, mature artist who is prepared to write his final fictions in the last decade or so of his creative life."

From a mythological/psychological point of view Begiebing has written an original study of the archetypal allegory that underlies the apparent realism of Mailer's fiction. He identifies the foundation on which Mailer has built his themes as "his life-long obsession with the discovery of the self." Good use is made of the Jungian perspective to provide critical analysis of Mailer's cultural purposes and the personal role it plays in his later journalistic nonfiction. Begiebing lucidly considers the nature of the allegorical impulse in Mailer's work and the similarities between the ideas of Jung and Mailer, which he sees as largely coincidental. He convincingly demonstrates that "an analysis of archetypal imagery helps us to understand a work's symbolic design" and allows us to "illuminate ramifications [...] we would otherwise miss." K.S.

48. BEGIEBING, Robert J. "Norman Mailer's *Why Are We in Vietnam?*: The Ritual of Regeneration." *American Imago* 37:1 (1980) 12-37.

Reading Mailer's novel (1967) as a hero's quest that fails, Begiebing briefly points out the archetypal aspects of D.J.'s bear-hunt and of Rusty as the Terrible Father.

49. BEGIEBING, Robert J. "Rebirth and Heroic Consciousness: Allegory and Archetype in the Works of Norman Mailer." (Ph.D. 1977 University of New Hampshire) 368 pp. *DAI* 38/05 A p.2782. Became book *Acts of Regeneration* (1980).

50. BENAMOU, Michel. *Wallace Stevens and the Symbolist Imagination*. Princeton: Princeton University Press, 1972. 109-139.

   In the final chapter major shifts in the imagery of Wallace Stevens' poetry are traced by means of word-counts and studied as a "psychological evolution." The essay is expanded from a paper in *Mundus Artium* 1 (1966). With recourse to Neumann and Jung, four phases are distinguished in Stevens' self-transformation. A preponderance of feminine imagery in the early poetry is followed by poems with many sun and hero images. Anima imagery returns in the third phase and is compared to the "mystic marriage" of masculine and feminine symbols in Jung's analysis of alchemical processes. In the final phase the search for a center of mental wholeness continues, but it leads Stevens "beyond the imagination's sea" to poems of "unsymbolized symbols," expressive "of mere being." The other essays in this collection consider the influence of French cubist painting and symbolist poetry on Stevens' work.

   The statistical approach seems promising, but the outcome is rather vague

51. *BENERT, Annette Larson. "The Dark Sources of Love: A Jungian Reading of Two Early James Novels." *University of Hartford Studies in Literature* 12:2 (1980) 99-123.

   The intricate development of character and point of view in Henry James's fiction finds an analogue in Jung's psychological investigations of the "complex, shifting nature of human reality." Benert analyzes the main characters in *Roderick Hudson* (1875) and *The Portrait of a Lady* (1881) in the light of Jung's notions of anima and animus projection, and of Eros and Logos as the principles of relatedness and the capacity for reflection in the human psyche. Always emphasizing the emotional development of individuals, James explicitly attributes the failure of a relationship to a "failure of perception." Roderick succumbs to his own illusions by failing to see that he merely projects onto Christina his own inner picture of the idealized woman. Isabel Archer acquires self-knowledge by learning the hard way that the persons she admires represent the negative sides of her own personality: Madame Merle, "the polished *persona* that Isabel all but becomes," and the man she marries, Gilbert Osmond, "the anti-self to which Isabel's negative animus" has logically driven her.

This perceptive literary analysis makes fine use of Jung's concepts and does justice to the psychological subtlety of James's character creations.

52.   BENERT, Annette Larson. "The Forces of Fear: Kesey's Anatomy of Insanity." *Lex et Scientia* 13:1-2 (1977) 22-26.

Ken Kesey's novel *One Flew over the Cuckoo's Nest* (1962) compellingly embodies "important strands of American psychic life-fear of women, fear of the machine, and glorification of the hero who conquers both." This essay analyzes how the inmates of the mental hospital, "in the language of analytic psychology," project their unlived femininity and power drives onto the women, blacks, and machines surrounding them. Big Nurse is for them the Terrible Mother of ancient mythology; they have to resist the Devouring Dragon of threatening technology; and McMurphy enters their nightmare world as the Savior "whose reluctant heroism earns him an electronic crucifixion."

The psychology of the characters and the symbolism in the novel are ably expounded.

53.   BENERT, Annette Larson. "Passion and Perception: A Jungian Reading of Henry James." (Ph.D. 1975 Lehigh University) 365 pp. *DAI* 36/09 A p.6095.

54.   *BENERT, Annette Larson. "Public Means and Private Ends: The Psychodynamics of Reform in James's Middle-Period Novels." *Studies in the Novel* 12:4 (1980) 327-343.

Even when Henry James is concerned with large social issues his view of political reality "begins in the jungles" of the individual human psyche. *The Bostonians* (1886) and *The Princess Casamassima* (1886) both depict political reform that "fails for the same reason that any human behavior fails in James's works, because of the primary failures of knowledge, particularly self-knowledge, and of relationship, particularly intimate, sexual relationship." Benert shows how closely "the dynamics of Jamesian narrative" correlate with Jung's psychosexual character typology. For both, the psyche is androgynous, and the adjectives "masculine" and "feminine" are linked with "Logos" qualities of discrimination and "Eros" qualities of involvement, respectively. Both writers "associate the disintegration of modern society with the weakening or devaluation of the feminine principle."

Benert argues that James bases these narratives, which move from the impulse to reform through political activity to climactic disintegration, upon three motivating principles: "(1) a private mythology upon which the protagonists' lives and relationships are based; (2) a primary homosexual bonding allied to the dominant political organization; and (3) a basically masculine brutality that blights the very movement it aims to support." In both novels there are triangular relationships with "a mythic or archetypal aura" involving competition between a powerful man and woman for the soul of a young person of mysterious origin. The main characters are only capable of deep emotional ties with members of their own sex, because (in very unorthodox Jungian terms) they unconsciously project onto their partners, not their individual contrasexual psychic qualities, but their own "unclaimed," insufficiently recognized, "femininity" or "masculinity." Olive in *The Bostonians* identifies so much with her masculine qualities that she projects her own anima onto very feminine women, while Hyacinth in *The Princess Casamassima*, with his "finely differentiated Eros," is drawn to masculine women and projects his animus in particular onto the brutally rational political leader of his anarchist group. Both James and Jung ascribe the destructive capacities and "spiritual inferiority" of the political fanatic to his "dissociated intellect," the "Logos gone mad."

A penetrating Jungian reading of the subtle complexities of James's fictional characters. Benert rightly and imaginatively goes beyond orthodox Jungian theory in "freeing" Jung's anima/animus and Eros/Logos conceptions from gender identity in order to "allow closer description of James's characters."

55. BENOIT, Ray. "The Mind's Return: Whitman, Teilhard, and Jung." *Walt Whitman Review* 13 (1976) 21-28.
Rpt. as "Whitman, Teilhard, and Jung" in *The Continuous Flame*: *Teilhard in the Great Traditions*. Ed. Harry J. Cargas. St.Louis, Mo.: Herder, 1969. 79-89.

Whitman's romantic visions of the universal democratic society as expressed in *Democratic Vistas* (1871) and the poem "Passage to India" find striking parallels in Teilhard de Chardin's views of a spiritual evolution of the universe to the point where geo-biological complexity will have developed into psychic unity, and in Jung's psychological principle of the syzygy, "the tension of opposites from which the divine child is born as the symbol of unity." Whitman's Democracy, Teilhard's Noosphere and Jung's Self are seen as analogous terms pointing to the unification of spiritualized matter and embodied spirit, as in the Christian Incarnation.

56. BENSON, James D. "*Romola* and the Individuation Process." *Colby Library Quarterly* 14:2 (1978) 54-71.
Against the usual critical strictures of the labored intellectuality of George Eliot's novel *Romola* (1863) it is argued

that a Jungian analysis shows its two stories to be structurally interrelated and symbolically focused on Romola's psychological development. The integration of the opposites in her character follows the stages of the individuation process: projection of her shadow on Tito and of her animus on Savonarola, and consequent withdrawal from both. In the chapters "Drifting Away" and "Romola's Waking" Romola's struggles with her conscience entail a psychological descent into the darkness of the unconscious and the attainment of a measure of wholeness, ultimately symbolized by her adoption of Tito's children. In contrast, Tito's repression of his shadow sides, shown in his abandoning of his father, leads to his being literally and symbolically destroyed by his unconscious.

This very full Jungian explication becomes a plea for greater appreciation of the novel's artistic qualities, because Eliot "wove her psychological insights into a meaningful mythic pattern that more closely approximates a moral-aesthetic whole than is generally recognized." The question remains in how far the neatness of the Jungian psychological scheme validates claims for greater artistic force and coherence than most critics have accorded this novel.

57.   BERENSON, William L. "Emerson and Self-Education: A Jungian Analysis." (Ph.D. 1986 University of Kansas) 512 pp. *DAI* 47/06 A p.2073.

58.   BERETS, Ralph. "A Jungian Interpretation of the Dream Sequence in Doris Lessing's *The Summer before the Dark*." *Modern Fiction Studies* 26:1 (1980) 117-129.

Stripped of her social persona of loving mother and wife during a summer away from her family, the heroine of Lessing's novel (1973) confronts her lack of self-definition. Under the pressure of unusual outward experiences Kate Brown embarks on an inner journey of psychic development that is suggested through a series of dreams about a stranded seal she must carry back to the sea through cold and darkness. Detailed analysis of these dreams shows that the novel must be read as Kate's progress toward greater psychological wholeness and "liberation of herself and her unconscious desires." Freudian readings that view Kate as another of Lessing's failed and frustrated women characters must be rejected as misinterpretations of Lessing's psychological theme, which is clearly Jungian oriented.

Though the case is at times overstated and some details seem questionable, the Jungian interpretation of the dreamsequence enhances the novel's meaning.

59. BERNSTEIN, Gene M. "Keats's 'Ode on a Grecian Urn': Individuation and the Mandala." *Massachusetts Studies in English* 4:1 (1973) 24-30.

The ode was written at the time when Keats was quickly maturing under distressful circumstances. In terms of an individuation process the urn is therefore seen as a mandala symbol that reconciles the poem's paradoxes, which center around "the intertwining of the eternal and the present." The urn's roundness is related to the "fourfold square" of human activities depicted on it: "love, art, religion and communal life."

This argument disregards, for one thing, that an urn in three dimensions hardly looks like a mandala. The mandala elements of spatial symmetry and geometric quaternity are also absent from the ode's organic imagery.

60. *BICKMAN, Martin. "Animatopoiea: Morella as Siren of the Self." *Poe Studies* 8:2 (1975) 29-32.

In Poe's tales woman often figures as the female soul mate, the anima, who in the attractions and repulsions of her wild, elusive character embodies both man's longing to encounter the depths of his unconscious and at the same time his fear that this will lead to the loss of his limited ego-consciousness. The wasting away of mother and daughter in "Morella" meaningfully suggests the narrator's own psychic disintegration through repression of the feminine within him. In other works, however, Poe envisages a final "luminous self-awareness that accompanies proper individuation" and even the tale "Morella" delineates "the very subtle but very real differences between creative mysticism and psychosis." It is argued that Jung's theory of the individuation process developes a typically Romantic thought pattern of unity-division-reintegration which is equally basic to Poe's philosophy, and that consequently Poe's great theme of psychic dissolution involves the complementary vision of psychic expansion, of a balanced, integrated soul at one with itself and the universe.

This brief article penetratingly argues the productiveness of a Jungian approach to Poe's tales. The idea is worked out in Bickman's book *The Unsounded Centre* (1980).

61. *BICKMAN, Martin. "Kora in Heaven: Love and Death in the Poetry of Emily Dickinson." *Emily Dickinson Bulletin* 32 (second half 1977) 79-104.

An earlier version of the excellent chapter on Dickinson in Bickman's book *The Unsounded Centre* (1980). The article is preceded by the author's own abstract: "Much critical comment about the nature of E.D.'s poetry can be reconciled if we view the poems as 'mythological ideas,' in K. Kerényi's use of the term, where 'opposites' such as the sexual and the spiritual, love and death, are comprehended. With the help of Jungian theory and empirical and psychological studies, the ambivalences and interrelations in the 'death-as-suitor' poems can be delineated. The psychological configuration uncovered here can be fruitfully juxtaposed with the Persephone myth, a juxtaposition that links this group of poems with other important groups, such as those dealing with Indian summer and the cycle of the seasons. Taken together, the poems chart a journey from a limited, ego-centered awareness to a consciousness that encompasses the entire psychic realm."

62. BICKMAN, Martin. "Melville and the Mind." In *A Companion to Melville Studies*. Ed. John Bryant. Westport, Conn.: Greenwood Press, 1986. 515-541.

A critical survey of important psychological criticism Freudian, Jungian, Lawrentian, Lacanian, or otherwise of Melville and his works. The "four major pieces" of the pioneer of Melville criticism, Henry A. Murray (q.v.), are given special attention. Jungian critics discussed include James Kirsch, Edward Edinger, and Ralph Maud (qq.v.). The potential for literary criticism of James Hillman's archetypal psychology is noted. There is an extensive bibliography.

63. BICKMAN, Martin. "Occult Traditions and American Romanticism: A Jungian Perspective." In *Literature and the Occult: Essays in Comparative Literature*. Ed. Luanne Frank. Arlington: University of Texas at Arlington, 1977. 54-64.

Both American Romanticism and Jungian psychology revitalize the previously occulted illuminist traditions of Gnosticism, Hermeticism, and Neo-Platonism. The "movement toward interiorization" of the Romantics "reaches a culmination in Jung's theory of the development of consciousness." Hence Jung's description of the process of individuation forms a useful analytic and conceptual tool for explaining the mythic symbolism of the soul's integration in Poe's "To Helen" and the quaternity symbols of Whitman in "Chanting the Square Deific."

64. *BICKMAN, Martin. *The Unsounded Centre: Jungian Studies in American Romanticism*. Chapel Hill: University of North Carolina Press, 1980. ix,182 pp.

New edition with new title and chapter on Melville added: *American Romantic Psychology: Poe, Emerson, Whitman, Dickinson, Melville*. Dallas, Texas: Spring Publications, 1988.

"This book is an approach to American Romanticism through Jungian psychology." At the same time, "the psychology itself is viewed as another formulation [...] of the confluence of traditions that shaped American Romanticism." Consequently the discussion of central concepts and symbols in the work of Poe, Emerson, Whitman and Dickinson not only provides psychological and literary analysis of some of the more enigmatic stories and poems, but also "illuminates the origins and the nature of [Jungian] psychology." The American Romantic writers "in the very process of writing their works [...] advanced the exploration of the psyche," and the psychological reading of literature may therefore shed light both ways, if the method is used flexibly and creatively.

In his methodical introduction Bickman shows how both Emerson and Jung see the symbol as a bridge between conscious and unconscious, as the "means of transposing the unknown into at least the suspected, the intuited, the embodied." The method for clarifying the highly symbolic texts is that of "amplification" in Jung's sense, the juxtaposing of illustrative or complementary analogues from myths, psychology or the works of the different authors themselves. The general pattern of "unity-differentiation-restored harmony," underlying Romantic thought, is traced in the key works of Poe, Emerson and Whitman, and its "congruence" with Jung's theory of the development of consciousness is demonstrated.

Chapters are devoted to each of the Romantics separately. First Poe's vision of the feminine as the contrasexual element is explored in the "transformative character" of anima imagery in poems like "To Helen," and in the ego disintegration of the male characters, who reject or repress the anima, in tales like "Morella" and "Ligeia" with their horrifying "return of the repressed." A corresponding examination of the masculine in a number of Emily Dickinson's poems, in which death figures as a suitor, brings out how the sexual and spiritual are inextricably fused, and how the images of death, sacred marriage and rebirth in her poetry (illuminatingly amplified with the Persephone myth and the Greek Eleusinian mysteries) became "symbolical enactments in the drama of a mind moving toward individuation." In another chapter Emerson and Jung (both "deliberately unsystematic thinkers") are allowed to illuminate each other by considering "the relationship between psychological dynamics and literary style and structure" in three of Emerson's essays. The analysis of the complex Whitman poems "The Sleepers" and "Out of the Cradle Endlessly Rocking" argues that their regressive eroticism and the reliving of memories from childhood are shot through with images of widening consciousness, suggesting the poet-singer's "future expansion of self" in the artist's communion with his audience.

Full praise must go to the sensitive detail of Bickman's discussions of individual texts, and to his intelligent elaboration of the book's central thesis. He shows a healthy awareness of the dangers involved in applying any critical thesis, and especially a psychological scheme, to literary texts. His book surveys the whole field of scholarship that has dealt with symbolism in the American Romantics, and he builds on a range of valuable earlier Jungian studies in this field, particularly the essays of Barton Levi St. Armand on Poe. Together with Albert Gelpi's fine study of the same writers, *The Tenth Muse* (1975), Bickman's compressed, yet rich and suggestive book exemplifies and extends the critical insights that have been won from Jungian interpretations of the American Romantics.

65. BICKMAN, Martin E. "Voyages of the Mind's Return: A Jungian Study of Poe, Emerson, Whitman, and Dickinson" (Ph.D. 1974 University of Pennsylvania) 174 pp. *DAI* 36/01 A p.266.
Became book *The Unsounded Centre: Jungian Studies in American Romanticism* (1980).

66. BISHOP, Nadean Hawkins. "The Mother Archetype in Arnold's *Merope* and Swinburne's *Atalanta in Calydon.*" (Ph.D. 1972 University of Wisconsin, Madison) 332 pp. *DAI* 33/12 A p.6862.

67. BLOCK, Sandra J. "The Archetypal Feminine in the Poetry of Denise Levertov" (Ph.D. 1978 Kansas State University) 488 pp. *DAI* 39/05 A p.2936.

68. BLOOM, Clive. *The 'Occult' Experience and the New Criticism: Demonism, Sexuality and the Hidden in Literature*. Brighton, England: Harvester Press, 1986. 256 pp.
Draws on the theories of Jung, Freud, de Saussure and Derrida in order to elucidate the presence of the occult in Blake, Wordsworth, Emily Brontë, Eliot, Yeats and Kafka.

69. BLOOMINGDALE, Judith. "Alice as Anima: The Image of Woman in Carroll's Classics." In *Aspects of Alice: Lewis Carroll's Dreamchild as Seen through the Critics' Looking-Glasses*. Ed. Robert Phillips. New York: Vanguard Press, 1971. 378-390.
The argument of this essay is summed up as follows: *Alice's Adventures in Wonderland* (1865) and *Through the Looking-Glass* (1871) can best be described as the harrowing of the Victorian Hell. Alice herself is Carroll's Beatrice, the Muse of his Comedy. Her fall down the rabbithole is that of Eve - Adam's soul mate, or *anima* - and her ultimate coronation as Queen of the Looking-Glass World is

an unconscious anticipation of the Assumption of Mary as Queen of Heaven, which became Catholic dogma in 1950." Jung is freely quoted and Freud invoked when Dodgson's personal life is related to the figures and situations in his books. Mother complex, Oedipus fixation and child archetype help explain his "precarious development of masculine identity" and his choice of a girl child as a heroine. The central riddle of *Wonderland* is that of the Cheshire Cat's grin, symbol of the Eternal Feminine. The Duchess and the Queen of Hearts play the role of the Terrible Mother. In the Looking-Glass world Alice finds herself on "a higher plain of existence." The White Knight as "positive *animus*" is the gentle, innocent servant of his Lady. "As absurd hero of his age, [he] sums up the history of Western civilisation: he is at once Christ, St.George, the Knight of the Grail, Lancelot, Don Quixote, and finally modern man."

The boisterous banquet at the coronation of Queen Alice leaves the reader of this essay with a deadly surfeit of symbols. Carroll's ironic topsy-turvy world requires cautious psychological interpretation. The psychological reading of his life is as full of sweeping claims as the Jungian explanations of Alice's adventures.

70.   *BLOTNER, Joseph L. "Mythic Patterns in *To the Lighthouse*." *PMLA* 71 (1956) 547-562.
Rpt. in *Myth and Literature: Contemporary Theory and Practice.* Ed. John B.Vickery. Lincoln: University of Nebraska Press, 1966. 243-255.

Virginia Woolf's novel (1927) contains correspondences with the myths of Oedipus and Demeter-Kore as interpreted by Freud on the one hand, and Jung and Kerényi on the other. The central character, Mrs. Ramsay, has physical attributes and psychic qualities reminiscent of the goddesses Rhea, Demeter and Persephone, the mother-daughter-maiden figures of Greek mythology, who encompass the life-giving feminine in its relations to a death-dealing male principle. Symbolically Mrs. Ramsay's fertility triumphs over death in the resurgence of Lily's creativity and the relation established between Mr. Ramsay and his son during the voyage to the lighthouse. The mythic pattern is a flexible "framework within boundaries and by virtue of whose spatial ordering the symbolic people, passages, and phrases of the book can be seen to assume a relationship to each other which illuminates their reciprocal functions and meanings."

A cautious and sensitive use of the archetypal approach.

71. BLY, Robert. "Developing the Underneath" and "The Network and the Communication." *American Poetry Review* 2:6 (1973) 44-45 and 3:1 (1974) 19-21.

   In these two columns Robert Bly writes wise words about the Jungian "four ways of grasping the world" and the need for poets (and other humans) to develop their weakest function, which is "the channel opening you to the rest of humanity." Too often people only relate in superficial "networks" through their dominant functions. Bly takes his examples from writers past and present.

72. BLY, Robert. *Sleepers Joining Hands*. New York: Harper & Row, 1973. 67 pp.

   In his volume of poems *Sleepers Joining Hands* Robert Bly inserts a prose piece, called "I Came Out of the Mother Naked," in which he sets down thoughts about the "psychic archaeology" of mother consciousness in the history of human culture and in his own poetry. Following Bachofen, Jung and Neumann he talks about the replacement of Great Mother cultures by patriarchies and about the different forms the mythic mother has taken in religion, mythology and literature, distinguishing besides the Great Mother and the Good Mother also the Dancing or Ecstatic Mother and the Stone or Teeth Mother. The latter's fierce destructiveness is seen at work in Bly's poem about the Vietnam war, "The Teeth Mother Naked at Last," in this volume. (See also the section "Talk about the Great Mother" in Bly's book of essays, talks and interviews *Talking All Morning*. Ann Arbor: University of Michigan Press, 1980. 207-237.)

73. *BODKIN, Maud. *Archetypal Patterns in Poetry: Psychological Studies in Imagination*. London: Oxford University Press, 1934. xiv,340 pp.
   Rpt. New York: Knopf, 1958. xvi,324 pp.

   This is the pioneering study in the application of Jungian psychology to the interpretation of poetry. Bodkin draws on a number of psychologists, among whom Freud (Oedipus complex, superego, life and death instincts), but she bases her psychological studies of individual poems and plays on Jung's concepts of the archetypes and the collective unconscious. Her aim is to test Jung's hypothesis that "the special emotional significance possessed by certain poems" is due "to the stirring in the reader's mind, within or beneath his conscious response, of unconscious forces which he terms 'primordial images', or archetypes." She argues from her own subjective reactions to "the great themes of poetry" as well as from responses of such readers of Shakespeare as A.C. Bradley, Gilbert Murray, and Ernest Jones.

The "persistent themes or archetypal patterns" in great poetry are studied in two ways: by exploring an archetype in a particular work (extensive analysis of the rebirth theme in "The Ancient Mariner"), or by comparing variants of an archetype in a number of works (the feminine in Homer, Virgil, Dante and Goethe). There are chapters on the essential form of tragic drama; on the Paradise-Hades, or heaven-hell archetype, illustrated from Coleridge, Milton, William Morris, Virgil and Dante; on the image of the devil, the hero and God; and finally, on patterns in sacred and contemporary literature (Lawrence, Woolf, Eliot). The last chapter considers the relation with poetry and music, dance and religion, and a plea is made for basing the psychological analysis of poetry on a full awareness of "the emotional and intuitive experience communicated."

This first extensive Jungian exploration of literary texts is a rich, sensitive and honest book. It is curious that for many years Bodkin's study attracted hardly any attention in literary and psychological circles. In his very appreciative chapter on "Maud Bodkin and Psychological Criticism" (in *The Armed Vision*, 1948. q.v.) Stanley Hyman discusses the possible reasons for this neglect. The academic world was apparently shy of an amateur student of literature, neither professional psychologist nor professional critic, who made eclectic use of Freud, Jung and other psychologists, who based herself frankly on the "free response and introspection" of her own and others' readings of great literature, and who was ready to discuss the moral and religious implications of these personal and at the same time "suprapersonal" experiences. Even if the earnestness with which Maud Bodkin offers her personal impressions may at times seem somewhat naïve, the depth and originality of her criticism has since been recognized, just as certain of her ideas have been taken up by later schools of criticism. In the 1960s Norman Holland's psychoanalytic studies of literary reception developed Bodkin's experiments in comparing her own associations with the emotional responses of other readers. (See for a balanced critique of Bodkin's work Simon O. Lesser's review of the 1958 paperback reissue: "Homage to Maud Bodkin" in *Literature and Psychology* 8:3 (1958) 44-45.)

74.   BODKIN, Maud. "Archetypal Patterns in Tragic Poetry." *British Journal of Psychology* 21 (1930) 183-202.
      This article became the first chapter of her book *Archetypal Patterns in Poetry* (1934).

75.   BODKIN, Maud. "Literary Criticism and the Study of the Unconscious." *The Monist* 37 (1927) 445-468.

Developing clues from the book *Art and the Unconscious* (1925) by the philosopher John M. Thorburn (q.v.) and using one of her own dreams for illustration, Maud Bodkin considers how far the new methods of Freud, Jung and others "can throw light upon the nature of poetry and all forms of imaginative literature." The study of dreams suggests analogies with the creative mind of the artist. The unity of unconscious motif discovered by dream analysis is paralleled by the universal motifs, Jung's archaic images or archetypes, to be discerned below the conscious intentions of the artist. A comparison between Marlowe's and Goethe's version of the Faust legend suggests the force of the archetypal mythological theme. The genesis of Ibsen's play *The Wild Duck* exemplifies the involuntary interaction of conscious and unconscious elements in the individual poet's creation. In all "complete creative thinking" unconscious factors play a decisive part. Yet the artist's thought is marked off by a command over the particular medium in which dreams and fantasies are expressed. Drama, dance and poetic song share an expressive language of bodily rhythms that reflects "the instinctive urgencies" of the life of the individual and of his age. The new psychology of the unconscious will help the literary critic discover forces within the human mind that shape the symbolism and the forms of literature. "We need a fuller study of works of art in comparison with dreams and myth, religious symbol and philosophic system with all forms in which the creative energies of the mind find expression."

The careful distinctions drawn in this essay contain the germinal ideas as well as the program for Maud Bodkin's later writings.

76. BODKIN, Maud. "Literature and the Individual Reader." *Literature and Psychology* 10:2 (1960) 39-44.

Literature appeals to readers of Maud Bodkin's type in the first place through "word-music" and as a symbolic expression of conflicts present in the mind of the writer. In some of Milton's poetry, telling of "things invisible," and in passages of Shakespearean tragedy this music makes the reader respond to "energies of the human spirit in a form which may be termed archetypal" in Jung's sense. Even agnostics intuitively react to the rebirth pattern in the story of the life and death of Jesus. It is suggested that similarly the poetic presentation of the hero's death in great tragedies is felt more as a release and a passing to some new existence than as a final extinction.

77. BODKIN, Maud. *Studies of Type-Images in Poetry, Religion and Philosophy*. London: Oxford University Press, 1951. xii,184.

In her last book Bodkin pursues her investigation of archetypal patterns, or type-images as she prefers to call them here, into the fields of religion and philosophy. Sharing Jung's belief in the "creative activity" of the individual mind, she argues with many illustrations from world literature that the encounter with "the archetypes of saving wisdom and spiritual rebirth" (as imaged, for instance, in Eliot's *Murder in the Cathedral* and Yeats's "The Second Coming") may give those "who cannot accept the dogmas of any religion" experience of the Divine and "faith in the existence of God."

78.   BOE, John. "To Kill Mercutio: Thoughts on Shakespeare's Psychological Development." *Quadrant* 8:2 (1975) 97-105.
      Aspects of Shakespeare's own psychology are deduced from speeches by Mercutio, Posthumus, Hamlet, Prospero, Caliban and other characters in the plays. His art is "an expression of the unconscious unclouded with ego elements," but he had to kill the Mercutio of light-hearted word-play within himself before he wakened, like Lear, "to the real mysteries of life."
      An inconsequential article that demonstrates the perils of losing sight of dramatic context and the way characters and their speeches function within the plays.

79.   BOE, John. "Jack London, the Wolf and Jung." *Psychological Perspectives* 11:2 (1980) 133-136.
      A brief piece about the wolf in Jack London's stories as the symbol of London's shadow sides, and about his ego's inadequate "relationship with the self."

80.   BOE, John. "Pastoral and the Unconscious." (Ph.D. 1974 University of California, Berkeley) No abstract in *DAI*.
      Jungian psychology is used to argue that the pastoral journey from city to country (in Virgil and the Renaissance) can be understood in terms of a journey from conscious to unconscious. Chapters on Sidney's *Arcadia* and Shakespeare's *As You Like It*, *Cymbeline*, *The Winter's Tale* and *The Tempest*.

81.   BOEWE, Charles. "Myth and Literary Studies." *University Of Kansas City Review* 27:3 (1961) 191-196.
      An attempt to formulate precise definitions of the terms image, symbol and myth, often too loosely used by critics studying literature in the context of its social and cultural relevance. When discussing "image", the Jungian "primordial image" is summarily dismissed as a somewhat unnecessary concept that "tells us little

about the social and cultural context" of the literature to which it is applied.

But who claims that this is what the archetype should be used for?

82. BOLLING, Douglass. "Imagery in Charles Williams' *Many Dimensions*." *Four Quarters* 23:1 (1972) 21-27.

The symbolism of body imagery in Charles Williams's novel *Many Dimensions* (1931) is analyzed to argue Chloe's archetypal role as a savior and earth mother who overcomes psychic imbalance in herself.

83. BOLLING, Douglass. "Structure and Theme in *Briefing for a Descent into Hell*." *Contemporary Literature* 14:4 (1973) 550-564.
Rpt. in *Doris Lessing: Critical Studies*. Eds. Annis Pratt and L.S. Dembo. Madison: University of Wisconsin Press, 1973. 133-147.

The protagonist's archetypal descent into the darkness of the unconscious is suggested in the first half of Lessing's novel (1971) through the mythical symbolism of visionary dream experiences during an "exploration of his inner space" that takes place while he is being treated in a psychiatric hospital for complete loss of memory. These "deranged" experiences form the outermost expansion of a creative spiral of his total psyche, which in the second movement of the novel contracts under the influence of electric shock therapy into his return to the spiritual sterility of his normal life. The theme of the loss of psychic wholeness in a "demythologized and dehumanized society" is reflected in the contrast between the lyrical, oracular style of the first part and the dry exchanges of doctor's reports and letters in the second part of the novel.

Good use has been made of Laing, Jung and Eliade to clarify the tightly joined symbolism of theme and structure in Lessing's novel.

84. BOLLING, Douglass. "The Journey into Self: Charles Williams' *The Place of the Lion*." *The Cresset* (Valparaiso) 37:6 (1974) 14-18.

An analysis of a major episode in Williams' novel *The Place of the Lion* (1931) to demonstrate his "use of Jungian insight." Damaris Tighe's struggle with a winged creature in her study symbolizes in a dialectic interplay of persona, shadow, and animus "her psychological and spiritual transformation [...] from a sterile and debilitating egoism and intellectualism to the threshold of maturity and wholeness."

85. BONNEY, William W. *"Christmas on the Nan-Shan*: Joseph Conrad and 'the New Seamanship'." *Conradiana* 10:1 (1978) 17-39.

This psychological/mythical reading of Conrad's *Typhoon* (1903) views the limitations of Captain MacWhirr's character in the context of a story that becomes a paradigm of the struggle between light and darkness in its clash between "conscious simplicity and undifferentiated chaos." The external collision with the typhoon dramatizes an inner conflict, "a re-enactment in the phenomenal world of MacWhirr's unrealized, and therefore potentially destructive, irrationality."

86. BOYD, John D. "Gabriel Conroy's Secret Sharer." *Studies in Short Fiction* 17:4 (1980) 499-501.

Brief article mistakenly suggesting that James Joyce's short story "The Dead" might be read as an "archetypal story" of psychological growth, if its ambiguous ending is understood as Gabriel Conroy confronting his own "shadow-figure" in his wife's memory of her long-dead lover.

87. BOYD, Nancy Willnet Cramer. "Plunging Through Baffling Wood: Melville's *Mardi* and Jungian Archetypes." (Ph.D. 1983 Bowling Green State University) 225 pp. *DAI* 45/05 A p.1398.

88. BRACEWELL, Marilyn. "From Androgyny to Community in the Poetry of Adrienne Rich." (Ph.D. 1980 University of Texas, Austin) 258 pp. *DAI* 41/04 A p.1591.

89. BRADSHAW, Graham. "Ted Hughes' Crow as Trickster-Hero." In *The Fool and the Trickster*: Studies in Honour of Enid Welsford. Ed. Paul V.A. Williams. Cambridge, England: Brewer, 1979. 83-108, 134-137.

This critical discussion of Hughes' poetic persona in the Crow poems considers the parallels between Crow and the hero of North American trickster myths, who is both "the blasphemous transgressor and a benefactor or culture-hero." At the same time Crow undergoes trials that constitute a quest aiming (in Hughes' words) "to locate and release his own creator, God's nameless hidden prisoner." Bradshaw sees this earlier creator as the Great Goddess or "Nature whose essential ambivalence is obliterated by Christian and Platonic dualisms." If this is the theme of *Crow* as a whole, it suggests how and why Hughes relates the trickster to "the ambivalent primaeval Goddess, in pursuing the correspondence between Trickster, Hero, and Shaman." What Hughes provides is "a poetic diagnosis of the effects of the suppression of the mother myths in Occidental civilizations." In Jungian terms Crow as trickster-hero is the collective shadow figure that the higher consciousness has neglected or repressed, and the trickster's relation to the Goddess is that of the shadow to the anima "in a liberating development of consciousness."

Discerning analysis of the psychology of Crow.

90. BRANDABUR, Agnes McSharry. "The Faust Theme and the Descent into Hell." (Ph.D. 1971 University of Illinois, Urbana-Champaign) 170 pp. *DAI* 32/10 A p.5775. (Thomas Mann, myth criticism)

91. BRANTLINGER, Patrick. "Romances, Novels and Psychoanalysis." In *The Practice of Psychoanalytic Criticism*. Ed. Leonard Tennenhouse. Detroit: Wayne State University Press, 1976. 18-45.

The psychologizing character of both romances and novels, the similarities and differences in the psychological functions of the two genres are considered. Using examples from 19th century fiction it is argued that romances embody wishfulfillments, regressive fantasies, dreams and illusions, whereas the realistic novel aims at disillusionment and the unmasking of the infantile and irrational. Both art forms, however, like all mental activity, have their roots in the unconscious. The writings of Freud and Jung on literature are reviewed. It is found that Jung claims too much direct psychic truth for all forms of literature, Freud perhaps too little. "The claims to maturity, objectivity, and rationality of realistic writers are no more to be accepted at face value than are the opposite claims of romancers and surrealists to be expressing unconscious contents without the mediation of secondary processes." Because all art is fantasy, there is no way of asserting the esthetic, moral or psychological superiority of one form over another. The quality of both novels and romances will in the end "depend largely on the truth and subtlety of the rational understanding which their authors bring to them."

The detail and subtlety of this paper are persuasive, and its contribution to genre study is original.

92. BRAY, Mary K. "Mandalic Activism: An Approach to Structure, Theme, and Tone in Four Novels by Phillip K. Dick." *Extrapolation* 21:2 (1980) 146-157.

The notion (derived from Jung) that a mandala is a centering image symbolizing "unity in diversity and interconnectedness," a paradigm of the nature of Being manifesting itself in opposites, is applied in a fairly abstract analysis of Dick's science fiction as a blend of "'mandalic awareness' and social activism, of Eastern and Western modes of perception and experience."

93.   BRESLIN, Paul. "How to Read the New Contemporary Poem." *The American Scholar* 47:3 (1978) 357-370.

After the "confessional" poetry of the sixties Breslin sees in the seventies a "new surrealism" in the work of poets like W. S. Merwin, Robert Bly, James Wright, and many younger poets. The new style is characterized by a symbolism of "interior revelation" and its general theme is that of "a voyage inward, a quest for union with the unconscious." In a list of recurrent images Breslin notes the correspondence with Jungian archetypes: "their significance is innate and prior to context." Key images of cave, stone and bones in well-known poems like "The Jewel" by James Wright and "Turning Inward at Last" by Robert Bly have analogues in the "big" dreams, recounted in Jung's *Memories, Dreams, Reflections* (1960), that led him to formulate his theory of the collective unconscious. The rise of this new poetry is related to the popular radicalism of the 1960s and the counterculture's emphasis on "recovery of the repressed through the exploration of one's own psyche." Breslin warns against the solipsistic tendencies inherent in the new movement.

94.   *BRIVIC, Sheldon R. *Joyce between Freud and Jung.* Port Washington, N.Y.: Kennikat Press, 1980. 226 pp.

The purpose of this study is to examine the development of Joyce's mind and works seen as a "sweeping movement from bitterness and rejection to good humor and acceptance," and as "a steady shift from naturalism and social criticism [in *The Dubliners*] to symbolism and myth in *Ulysses* and *Finnegans Wake*." The main tool used "to show how Joyce's mind was formed and to explore its unconscious aspects" is Freudian psychoanalysis, which "tells better than any other method where mental life comes from." However, "it can't tell where it goes," and it is Jungian psychology that provides the best means of comprehending the sense of purpose and of "the affirmation of human value and love that readers find in Joyce's later works."

The first third of Brivic's book examines *Portrait of the Artist as a Young Man* (1916) from a Freudian perspective and establishes the origins of Stephen's (and Joyce's) obsessions in his Oedipal family ties. The next third analyzes Joyce's treatment of love in the play *Exiles* (1918) in terms resembling those of Jung. The logic of interacting opposites and of the need for spiritual rebirth explain the main theme of Joyce's life and writings: "the individual [who] paradoxically achieves creative relation to the world by means of separation." In order to stay spiritually alive people must confront their opposites and risk alienation and death, as Richard Rowan in *Exiles* achieves rebirth and spiritual enlargement by following the mythical path of freedom and exile in his relations with Bertha.

In the final part of his book Brivic makes extensive use of Jung's *Psychological Types* to explore the complementary natures of Stephen, introverted intuitive with thinking as his secondary function, and Bloom, the extraverted sensation and feeling type. By collision of the opposites of Stephen and Bloom, and their relations to the feminine, self-development is promoted, and change toward wholeness. Joyce links the characters and the events in *Ulysses* (1922) through meaningful coincidences, which find their explanatory parallel in Jung's idea of synchronicity as the transcendent principle of meaning.

Granted the assumption that there is a good deal of Joyce himself in his literary characters, Brivic has written a very able psychological study that sheds light on "the nature and development of Joyce's mind as reflected in his work." The Freudian and Jungian interpretations clearly reinforce and complement each other. It is salutary to find a critic who can make fruitful use of both Freud and Jung in analyzing the works of an author who himself managed "in piercing through conventional assumptions about human relations and mental experience to reveal new areas of psychological reality." Just as it is amusing to hear that, when at one point Stephen calls on a female spirit, this "female soul or *anima* [...] goes through a Jungo-Freudian transformation to become his mother."

95. BROOKS, Ellen W. "Fragmentation and Integration: A Study of Doris Lessing's Fiction." (Ph.D. 1971 New York University) 569 pp. *DAI* 32/07 A p.3989.

96. BROOKS, Harold F. "W.B. Yeats: 'The Tower'." *Durham University Journal* 73:1 (1980) 9-21 [n.s. 42 (1980-81)].

An elaborate explication of Yeats's poem "The Tower" with its impassioned expression of the need for the poet to perfect his soul now that "decrepit age" threatens both him and his "fantastical imagination." The solution Yeats proposes to himself in the poem is linked to Jung's discussion of the problems of the second half of life in his commentary (1929) on the Chinese wisdom book *The Secret of the Golden Flower*. Life's conflicts may be transcended by creative detachment without denying the significance of past experiences.

97. BROWN, Daniel R. "A Look at Archetypal Criticism." *Journal of Aesthetics and Art Criticism* 28:4 (1970) 465-472.

A general discussion of the uses and abuses of archetypal criticism in literary studies. If flexibly applied, it has the advantage that its psychological approach combines essential "demands of human thinking - the analytical and the spiritual."

98. BROWN, Eric D. "Archetypes of Transformation: A Jungian analysis of Chaucer's 'Wife of Bath's Tale' and 'Clerk's Tale'." (Ph.D. 1972 Pennsylvania State University) 209 pp. *DAI* 33/10 A p.5672.

99. BROWN, Eric D. "Symbols of Transformation: A Specific Archetypal Examination of *The Wife of Bath's Tale*." *Chaucer Review* 12:4 (1978) 202-217.
The transformation of hag into maiden seen in the archetypal light of the knight's psychic growth. The rape, the riddle and the loathly mother figure suggest his hostility toward and fear of the unconscious. Acceptance of the hag and his own shadow side crown the knight's search for the anima with his symbolic renewal in his union with the beautiful young maid.

100. BROWN, Eric D. "Transformation and *The Wife of Bath's Tale*: A Jungian Discussion." *Chaucer Review* 10:4 (1976) 303-315.
Prolegomenon to an archetypal analysis of Chaucer's tale. With a variety of quotations from Jung on psychic transformation it is argued that the tale of the hag turning into bright maiden shows levels ranging from the factual ugliness-beauty, winter-spring elements to the analogical symbolism of sun-fertility consciousness arising from the dark, frightening, unshapen unconscious. The world-wide distribution of the story may be related to its union of opposites in a rite of renewal that leads to a release of psychic energy. Comparison of the various analogues thus suggests a common mythical-psychological framework that may aid the understanding of Chaucer's work.

101. BROWN, Harriette Grissom. "Animus and the Fiction of Anaïs Nin: A Feminine Interpretation of Logos." (Ph.D. 1980 Emory University) 397 pp. *DAI* 41/04 A p.1579.

102. BROWN, P.L.R. "Psychological Aspects of Some Yeatsian Concepts." *Mosaic* 11:1 (1977) 21-35.
The remarkable parallels between Yeats's system and Jung's psychology are approached from the viewpoint that "Yeats's system is not an analogue but a direct representation of reality," since the world of Spirits and Daimons developed in *A Vision* (1925) is "an elaborate dramatization of unconscious processes" as described by Jung. Yeats's Daimon experienced as a living reality corresponds in psychological terms with a Jungian archetype constellated as a personalized autonomous complex. Yeats's quest for the daimonic

Self and for artistic symbols expressing Unity of Being are the Jungian search for a healthy balance between conscious and unconscious, ego and daimon.

103. *BROWN, Russel, M. and Donna A. Bennett. "Magnus Eisengrim: The Shadow of the Trickster in the Novels of Robertson Davies." *Modern Fiction Studies* 22:3 (1976) 347-363.

In contrast with the traditional picture of man struggling and suffering in the wilderness, a positive trickster figure has been a frequent character in Canadian fiction since the 1950s. Combining "folly and guile, cleverness with recklessness" and liberating other characters from the psychic traps of social conventions, the comic trickster serves as "an anti-Job." The "most fully developed fictional investigation of the trickster yet to appear" is to be found in Robertson Davies' *Deptford Trilogy* (1970-1975). With the help of Jung's archetypal theory and his essay "On the Psychology of the Trickster Figure" the authors show how in *Fifth Business* (1970) the trickster-magician Magnus Eisengrim leads both the spiritual Dunstan Ramsay and the materialistic Boy Staunton to recognition of their shadow sides. The confrontation with his subconscious wishes drives Boy to suicide, while his son David and Dunstan learn from Eisengrim and his *femme inspiratrice* Liesl to reach for psychic wholeness, integration of mind and shadow, of spirit and body.

Penetrating character analysis that makes exellent use of Jung's theories. The emergence of the literary trickster in recent Canadian fiction is related to artists' views of general cultural developments in modern society.

104. BRUNNER, Cornelia. *Anima as Fate*. Dallas, Tex.: Spring Publications, 1986. xv,225 pp. Translated from the German *Die Anima als Schicksalsproblem des Mannes*. Zurich: Rascher Verlag, 1963.

Contains a lengthy psychological interpretation of Rider Haggard's *She*.

105. BUCHSBAUM, Betty. "Wallace Stevens: The Wisdom of the Body in Old Age." *Southern Review* (Baton Rouge) 15:4 (1979) 953-967.

To explain the sense of "wholeness" in the heroes of Stevens' late poems the critic pursues the parallel with Jungian individuation. The "wisdom" of Penelope in the poem "The World is Meditation" and of the dying Santayana in "To an Old Philosopher in Rome" is related to their embodying the archetypes of the anima expressing life, and of the wise old man who personifies meaning.

106. BURKE, J. David. "Images of Love in the Lyrics of Popular Songs of the 1960s: A Jungian Perspective in Ethics." (Ph.D. 1980 University of Southern California) *DAI* 41/04 A p.1644.

107. BURKE, Kenneth. "Symbolism as a Realistic Mode: 'De-Psychoanalyzing' Logologized." *Psychocultural Review* 3:1 (1979) 25-37.

Burke gives final definition to a theory developed in earlier books, particularly in the chapter "Archetype and Entelechy" of *Dramatism and Development* (1972), where he criticized the Freudian Oedipal archetype. Distinguishing between Platonic archetypes as idealistic and Aristotelian entelechies as realistic, he here argues that the Freudian and Jungian archetypes, unnecessarily conceived in terms of actual origins, "overstress [...] the 'archaic' or 'primordial' where the real issue, as viewed 'logologically' (i.e. from the point of view of symbolic theory), involves but an 'entelechial' perfecting of symbol-systems." Instead of the archetypes of psychological idealism "Logological Realism" posits entelechy or the striving after perfection as the realistic principle of symbolic motivation.

108. BURLESON, Donald R. *H.P.Lovecraft: A Critical Study*. Westport, Conn.: Greenwood Press, 1983. xi,243.

This study of Lovecraft's fiction blends a number of critical approaches, including formalist, philosophical, biographical, Jungian, and mythical-archetypal. The horror stories "The Outsider", "The Rats in the Walls" and "The Shadow out of Time" are analyzed in Jungian terms as the descent to the most primitive levels of the collective unconscious and the destructive confrontation with the archetypal shadow.

109. BURROWS, David J., Frederick R. Lapides and John T. Schawcross, eds. *Myths and Motifs in Literature*. New York: Free Press, 1973. xxii,470.

An anthology illustrating "commonly accepted archetypes" in various genres of world literature from Homer to John Barth. There is an introduction to archetypal theory with selections from Bodkin, Fiedler, Fromm, Frazer and Frye. The selections are grouped under the main headings "The Cycle of Life" and "Archetypal Characters."

110. BURROWS, J.F. "Archetypes and Stereotypes: *Riders in the Chariot*." *Southerly* 25:1 (1965) 46-68.

An exploration of the wide range of mythic elements in Patrick White's novel *Riders in the Chariot* (1961) from Himmelfarb's

Messianism to Dubbo's Christian vision, from Miss Hare's portrayal with "subdued echoes of Eve" to Mrs. Godbold as Magna Mater, pure and simple. It is suggested that White's "myths carry strong, sometimes blatant, Jungian overtones."

111. BURWELL, Rose M. "Joyce Carol Oates' First Novel." *Canadian Literature* 73 (1977) 54-67.

With Shuddering Fall (1964) should not be seen as a novel on madness and violence in the naturalist or social realist mode, but as a psychological novel in which theme and structure are provided, as in all Oates' later novels, by the search for self-realization of the major characters. High school drop-out Karen Herz, daughter of Eden County's largest landowner, rebels against the constricting conventions of family and church by entering a relationship full of emotional and physical violence with a racing-car driver. His self-chosen death on the track and her subsequent breakdown and "self-cure" are viewed as experiences in a Jungian maturation process, in which the darker forces of the unconscious are integrated into greater psychic wholeness. Though returning to her rural community as an alien and misfit, Karen has achieved personal integrity and moral independence.

Thorough-going psychological reading of this novel.

112. BURWELL, Rose M. "The Process of Individuation as Narrative Structure: Joyce Carol Oates' *Do With Me What You Will*". *Critique: Studies in Modern Fiction* 17:2 (1975) 93-106.

"The distinctly Jungian development of the novel's protagonist" is pursued in the stages of her growth from passivity to ruthless self-determination. Elena's moral and emotional struggle involves the realization that she must either reach a measure of personal wholeness or submit to psychic disintegration. The novel's overt symbolism helps to express how she learns to value positively the shadow aspects of her personality repressed by family and society: her potential for sexual fulfillment and for exercising her own free will.

Good Jungian interpretation, but the claim that the stages of the individuation process provide the narrative structure of this novel (1973) has not really been worked out.

113. BUSS, Helen M. *Mother and Daughter Relationships in the Manawaka Works of Margaret Laurence*. Victoria, B.C.: University of Victoria, 1985.

Employs a Jungian archetypal approach to explore the development of the mother-daughter relationships in Laurence's novels.

114. BUTLER, Richard E. "Jungian and Oriental Symbolism in Joseph
Conrad's *Victory*." *Conradiana* 3: 2/3 (1971-1972) 36-54.

In the teeth of those critics who consider it "an awkward
popular romance," Conrad's novel (1915) is claimed to be "a
masterful dramatization" of the philosophical concept of solipsism.
Critical attacks on the structure, characterization and language of
the novel are irrelevant if the novel's very "Eastern" and
archetypal symbolism has not been understood. Jung's theory of
archetypes and his commentary on a book of Chinese philosophy
offers clues to such an understanding. The isolation in which the
main character Heyst lives is caused and intensified by the lack of
pschychological balance shown in his undissolved father complex
and obsessive anima and shadow projections. Conrad's symbolical
language makes Lena into Heyst's anima and the trio of
melodramatic villains into destructive shadow figures. Mandala
symbolism in the form of circular structure and character
quaternities suggests that, in spite of apparent failure, "victory" is
achieved, not only (ironically) by Lena in sacrificing herself for
Heyst, but by Heyst himself in the sense that death brings him
final enlightenment, a kind of Oriental unity in emptiness and the
birth of a psychologically superior personality.

The self-defeating conclusion of this analysis is that Conrad
may have meant "the essence of Heyst's victory" to be a mystical
"nothing," because the experience "of coming to terms with the
disparate aspects of one's personality is entirely personal and
incommunicable." Jung's archetypal theory is enthusiastically but
naïvely applied. A novelistic character does not automatically
become an artistic success if it can be shown to embody archetypal
symbolism.

115. BUTTERICK, George F. *A Guide to the Maximus Poems of Charles
Olson*. Berkeley: University of California Press, 1978. lxvi,816 pp.

Locates the principal passages in Jung which Olson made direct
use of in his *Maximus Poems*, but does not discuss their
significance nor give Jung in the index.

116. BYARS, John A. "The Initiation of Alan Sillitoe's Long-Distance
Runner." *Modern Fiction Studies* 22:4 (1976-77) 584-591.

In Sillitoe's story "The Loneliness of the Long-Distance
Runner" (1959) the protagonist decides deliberately to lose the All-
England race in which he is taking part. This decision may be seen
symbolically as part of his ordeal of strength in an initiation rite.
Other aspects of his individuation are his re-experiencing of his
father's death and his refusal to conform to the authority of his
surrogate father, the governor of the Borstal institution.

117. *CALLAN, Edward. "Allegory in Auden's *The Age of Anxiety.*" *Twentieth Century Literature* 10:4 (1965) 155-165.

For a full understanding of W.H. Auden's dramatic allegory *The Age of Anxiety: A Baroque Eclogue* (1947) it is necessary to see how its two levels of allegory embody the psychological theories of Jung and the existentialist philosophies of Heidegger, Jaspers, and Kierkegaard. The discussions and actions of four strangers who meet in a Third Avenue bar dramatize the progression of a collective psyche exemplifying modern man's "anxiety in time." From a state of disintegration of the four psychic faculties, the allegorical characters move "through a surrealistic dream-journey" and experiences of sexual eros and spiritual love in the direction of "wholeness."

"This outline of Auden's debt to Jung," particularly to *Modern Man in Search of a Soul* (1933), provides a clear analysis of the psychological structuring of Auden's dramatic poem.

118. CALLAN, Edward. *Auden: A Carnival of Intellect.* New York: Oxford University Press, 1983.

Not a Jungian study of Auden's work, but incorporates Callan's earlier essays and attempts to show Jung's influence on Auden from an early date.

119. CALLAN, Edward. "W.H. Auden's First Dramatization of Jung: The Charade of the Loving and Terrible Mothers." *Comparative Drama* 11:4 (1978) 287-302.

Though the underlying theme is that of the Freudian Eros and Thanatos, much of the substance of Auden's poetic play *Paid on Both Sides* (1930) may have been directly derived from Jung's *Symbols of Transformation*. The play presents us with an archetypal hero in his journey from birth to death, and with loving and terrible mothers who mourn dead husbands, give birth to a son or instigate his killing. The significant action takes place in the unconscious of the hero as suggested in the central dream-scene, where Auden uses figures from the ancient mummers' plays with their ritual killing and reviving of the vegetation spirit. Auden adds manifestations of the unconscious such as an androgynous Man-Woman, and Bo and Po, spokesman respectively for the extraverted urges and the introverted tendencies. Like T.S. Eliot, Auden ransacked, though "rather more indiscriminately," Jessie Weston's *From Ritual to Romance* and Frazer's *The Golden Bough*. His allegorical charade explores the same psychic territory as Eliot's poem, more positively but with considerably less artistic effect. Auden's use of similar Jungian themes in later, more mature works is indicated.

120. *CAMPBELL, Joseph. "The Interpretation of Symbolic Forms." In *The Binding of Proteus: Perspectives on Myth and the Literary Process*. Eds. Marjorie W. McCune, Tucker Orbison and Philip M. Withim. Lewisburg: Bucknell University Press, 1980. 35-59.

Without quoting Jung overmuch Campbell develops the fundamentally Jungian view that symbols shared by the world's religions and mythologies should not be interpreted literally and historically, but psychologically and poetically. "The documents of religion [...] are to be read as poetry." With examples drawn from Jewish, Christian and Buddhist teaching, from Germanic, Central American and Near Eastern myth, as well as from Sufi mysticism, he demonstrates how ubiquitous symbols like the cross, the crucifixion, the tree of life and the fall of man have similar psychological meanings in different religions. Campbell clinches his argument with a discussion of the seven stages or chakras of the lotus ladder of Kundalini yoga, symbols of the archetypal steps in the ascent of human consciousness. He stresses the relevance for our Western arts and religions of "the transformations of human insight by the vitalizing energies of the psyche rising from states conditioned by fear and desire to those of rapture and transcendent light."

This paper, both down-to-earth and mystical, may well be read as a masterly summary of Campbell's seminal thinking and writing about mythic symbolism. It was presented in 1974 at a Bucknell University program on Myth and Literature. A more extended version of the psychological reading of Kundalini yoga also forms the center-piece of Campbell's *The Mythic Image* in the Bollingen Series (1974).

121. *CAMPBELL, Joseph. *The Masks of God*. Vol. 1 *Primitive Mythology* (1959, xv,504 pp.), vol. 2 *Oriental Mythology* (1962, x,561 pp.), vol. 3 *Occidental Mythology* (1964, x,564 pp.), vol. 4 *Creative Mythology* (1968, xvii,730 pp.). New York: Viking Press, 1959-1968.

In the four volumes of *The Masks of God* Joseph Campbell develops his masterly survey and interpretation of the main themes that underlie the world's myths and the unity of man's spiritual thinking. With a wealth of well-digested detail from the philosophical, religious and artistic history of Western culture since the early Middle Ages, the final volume, *Creative Mythology*, shows how our Western "civilization of the individual" created its own mythology. In tracing the great mythic symbols of modern man, Campbell uses for his main texts the legends of Tristan and Isolt and of the Quest for the Holy Grail, in the thirteenth century versions of the poets Gottfried von Strassburg (*Tristan*, c1210) and Wolfram von Eschenbach (*Parzival*, c1205), and the twentieth century novels of James Joyce, *Ulysses* (1922), and Thomas Mann, *The Magic Mountain* (1924). Campbell's analysis throughout is in sympathy with the interpretations of the psyche and its archetypal symbols by C.G. Jung, who was the exact contemporary of Joyce and Mann.

122. CAMPBELL, Joseph. "Mythological Themes in Creative Literature and Art." *Myth, Dreams, and Religion.* Ed. Joseph Campbell. New York: Dutton, 1970. 138-175.

Distinguishing four functions of the world's great mythologies (mystical, cosmological, sociological and psychological), Campbell argues that what remains alive are not the outmoded cosmological and sociological religious traditions, but the archetypal metaphysical and psychological symbols that are expressed through "the authentic creative way of art." To illustrate how the timeless "archetypes of mythology" arising from the collective unconscious are revitalized in European literature, Campbell traces the theme of the hero who attains individuation by learning "to act out of a center of life within" in James Joyce's *A Portrait of the Artist as a Young Man* (1916), Thomas Mann's *The Magic Mountain* (1924), and in the Grail myth that informs T.S. Eliot's poem *The Waste Land* (1922).

123. CAMPBELL, Joseph. "The Occult in Myth and Literature." In *Literature and the Occult: Essays in Comparative Literature.* Ed. Luanne Frank. Arlington: University of Texas at Arlington, 1977. 3-18.

In the opening address to a conference on literature and the occult (University of Texas at Arlington, 1975) Joseph Campbell presents a magisterial overview of the development of mythology and religion. In our Western world the sense of the immanence of the hidden or "occult", and of the micro-macrocosmic mysterious unity of man and universe has receded before monotheism with its super-natural god and the impact of scientific thinking. The resurgence of mythological thinking is illustrated from the use of mythology and the occult in the novels of Thomas Mann and James Joyce, both "profoundly influenced by Jung's publication of his theory of psychological archetypes."

124. CAMPBELL, Joseph and Henry M. Robinson. *A Skeleton Key to* Finnegans Wake. New York: Harcourt, Brace, 1944. xiii,365 pp.

In their spirited commentary, printed alongside the condensed text of James Joyce's "running riddle," the authors of this reader's guide to *Finnegans Wake* (1939) mention Freud a few times and Jung only once. Yet their interpretations fully recognize that Joyce developed his literary techniques and his new language in order to give expression to that "new dimension of human experience the unconscious mind." Viewing the book as a "dream confessional" and "treasury of myth," Campbell and Robinson explicate its archetypal characters and themes. They ascribe to Joyce the very Jungian belief that "in the noncerebral part of man dwells an intelligence which is the most important organ of human wisdom." In fact as Thomas Cowan (q.v.) wrote: this "first effort at a total explication" of Joyce's book drew "heavily on Jungian structural analysis" and "set the canon of interpretation [...] firmly in mythological terms."

125. CAMPBELL, Josie P. "The Woman as Hero in Margaret Atwood's *Surfacing*." *Mosaic* 11:3 (1978) 17-28.
   Admirably detailed analysis of the structure and meaning of Atwood's novel *Surfacing* (1972) in terms of Joseph Campbell's interpretation of the myth of the heroic quest. Structurally, in its division into three parts of separation, initiation and return, and thematically, in the unnamed heroine's quest for her lost father and the "ghosts" of her past, the novel's mythic pattern embodies, symbolizes and explores the protagonist's development towards self-awareness and self-realization.

126. CAMPO, Allen. "The Woman of Prey." In *Benchmark and Blaze: The Emergence of William Everson*. Ed. Lee Bartlett. Metuchen, N.J.: Scarecrow Press, 1979. 117-136.
   In two poems from *The Hazard of Holiness* (1962) by Brother Antoninus (William Everson), the anima is steeped in the shadow. In "Judith and Holofernes" and "The Beheading of John the Baptist," the anima is destructive. A contemporaneous poem, "The Last Crusade," was withheld from publication until 1969, and treats an overly curious feminine, seized by the masculine; an inadvertent but horrifying father-daughter incest is discovered. Two more poems of the anima sirens - and succubi visiting celibate monks - are treated. J.K.

127. CARGAS, Harry J. "The Love Poet." In *Benchmark and Blaze: The Emergence of William Everson*. Ed. Lee Bartlett. Metuchen, N.J.: Scarecrow Press, 1979. 102-107.
   The erotic mysticism of Brother Antoninus (William Everson) is presented in Jungian terms of the completion of a man "by finding in a woman that which comes closest to the feminine element in his unconscious." As Antoninus puts it: "[...] it's always been through a woman's hands that I discovered God at ever deepening levels." J.K.

128. CARGILL, Oscar. "Fusion-Point of Jung and Nietzsche." In
      Intellectual America: Ideas on the March. New York: Macmillan,
      1941. 696-702.
      Rpt. in *O'Neill and His Plays: Four Decades of Criticism*. Ed. Oscar
      Cargill et al. New York: New York University Press, 1961. 408-414.
          O'Neill read books by Freud and Jung, and deliberately
      employed depth psychology in his plays. To understand why the
      characters in *The Great God Brown* (1925) wear masks, one needs
      to know something about Jung's notion of the persona. The
      "antithetical dualism" in the character of Dion Anthony is
      symbolized by the scoffing, sensual Dionysian mask he presents to
      the world, which hides and balances the inner face of this sensitive
      artist and mythic St. Anthony. In *Lazarus Laughed* (1926), O'Neill's
      "theatrical masterpiece," he draws on Jung's *Psychological Types* for
      characterization. Pompeia for instance, the emperor's mistress,
      "wears a mask of evil beauty and perverted passion" over a girlish
      mouth "set in an expression of agonized self-loathing," animus
      balancing persona. The philosophy of this play, moreover, makes it
      a Nietzschean tragedy that combines the Apollonian and the
      Dionysian.
          A brief, incisive essay, inviting further psychological
      interpretation of O'Neill's plays.

129. CARLSON, Eric W. "'William Wilson': The Double as Primal Self."
      Topic 30 16 (1976) 35-40.
          Poe's tale "William Wilson" (1839) "deserves to be read as one
      of his psycho-epic visions of the primal, unified Self suffering
      internal split, conflict, and disintegration." Jung's concepts of
      shadow and self are superficially applied to this story about a man
      who kills his Double.

130. CARPENTER, Barbara. "Epoch and Archetype: Metaphors of
      Transcendence in the Fiction of John Fowles." (Ph.D. 1982 Tulane
      University) 248 pp. *DAI* 44/01 A p.165.

131. CARSON, Joan. "Visionary Experience in *Wuthering Heights*."
      Psychoanalytic Review 62:1 (1975) 131-151.
          To elucidate the strangeness and emotional power of Emily
      Brontë's novel it is read on three levels. Main pattern of the
      literal action is the return of Catherine and Heathcliff to the
      "preternatural world" of their intense childhood relationship. The
      significant images of window, bed and coffin recur in passages
      dramatizing this backward drive. On the psychological level these
      indicate that the parallel desires for death and childhood constitute
      "a regressional tendency of the libidinal energy" expressed in

traditional womb imagery. On the archetypal third level this regression towards "the primal situation" may be viewed symbolically as the "primordial vision" of progression towards spiritual rebirth. In terms of archetypes Heathcliff functions as Catherine's animus-projection, and the "soul-image" relationship of the two children brought up as brother and sister lends their love mythical force. It associates them with the symbolic incest of Osiris and Isis, and with the sun god's rebirth after his night sea journey.

Good use is made of Jung and Otto Rank, and convincing symbolic details are found in plot and imagery to support this archetypal reading.

132. CARTER, Nancy C. "Demeter and Persephone in Margaret Atwood's Novels: Mother-Daughter Transformations." *Journal of Analytical Psychology* 24:4 (1979) 326-342.

Margaret Atwood's novels *Edible Woman* (1969), *Surfacing* (1972) and *Lady Oracle* (1976) are interpreted according to Jung, Kerényi and Neumann's explanations of the Demeter-Persephone myth. Her protagonists must integrate the Mother/Demeter aspect of themselves (representing mature womanhood) with the Daughter/Persephone (the innocent maiden) in order to become complete individuals who are aware of their participation in the "universal cycle of birth-death-rebirth." K.S.

133. CARTER, Steve. "Caddy and Quentin: Anima and Animus Orbited Nice." *University of Hartford Studies in Literature* 12:2 (1980) 124-142.

The essay compares Freudian and Jungian interpretations of Faulkner's *The Sound and the Fury* (1929), and works out a Jungian view of Caddy and Quentin as two "mutually complementary characters" who are not merely "pathological misfits." Reflecting the male-female dichotomy of all Faulkner's relationships between earthy women and spiritual-mental men, Caddy and Quentin neurotically project onto each other their own unconscious sides, the psychological qualities each is lacking. Caddy's "frantic promiscuity" is a means of projecting her repressed power-seeking animus onto men aspiring to power and self-control, while Quentin's anima-obsession of incest with Caddy is an attempt to get in touch with his own feelings. If both are seen as actually striving for psychic wholeness, however unbalanced and misdirected their attempts, they become in Jung's sense the archetypal anima-animus pair, the "syzygy" that embodies man's unrealized potential for integrating and reconciling the seemingly "irreconcilable opposites" of life.

Thoroughly Jungian, though very schematically drawn perspective on the psychology of Faulkner's characters.

134. CARTER, Steve. "The Metaphor of Assimilation and 'Rise O Days from Your Fathomless Deeps'." *Walt Whitman Review* 24:4 (1978) 155-161.

   Whitman's conception of the evolutionary growth of the personality through time is best explained with the help of Jung's model of the process of individuation. The metaphor of assimilation, representing the gradual appropriation by the ego of so far unconscious elements of the self, occurs throughout the poems in *Leaves of Grass* (1855). The use of this metaphor to express how soul and body in "oneness " feed on life and grow toward higher levels of being is traced in "Rise O Days."

135. CASTY, Alan. "Tennessee Williams and the Small Hands of the Rain." *Mad River Review* 1:3 (1965) 27-43.

   A critical examination of Tennessee Williams' plays, in which Jung's concept of the mandala as a symbol of integrated wholeness is unorthodoxly used as an ideal against which to measure the tensions between the "sexual and spiritual poles" in the inner life of the main characters.

136. CEDERSTROM, Lorelei. "Doris Lessing's Use of Satire in *The Summer before the Dark*." *Modern Fiction Studies* 26:1 (1980) 131-145.

   In the course of an analysis of Lessing's novel as presenting a satirical view of Ruth Brown's summer of self-discovery it is argued (quoting Jung) that her series of dreams, which several critics have termed Jungian, is not symbolical but allegorical, and in its simplicity "a reflection of Kate's shallowness." For the same reasons Kate's journey with Jeffrey turns into "a parody of the archetypal journey to the center."

   The article claims that this novel is a satire rather than a fictionalization of individuation.

137. CEDERSTROM, Lorelei. "From Marxism to Myth: A Developmental Study of the Novels of Doris Lessing." (Ph.D. 1978 University of Manitoba, Canada) *DAI* 38/12 A p.7320.

138. *CEDERSTROM, Lorelei. "'Inner Space' Landscape: Doris Lessing's *Memoirs of a Survivor*." *Mosaic* 13:3-4 (1980) 115-132.

   Doris Lessing's novel *Memoirs of a Survivor* (1975) has been read as futuristic science fiction, giving an impression of our technological society disintegrating in a city that collapses into anarchy, with a protagonist who through the walls of her appartment has mysterious visions of other rooms harboring a harmonious natural world. The surface level of the story is, however, better understood as "mythic narrative," as "a symbolic portrait of the ego in a time of cultural failure," an inner landscape where "each person is a personified projection of an aspect of the protagonist's personality." The relationship between the protagonist and the girl Emily, who symbolizes her younger personality, "explores the growth and development of the feminine psyche." While assessing the stereotyped social patterns through which Emily moves in the course of the story, the protagonist confronts the inadequacies of her own ego-structure and is transformed by communicating with "the transpersonal experience of the archetypal self" in the inner rooms of her unconscious.

This exemplary Jungian analysis of "the most Jungian" of Lessing's novels offers a subtle and coherent interpretation of its psychological symbolism. Cederstrom demonstrates how Lessing uses Jung's description of the structure of the psyche as the basis of her symbols. From a psychological viewpoint, the story meaningfully moves on levels of interaction between Ego and Self, with the characters existing "primarily on the plane of projection," and a protagonist who achieves individuation by vitalizing her "links with a living symbolic heritage." Not only does Lessing make "use of all the techniques and symbols of psychic exploration which she developed in her earlier novels," but by presenting a survivor's "healing vision" she gives this novel a profound social significance for a world that is losing touch with its collective symbols of psychic wholeness.

139. CEDERSTROM, Lorelei. "The Process of Individuation in *The Golden Notebook*." *Gradiva* 2:1 (1979) 41-54.

In a seemingly structureless welter of fragmented notebook sections Lessing's novel (1962) suggests Anna Wulf's descent into chaos and madness, yet there is also a carefully constructed movement that shows how her breakdown initiates a process of psychological regrowth. For the woman artist in the collapsing social structure of our patriarchal culture it is particularly difficult to find her individual self and accept "the person within." Each of the notebooks Anna keeps embodies a different stage or problem in the development of her personality.

In the Black Notebook Anna confronts her own inner chaos in the morbid memories of her youth in Africa that provided her with the materials for her first successful novel. The Red Notebook deals with her search for a substitute Great Father in the collective ideology of the communist party. The Yellow Notebook gives the stories about Ella, Anna's own shadow figure, who is herself a writer. The Blue Notebook is the key to her inner development in showing how Anna's analysis with the Jungian analyst Mrs. Marks puts her into touch with the collective unconscious through dream encounters with spirit goblin, wise old woman and animus. When in the Golden Notebook her writer's block is broken by a friend, acting as positive animus, disintegration is turned into creative wholeness.

Able discussion of the lessons Anna learns from her unconscious.

140. CELLI, John P. "The Uses of the Term 'Archetype' in Contemparary Literary Criticism." (Ph.D. 1974 Kansas State University) 239 pp. *DAI* 36/01 A p.304.

141. CHAPMAN, Edgar L. "The Mandala Design of Patrick White's *Riders in the Chariot.*" *Texas Studies in Literature and Language* 21:2 (1979) 186-202.

The religious character of White's novel (1961) is emphasized by viewing the chief symbol of the divine chariot with its four riders as a cosmic mandala, archetype of unity and transcendence. The major characters form a quaternity of mystic visionaries seeking "for a perception of the infinite" in "the cultural and spiritual wasteland of Australia." Their portrayal is patterned by associating each of them with one of the four elements, with a particular sense, and with one of Jung's four psychological functions.

142. *CHAPMAN, Marilyn. "Female Archetypes in *Fifth Business.*" *Canadian Literature* 80 (1979) 131-138.

Robertson Davies' novel (1970) is based on "implicit Jungian principles." Some of these are clearly manifested in Ramsay's relationships with the four most important women in his life, who correspond to the four stages Jung distinguishes in anima development. The nurse Diana, who mothers him when he is a war casualty, is the Eve figure; the young circus beauty Faustina is the erotically tempting Helen; the deranged but saintly Mary Dempster, to whom he remains devoted through life, appears to him on the battlefield as the Madonna; and the complex Liesl, manageress of the magic show, is the ugly, devilish, but powerful Sapientia figure whose intuitive wisdom uncovers the middle-aged Ramsay's "unlived life" and works his maturity.

A very pertinent demonstration of how these women, real enough as novelistic characters, in Ramsay's psychological development "sometimes function as Jungian archetypes."

143. CHARD, Jean M. "Some Elements of Myth and Mysticism in C.S. Lewis' Novel *Till We Have Faces*." *Mythlore* 5:2 (1978) 15-18.
    Jungian psychology, Greek and Babylonian mythology, Sufi mysticism, and alchemical lore illuminate the symbolism of Lewis' novel (1956) and its themes of body-soul relationship, sterility and fertility, and the doctrine of substitution.

144. CHARTERS, Ann. "I, Maximus: Charles Olson as Mythologist." *Modern Poetry Studies* 2:2 (1971) 49-60.
    A tribute to Charles Olson, who at Black Mountain College taught his disciples, and in his poetry urged his readers to do what Jung had said, and what Olson called "causal mythology": "Every man must discover his own mythology in order to effect the most complete development of his individuality." In his early theater piece *Appolonius of Tyana* Olson dramatized "mythology as an explicitly moral exercise." Later in *The Maximus Poems* (1953-1968) he created the "homo maximus" as "a hero to mythologize his own experience" and project his view of the individuating poet.

145. CHAYES, Irene H. "Little Girls Lost: Problems of a Romantic Archetype." *Bulletin of the New York Public Library* 67:9 (1963) 579-592.
    Rpt. in *Blake: A Collection of Critical Essays*. Ed. Northrop Frye. Englewood Cliffs: Prentice-Hall, 1966. 65-78.
    Persephone, lost daughter and queen of the underworld, is the archetypal image (as described by Jung and Kerényi) underlying the many other images evoked by the symbolical maiden in Blake's poems "The Little Girl Lost" and "The Little Girl Found." The shift from a renewal of seasonal life in the Greek myth to the Christian awakening of the girl and her parents to a totally new life illustrates how "the broad mythological archetype is modified into a Romantic literary archetype."
    The discovery of similar Romantic Persephones in Wordsworth's "Lucy Gray" and Keats's "The Eve of St. Agnes" is less convincing than Chayes's reading of Blake.

146. CHOUINARD, Timothy. "Eliot's 'Oeuvre', Bradley's 'Finite Centres', and Jung's Anima Concept." *Journal of Analytical Psychology* 16:1 (1971) 48-68.
    The central problem of T.S. Eliot's work is defined as reconciling the "demands of the feminine with those of the masculine, and, with this, the requirements of every human's need for communication with the Absolute as well as with the sensual." While tracing imagery related to women through Eliot's major poems and plays, Chouinard draws a parallel with the Jungian

theory of the four stages of anima development in the individuation process. "Prufrock" reflects the negative phase (Eve), *The Waste Land* that of the ambiguous Helen. In *Ash Wednesday* the anima is spiritualized in the figure of Mary in the garden. In *Four Quartets* "an intellectual and poetic individuation unfolds," and in the plays the poet approximates the final Sapientia phase of personality development.

Using a considerably chastened vocabulary (compared with his other essay), Chouinard provides a perceptive analysis of an important aspect of the "unique human content" of Eliot's art.

147. CHOUINARD, Timothy. "The Symbol and the Archetype in Analytical Psychology and Literary Criticism." *Journal of Analytical Psychology* 15:2 (1970) 155-164.

The author wishes to clarify the terms "archetype" and "symbol" for the "psycho-literary mêlée" of "inexperienced, rash, and irresponsible" critics who misunderstand Jung. In somewhat muddled and bombastic philosophical jargon he follows Erich Kahler in distinguishing "descending" (author's unconscious use) and "ascending" (conscious variation of archetypal form) symbols. In the end little more is revealed than that "all archetypes are symbolic but not all symbols are archetypal."

148. CHRISTY, McVay. "Journey to the Center: The Archetypal Nature of Melville's 'Piazza'." *Higginson Journal* 20:2 (1978) 21-28.

The mariner's journey to fairyland in Melville's story "The Piazza" (1856) is a failed quest for enlightenment and individuation. The mountain is "an archetypal image of the *axis mundi*," the worms in the plant represent the shadow, and the condors on the mountain are "symbols of transcendence" which lead him to Marianna, a negative anima. His failure to recognize either his shadow or his negative anima dooms this search for the self. K.S.

149. CLARK, Charles C. "*A Name for Evil*: A Search for Order." *Mississippi Quarterly* 23:4 (1970) 371-382.

Andrew Lytle's *A Name for Evil* (1947), modeled on Henry James's ghost story *The Turn of the Screw*, is a different sort of psychological novel in that it illustrates the destructive effects of a distorted view of tradition. The psychotic Henry Brent, who has been fighting off the ghost of his satanic ancestor Major Brent, in the end becomes the force of evil he has created in his own mind, when he causes the death of his wife. His reconstructed garden is both a Christian and a Jungian symbol, an Edenic mandala attempting to achieve order in life. With its covered spring and graves, however, it is an inversion of the fountain of life, symbolic of the cause of Henry's problems, his solipsism. K.S.

150. CLARKE, Delia. "*Raintree County*: Psychological Symbolism, Archetype, and Myth." *Thoth* 11:1 (1970) 31-39.

Ross Lockridge Jr.'s novel, *Raintree County* (1948), is explained in terms of Jungian archetypes and Freudian symbolism. During the course of the story John Shawnessy experiences a symbolic death and rebirth in the swamp and in the mistaken report of his death in battle, encounters the collective unconscious through "mr. shawnessy", makes a "night journey" to New York where he discovers the sordid side of life, and meets his shadow in the form of Jerusalem Webster Stiles. On the mythic level, Shawnessy's quest is "a ritual search for a lost and vaguely remembered Eden." K.S.

151. CLAYBOROUGH, Arthur. *The Grotesque in English Literature*. Oxford: Clarendon Press, 1965. x,266 pp.

This study of various types of grotesque art in the work of Swift, Coleridge and Dickens is preceded by a lengthy examination of the semantic history of the term "grotesque" and of attempts at definition by writers on aesthetic theory from Kant to Wolfgang Kayser. Incongruity and strangeness being the two chief qualities of grotesque art, the idea is developed that the grotesque is "a product of the interaction of two contrasting sides of human nature: the practical, rational side, and the sense of the eternal." The psychological basis for this hypothesis is found in Jung's theories about the conscious-unconscious, progressive-regressive polarization of the human mind, and in his distinction between directed thinking and dream or fantasy thinking.

152. CLIFT, Jean Dalby. "Little Nell and the Lost Feminine: An Archetypal Analysis of Some Projections in Victorian Culture." (Ph.D. 1978 University of Denver) 238 pp. *DAI* 39/06 A p.3593. (Dickens)

153. COBB, Noel. *Prospero's Island: The Secret Alchemy at the Heart of The Tempest*. London: Coventure, 1984. 224 pp.

Blending the methods of history, alchemy, poetry and James Hillman's archetypal psychology, Cobb reads Shakespeare's play as "a celebration of the project which Jung termed individuation." He sees *The Tempest* as "the greatest mystery play of our tradition," steeped in alchemical imagery and profoundly influenced by Renaissance hermeticism. Archetypal patterns of gnosis are descried "within the crystal ball of Shakespeare's masterpiece."

154. COE, Richard N. *When the Grass Was Taller: Autobiography and the Experience of Childhood*. New Haven: Yale University Press, 1984. 352 pp.

A study that surveys 150 years of autobiographies of childhood and adolescence in European, American, Australian, and African literature. The analysis of the myths and "magic" of childhood experience owes much to Jung's theory of the archetypes of the collective unconscious.

155. COLEMAN, Elliott. "A Note on Joyce and Jung." *James Joyce Quarterly* 1:1 (1963) 11-16.

Coleman notes that Jung's anima-animus theory illuminates the relationship between Bloom and his wife Molly, as well as the Circe episode in *Ulysses* "with its series of transmutations in Bloom to the point of sexual transpositions in Bloom and Bella." He further speculates upon the possible influence on Jung of his reading of Joyce's *Ulysses* (1922) and of his acquaintance with Joyce and his schizoid daughter Lucia, whom Jung described in a letter as "classic examples" of his theories.

156. COLLINS, Carvel. "Are These Mandalas?" *Literature and Psychology* 3:5 (1953) 3-6.

Mandala symbolism is suggested in several of Faulkner's stories, among them *The Bear* (1942) and *Sartoris* (1929). The mandala elements in the final scene of *The Bear* support a reading of the story as the hero's initiation into maturity and his successful synthesis of civilized and primitive life.

157. COOK, Harry J. "The Individuation of a Poet: The Process of Becoming in Whitman's 'The Sleepers'." *Walt Whitman Review* 21:3 (1975) 101-110.

The mystic symbolism of Whitman's "The Sleepers" is illuminated when viewed in terms of Jung's individuation process. The poem moves from initial mental chaos and disjunction to psychic regeneration and healing in the last two sections. The dominating symbols of darkness, sea, soul, unity and mother are related to Jung's concepts of the collective unconscious, anima, objective self and chthonic mother. The analysis indicates the surfacing of archetypal contents into the conscious creative faculty of the poet.

158. COOK, Reginald. "The Forest of Goodman Brown's Night: A Reading of Hawthorne's 'Young Goodman Brown'." *New England Quarterly* 43:3 (1970) 473-481.

The haunted forest where Goodman Brown has his fearful dream of evil symbolizes the dark depth of his Puritan conscience that makes the diabolism "he should have recognized as only one of the powerful forces in the collective unconscious" into an exclusive "soul-torturing suspicion of human guilt" without possibility of redemption.

159. COOLEY, Dennis. "Antimacassared in the Wilderness: Art and Nature in *The Stone Angel.*" *Mosaic* 11:3 (1978) 29-46.
      With close attention to the text and the symbolic function of the imagery, a psychological portrait is developed of Hagar, the protagonist in Margaret Laurence's novel *The Stone Angel* (1968). The analysis demonstrates how well Jung's archetypes of individuation fit the description of the strongly inhibited, opinionated and life-denying Hagar, who lives by her persona. Only at the end of her life she "experiences a personal breakthrough," when she runs away to the cannery at "Shadow Point" at the seaside, where, communicating with a wise old man, for the first time she "opens up to her shadows" and "moves toward personal wholeness."

160. COOPER, David D. "Gertrude Stein's 'Magnificent Asparagus': Horizontal Vision and Unmeaning in *Tender Buttons.*" *Modern Fiction Studies* 20:3 (1974) 337-349.
      To explain the difficulties Jung had in reading Joyce's *Ulysses*, his division of artistic creation into the psychological and visionary modes is expanded into three types. Literature of Self-Expression, the expository mode, exemplified by Henry James, uses language as a focusing device to communicate ideas in "transparent" (which does not mean "simple") style and draws upon materials rooted in man's conscious life. Literature of Self-Discovery, the vertical visionary mode, exemplified by Walt Whitman, tries to communicate in a more opaque style the deeper meanings of intuitive impulses or spiritual motives that lie beneath or beyond consciousness. Literature of Discovery, the horizontal visionary mode, exemplified by Stein's *Tender Buttons* (1914) and Joyce's *Ulysses* (1922) is only concerned with sense impressions and exterior experience. It does not, like the other modes, proceed from the premise that there is chaos in the world and art creates order. "Chaos is the point."

161. COOPER, David D. "The Paradox of Spirit and Instinct: A Comparative Examination of the Psychologies of C.G. Jung and Sigmund Freud." (Ph.D. 1977 Brown University) 289 pp. *DAI* 38/12 A p.7330. (Gives interpretations of Whitman)

162. COOPER, David D. "The Poet as Elaborator: Analytical Psychology as a Critical Paradigm." *Critical Inquiry* 6:1 (1979) 51-63.

Hart Crane's poem "The Broken Tower" is an example of the "split consciousness fostered by the rupture between faith and knowledge" that is a common theme in modern poetry. To find symbols for expressing his alienated consciousness, the modern poet "in 'translating' his age [...] must assimilate the shadow and elaborate the psychological conflict individually as it is lived out collectively." Using Jung's commentary on Brother Klaus' creative "elaboration" of his "Trinity Vision" as a parallel, Cooper argues that analytical psychology offers a critical method for explicating the poet's creative response to similar numinous experiences in "a broken world."

163. COOPER, Douglas W. "Tennyson's *Idylls*: A Mythography of the Self." (Ph.D. 1966 University of Missouri, Columbia) 238 pp. *DAI* 27/10 A p.3423.

164. COOPER, James G. "The Womb of Time: Archetypal Patterns in the Novels of Jack London." *Jack London Newsletter* 8:1 (1975) 1-5 and 9:1 (1976) 16-28.

In these excerpts from his dissertation Cooper argues that the characters in London's tales and novels are archetypal symbols, created from the unconscious, rather than realistic portrayals of men and women. Prevailing theme is the Hero myth, the stages of which "occur in the same order generally as that described by Campbell, Rank, and Raglan."

165. COOPER, James G. "The Womb of Time: Archetypal Patterns in the Novels of Jack London." (Ph.D. 1974 Texas Tech University) 159 pp. *DAI* 35/04 A p.2261.

166. CORRIGAN, Matthew. "Chaucer's Failure with Woman: The Inadequacy of Criseyde." *Western Humanities Review* 23:2 (1969) 107-120.

Corrigan argues that in spite of all critical praise for Chaucer's *Troilus and Criseyde* the picture of Criseyde does not rise above the ambivalence of the medieval conception of woman as either courtly ideal or seductive devil. Modern psychology (Jung and Neumann) gives insight into man's fear of entanglement in his feminine unconscious and explains the force of male bias in the Middle Ages about the inferior second sex. Keeping within the psychological restrictions of his time, Chaucer does not suggest convincing feminine motivations, and he remains unsure how to account for Criseyde's transition from angel to devil.

The argument is unfair to Chaucer, since the author disregards the force of literary conventions, the nature of Chaucer's courtly audience, and his pictures of women in other poems, such as *The Legend of Good Women*.

167. COSGROVE, Edward G. "Coincidence, Symbols and Archetypes in Selected Short Fiction of Nathaniel Hawthorne." (Ph.D. 1979 Fordham University) 223 pp. *DAI* 40/02 A p.849.

168. COSTA, Richard H. *Malcolm Lowry*. New York: Twayne, 1972. Twayne's World Authors Series. 208 pp.

In 1948, after reading Lowry's novel *Under the Volcano* (1947), Jung invited the author to come and see him in Switzerland for treatment. Lack of money prevented Lowry from making the journey. Speculating on Jung's recognition of the strongly archetypal character of Lowry's novel, Costa devotes one chapter to a discussion of the archetypal motifs of fire and water, ravine and river, death and rebirth in Lowry's fiction. The alcoholic Consul in the mythical and autobiographical *Under the Volcano* may be seen as a Jungian "conductor" of archetypes from the unconscious, and embodiment of the "Everlasting Voyager" motif that also applies to Lowry's own life. The Consul's intense, clearsighted look into the dark side of his nature is part of Lowry's successful transformation of neurosis into art.

Brief but very pertinent analysis of the archetypal aspects of Lowry's life and work.

169. COURSEN, Herbert R. "The Death of Cordelia: A Jungian Approach." *Hebrew University Studies in Literature* 8:1 (1980) 1-12.

Lear's overconfident self-reliance is inflation of an ego that identifies with the royal persona and ignores the unconscious and the directives of the self within him. In a Britain ruled by Lear's egotism, abdication means the releasing of the repressed primitive aspects of greed and lust embodied in the figures of Edmund, Goneril and Regan. With the potential integrating force of Cordelia banished, Lear will have to discover through suffering within himself the anima qualities of compassion and kindness.

The Jungian approach becomes less helpful when Coursen suggests that there is a second case of inflation when, after capture by Edmund, Lear takes Cordelia along to prison and so forces her sacrifice. Ego inflation in a mad and broken king?

170. COURSEN, Herbert R. *The Compensatory Psyche: A Jungian Approach to Shakespeare*. Lanham, MD: University Press of America, 1986. 240 pp.

Shows that the tragedies dramatize Jung's concept of the compensatory psyche, the unconscious as a balance for consciousness, which was available to Shakespeare from "Christian psychology." Examines how dreams in Shakespeare's works function as psychological checks and balances to the ego, if permitted by the dreamer.

171. COWART, David. "The Tarzan Myth and Jung's Genesis of the Self." *Journal of American Culture* 2:2 (1979) 220-230.
In this explanation of Tarzan's lasting appeal Jung's essay "The Psychology of the Child Archetype" is cited as "probably the single best commentary on the Tarzan myth of the hero and the marvellous child." The novels *Tarzan of the Apes* (1912) and *Jungle Tales of Tarzan* (1919) by Edgar Rice Burroughs chronicle a number of archetypal hero-experiences, such as miraculous birth, and humble upbringing, the dual mother, defeat of monsters and anima encounters. In Tarzan's transition from beast to man, child to adult and his maturing from trickster to "something like a savior" he symbolizes Jung's views of man's psychological development in the early stages of life.

172. COWAN, James C. *D.H. Lawrence's American Journey: A Study in Literature and Myth*. Cleveland: Press of Case Western Reserve University, 1970. xi,161 pp.
Lawrence's fiction written during a three-year stay in New Mexico embodies his essentially religious search for symbols of personal and cultural regeneration. Among the patterns traced in both work and life are those of Joseph Campbell's mythic quest of the hero through symbolic death to rebirth, and of Jung's theory of the need for integration of the conscious and unconscious sides of the personality in the second half of life.
Pointed, tersely written analysis of Lawrence's ideas, values and relationships, and of the symbolism of his writings in this period, especially the stories in the volumes *St. Mawr* (1925) and *The Woman Who Rode Away* (1928), and the novel *The Plumed Serpent* (1926).

173. COWAN, James C. "Lawrence in Old and New Mexico: The Quest and the Art." (Ph.D. 1964 University of Oklahoma) 236 pp. *DAI* 25/06 p.3567.
Became book *D.H. Lawrence's American Journey: A Study in Literature and Myth* (1970).

174. COWAN, Thomas. "On Finnegans Wake." *Spring* (1972) 43-59. Rpt. in *Puer Papers*. Ed. James Hillman. Irving, Texas: Spring Publications, 1979. 224-237.

Maintaining that Joyce's "unreadable" book (1939) is profoundly Jungian, Cowan offers a series of notes on its archetypal themes in order "to show Jungians why the *Wake* ought to be read by them." He suggests that what Joyce called his "Jungfraud Messongebook" is a wholly "synchronistic uroboros" and "a huge mandala." Anna Livia Plurabelle is the anima and the archetypal wife-daughter-mother, Shem and Shaun are the archetypal twin brothers, while the relations between old man HCE and the younger men could be fruitfully examined in terms of James Hillman's writings on the senex-puer configuration. In the end "the *Wake* itself is Joyce's record of his own life-long painful journey toward individuation."

175. CRABTREE, Ursula M. "Facing the Bogeyman: A Comparative Study of the Motif of the Double in the Novels of Saul Bellow and Günter Grass." (Ph.D. 1978 University of California, Davis) 457 pp. *DAI* 39/03 A p.1532.

176. CRANE, R.S. *The Language of Criticism and the Structure of Poetry*. Toronto: University of Toronto Press, 1953. xxi,214 pp.

In this study of critical method and theory Crane devotes a chapter to a general discussion of the rise and application of "archetypal" criticism (Coomaraswamy, Maud Bodkin, Kenneth Burke, Edmund Wilson, Lionel Trilling, Richard Chase, Francis Fergusson, and Northrop Frye) in relation to twentieth century developments in cultural anthropology, theories of symbolism, and the depth psychology of Freud and Jung.

177. CREWS, Frederick. "Anaesthetic Criticism." In *Psychoanalysis and Literary Process*. Ed. Frederick Crews. Cambridge, Mass.: Winthrop, 1970. 1-24.
Rpt. in *Out of My System: Psychoanalysis, Ideology, and Critical Method*. New York: Oxford University Press, 1975. 63-87.

Crews's spirited defense of the possibility of "sound" psychoanalytic interpretations of literature entails the rejection of much reductive criticism by fellow-Freudians and of Norman Holland's procedure of fitting texts to a theoretical model of readers' responses. He attacks "anaesthetic" academic studies of motifs, genres, and literary history, as well as Northrop Frye's ideal of detached criticism and a classificatory framework derived from within literature itself. The good critic, for Crews, is evaluative, emotionally involved, and undergoes great literature as "a symbolic process of self-confrontation."

In the course of his influential and pointed critique of prevailing academic criticism, Crews scathingly and summarily dismisses the Jungian approach, because of the "nebulous, dignified, quasi-metaphysical" character of Jung's concepts. His judgment of Jungian psychology seems largely based on Edward Glover's cantankerous and confused book *Freud or Jung?* (1950) with its demonstration that "Jung's hypotheses are logically unnecessary and mutually contradictory." Crews's expression of his own views, however, seems to show affinities with Jung's central tenets of the reconciliation of opposites and the psyche's purposive drive towards meaning. One wonders what Crews thinks of Jung since his own drastic recantation of Freudianism ("The American Literary Critic Explains Why He Has Rejected Freud." *London Review of Books* 4 December 1980, 3-6).

178. CROW, John H. and Richard D. Ehrlich. "Words of Binding: Patterns of Integration in the Earthsea Trilogy." In *Ursula K. Le Guin.* Eds. Joseph D. Olander and Martin Harry Greenberg. New York: Taplinger, 1979. 200-224, 236-239.

The unifying vision in Ursula Le Guin's fantasy and science fiction is manifested in the structural patterns of her Earthsea trilogy. Three interacting patterns are analyzed: movement from social disorder to social order, dialectical form tending to balance, and the theme of individual human development. This third theme parallels Jung's process of individuation. The mythical events of the trilogy relate the adventures of the child Ged, who recieves his name from a wizard, conquers the shadow, descends into the underworld to rescue the anima from the Great Mother, and in the end becomes himself a wise old man who initiates another child, symbol of psychic wholeness. Ged's return on the back of a dragon suggests an alliance with the spirit and makes the hero "an archetypal representative of man's psychological journey from the birth of consciousness to the complete integration of the Self."

179. CROW, John H. "Dying Generations: Shifting Archetypal Patterns in Romantic and Victorian Poetry." (Ph.D. 1975 Emory University) 376 pp. *DAI* 36/05 A p.2841. (Coleridge, Shelley, Browning, Arnold, Swinburne)

180. CURRIE, R. Hector. "The Energies of Tragedy: Cosmic and Psychic." *Centennial Review* 11:2 (1967) 220-236.

Shakespeare's "psychic tragedy of stress" is opposed to the superior cosmic drama of Sophocles and Strindberg. Jung leads the way in exploring "the transcendent planes of myth and the deep strata of the subconscious." "Deriving from Vedic philosophy and

Jungian mythic study, the cosmic transcendence theory of tragedy which is here advanced strives to integrate such evidences of tragic affirmation as are discoverable in the works of Goethe, Nietzsche, Strindberg, and Artaud in a pan-cultural and transcendent matrix for cosmic tragedy. It identifies tragedy's ultimate action as an integration of the psyche of the hero in the cosmic energy of original chaos."

An essay in transcendent fustian.

181. CURRY, Ryder H. and Michael Porte. "The Surprising Unconscious of Edward Albee." *Drama Survey* 7:1-2 (1968-69) 59-68.

This reading of Albee's *Tiny Alice* (1965) proposes that the play "presents a challenge to faith in the God of Christendom, a challenge which takes the form of a Gnostic ritual whereby the soul is released from existence." Julian (whose transformation resembles that of his namesake the Emperor Julian, the Apostate) is the "sacrificial hero-victim in a rite of mystic union with Alice, the cosmic goddess," and he ultimately participates "in a rite of mystic union-release with the acosmic powers." The resemblance of the "mystery play", sprung from Albee's "surprising unconscious", to the mystery rituals of Gnostic sects in the early Christian era amounts for the authors of this article to "a total vindication of Jung's brilliant theory of the collective archetypes as the basis for artistic form."

Readers of this essay must decide for themselves how plausible is this interpretation of Albee's complicated symbolism. In spite of their quasi-scientific "proofs of character, proofs of action, and proofs of dialogue," the authors offer little actual evidence from the play to substantiate the verbiage of their sweeping claims.

182. DAKOSKE, Mary B. "Archetypal Images of the Family in Selected Modern Plays." (Ph.D. 1980 University of Notre Dame) 228 pp. *DAI* 41/06 A p.2598. (T.S. Eliot, Tennessee Williams, O'Neill, Pinter)

183. DAVIES, Robertson. "Gleams and Glooms." In *One Half of Robertson Davies*. Toronto: Macmillan, 1977. 223-247.

In a lecture on ghosts and the continued popularity of ghost stories Davies talks about the great changes brought about by the "Freudian revolution" in our thinking and believing. He explains why his interest in art and literature made him in the end prefer the Jungian point of view above the Freudian reductive, scientific outlook, for one thing because Jung really grapples with the problem of Evil.

184. *DAVIES, Robertson. "Jung and the Theatre." In *One Half of Robertson Davies*. Toronto: Macmillan, 1977. 143-160.

In the introduction to this paper, printed in a collection of his addresses and lectures, the Canadian novelist and dramatist Robertson Davies says: "although I deplore the partial and facile application of Jungian ideas to literary criticism, I know that a serious study of Jungian thought is one fruitful path of literary study." Starting from the idea that "the theatre is a house of dreams in which audiences gather to share a dream," Davies discusses "the archetypal power" and the Jungian elements of a number of popular nineteenth century melodramas. Among these are "the Fatal Man, the incubus-devil who destroys what he loves but who seeks Redemption" in Byron's *Manfred* (1816); the Shadow and Mercurius figures in Dion Boucicault's *The Colleen Bawn* (1860); the theme of "Renunciation" and the "redeemed Shadow" with implied homosexual feeling in one of the most celebrated of all melodramas, *The Only Way (1890)*, an adaptation from Charles Dickens' novel *A Tale of Two Cities* (1859); and the Wise Old Man as the ambiguous fairy-tale monster in *The Hunchback* (1832) by Bulwer-Lytton. Davies relates Jung's saying that "archetypes speak the language of high rhetoric, even of bombast" with the claim that, even if the effects might sometimes be crude, nineteenth century melodrama "tried to deal with much that was personal, subjective and psychologically daring." Finally, he observes that if we look in the twentieth century for Jungian archetypal material in melodramatic form, we shall find it "still vital and popular in the opera houses and ballet theatres of the world," and particularly in the works of Giuseppe Verdi.

A very interesting demonstration of the "Jungian content of effective drama."

185. DAVIES, Stevie. *Emily Brontë: The Artist as a Free Woman*. Manchester: Carcanet, 1983. 170 pp.

A personal meditation on the poems and the prose of Emily Brontë from a Jungian perspective which emphasizes the archetypal earth-mother, and interprets *Wuthering Heights* (1847) as a "myth of rebirth," of the soul seeking its "lost male counterpart," and as a myth of "universal forgiveness."

186. DAVIS, Robert I. "'In the Wide Deepe Wandring': The Archetypal Water-Motif in Spenser's *Faerie Queene*." (Ph.D. 1974 University of Pittsburgh) 183 pp. *DAI* 35/04 A p.2262.

187. DAY, Douglas. *Malcolm Lowry: A Biography*. London: Oxford University Press, 1974. 483 pp.

In the final chapter of this biography Day finds Jung's distinction between the psychological (or personalistic) and the visionary artist more helpful than Freud's theory of neurotic repression to explain both the source of the creative process and the nature of Lowry's artistic achievement. He sees *Under the Volcano* (1947) as a "successful fusion of both modes of artistic creation," the vision of the obscure but potent archetypal world and the evidence of ten years of "intelligent and sensitive shaping" of the material.

188. DAY, Robert A. "The Rebirth of Leggatt". *Literature and Psychology* 13:3 (1963) 74-81.

Conrad's *The Secret Sharer* (1912) seen as "a double narrative in which the captain's initiation into maturity is paralleled and complemented by a symbolic presentation of the archetype of rebirth" in Leggatt. The captain's assistance in Leggatt's rebirth as "a free man, a proud swimmer" points up the captain's own psychological growth. Maud Bodkin's analysis of the rebirth pattern in *The Ancient Mariner* serves for close comparison.

189. DEFALCO, Joseph M. "'The Great Good Place': A Journey into the Psyche." *Literature and Psychology* 8:2 (1958) 18-20.

The dream sequence in Henry James's short story (1900) analyzed as the protagonist's journey through "the deep recesses of the psyche, where the ego, overwhelmed by the pressures of the conscious world, is healed by the tender care of the Great Mother archetype and emerges reborn." The life-death-rebirth pattern is traced in the use of rain and bell images as unifying symbols in the stages of the journey.

190. DEFALCO, Joseph M. *The Hero in Hemingway's Short Stories*. Pittsburgh: University of Pittsburgh Press, 1963. xi,226 pp.

Below the realistic surface and the simple plots of Hemingway's short stories there is "the psychological level, or inner movement," where meaning is expressed through imagery and symbolic allusion. Jung's theory of the individuation process and Campbell's account of the stages of the mythic hero's journey offer explanatory parallels for the psychological development and intense inner conflicts of the typical Hemingway hero. Grouping the stories by theme, DeFalco shows how Nick Adams in the early stories is pictured as undergoing initiation and reaching the threshold to maturity. In later stories wounded war heroes are given symbolic stature by implied comparisons with the crippled figures of mythology and with Christ as archetypal hero. The marriage stories express the isolation and alienation of partners who fail to achieve selfhood in the maturation process. Finally, there are the stories in which Hemingway makes his men face the ultimate tests of life. Many settle for the contingencies of life, but some "strong" heroes, by the manner of their deaths, realize an ideal of self-fulfillment, as, for instance, the "complete bullfighter" in the story "The Undefeated" or the big game hunter in "The Short Happy Life of Francis Macomber."

In this study the Jungian approach is well used to clarify the symbolic and representative nature of Hemingway's heroes, who "catalogue the disillusionment of contemporary man in his struggle to come to terms with a world he cannot truly understand."

191. DEFALCO, Joseph M. "The Themes of Individuation in the Short Stories of Ernest Hemingway." (Ph.D. 1961 University of Florida) p.127. No abstract in *DAI*.
Became book *The Hero in Hemingway's Short Stories* (1963).

192. DEGROOT, Elisabeth M. "Archetypes in the Major Novels of Thomas Hardy and Their Literary Application." (Ph.D. 1967 New York University) 302 pp. *DAI* 28/03 A p.1048.

193. DELEO, James V. "A Jungian Perspective of the Drama and the Writings of Tennessee Williams." (Ph.D. 1976 California School of Professional Psychology, San Diego) 109 pp. *DAI* 38/09 B p.4448.

194. DEL FATTORE, Joan. "The Hidden Self: A Study of the Shadow Figure in American Short Fiction." (Ph.D. 1978 Pennsylvania State University) 217 pp. *DAI* 39/10 A p.6127. (Barth, Jackson, James, Malamud, O'Connor, Poe, Porter)

195. DEMETRAKOPOULOS, Stephanie A. "Anaïs Nin and the Feminine Quest for Consciousness: The Quelling of the Devouring Mother and the Ascension of the Sophia." *Bucknell Review* 24:1 (1978) 119-136. Rpt. in *Women, Literature and Criticism*. Ed. Harry R. Garvin. Lewisburg: Bucknell UP, 1978. 119-139.

The theories of Jung and Neumann are used to support the theory that Nin, indeed every female artist, is delayed in realizing her potential because of the influence of both her real mother and the archetypal Great Mother. Women internalize the self-sacrificing mother as a role model, causing them to be attracted to dependent men who drain their creative energy. Nin's own struggle with her mother is traced through her diaries and fiction, particularly *The Four-Chambered Heart* (1959).

Demetrakopoulos sees Nin's development of the self as reflected in the diaries as having universal appeal to other women experiencing the same conflicts. Nin's exploration of herself indicates the necessity for women to follow their own inner voices along paths that differ from those taken by men. At the end of her life Nin may be said to have reached "the highest stage of the feminine principle, the Sophia." K.S.

196. *DEMETRAKOPOULOS, Stephanie A. "Archetypal Constellations of Feminine Consciousness in Nin's First *Diary*." *Mosaic* 11:2 (1978) 121-137.

Describing herself as a third generation Jungian and applying several of James Hillman's ideas, the author traces the psychological progress in Anaïs Nin's first *Diary* (1966) as "Nin's raising of various archetypes and personal repressions into her conscious mind so that she can control and understand them." The role of Henry Miller, who embodies the trickster element for her, is especially stressed. His respect and constant affection strongly encouraged her development as woman and artist. The numinous force of a whole series of other characters presented in the *Diary* is explained through Nin's positive projections upon them of archetypes intrinsic in her own psyche, a process which enables her "to annex the deeper layers of the unconscious" (Jung's phrase). The *Diary* reveals to us this process of self-actualization in Nin's living out of, among others, the myths of Persephone, Demeter, Venus, Artemis and Hestia. Nin thus "embodies the feminine principle in many of its metamorphoses and she tells us how it feels and what it means to be a woman artist."

Good archetypal and psychological discussion of Nin's *Diary* "as a document of the growth of a psyche."

197. DEMETRAKOPOULOS, Stephanie. "The Iconography of Heroic Womanhood: An Interdisciplinary Illustration of the Great Mother and Sophia Archetypes in Renaissance Art and Drama." *Anima* 4:1 (1977) 3-15.

"One of the distinguishing characteristics of the Renaissance is the reemergence of a positive, life-enhancing feminine principle." In some of the greatest art of the period the Great Good Mother archetype figures as the Sophia, highest embodiment of the anima, embracing natural female sexuality and fertility as well as feminine goodness, wisdom, and spirituality. This "heroic womanhood" finds expression in some of the most famous paintings of Botticelli, da Vinci, and other Italian masters. It is found in its fullest complexity in literary works: Shakespeare's portrayal of Imogen in *Cymbeline* and, in particular, Webster's Duchess of Malfi, "perhaps the best example of the Sophia in all literature."

198. DEMETRAKOPOULOS,Stephanie."TheMetaphysicsofMatrilinearity
in Women's Autobiography: Studies of Mead's *Blackberry Winter*,
Hellman's *Pentimento*, Angelou's *I Know Why the Caged Bird Sings*,
and Kingston's *The Woman Warrior*." In *Women's Autobiography:
Essays in Criticism*. Ed. E. Jelinek. Bloomington: Indiana University
Press, 1980. 180-205.

   The influence of mothers, grandmothers or aunts in a child's
home life ("the matriarchal realm") and the ways in which mother-
daughter relationships pattern a girl's inner experiences
("matrilinear consciousness") are studied in four women's
autobiographies (Margaret Mead, 1972; Lillian Hellman, 1973; Maya
Angelou, 1973; Maxine Hong Kingston, 1977). The degree of
meaningful connectedness reached in life, as described by each of
these four women, is viewed under the universal dimensions of a
woman's psyche as imaged in the Demeter/Kore archetype of the
mother-daughter bond, ritualized in the Eleusinian mysteries, and in
the archetype of the sheltering Great Good Mother.

   In spite of some rather abstract terminology, Demetrakopoulos
very concretely applies archetypal and mythological categories in
her lucid analysis of feminine psychology in these autobiographies.
She emphasizes how in the twentieth century "woman's mythos is
taking shape" as psychic necessity, when these writers, while
describing their lives, show the need for women to forge their
individual identities from the matriarchal realm.

199. DEMOTT, Robert. "Toward a Redefinition of *To a God Unknown*."
University of Windsor Review 8:2 (1973) 34-53.
Rpt. with minor revisions in *A Study Guide to Steinbeck: A
Handbook to His Major Works*. Ed. Tetsumaro Hayashi. Metuchen,
N.J.: Scarecrow Press, 1974. 187-210.

   Careful analysis of Steinbeck's "visionary" novel (1933), viewed
its mythical symbolism in Jungian psychological perspective. The
novel's hero, Joseph Wayne, moves in a symbolic landscape, in
which the mythology of his relation with the land and with the
fertility and drought of the natural cycle is at the same time his
progressive journey into the collective unconscious, the unknown
god within him. Through his final self-sacrifice Wayne not only
releases the psychic energy which as an archetypal wedding of
mother earth and primal man restores fertility to the land, but also
achieves the wholeness of complete individuation, the synthesis of
his consciousness with the creative unconscious upon which "the
cyclical continuance of man and nature depends."

200. DEMOUY, Jane Kraus. *Katherine Anne Porter's Women: The Eye of
Her Fiction*. Austin: University of Texas Press, 1983. 228 pp.

Psychological and archetypal analysis that makes use of Freud, Jung and Neumann, and identifies the main theme of Porter's fiction as a conflict of female identity, the impossibility of full integration or individuation for woman.

201. DETWEILER, Robert. "Patterns of Rebirth in *Henderson the Rain King.*" *Modern Fiction Studies* 12:4 (1966-67) 405-414.

The structural and thematic unity of Bellow's novel (1959) is focused in the concept of a rebirth through imagination, leading to spiritual and moral redemption. The process of Henderson's rebirth is viewed from four angles: the animal imagery, the psychological symbols, the pattern of the hero myth and the archetypal dying king, and finally the pervasive irony of the comical-paradoxical affirmation of life that gives the novel its disturbing profundity.

202. DIAMOND, Ruth. "The Archetype of Death and Renewal in *I Never Promised You a Rose Garden.*" *Perspectives in Psychiatric Care* 8:1 (1975) 21-24.

During her descent into insanity, the heroine of Hannah Green's novel (1964) experiences an archetypal voyage to the underworld, followed by rebirth into the world of the living. Schizophrenia "is a process in which the ego dies to the world of reality and finds itself trapped in the inner world of the unconscious." Here Deborah encounters her "inner archetypes." She recovers after a dream encounter with the self, indicating "the existence of powerful forces in the human psyche which can carry us to salvation and individuation." K.S.

203. DICKERSON, Lucia. "Portrait of the Artist as a Jung Man." *Kenyon Review* 21:1 (1959) 58-83.

A spirited attempt to decode the complex hidden symbolism of *The Snow Pasture* (1949) and *The Young May Moon* (1950) by the English novelist P.H. Newby. In a way the books are "symbolic psychological histories comprehensible only to the Jung adept." Four main symbolic systems have been used "contrapuntally" : "the Classical, the Celtic, the Alchemical, and the Jungian." In her detailed explications the author detaches "the familiar archetypal figures from the welter of Greek myth, Celtic folklore, mediaeval alchemy, and Pythagorean number mystique." In both novels the characters and the symbolism suggest "the projection of the unconscious parts of the personality" and the collision of opposites in a Jungian individuation process, which is further related to rebirth and mystic enlightenment in Zen Buddhism.

204. *DIGBY, George Wingfield. *Symbol and Image in William Blake*. Oxford: Clarendon Press, 1957. xx,143 pp., 77 plates.

This book is devoted to the elucidation of Blake's symbols and ideas in his early sequence of pictures *The Gates of Paradise* (engraved 1793, text added in later edition) and the so-called Arlington Court picture, a water-color painted in 1821, representing the central theme of Blake's art, regeneration. To grasp the spiritual intent of his symbolism Blake must be approached imaginatively rather than analytically. Digby draws on all of the poetic and pictorial works for amplification and often brings in comparisons with Indian mythology, Chinese philosophy and Jungian psychology, since Blake's images and symbols can only be understood "in relation to the psychological, or religious aim of his work." In a chapter "On the Understanding of Blake's Art" Digby explains how Blake attempts to grasp in a "unitive vision" the opposites of man's irrational instincts and the rational, conscious sides of his mind. As a result the poems and pictures embody "the great archetypal principles and images - the *eternal attributes*, as Blake calls them."

Digby writes lucidly about the complex visions of Blake's "intuitive imagination" and his commentary on the pictures provides an excellent guide to Blake's symbolism. Jung's general theory of symbols is imaginatively used to explain aspects of Blake's art. Anima and puer aeternus as images of "creative possibility" clarify the "redeeming symbols" in these pictures.

205. DIPIPPO, Albert E. "Pastoralism as Archetypal Idea, Concept, and Protest." (Ph.D. 1975 University of Southern California) 153 pp. *DAI* 36/06 A p.3648.

206. DJWA, Sandra. "False Gods and the True Covenant: Thematic Continuity between Margaret Laurence and Sinclair Ross." *Journal of Canadian Fiction* 1:4 (1972) 43-50.
Rpt. in *Margaret Laurence*. Ed. William New. Toronto: McGraw-Hill Ryerson, 1977. 66-84.

The Canadian novelists Sinclair Ross and Margaret Laurence share a vision of the "ironic discrepancy between the spirit and the letter" of small-town puritan religion. Both writers use Biblical allusions "to provide a resonating mythic framework" for an essentially psychological analysis of character. Like Jung, they see "the growth of the god-like spirit or psyche within the individual" as synonymous with self-realization, and religion as a "numinous experience" which can lead to psychological change.

207. DOCKERY, Carl. D. "The Myth of the Shadow in the Fantasies of Williams, Lewis, and Tolkien." (Ph.D. 1975 Auburn University) 180 pp. *DAI* 36/06 A p.3727.

208. DOGGETT, Frank. *Stevens' Poetry of Thought*. Baltimore: Johns Hopkins Press, 1966. xiii,223 pp.

In the "inner discourse" of his poems Stevens often addresses projections of "the interior life," personifications embodying "human feelings in the shape of the hero, the child, the father, the mother, the maiden." The chapter "Variations on a Nude" considers the relevance of Jung's anima concept to an understanding of the persistent image of the symbolic woman as an archetypal and "incipient mythic" figure.

209. DOLL, Mary Aswell. "Samuel Beckett and Archetypal Consciousness." (Ph.D. 1980 Syracuse University) 328 pp. *DAI* 41/06 A p.2598.

210. DOOLEY, David J. "Baptizing the Devil: *Fifth Business*." Chapter 9 of *Moral Vision in the Canadian Novel*. Toronto: Clarke, Irwin, 1979. 109-122.

In a collection of essays on the "moral contexts" created by eleven Canadian novelists, Dooley considers in how far Robertson Davies' "provocative novel" *Fifth Business* (1970) may be seen as a Jungian parable, illustrating psychologically more and less mature approaches to life. Three somewhat "unreal characters" prove Davies' Jungian point. The saintly Mrs. Dempster, the devilish Liesl and the unorthodox priest Padre Blazon teach Dunstan Ramsay that the opposites of psychic life, conscious and unconscious, good and evil, must be brought into harmony; that "evil is as positive a factor as good, especially for individuation." Like Jung, Davies raises the question whether "the ultimate sanction of religion is its psychological utility," and does not answer it.

211. DOWNING, Christine. "Revisioning Autobiography: The Bequest of Freud and Jung." *Soundings* 60:2 (1977) 210-228.

Explores the poetic and mythic dimensions of Freud's *The Interpretation of Dreams* (1900) and Jung's *Memories, Dreams, Reflections* (1962) as innovative autobiographical ventures. "The discovery of the unconscious leads to a new sense of the form and content of autobiography," as dreams and other imaginal events become part of the "psyche's search to understand itself," in awareness of the "fictiveness of the unity of the self."

Extremely interesting and lucid discussion of the "radically new conception of self" emerging from Freud's and Jung's writings.

212. *DREW, Elizabeth. *T.S. Eliot: The Design of His Poetry*. New York: Charles Scribner, 1949. 216 pp.

After a sympathetic and critical summary of the central concepts of Jungian psychology, Drew studies the ordering of sensuous symbolism into pattern as the basis of Eliot's poetic technique and of his "mythical method." Her analysis of key poems in Eliot's work does not wholly depend on Jung, but she draws a general parallel between the sequence in which the symbols "arise in the course of the poetry, their inter-relationships, and their final resolution into the design of *Four Quartets*," and Jung's description of the order in which the archetypal symbols appear in the process of psychic integration of the personality as it finds expression in dreams and myths.

The picture of aimless and sordid city-life in the early poems culminates in the sterile degeneration and need for regeneration expressed in *The Waste Land* (1922), where the central symbol of the sea-change ("those are pearls that were his eyes") suggests the sea in its destructive and creative aspects as archetype of psychic death and rebirth. In *The Hollow Men* (1925) spiritual stagnation is symbolically characterized in the paralysing meeting with the Shadow and a new redeeming symbol from the unconscious is glimpsed in the appearance of the "multifoliate rose, the hope only of empty men." Especially in *Ash Wednesday* (1930) the parallel with Jung's archetypes of transformation offers insights into the symbolic functioning of Lady, garden, rose, fountain, yew trees and leopards. The extraordinary intensity of feeling created in "Marina" is related to the dream-image of the birth of the miraculous child as the beginning of new spiritual experience and as a symbol of "supreme vital intensity." And the sense of the ambiguity of rebirth in the other *Ariel Poems* is connected with Jung's idea that the psychic renewal involves a reversal and destruction of old values that "resembles a devastation."

In the explication of *Four Quartets* (1943), Jung's view of the final stage of the process of psychological integration as the attaining of a new centre of being offers a suggestive analogue to Eliot's poetic exploration of the inner pattern centering in the Incarnation, the point of intersection between our life in the world of time and the timeless reality that transcends and gives meaning to human existence. The mandala symbol, in its circle divided into four equal parts circulating round a center, visualizes this sense of psychic wholeness as much as Eliot's use of "fourness" in many aspects of *Four Quartets* and its image of the "still point of the turning world."

This is the first Jungian study of a writer's creative work in its totality (if we leave aside the plays). It is at once a very fine study of Eliot's poetry and a model of the successful application of psychological notions to the elucidation of literary texts. In her introduction Drew emphasizes the limitations that make psychology "a poor instrument" for literary criticism, yet her sensitive readings of Eliot's poems make excellent use of the insights derived from the suggestive parallels with Jung's psychology.

213. DRISCOLL, James P. *Identity in Shakespearean Drama*. Lewisburg, Pa.: Bucknell University Press, 1983. 202 pp.

A Jungian approach to Shakespeare's characters, their self-knowledge and sense of identity.

214. DUCHARME, Robert. *Art and Idea in the Novels of Bernard Malamud: Toward The Fixer*. The Hague: Mouton, 1974. 151 pp.

The archetype of the Waste Land occurs in the mythic structure of each of Malamud's first four novels and the central realistic figures parallel mythic heroes (Percival, St. Francis, Adam, Christ). The ironic handling of the controlling archetypes is discussed, as well as the father-son motif, and Malamud's development of the themes of suffering and responsibility. For his interpretation Ducharme has made use of the findings of anthropology (Frazer, Roheim), scholars of the hero myth (Rank, Campbell), and the depth psychologists (principally Freud and, to some extent, Jung).

215. DUDEK, Louis. "The Psychology of Literature." *Canadian Literature* 72 (1977) 5-20.

The archetypal "visionary view of literature" of Jung and Northrop Frye, in search of abstract underlying unity, is rejected in favour of a view of art as a "method of thinking with things," and of meaning as "multi-faceted and actual." The problem of how "the imagination in its deepest working" generalizes the particular into larger perspectives is solved by giving art in the first place biographical meaning as "the concrete symbolic representation of the tensions and dilemmas in the mind of the author."

However, when discussing how the work of literature as the "creative crisis" of the individual suffering artist can meaningfully express the experiences of a whole society and even of later generations, the author, in spite of himself, is back with the problem tackled by Jung and Frye.

216. DUNCAN-JOHNSTONE, L.A. "A Psychological Study of William Blake." Guild Lecture No. 40. London: Guild of Pastoral Psychology, 1945. 28 pp.

Brief explanation of the archetypal structure of Blake's complicated myth in his Prophetic Books. The gods and gigantic figures in *Vala or the Four Zoas, Milton*, and *Jerusalem* may be understood in Jungian terms as psychic manifestations, archetypal images and activities of the soul. Albion, universal man, in his fourfold unity was one with the universe. After the Fall his divine life-giving powers, the Zoas, become four disunited warring gods. This psychological struggle of "Man at war with himself" is further dramatized by splitting off from each Zoa, and from Albion, first their Emanations, or feminine counterparts, and then the Spectres, symbolizing consciousness divorced from the unconscious. The Spectre of man is his Reasoning Power, set up as a god, but in Blake's view "the abstract objecting power that negatives everything." Only what Blake calls man's "humanity" (with his faculty of Imagination as "the whole-making spirit") can defeat the Spectre and restore the opposites to wholeness, a *religio* of consciousness and the unconscious.

217. DUNCAN, Joseph E. "Archetypal Criticism in English, 1946-1980." *Bulletin of Bibliography* 40:4 (1983) 206-230.

In this bibliography of 330 titles "archetype" is understood as "a recurrent pattern, like the quest, the scapegoat, or the 'shadow' of Carl Jung's psychology." Included are "critical works dealing primarily with an identifiable and widely recurrent pattern," but not "those dealing with either a particular myth or the general nature of mythology." Postwar archetypal criticism is seen as rooted in the works of anthropologist Sir James Frazer and psychologist Carl Jung, while Northrop Frye's prolific writings on "archetypes as purely literary structures" have been particularly influential.

The bibliography is divided into four sections: 1. Works influencing literary criticism (citing books by Campbell, Eliade, Frazer, Jung, Neumann, Raglan, and Rank); 2. General works of criticism; 3. Individual writers (authors covered are English or American); 4. Textbooks. The contents of each book or article are very briefly indicated. There are 146 specifically Jungian titles in this bibliography.

218. *DUNCAN, Joseph. E. "Archetypes in Milton's Earthly Paradise." In *Milton Studies*. Vol. 14. Ed. James D. Simmonds. Pittsburgh, Pa.: University of Pittsburgh Press, 1980. 25-58.

Milton's depiction of the earthly paradise in *Paradise Lost* is examined through three different but related archetypal approaches. In the contexts of anthropology, psychology and literary criticism, focusing on the studies of Mircea Eliade, Carl Jung, and Northrop Frye, Duncan shows that Milton's Paradise is "an intensive concentration of patterns central to the life of religion, the life of the psyche, and the life of the Western literary tradition." For "Eliade and Frye, paradise itself is central; for Jung, paradise can be a symbol of the mother and of the inner center of the self." Among the major patterns relating to paradise, discussed by these authors and also found in Milton, are: "the *axis mundi* and world mountain, the sacred place and the sacred marriage, the maternal nature of paradise, the emergence and expansion of consciousness, the quest for 'identity' and the 'analogy of innocence'." In the section on Jung, Duncan establishes, with a variety of citations, how Jung "sees paradise as a symbol of the mother archetype and of individuation, the integration of the conscious and unconscious within the individual; paradise is also closely associated with the mandala and the archetype of quaternity."

In this meticulously researched essay Duncan demonstrates with a wealth of references the rich archetypal "complexity of Eve, the garden, and *Paradise Lost*." The notes form a valuable bibliography of the subject.

219. DUPLESSIS, Rachel Blau. "The Critique of Consciousness and Myth in Levertov, Rich, and Rukeyser." *Feminist Studies* 3 (1975)199-221.
      These three poets are seen as questioning the role of the individual consciousness in history. In particular, Rich and Rukeyser doubt the validity of the old patriarchal myths, and try to develop new ones which are more relevant to the experience of women. Their poems express "the creative antagonism of the woman-hero to traditional consciousness and old patterns of myth" as elaborated, for instance, in Erich Neumann's views of the development of masculine consciousness, or in the myth of Perseus' struggle with "wicked" female power. The author discusses a selection of important poems which offer "in fact reinventions of myth, appropriating and rediscovering the essential mythic experiences: journey, rebirth, transformation, and centering." K.S.

220. EDDINS, Dwight. "John Fowles: Existence as Authorship." *Contemporary Literature* 17:2 (1976) 204-222.
      In a highly abstract "metafictional" analysis of the first three novels by John Fowles, the idea is pursued that the author "involves his characters in initiations designed to make them the existential authors of their own lives." The novels are "artistic constructs" of overlapping "psychodramas," in which in a sense the characters write the "novels" of their own lives. The movement in each novel is from "eidetic images" of artificial art to "contingent images" of natural everyday existence. In the efforts of the

characters to achieve the freedom of "authentic existence" the anima and animus archetypes play constructive roles.

221. EDEL, Leon. "Literature and Psychology." In *Comparative Literature: Method and Perspective*. Eds. Newton P. Stallknecht and Horst Frenz. Carbondale: Southern Illinois University Press, 1961. 96-115.

This collection of essays introduced what was at the time "a young discipline." In "Literature and Psychology" Leon Edel suggests that the rise of psychoanalysis has an independent parallel in the early twentieth century "stream of consciousness" novels. Later, Freud's writings directly fertilize imaginative writers. Psychoanalysis has contributed to three facets of literary study: literary criticism, the study of the creative process, and literary biography. As examples of the first, Ernest Jones's Hamlet essay and Maud Bodkin's *Archetypal Patterns in Poetry* (1934) are mentioned. Bodkin "has had a profound influence," although "often the individual qualities of a work are obscured in favor of universal patterns." In general Edel feels that "much of the literary use of psychoanalysis has been to date rather crude and primitive, tending to simplify material highly complex and to make stereotypes of creative personality."

222. EDINGER, Edward F. *Encounter with Self: A Jungian Commentary on William Blake's Illustrations of the Book of Job*. Toronto: Inner City Books, 1986. 74 pp.

223. EDINGER, Edward F. "Helen of Troy." In *A Well of Living Waters: A Festschrift for Hilde Kirsch*. Ed. Rhoda Head et al. Los Angeles: C.G. Jung Institute, 1977. 120-127.

A slight sketch of the development of the figure of the archetypal feminine in the literary tradition from Homer's Helen to the spiritualized Eros of eternal womanhood at the end of Goethe's *Faust*. In Jung's psychological outline of the evolution of the anima, Marlowe's Faustus would represent a case of arrested individuation. He merely follows "the anima of his desirousness until she leads him to hell." There is no transformation.

224. EDINGER, Edward F. *Melville's Moby-Dick: A Jungian Commentary. An American Nekyia*. New York: New Directions, 1975. 150 pp. The material of this book appeared in four instalments in *Quadrant* 7:2 (1974) 7-33, 8:1 (1975) 5-32, 9:1 (1976) 17-47, 9:2 (1976) 35-58.

This ambitious "psychological study" of *Moby-Dick* (1851) attempts to fulfill three aims: to elucidate the psychological significance of Melville's greatest work, to demonstrate the methods of analytical psychology in dealing with symbolic forms, and to present "the basic orientation, or *Weltanschauung*" underlying the Jungian therapeutic approach. Its method is to "approach the novel as a psychological document, a record in psychological imagery of an intense inner experience as though it were a dream which needs interpretation and elaboration of its images for their meaning to emerge fully." The largely archetypal interpretation is complimented with insights from causalistic personal (i.e. Freudian) psychology. Written in an age when traditional religion was beginning to lose "its capacity to carry living meaning," *Moby-Dick* is also seen as "a document of our civilization in transition." It expresses "Melville's personal experience of simultaneously losing religious projections and discovering the transpersonal contents of the unconscious."

After a chapter on Melville's life and background we are taken through the novel in chapters that follow the story as a psychological progression, its archetypal aspects amplified with biblical and mythological parallels. At the same time each chapter illustrates one or more specific Jungian concepts so that the whole book may also be read as a primer of Jungian psychology. From Ishmael, prototype of modern alienated man, who sets out on the "night sea journey" or descent into the unconscious that may lead to individuation, we move to Queequeg as the positive shadow. Both characters are related to Melville's personal psychology and seen as symbolizing aspects of the psyche of 19th century America. By unraveling the rich network of allusions surrounding Ahab and the white whale, Edinger illuminates the archetypal force of Melville's antagonists: Ahab, the inflated Promethean sun-hero, whose "ego-self identification" must be dissolved, who Osiris-like must be dismembered to be transformed, and the multiple-meaninged white-black whale, incarnation of dark evil, but also symbol of the self in its union of opposites: its whiteness related to the Spirit Father of the Christian Deity, its black hooded head associated with the Sphinx and the Medusa of the Mother archetype. Ahab's pact with the devil is embodied in his evil shadow Fedallah, who paradoxically guides Ahab to his encounter with the numinous. Before Moby-Dick carries Ahab into the depths of the sea (and of the unconscious) Melville's descriptions abound with transformational symbols of death and rebirth. Edinger sees Ahab's death ultimately as a reconnection "with the whale as Great Mother," a reconciliation of opposites, out of which comes (for Melville) the possibility of psychological rebirth.

This study by a "depth psychotherapist" is an uneven book. Edinger provides many penetrating insights into the symbolism of the "linked analogies" and the emotional and intellectual import of Melville's masterpiece. Particularly good are his observations on Ahab as "a study in the psychology of resentment," and "the acute,

tortured awareness of radical evil as an aspect of God" that runs
through all of *Moby-Dick*, its core being the Job archetype, which
in psychological terms is "the ego's experience of being wounded by
encounter with the Self." Illuminating is the discussion of Fedallah
as paradoxically the avenging angel of an apparently malevolent
deity.

These virtues, however, are offset by considerable weaknesses
springing from the narrowly psychological viewpoint. By using the
book as a quarry for illustrations to the major tenets of Jungian
psychology, Edinger is led into contradictions and distortions, not
only of literary effects, but also of psychological meanings. To
simply assume the work of art to be "a living psychic product of
the autonomous imagination," not subject to the "deliberate
contrivance of the conscious will," when obviously every great
novel is a combination of the two, is to court at least occasional
critical disaster. Ishmael, for instance, is taken to task for "the
careless, flippant attitude" with which he announces his decision to
go to sea, and equally, for the "suspicious speed" with which he
"turns his back upon the whole Judeo-Christian heritage" and
becomes a pagan idolator when joining in Queequeg's religious
ceremonies. To miss Melville's humor and irony as part of his
narrative strategy leads to overly moralizing comments, just as
Melville's famous remark in a letter to Hawthorne "I stand for the
heart. To the dogs with the head!" seems hardly to make "evident"
that "Melville was cut off from a full masculine functioning of
discriminating rationality." And can we take the psychologist
seriously when he tells us that Ishmael's rapturous description of
the enchanting peacefulness of life in the ship's masthead on a
gently rolling sea must be read as the "inflated state of passive
identification with the unconscious?"

The Jungian framework leads to questionable identifications.
Melville's own psychology may be reflected in the four officers he
created for the *Pequod*, but is his superior function, thinking,
embodied in monomaniac Ahab? To argue this in relation to Ahab
and in contrast to Melville's remark "I stand for the heart,"
Edinger develops the tortuous argument that Ahab presents
Melville's "potential superior function," and that on the *Pequod* we
have "the dictatorship of a crippled superior function." Since
Ishmael does not fit into the foursome of the ship's officers,
Edinger fails to relate him to the novel's inclusive psyche. This
becomes awkward at the end of the book, when the Jungian schema
reaches the final stage of the individuation process. Ahab's fire
speech is seen as another sign of Ahab's self-reflection and psychic
growth that warrants the conclusion that "Ahab, although he dies,
is healed." It is one of Edinger's apodictic statements that

disregard the actual narrative. Edinger has written a stimulating and readable book that falls short of being the definitive Jungian interpretation of *Moby-Dick*.

225. EDINGER, Edward F. "Ralph Waldo Emerson: Naturalist of the Soul." *Spring* (1965) 77-99.

"Emerson was a kind of intuitive proto-psychologist." Anticipating Jung, he discusses in his writings many archetypal patterns of life. His understanding of symbolism makes him appreciate the function of myths and dreams. His concept of the Over-Soul corresponds to Jung's collective unconscious. There are passages in his essays that give us psychological descriptions of what Jung later called self, mandala, synchronicity and psychic wholeness.

226. EDINGER, Edward F. "*Romeo and Juliet*: A Coniunctio Drama." In *The Shaman from Elko: Papers in Honor of Joseph L. Henderson on His Seventy-Fifth Birthday.* Ed. Gareth Hill et al. San Francisco: C.G. Jung Institute of San Francisco, 1978. 67-80.

The symbolism of the alchemical *coniunctio oppositorum* is applied to the play's conflicts and paradoxes. Because the immature egos of Romeo and Juliet identify too willingly with the transpersonal forces, they become sacrificial victims in the archetypal drama of marriage to death. However, in the symbolical process death is followed by rebirth into fuller consciousness. This is suggested through Shakespeare's persistent references to light and beauty, and it helps to explain why the play leaves us "with the definite sense of life and love triumphant over death."

227. *EISENSTEIN, Samuel A. *Boarding the Ship of Death: D.H. Lawrence's Quester Heroes.* The Hague: Mouton, 1974. 171 pp.

The less successful novels, which are closer to Lawrence's own experiences, show better than the artistically more achieved works the continuity of character in his work as a whole. The constant theme is self-realization, which may mean a development towards greater wholeness or disintegration in the failure or qualified success of a hero struggling to free his own creative potential. Eisenstein pursues this "intuitive design" in the creation of Lawrence's characters from the hero of *The Trespassers* (1912), who hangs himself, through the other early novels *The White Peacock* (1911) and *The Lost Girl* (1920), short stories like "The Woman Who Rode Away" and the later novels *Aaron's Rod* (1922) and *Kangaroo* (1922), to the Jesus-Osiris of "The Man Who Died," who is resurrected into physical life to become "Lawrence's perfected hero."

"The greatest challenge for Lawrence was to portray woman coming into being, and man springing from her," attempting to make "his own life apart from her." There are obvious parallels (often pointed to by Lawrence himself) with the quester heroes of myth and religion, with Earth Mothers, strong with unconscious life, and with the painful journeys of their sons through psychic initiation, death and rebirth to independence and greater consciousness. Eisenstein draws on a wide range of studies in anthropology, mythology and Eastern and Western religions to amplify and illuminate such recurring symbols in Lawrence's novels and stories as "the moonrites, together with the rabbit symbol," pointing toward "the possibility of a reconciliation of conscious and unconscious, *eros* and *thanatos*"; the horses, grooms and gamekeepers "who are in instinctive rapport with the wild things of the earth"; and the phoenix and other birds symbolizing rebirth.

At one point Eisenstein formulates his purpose as "showing that the success or failure of every character is a case study in the process of individuation." This sounds like a dangerously limiting critical program, but in fact his study admirably opens up the mythical, psychological and religious dimensions of the characters and the symbolism in Lawrence's work. He makes particularly good use of the relevant books of Jung and Neumann, and of Esther Harding's *Woman's Mysteries: Ancient and Modern* (q.v.).

228. EISENSTEIN, Samuel A. "The Quester Hero: A Study of Creative Evolution in the Fiction of D.H. Lawrence." (Ph.D. 1965 University of California, Los Angeles) 304 pp. *DAI* 26/07 A p.3950.
Became book *Boarding the Ship of Death: D.H. Lawrence's Quester Heroes* (1974).

229. *ELIAS-BUTTON, Karen. "Journey into an Archetype: The Dark Mother in Contemporary Women's Poetry." *Anima* 4:2 (1978) 5-11.
Feminist critiques of Jungian archetypes as perpetuating patriarchal hierarchies are signalized in articles by Naomi Goldenberg and poems by Susan Griffin. Women writers are attempting a redefinition of the feminine in which the dark side of the archetype of the Great Mother is not merely seen as destructive, but is positively valued as a necessary aspect of the complexity of feminine creativeness. In Sylvia Plath and Anne Sexton the "terrible" mother still appears as a wholly negative figure. Poems by later poets like Robin Morgan, May Sarton and Adrienne Rich illustrate the process of rediscovering a matriarchal mythology, in which symbols of the mother-goddesses, like the Erinyes, "speak judgment and tenderness at the same time."

This article is an example of the productive interaction of feminist criticism and analytical psychology.

230. ELLISON, Jerome. "How to Catch a Whale: Evil, Melville, and the Evolution of Consciousness." *Michigan Quarterly Review* 6:2 (1967) 85-89.

A plea for a new type of "evolutionary" literary criticism that will place the literary work in the wide context of theories about man's evolving consciousness (notably developed by Jung). Melville's work is an example of literature as a "veritable battleground of the evolutionary war" between the primitive and the civilized, the evil and the good, witness the recurrence of the devil-archetype in his novels, most forcefully as Ahab in *Moby-Dick*. Seen in the perspective of man's historical development toward fuller consciousness, Melville's grappling with the problems of evil is more than a lifelong painful struggle. It is a positive part of literature's "central role in the evolutionary advance."

In the course of his inflated argument the author mistakenly identifies Jung's archetypes with "primitive emotions and impulses."

231. ELLWOOD, Gracía F. "The Good Guys and the Bad Guys." *Tolkien Journal* 3:4 (1969) 9-11.

"The universality and religious character" of Tolkien's *The Lord of the Rings* is briefly argued in parallels from Jungian archetypes, Campbell's hero myth, and initiation rituals as described by Eliade.

232. ELLWOOD, Gracía F. "The Good Guys: A Study in Christ-Imagery." In *Good News from Tolkien's Middle-earth*. Grand Rapids, Mi.: Eerdmans, 1970. 87-142.

An essay on Christian parallels in *The Lord of the Rings* (1954-55). The lack of characterization in Tolkien's fantasy is explained by pointing out that its characters are archetypal figures taking part in a typical hero myth. Incorporates the author's article on "The Good Guys and the Bad Guys" in the *Tolkien Journal*.

233. *EMMETT, Paul. "The Reader's Voyage through *Travesty*." *Chicago Review* 28:2 (1976) 172-187.

John Hawkes' novel *Travesty* (1976) is seen as a powerful blend of epistemology, myth and humor. The reader's apparently unanswerable questions about the anonymous narrator's motivations make the book a "labyrinth of epistemological chaos" with "myth as the thread out of the maze." The novel consists mostly of the narrator's long monologue during a suicidal car-drive involving his daughter and her lover. Employing many of the Freudian dream structures Hawkes makes his story simulate a dreamlike product of the unconscious, his aim being to write "an authentic myth-making novel." In the light of Jung's *Symbols of Transformation* ("important to much of Hawkes' fiction") the narrator's "descent into death" is read as a mythic journey that is a projection of an inner search for psychic unity, self-knowledge and lost innocence. The narrator regresses back to childhood through memories of the past and makes an imaginary journey forward to his absent wife, whose function as archetypal anima and terrible mother is analysed. "The labyrinthine form of the narrator's monologue is a metaphor for his journey through a maze of conscious impediments toward his unconscious inner self and the rediscovery of paradisiac innocence."

The article provides an enlightening travel guide for the reader's journey of discovery through "the true mythic density of Hawkes' novel."

234. ESMONDE, Margaret P. "The Master Pattern: The Psychological Journey in the Earthsea Trilogy." In *Ursula K. Le Guin*. Eds. Joseph D. Olander and Martin H. Greenberg. New York: Taplinger, 1979. 15-35.

The Earthsea trilogy is seen as embodying the "master pattern" for all of Ursula K. Le Guin's fiction: the Jungian archetypal journey toward integration. In each of these three novels, an archetypal wise old man helps the protagonist face the shadow and accept mortality as an aspect of life, thus completing the development of the self. K.S.

235. *ETHERINGTON, Norman A. "Rider Haggard, Imperialism and the Layered Personality." *Victorian Studies* 22:1 (1978) 71-87.

Etherington refutes the charges of imperialism made against Haggard for such books as *King Solomon's Mines* (1885) and *She* (1887). Freud and Jung took a particular interest in Haggard's romances because their own models of the psyche correspond closely to Haggard's view that the human personality consists of several layers ranging from the superficially civilized to the barbarous. The popularity of these novels is accounted for by the theory that "the beasts which Victorians feared to encounter in themselves could be contemplated at a safe remove."

A very readable discussion of the psychology of Rider Haggard's romances and of what attracted Freud and Jung. K.S.

236. EVANS, David L. "Henry's Hell: The Night Journey in *The Red Badge of Courage*." *Proceedings of the Utah Academy of Sciences, Arts and Letters* 44:1 (1967) 159-166.

The hero of Stephen Crane's novel (1893), Henry Fleming, experiences the isolation from his comrades, and the symbolic death and rebirth of the archetypal Night Journey. As a result, he overcomes his cowardice and is accepted by his fellow soldiers. The Night Journey has become a common element in war literature, with the heroes arriving "at an understanding of their responsibility to others; the descent within the self leads to the outer world." In Henry's case, he moves too far in this direction, becoming a "war devil." Balance comes only afterwards, in his looking forward to a peaceful future. K.S.

237. EVANS, Oliver and Harry Finestone, eds. *The World of the Short Story: Archetypes in Action.* New York: Alfred A. Knopf, 1971. xi,581 pp.

An interesting and unusual selection of 57 short stories from many parts of the world, half of them translations from non-English-speaking cultures. The stories are arranged according to archetypal characters (fatal woman, earth-mother, scapegoat, alter ego) and archetypal themes (search, wisdom, transformation, prophecy and fulfillment, initiation, return to the womb). The introduction traces the notion of archetype as "primordial idea" through Western literature back to Plato and provides an outline of Jung's theory of archetypes. In the headnotes the psychological and anthropological aspects of each archetype are further discussed and many other striking literary treatments, mostly from the literatures of the Western world, are noted.

238. EVERSON, William (Brother Antoninus). *Archetype West: The Pacific Coast as a Literary Region.* Berkeley: Oyez, 1976. xiv,181 pp.

A survey of the literature of California, Oregon and Washington State, with specific attention to both literary and popular images of the Western writer. Jung's notion of the archetype is adopted, yet most technical terms from analytical psychology are replaced by more specifically literary criticism. Still, Everson urges that "intangible psychic forces in unconscious collective life [...] shape the substance of our responses, and become, through accumulation of experience, repository images, established symbolic forms." Writing for the non-specialist (literary or psychological), Everson fuses the analytic method of Jung with the more cultural bias of Northrop Frye, though naming the former only once and the latter not at all. J.K.

239. EVERSON,William (Brother Antoninus). *Birth of a Poet: The Santa Cruz Meditations.* Ed. Lee Bartlett. Santa Barbara, Ca.: Black Sparrow, 1982. 197 pp.

These transcripts are course lectures, called meditations because they were spoken without notes, the speaker pacing a wide circle in an auditorium among his students. Using Campbell's model of the monomythic journey of the hero, Everson expatiates on his personal vocation as a poet, his years before and after the two decades as a monk, and on writing as self-discovery. He required his students to maintain a dream journal and look for their charismatic vocations - as poets, healers, teachers, musicians, or lawyers and public leaders. Selected contents: The Way In, Myth and Dream, Free Will, The Power of the Negative, The New Adam, The American Shaman, The Archetype of the West, Landscape and Eros, Sacred Space. J.K.

240. EVERSON, William (Brother Antoninus). "Dionysus and the Beat Generation." In *Earth Poetry: Selected Essays and Interviews of William Everson, 1950-1977*. Ed. Lee Bartlett. Berkeley: Oyez, 1980. 21-28. Orig. in *Fresno*, Summer 1959.
Rpt. in *The Beats: Essays in Criticism*. Ed. Lee Bartlett. Jefferson, N.C.: McFarland, 1981.
A fusion of Catholic and Jungian notions of an archetypal expiation or catharsis resolving the Apollonian-Dionysian split. "Civilization-as-usual [...] is no longer capable of stemming the uprush of ecstatic forces from the repressed instinctual and spiritual life of man." Writing when he was a monk, Everson/Antoninus looks at the life and writings of his fellow Beat poets and concludes "that only a supernatural culture, the culture of basic Christian mystical life [...] is capable of healing the disordered human psyche." J.K.

241. EVERSON, William. (Brother Antoninus). *Robinson Jeffers: Fragments of an Older Fury*. Berkeley: Oyez, 1968.
Celebratory discussion of Jeffers' mythic qualities. Jung and Campbell are invoked in the essay "The Far-Cast Spear" which provides an introduction to Jeffers' long poem "The Women at Point Sur" (1927).

242. EWALD, Robert J. "The Jungian Archetype of the Fairy Mistress in Medieval Romance." (Ph.D. 1977 Bowling Green State University) 204 pp. *DAI* 38/09 A p.5451.

243. FABRICIUS, Johannes. *The Unconscious and Mr. Eliot: A Study in Expressionism.* Copenhagen: Nyt Nordisk Forlag Arnold Busck, 1967. 160 pp.
T.S. Eliot is seen as a leading representative of Expressionism, the artistic movement that "represents an eruption of the collective unconscious into the conscious strata of modern civilization." The thesis here is that the unconscious is "the creative matrix and

spiritual focus of T.S. Eliot's poetry." Film became the main medium of Expressionist art because its technique of cross-cutting and parallel montage of dreamlike symbolic images allows of direct expression of the unconscious. Applying the new filmic techniques Eliot's revolutionary expressionist poem *The Waste Land* (1922) achieves a synthesis of and "interaction between consciousness and the collective unconscious." Eliot's key notions of "tradition" and "impersonal art" are related to the collective unconscious in that he rejects the personal, and aims at the universal and timeless, while his meditative poetry follows Dante in the "higher dream" and "vision" that release archetypal imagery from the deep unconscious. Both Eliot and Jung conceive of the symbol ultimately "as a final or transcendent function of religious quality." The essential religious nature of Expressionist drama is found in the mythic/ritual level underneath the surface realism of Eliot's later plays, in *The Family Reunion* (1939) conveyed through its symbolism of "the unconscious dynamics of incestuous rebirth and reunion."

This is an odd collection of genuine insights into the important role of the unconscious in Eliot's art embedded in sketchy arguments, repetitive statements, and undigested generalizations. Half of the text consists of strings of lengthy quotations from Eliot's critical prose-writings (many of them interestingly culled from periodicals like *The Egoist*, *The Athenaeum*, and *The Dial*), which, however, are too often left to speak for themselves.

244. *FALK, Doris V. *Eugene O'Neill and the Tragic Tension: An Interpretive Study of the Plays.* New Brunswick, N.J.: Rutgers University Press, 1958. vii,211 pp.
Second edition with new material: New York: Gordian Press, 1982. 223 pp.

In her searching study of O'Neill's work Doris Falk emphasizes the psychological pattern of the plays. "O'Neill is chiefly concerned with the resolution of inner conflicts" to such an extent that "the real action in the plays takes place within the mind of the protagonist." Themes and symbols were strongly influenced by the new psychology. "Though no deep student of psychoanalysis," O'Neill knew the outlines of Freudian theory and had read several books on the subject, but, he said, "Jung is the only one of the lot who interests me. Some of his suggestions I find extraordinarily illuminating in the light of my own experience with hidden motives." Most important among the many Jungian ideas O'Neill uses are the conceptions of "the existence and power of the unconscious" as an autonomous force, and of psychic life as perpetual tension between opposites, the conflict and pain of which is "the source of all change and growth." To reconcile his unconscious needs with those of the conscious ego man must find self-knowledge. The failure to know themselves leads many characters in O'Neill's plays to self-destruction.

As important as the conscious echoes of Jung's thoughts are O'Neill's unconscious anticipations of the findings of the Neo-Freudians, Karen Horney and Erich Fromm. In the earlier plays the theme is often that of the false ego-image hidden behind an aggressive mask (analogous to Horney's theory of "neurotic pride"), and in the later plays the repression of sexual drives is added to the conflict between reality and illusion. That O'Neill draws heavily on ideas and symbols from Jungian psychology is demonstrated in the analyses of *The Emperor Jones* (1921) with its dramatization of aspects of the collective and personal unconscious, and of *The Great God Brown* (1925) with its persona and shadow characters. Falk does not lose sight of the artistic limitations of O'Neill's work. She observes, for instance, that "in his effort to make his characters symbolic, O'Neill has often confined them to almost diagrammatical representations" of Jungian anima and animus types.

245. FARRELL, Leigh A. Dawes. "The Archetypal Image: An Interpretation of the Poetry of Theodore Roethke, Arthur Rimbaud, W.B. Yeats, and Robert Frost." (Ph.D. 1983 University of Washington) 245 pp. *DAI* 44/11 A p.3377.

246. FARRINGTON, Lorna Dishington. "*Empedocles on Etna*: A Jungian Perspective." (D.A. 1970 Carnegie-Mellon University) 67 pp. *DAI* 31/05 A p.2341. (Arnold)

247. FEINBERG, Susan. "Whitman's 'Out of the Cradle Endlessly Rocking'." *Explicator* 37:1 (1978) 35-36.

A note suggesting a reading of the poem in terms of the individuation process. The boy persona regresses at the sea's edge to a womb-like stage. He identifies with shadow birds that produce four eggs, and the incessantly moaning mother-sea becomes his anima spirit that inspires the insights of the poet's harmonious, mature work.

248. *FERGUSON, Suzanne. "Fishing the Deep Sea: Archetypal Patterns in Thomas' 'Ballad of the Long-Legged Bait'." *Modern Poetry Studies* 6:1 (1975) 102-114.

On a level more fundamental than Dylan Thomas' own description of the theme of his puzzling poem as the "search for sexual experience," the "Ballad of the Long-Legged Bait" is given a depth reading. Some lyrical passages from Jung's essay "Archetypes of the Collective Unconscious," describing the meeting with the unconscious in terms of sea-fishing images and "the chaotic urge to life" evolving into meaningfulness, provide striking parallels with Thomas' poetic metaphors. In this light the poem symbolizes the narrator's quest for individuation, and the fishing-trip is the mythological voyage of rebirth. The fisherman's struggle with his "transformative" feminine aspect - the long-legged bait he catches and throws back into the sea - leaves him in the last stanza as the individuated self at the door of his home on land with "his long-legged heart in his hand."

This informed Jungian interpretation makes sense of the metaphoric density and the welter of paradoxes in Thomas' long poem, which has been given a bewildering variety of readings.

249. FIEDLER, Leslie A. "Archetype and Signature." *Sewanee Review* 60:2 (1952) 253-273.
Rpt. in *No! In Thunder: Essays on Myth and Literature*. Boston: Beacon Press, 1960. 309-328.
Rpt. in *Art and Psychoanalysis*. Ed. William Phillips. New York: Criterion Books, 1957. 454-472.

Fiedler stages a lively attack on extreme new-critical views of the work of art as a self-contained "set of mutually interrelated references," and reaffirms the relationship between the writer's life and his work. He distinguishes between Archetype and Signature. Upon the mythical/archetypal basis of the poem ("any of the immemorial patterns of response to the human situation in its most permanent aspects") the poet imposes his Signature, "the sum total of individuating factors in a work, the sign of the Persona or Personality, through which an Archetype is rendered." The transformations of the archetypal poet "as Scape-Hero" are considered in Western literature from Homer down to our modern age. The greatest writers are those "capable (like Shakespeare) of at once realizing utterly the archetypal implications of his material, and of formally embodying it in a lucid and unmistakable Signature."

An incisive and influential essay.

250. FIEDLER, Leslie A. *Love and Death in the American Novel*. New York: Criterion Books, 1960. xxxiv,603 pp.

Fiedler's provocative study of death, incest and innocent homosexuality in the classic American novel emphasizes "the neglected contexts of American fiction, largely depth-psychological and anthropological." In his introduction he acknowledges his general debt to Freud and Jung, who provided "much of my basic vocabulary; I cannot imagine myself beginning the kind of investigation I have undertaken without the concepts of the conscious and the unconscious, the Oedipus complex, the archetypes, etc. Only my awareness of how syncretically I have yoked together and how cavalierly I have transformed my borrowings prevents my making more specific acknowledgements." Fiedler's commixture of Freudian and Jungian concepts adds to the penetration and liveliness of his extensive analysis of the psychological, mythical and archetypal aspects of Cooper's *Leatherstocking Tales*, Hawthorne's *The Scarlet Letter*, Melville's *Moby-Dick* and Twain's *Huckleberry Finn*.

251. FIEDLER, Leslie A. *No! In Thunder: Essays on Myth and Literature*. Boston: Beacon Press, 1960. 336 pp.
Stimulating studies of mythical archetypes in American fiction, generally indebted to Freudian and Jungian concepts.

252. FINN, Kay. "Archetypal Symbolism in the Major Novels of Thomas Hardy." (Ph.D. 1970 Wayne State University) 163 pp. *DAI* 31/07 A p.3545.

253. FITZPATRICK, William P. "The Myth of Creation: Joyce, Jung, and *Ulysses*." *James Joyce Quarterly* 11:2 (1974) 123-144.
Underlying the multi-leveled mythopoeia of James Joyce's *Ulysses* (1922) is the myth of creation. "The very act of artistic creation, the novel itself," is mythicized in the development of the young artist Stephen, who forms with Bloom and Molly the pattern of the archetypal family. Stephen has to dissociate himself from the repressive maternal influences of mother, nation and church, and establish a symbolic relationship with Molly, "fertile living anima" figure, before he can achieve creative activity. This development is traced in the mythic symbolism of three crucial episodes: "The Oxen of the Sun" with its "symbolic affiliation of birth and gestation"; "Circe", the descent into chaos which, in Jung's terms, is "a kind of symbolic incest that is preliminary to rebirth and freedom"; and "Penelope" in which Molly's reverie expresses the feminine life force, "the basic pulsing stuff of experience, from which the artist may begin his creation."
Drawing on Jung, Eliade and Vico, the essay provides a clear perspective on the mythic dimensions of *Ulysses*.

254. FLEISSNER, Robert F. "'Kubla Khan' as an Integrationist Poem." *Negro American Literature Forum* 8:3 (1974) 254-256.
Fanciful article that pushes Coleridge's Abyssinian maid as a symbol of spiritual and racial integration by pointing to the archetypal imagery of dome, river and fountain in relation to the wailing woman and dulcimer damsel as anima figures. The

Coleridgean reconciliation of opposites in the poem suggests the harmony of an unconscious "communal and anti-racist longing."

255. FOLEY, John M. "*Beowulf* and the Psychohistory of Anglo-Saxon Culture." *American Imago* 34:1 (1977) 133-153.

   This "psychohistorical" analysis of *Beowulf* views the orally transmitted epic as "educative and even therapeutic" for its audience. The narrative or "autotypal" level is distinguished from the underlying "unconscious myth-generating" or "archetypal" level. The latter "reflects in symbol" the hero's "ontogenic" progression from mother dependence to "psychological manhood" through dismembering the Oedipal father monster.

   Concepts from Jung and Neumann are appropriated in this pretentiously worded essay.

256. FOSTER, Genevieve W. "The Archetypal Imagery of T.S. Eliot." *PMLA* 60:2 (1945) 567-585.

   Early attempt to outline a Jungian interpretation of basic images in Eliot's poetry before *Four Quartets*. Following Jung's method of interpreting dreams both on the objective and subjective levels, the poems are seen to express, socially, a criticism of modern European society and, individually, the search for completeness of personality. *The Waste Land*, *The Hollow Men* and *Ash Wednesday* describe the quest for a new vision in a society that has overvalued intellectual qualities, facts and logic at the expense of feeling and intuition. The compensating poetic images from the unconscious are particularly those of the Grail quest, life-giving water, the vision of eyes, rose and star, and the establishing of a new relation with the feminine principle of the anima: lady, sister and mother in *Ash Wednesday*, or daughter in "Marina." Redeeming and integrating images begin to appear in "Journey of the Magi","A Song for Simeon" and "Triumphal March" in the mythical figures of the divine child and of the hero "at the still point of the turning world." Eliot's poems embody a Jungian process of individuation urging both the healing of the "insufficiency and one-sidedness of the age" and the integration of the conscious and unconscious sides of the poet's own personality.

   This stimulating article expresses indebtedness to Esther Harding's psychological interpretation of *The Waste Land* in her book *Woman's Mysteries* (q.v.), and in its turn inspired the study of Eliot's poetry by Elizabeth Drew.

257. FRANTZ, Gilda. "The Orphan." In *A Well of Living Waters: A Festschrift for Hilde Kirsch*. Ed. Rhoda Head, et al. Los Angeles: Jung Institute, 1977. 15-19.

Henderson's journey into darkest Africa in Saul Bellow's novel
Henderson the Rain King (1959) leads him from the chaos of his
ego-ridden existence into friendship with King Dafu, who in
appealing to his imagination awakens his inner Self. Jung tells us
that out of the union of chaos and the *imaginatio* was born the
alchemist's stone, often called the Orphan or the One. It is no
accident that on the plane home Henderson picks up an orphan
child, symbol of the renewed energy and meaning of his life.

258. FRENCH, Frank G. "Archetypal Variations in European Faust
Literature." (Ph.D. 1979 New York University) 285 pp. *DAI* 40/03 A
p.1450. (Marlowe, Byron, Sayers, I.A. Richards, Durrell)

259. FRIEDMAN, Norman. "Imagery: From Sensation to Symbol." *Journal
of Aesthetics and Art History* 12:1 (1953) 25-37.
A brief and very general historical survey is given of the study
of the poetic image from its beginnings in the nineteenth century
psychology of perception to recent theories about the nature of
metaphor and symbol. It is argued that the early studies of
recurring imagery develop under the influence of Frazer and Jung
into investigations of themes and symbols as literary archetypes. A
list of archetypal patterns is appended in an attempt to offer both
"a working definition of imagery and a comprehensive frame for the
interpretation of literature."

260. FRIEDMAN, Susan Stanford. "Mythology, Psychoanalysis, and the
Occult in the Late Poetry of H.D." (Ph.D. 1973 University of
Wisconsin, Madison.) 517 pp. *DAI* 34/10 A p.6638.
Became book *Psyche Reborn: The Emergence of H.D.* (Bloomington:
Indiana University Press, 1981).

261. FRITZ, Donald W. "The Animus-Possessed Wife of Bath." *Journal of
Analytical Psychology* 25:2 (1980) 163-180.
The aggressive behaviour of the character in Chaucer's
Canterbury Tales is interpreted as "a classic case of the animus-
ridden woman" who has not consciously assimilated her recessive
masculine side, but shows her primitive masculinity in her
opinionated, domineering, ruthless and erotic assertiveness. The tale
told by the Wife of Bath is said to reflect her psychology
accurately by reading "the Loathly Lady as a symbol of the
feminine principle within the Wife and the knight as symbolising
her animus." The miraculous transformation of hag to lovely maiden
then represents the Wife's unconscious desire for real virginity and
suggests the possibility of true integration of the male and female
components in her. That she herself "cannot follow the direction of

her inner guiding spirit" makes her into something of a tragic figure, for which, however, the male-dominated world in which she lives is to blame.

This ponderous application of Jung's views of the negative animus tends to lose sight of the shrewdness, the humor and irony of Chaucer's portrait.

262. FRYE, Northrop. *Anatomy of Criticism: Four Essays*. Princeton: Princeton University Press, 1957. ix,383 pp.

In the grand sweep of his "synoptic view of the scope, theory, principles, and techniques of literary criticism" with its multileveled schema of classifications, Frye distinguishes archetypal criticism as one of his four main classes and develops for it a "theory of myths." He borrows the term "archetype" from Jung and occasionally refers to its psychological meaning. In discussing the "mythos of summer", for instance, he says that the form of "the quest-romance is the search of the libido or desiring self for fulfillment." And within the genre of drama Jungian archetypes are said to "throw a great deal of light on the characterization of modern allegorical, psychic, and expressionist dramas." But on the whole symbols, myths, and archetypes are for Frye strictly literary concepts. He uses "archetype" in the sense of "recurrent image or theme," and dismisses Jung's theory of the collective unconscious as "an unnecessary hypothesis in literary criticism."

263. FRYE, Northrop. "Expanding Eyes." *Critical Inquiry* 2:2 (1975-76) 199-216.

Frye reviews his own development as cultural and literary critic, stressing the influence of Blake on his thought and imagination. He considers the impact of Spengler, Frazer and Jung on the thinking of the age and indicates the points of contact and difference between Jung's theories and his own. The view of literature set out in *Anatomy of Criticism* (1957) has many points in common with the coordinated symbolism of a mandala vision. As a psychologist, however, Jung is concerned with "existential archetypes," while Frye is dealing with imaginative ones. Jung's work on alchemy shows that the spiritual seeker and the poet use the same kind of symbolism and "perhaps we cannot fully understand either without some reference to the other."

264. FRYE, Northrop. *Northrop Frye on Culture and Literature: A Collection of Review Essays*. Ed. Robert Denham. Chicago: University of Chicago Press, 1979. viii,264 pp.

Among these reprints of Frye's reviews of influential twentieth-century books and thinkers, there are two essays in which he defines his views of, and relation to, Jung's thinking. In "Forming Fours" (originally in *Hudson Review* 6:4 (1954) 611-619) he provides a discerning summary of Jung's archetypal system and explains its religious and philosophical implications. He criticizes Jung's practice of "turning every mythopoeic structure he has studied into a vast allegory of his own techniques of psychotherapy," but is prepared to claim that Jung's *Psychology and Alchemy* (1944) is "a grammar of literary symbolism which for all serious students of literature is as important as it is endlessly fascinating."

In the other essay, called "World Enough without Time" (*Hudson Review* 12:3 (1959) 423-431), Frye discusses Jung's influence as "one of the seminal thinkers of our time" while reviewing a selection of papers from the Eranos Yearbooks and five of Mircea Eliade's studies in comparative religious symbolism.

In his introduction the editor indicates the indebtedness of Frye's archetypal criticism to the anthropology of Frazer and the psychology of Jung, as well as the distinctions that have to be made between Jung's psychological concepts and Frye's literary archetypes.

265. FURNISS, James M. "Coherence in Wallace Stevens' *Notes toward a Supreme Fiction* Revealed through the Model of Jung's Transcendent Function." (Ph.D. 1986 University of Connecticut) 247 pp. *DAI* 47/09 A p.3424.

266. FYLER, Anson C., Jr. "Self-Unification: An Archetypal Analysis of Prospero in Shakespeare's *The Tempest*." *Hartford Studies in Literature* 3:1 (1977) 45-50.

The Tempest is analyzed in terms of archetypal patterns "seen as a process of the self-unification" of Prospero. Starting with rejection of the false unity with the evil mother (the witch Sycorax), and developing through confrontation with man's amoral nature projected onto others as the shadow, differentiation of man's "dualistic sexual nature" and acceptance of "the necessary duplicity and finality of nature" in the archetype of the wise old man, the process ends with the actualization of the self in the unifying symbol of the island as mandala.

Although, as other interpreters have shown, aspects of Jung's individuation process apply very well to a psychological reading of Shakespeare's play, Fyler makes fanciful use of Jungian concepts. A few examples: Prospero's "expulsion from Milan has dealt a crushing blow to his masculine spirit or animus, and has left him with only a bisexual self-image of being both father and mother to Miranda"; Ariel functions as "a substitute asexual animus"; the tempest serves "to bring the collective male images which make up the whole of Prospero's animus into the consciousness of the island."

267. GABBARD, Lucina P. "Albee's *Seascape*: An Adult Fairy Tale." *Modern Drama* 21:3 (1978) 307-317.

With the help of Jung and Campbell it is argued that Albee's play (1975) can be interpreted as a rite of passage in which the protagonists advance to their next stage of life. Like the lizards emerging from the primordial sea to become conscious beings, Charlie and Nancy overcome their fear of the unknown and accept the inevitability of death. K.S.

268. GALLANT, Christine. "The Archetypal Feminine in Emily Brontë's Poetry." *Women's Studies* 7:1-2 (1980) 79-94.

In the dominant, passionate women of her Gondal poems Emily Brontë explores the archetypal feminine "in Jung's sense." Most of the poems are interior monologues expressing strong emotions in the face of inevitable extinction. This relates the speakers to earth mothers and nature goddesses for whom "dissolution and death are the grounds for life" maintained in the cycles of nature.

269. GALLANT, Christine. *Blake and the Assimilation of Chaos.* Princeton: Princeton University Press, 1978. xi,198 pp.

Blake's prophetic poems envision radical changes in the social, political and religious life of his days, but his myths must in the first place be read as symbolic of man's "psychic drama." This is repeatedly indicated by Blake himself when he says that the figures and events of his myths live "in the Human Brain." Christine Gallant begins her psychological reading of Blake's work by pointing out that common intellectual roots and preconceptions structure the thinking of both the Romantic poet and "the neo-Romantic psychologist" Jung, their scholarly background including "ancient mythology, alchemy, Gnosticism, and neo-Platonism." She warns, however, against too easy equations of Blake's and Jung's archetypal "systems," in spite of the obvious similarities of the four Zoas with the four personality functions, of Emanation with anima, and of Blake's Regeneration with Jung's individuation.

Gallant's thesis is that "through attention to the changing pattern of Jungian archetypes" in the course of the composition of his longer poems "one can see the profound changes occurring in Blake's myth as it expanded from a closed, static system to a dynamic, ongoing process." In the early Lambeth books and Prophecies the promise of the American and French revolutions fires the hope that social disorder may be replaced by the millennium of static universal harmony. But under the pressure of disappointing outward political events and inner necessities Blake's conception of the relationship between chaos and order develops into the insight that they are "Contraries" whose cosmic polarity is essential to life. In the later long prophetic poems *The Four Zoas*, *Milton* and *Jerusalem*, Los and other mythical figures, fallen from a "perfect unity," descend into the "Void," and undergo "a complete psychological dissociation," before they are regenerated in an apocalyptic resurrection.

Psychologically, the movement is not towards the opposing of the chaotic unconscious, but towards the acceptance and assimilation of chaos. In Jungian terms, "consciousness begins to incorporate the unconscious"; in Blake's terms, Chaos, "if enter'd into," produces, not extinguishes, life. That is why in *The Four Zoas* Urizen assumes the guise of Antichrist who, in his vigor, is conceived as the complement of Christ and a "manifestation of the dark aspect of the self." Mythically, the dragon's darkness is seen to be a form of energy. The Jungian concepts of the bipolar archetypes and the fourfold mandala of psychic wholeness help to explain the alternating "prolific" and "devouring" functions of the feminine "Emanations" in Blake's myth, as well as the appearance of mandala constellations at various points when the void seems to overwhelm the Zoas. When Los (Blake) builds the fourfold city of Golgonooza in the final vision of *Jerusalem*, it is a thoroughly "humanized" vision of Eternity of which "dim Chaos brightened" is an essential part.

Christine Gallant's lucidly written Jungian study makes beautiful general sense of the confusing complexities of Blake's poems. Perhaps too much so. Only a Blake specialist will be able to judge how convincing are all the details of her reading of Blakean myth. There certainly seems to be a greater integration of psychic elements in the later prophetic books, and Jung's archetypes and individuation process offer useful analogues for psychological interpretation. But Blake scholars have questioned Gallant's total identification of Blake's chaos with the Jungian unconscious, since Blake calls so many different things chaotic, and in the end his imaginative vision aims at triumphing over chaos rather than at incorporating it. Gallant has demonstrated "the attractiveness of Jungian psychology as a potential tool for analyzing Blake's works" (Tannenbaum), but in spite of her own warnings against imposing Jung's system upon Blake's, she has perhaps not escaped some oversimplification while applying Jung's individuation theory as an exclusive means of interpreting the psychology of Blake's mythmaking process. See for a lengthy, largely critical review: Leslie Tannenbaum in *Blake* 13:4 (1980) 200-202.

The scholarly strictures, however, do not invalidate the many perceptive and valuable insights contained in Gallant's well-reasoned Jungian analysis.

270. GALLANT, Christine Condit. "Regeneration Through Archetype: William Blake's Changing Myth in *The Four Zoas*." (Ph.D. 1976 University of Minnesota) 248 pp. *DAI* 38/06 A p.3480. Became book *Blake and the Assimilation of Chaos* (1978).

271. GARCIA, Wilma Thackston. "Mothers and Others: Myths of the Female in the Works of Melville, Twain, and Hemingway." (Ph.D. 1983 Wayne State University) 237 pp. *DAI* 45/01 A p.182.

272. GARNETT, George R. "*Under the Volcano*: The Myth of the Hero." *Canadian Literature* 84 (1980) 31-40.
    With apt quotations from Jung it is argued that the Consul's tragic quest is a modern version of the myth of the Promethean hero. Lowry's novel (1947) concentrates on the trials of initiation, the crucial middle stage of the hero's journey. Though the Consul's struggle with the shadow aspects of his personality ends in failure, it is the intensity of Lowry's vitalization of the myth that counts. The autobiographical elements in the story make us see Lowry himself as "the hero who wrests meaning from the chaos of life" through his successful attempt in this great novel "to dream (in Jung's words) the myth onwards and give it a modern dress." Good discussion of the novel's archetypal force.

273. GATES, Charlene E. "The Tarot Trumps: Their Origin, Archetypal Imagery, and Use in Some Works of English Literature." (Ph.D. 1982 University of Oregon) 246 pp. *DAI* 43/06 A p.1978. (T.S. Eliot, Charles Williams)

274. *GELPI, Albert. "Adrienne Rich: The Poetics of Change." In *American Poetry since 1960: Some Critical Perspectives*. Ed. Robert B. Shaw. Cheadle, Cheshire: Carcanet Press, 1973. 123-143.
    A study of the development of the poet's themes, techniques and imagery, tracing the change from her earlier poetry of aesthetic distance to the later more personal and political commitment which finds its focus in the theme of the woman poet in late-twentieth-century America. The self-image projected in the later poems is archetypal: at first the poet tends to imagine herself in terms of her animus, identifying the possibilities of self-realization with "masculine" qualities and the controlling consciousness, but later the animus is assimilated into her identity as a woman and comes to be seen as the mediating power within

herself through which psychic experience can emerge into the images and rhythms of the poem. The deepening subjectivity expresses itself in dreams and in dream imagery, yet at the same time there is a searching engagement with people, social forces, the problem of death, and with the question of the "validity and efficacy of language."

Eloquent and penetrating. Gelpi claims for Adrienne Rich a central place in the contemporary poetry scene and considers the importance of the woman artist who lives out aspects of our collective destiny. He also raises the question of the striking frequency with which artists in their struggle for self-realization have identified themselves with their anima or animus.

275.   *GELPI, Albert. "Emily Dickinson and the Deerslayer: The Dilemma of the Woman Poet in America." *San José Studies* 3:2 (1977) 80-95. Rpt. in *Shakespeare's Sisters: Feminist Essays on Women Poets*. Eds. Sandra M. Gilbert and Susan Gubar. Bloomington: Indiana University Press, 1979. 122-134.

In some of her most ecstatic poems Dickinson celebrates her experience of womanhood as an identification with, or a summoning to the fullness of life through, a male figure who must not be seen as a real man, but as the animus, the archetypal factor in her inner life. In the famous "My Life had stood - a Loaded Gun - " he figures as a hunter and woodsman in terms of the American myth of the frontier pioneer. Becoming like him a deerslayer, a link with Cooper's version of the myth, the poet sacrifices womanhood experience as a lover, wife and mother to find psychic fulfillment and artistic inspiration through the animus-figure of her masculine muse. In other poems her wifehood is accomplished, not through creative denial of her womanhood, but through a secret, mystic wedding to the animus "on peculiarly private terms withdrawn from the risks and dangers of contact with actual men in a man-dominated culture." Adrienne Rich's poem on Dickinson "I am in Danger - Sir" is discussed to show how a hundred years later in a vastly changed, though still patriarchal society women poets can at least sing out "on their own premises" what Dickinson could only write about in the isolation of her upstairs bedchamber.

Sensitive and subtle approach to this key aspect of Dickinson's poetry.

276.   *GELPI, Albert. "Everson/Antoninus: Contending with the Shadow." *Sequoia* (Stanford, Ca.) (Winter, 1977). Rpt. as the Afterword to Everson's collected Catholic verse *The Veritable Years: 1949-1966*.

Rpt. in *Benchmark and Blaze: The Emergence of William Everson.*
Ed. Lee Bartlett. Metuchen, N.J.: Scarecrow Press, 1979. 179-193.
After sketching the contours of William Everson's pre-Catholic
poetry of the vineyard and as war protester, Gelpi shows how in
his later work the erotic mysticism of the converted monk
Antoninus grapples with the dark shadow of his passions and the
woman within, "the feminine component of his psyche which
mediates his passional, instinctual and poetic life." "And if trusted
and loved, [the anima] can free him of enslavement to the shadow,
mediating the unconscious and the passions, drawing them from
blind automation into activity and actualization in masculine
consciousness." It is an attaining of Selfhood that means
"participation in the Godhead."
  Gelpi's fine essay on the development of the unorthodox
Christian poet and his poetry of erotic spirituality is concluded
with a bold fusion of Catholic theology and Jungian theory:
"Expressed in the archetypal terms of the human psyche, the
Incarnation is God entering into, permeating and operating through
the feminine, just as the Annunciation proclaims." J.K.

277. *GELPI, Albert. *The Tenth Muse: The Psyche of the American Poet.*
Cambridge, Mass.: Harvard University Press, 1975. xx,327 pp.
  In this brilliant book Gelpi studies the work of the five major
American poets before the twentieth century: Taylor, Emerson, Poe,
Whitman, and Dickinson. His purpose is to combine "a literary-
historical and textual reading of the poems with a psychological
sensitivity." "The writing of the poem was for the poet an effort at
integrating the conscious and unconscious aspects of his psyche." If
the critic is to "extend the poem, open it to new depths," a
responsiveness is needed "to approaches which trusted, affirmed,
and worked from the unconscious."
  For his interpretations Gelpi finds fruitful support in Jung and
Jungians like Erich Neumann, Marie-Louise von Franz and James
Hillman. With Jung, Gelpi believes that "the language and
imaginative expression are the substantive [...] means whereby poets
[...] strive toward psychological wholeness and completion." He
discusses the similarity of Emerson's notions of "aboriginal Self"
and "Over-Soul" with Jung's collective unconscious; Whitman's
differentiation between individual ego and transcendent Self; the
positive function of neurosis as impetus for psychic growth; and the
"lifelong contention of eros and psyche" in the work of Whitman
and Dickinson. Successful self-realization issues from the
reconciliation of feminine and masculine aspects in these poets, a
process in which "Whitman's anima and Dickinson's animus became

the channels through which their psychic energy found characteristic form and expression in words."

The strength of this book is its sensitive eclecticism. Though the overall psychological view is essentially Jungian, in his perceptive readings of the poems and the poets' minds Gelpi draws on other psychologies as well, and applies the models only when they can help to achieve insight.

278. GIBBONS, Kathryn G. "Quentin's Shadows." *Literature and Psychology* 12:1 (1962) 16-24.

Faulkner's thematic use of shadow symbolism in the Quentin section of *The Sound and the Fury* (1929) is looked at in Jungian terms. Quentin projects his own shadow qualities onto his sister's lovers. His relation to figures representing anima and wise old man as well as the picture of an incomplete mandala exemplify his lack of personal integration and drift toward death.

Superficial treatment of the archetypes leaves this article the mere beginning of a Jungian interpretation.

279. GIBBS, Charles K., Jr. "Myth and Creativity in *Moby-Dick*." (Ph.D. 1973 University of Massachusetts) 211 pp. *DAI* 34/07 A p.4200.

280. GIBSON, Donald B. *The Fiction of Stephen Crane*. Carbondale: Southern Illinois University Press, 1968. xviii,169 pp.

The attainment of identity by Crane's heroes is, in a very general way, discussed in terms drawn from Neumann's *The Origins and History of Consciousness*.

281. GILBERTSON, Michael K. "An Archetypal Analysis of Byron's *Don Juan*. (Ph.D. 1983 Arizona State University) 202 pp. *DAI* 44/03 A p.758.

282. GODARD, Jerry C. *Mental Forms Creating: William Blake Anticipates Freud, Jung and Rank*. Lanham, MD: University Press of America, 1985. 186 pp.

Argues that Blake in his poetry anticipated the most important concepts about human nature which were developed in the twentieth century by Freud, Jung and Otto Rank.

283. GODDARD, Harold C. *The Meaning of Shakespeare*. 2 vols. Chicago: University of Chicago Press, 1951. xiii,394 and v,230 pp.

In this stimulating and enlightening book on Shakespeare, Goddard considers his works as parts of the larger whole formed by the "integrity" of the poet's imagination. The plays are seen as a "kind of unconscious record" of Shakespeare's inner life, and at the same time as "works of the Imagination in the widest and deepest sense." Whether Goddard traces the themes of dream, play, love, and art in the comedies, or those of chaos, force, passion and death pitted against imaginative vision, love, forgiveness and life in the tragedies, the psychological is only one aspect of readings that take in the moral, the aesthetic, and the human as well. In his "Word to the Reader" he acknowledges his profound indebtedness to "those recent explorers in the realm of the unconscious among the wisest of whom are Samuel Butler, William James, and Carl G. Jung." In this guide for the reader of Shakespeare there is naturally no Jungian analysis of any one play, but the debt shows in many ways. For example, in the discussion of symbols as mediators between the conscious and unconscious sides of the mind, or in Goddard's view of Prospero as the "integrated man" and Ariel as the "union of the masculine and feminine elements of the soul," or the working of the unconscious in Hamlet and "his perfidy to the feminine element in his own nature."

284. GOETSCH, Robert S. "Critical Methodologies: Jungianism and Structuralism." (Ph.D. 1978 University of Nebraska, Lincoln) 308 pp. *DAI* 39/11 A p.6745.

285. GOLDEN, Kenneth L. "The Problem of Opposites in Five Fictional Narratives: Jungian Psychology and Comparative Mythology in Modern Literature." (Ph.D. 1978 University of Southern Mississippi) 244 pp. *DAI* 39/09 A p.5502. (Conrad, *Heart of Darkness*; Lawrence, *Women in Love*; Faulkner, *Absalom, Absalom*)

286. GOLDIE, Terry. "The Folkloric Background of Robertson Davies' Deptford Trilogy." In *Studies in Robertson Davies' Deptford Trilogy*. Eds. Robert Laurence and Samuel Macey. Victoria, B.C.: University of Victoria, 1980. 22-31.

The "Jungian pattern" of balanced opposites in Davies' trilogy of novels is explored through the "folkloric" allusions to saints' legends, the magus tale and the philosopher's stone of the alchemists.

287. GORDON, Rosemary. "Look! He Has Come Through! D.H. Lawrence, Women and Individuation." *Journal of Analytical Psychology* 23:3 (1978) 258-274.

On the basis of Lawrence's life and work, Gordon shows that he had failed to differentiate the three principal roles of women: mother, beloved and death-giver. As a result, "all of them remain highly charged emotionally, a characteristic of those images that have remained predominantly archetypal and insufficiently humanized." Lawrence was gripped by opposing forces - the urge to fuse with another human being and the need to be independent - caused by his need both to submit to and rebel against the powerful mother image. Among the confusions of Lawrence's life, this polarity (to use Lawrence's notion) or complementarity (in Jung's terms) is seen as part of "strong synthesizing impulses which drove him on towards even greater integration and individuation." An analyst's optimistic view of the degree of psychic wholeness reached by Lawrence. K.S.

288. *GOSE, Elliott B., Jr. *Imagination Indulged: The Irrational in the Nineteenth Century Novel.* Montreal: McGill-Queen's University Press, 1972. xii,182 pp.

Gose explores the growing interest in the irrational in nineteenth century English fiction. Focusing on the symbolism in novels by Emily Brontë, Dickens, Hardy and Conrad he investigates "what happens when serious novelists start using motifs from romance, fairy tale, and dream to shift the emphasis in their fiction from verisimilitude of action to validity of feeling." The insights of depth psychology, particularly Jung's theory of archetypes, if "used discriminately," may help us see patterns "clearly in touch with the life of the novel and the imagination of the author." The fairy tale motifs of symbolic transformation and rebirth, which were assimilated by these Victorian authors into the mainstream of English fiction, embody truths about human nature that were ignored by an increasingly materialistic society.

The horrors of Matthew Lewis' *The Monk* (1795) are analyzed to show how the Gothic novel established "the practice of patterned fantasy and psychologically significant settings and action." The motif of the descent into a well to find truth at the bottom, exemplified in Grimm's fairy tale "Iron Hans," is traced as a key image in these novels concerned with the more or less successful "individual transformation" of the main characters. It is this theme that pervades the "irrationally imaginative view of reality" in *Wuthering Heights* (1847), as well as Dickens' joining of "conscious and unconscious, sophisticated and naïve, man and beast" in *Bleak House* with its archetypal deprived child, cruel stepmother, the numerous *alter ego* characters, and the good and bad old men. Hardy uses romance and nature rituals to illuminate the psyche of his characters in *The Return of the Native.* Conrad, in writing his novels, entered what he called his own "creative darkness." In Patusan he created for the hero of *Lord Jim* an archetypal world of the imagination in which Jim struggles to reconcile the demands of his inner and outer lives, and ultimately fails because he never comes to terms with his shadow side.

Gose's close readings of the imagery and symbolism of these novels excellently support his thesis. In the chapters on Dickens and Conrad he is particularly brilliant, not only on the symbolism of the novels but also on the psychology of their authors.

289. *GOSE, Elliott B., Jr. "Pure Exercise of Imagination: Archetypal Symbolism in *Lord Jim*." *PMLA* 79 (1964) 137-147.

The two opposed halves of Conrad's novel (1900) contrast Marlow's rational Western moral code with the Eastern dreamland of Patusan, where Stein advocates immersion in "the destructive element" of the unconscious. Close analysis of the light-dark imagery shows how Jim's life may be seen in terms of the myth of the birth of the hero: his plunge into the darkness of the unconscious and psychic death followed by a kind of rebirth from his guilt in Patusan. Quotations from Jung's writings on the structure of the unconscious throw light on the romantic, archetypal world of Patusan. Jim finds a great measure of psychic harmony in his life with anima and parent figures, guided by wise old man Stein, but he never comes to terms with the shadow. That is why he fails once more when confronted with his evil shadow brother, Gentleman Brown, another intense egoist. By accepting the role of savior in Patusan without assuming the necessary authority, Jim, instead of finding himself, succumbs to the negative forces of the unconscious. His immature self-idealization makes him choose the cold star light of eternity and sacrificial death instead of the warm fire of humanity in Jewel's love. Gose suggests that the novel is also Conrad's most thorough exploration of the conflict between romantic escapism and human responsibility within himself.

Subtle and illuminating examination of symbolic imagery in this novel.

290. *GOSE, Elliott B. "They Shall Have Arcana." *Canadian Literature* 21 (1964) 36-45.

The Christ-like protagonist in Gwendolyn MacEwen's novel *Julian the Magician* (1963) and the miracles he performs are compared with the Grimm folktale of "Iron Hans," the bewitched wild man who guards a gold treasure and helps a boy to become the savior of his country. Jung's interpretation of the alchemist's search to create gold out of base metal, and the symbolism of the trinity striving to include an opposite to become the complete quaternity, shed light on the novel's mythical and religious theme. Julian's crucifixion parallels Jung's unorthodox Christian view that the achievement of psychological wholeness is, as Julian puts it, the realization of the "conscious state of deity" within himself.

Astute reading of this novel.

291. GOSE, Elliott B., Jr. *The World of the Irish Wonder Tale: An Introduction to the Study of Fairy Tales*. Toronto: University of Toronto Press, 1985.
    Uses Jung, von Franz, and archetypal theory.

292. GOSELIN, Peter D. "Two Faces of Eve: Galadriel and Shelob as Anima Figures." *Mythlore* No. 21, 6:3 (1979) 3-4.
    The Queen of Lorien and the evil spider in Tolkien's *The Lord of the Rings* are "the two poles of the female principle," the ideal anima figure and the destructive "anima shadow."

293. GOULD, Eric. "The Gap between Myth and Literature." *Dalhousie Review* 58 (1978-1979) 723-736.
    A highly abstract discussion of the relationship between myth and literature. Myth should not be seen as "the essential reality behind the text," as is so often done, "no matter whether we are comparative mythologists, followers of Jung or Frye, Structuralists or Semiologists." Both myth and literature are sign systems that offer "homologies of the real." Of the two basic approaches to myth-and-literature studies, the Essentialist/Archetypalist and the Structuralist, the first (whether Freud, Jung, Frye or Fiedler) is dismissed as too narrow, "for it seeks an order determined by proving the worth of literature by the presence of psychological archetypes." The structuralist argument (Lévi-Strauss and Barthes) that myth is a metalanguage affords the possibility of a synthetic view, for in both mythic and literary thought language is "a second-order system" that is "vitally self-transforming."

294. GOULD, Eric. *Mythical Intentions in Modern Literature*. Princeton: Princeton University Press, 1981. xi,279 pp.
    A "post-Structuralist study" of myth that considers "the question of whether modern literature can attain the ontological status of myth as a superior treatment of fact." The archetypal theories of Jung and Frye are critically discussed and rejected in favor of views of myth as "superior reason" in the works of Lévi-Strauss, Barthes, and others.

295. GRAHAM, Dorothy B. Harbin. "The Archetypes of Individuation in Nathaniel Hawthorne's Life, the Major Romances, and 'Rappaccini's Daughter'." (Ph.D. 1985 Georgia State University) 221 pp. *DAI* 46/10 A p.3033.

296. GRANT, Patrick. "Tolkien: Archetype and Word." *Cross Currents* 22 (1973) 365-380.

Rpt. in *Tolkien: New Critical Perspectives*. Eds. Neil D. Isaacs and Rose A. Zimbardo. Lexington: University of Kentucky Press, 1981. 87-105.

This essay discusses the interest in Jung of Tolkien and his friends C.S. Lewis and Owen Barfield, and traces the archetypal patterns in *The Lord of the Rings* (1954-1955), in particular the quest of Frodo and Sam as a journey of individuation. However, the fairy story is "more than the inner psychodrama that a purely Jungian interpretation suggests," for with its "implicit motifs of Christian heroism, obedience, charity, and providence," it offers a "spiritual interpretation of heroism" that "derives largely from the tradition of Christian and epic poetry."

297. GRANT, William E. "Hawthorne's *Hamlet*: The Archetypal Structure of *The Blithedale Romance*." *Rocky Mountain Review of Language and Literature* 31:1 (1977) 1-15.

Making use of "the insights into literary structure offered by Freud, Jung, Kenneth Burke, Maud Bodkin and Ernest Jones," Grant tries to prove that Hawthorne's novel "follows a recognizable archetypal pattern [...] which generates a structural unity within an only apparently formless narrative." The archetypal pattern is that of the Oedipus complex, a conflict between generations that underlies both this novel and *Hamlet*. Here, Coverdale is Hamlet, Hollingsworth is Claudius, Moodie is Polonius, Zenobia is Gertrude and Priscilla is Ophelia. Westervelt represents Coverdale's shadow, and Zenobia is the "unincorporated sensual *shadow* of Priscilla's sexually repressed nature."

There is just criticism in the reviewer's remark that this interpretation "distorts the particularities of a text in tailoring it to the larger pattern." (*American Literary Scholarship*, 1977, p.29) K.S.

298. GRATTO, Joseph M. "William Carlos Williams and the Analytical Psychology of Carl G. Jung." (Ph.D. 1983 Emory University) 185 pp. *DAI* 44/03 A p.752.

299. GREBSTEIN, Sheldon N., ed. *Perspectives in Contemporary Criticism*. New York: Harper and Row, 1968. xvii,395 pp.

This collection of essays by American, English and other European literary critics comprises in five sections historical, formalist, sociocultural, psychological and mythopoeic criticism. The introductory essay of the section "The Psychological Critic" concentrates on the influence of Freud; that of "The Mythopoeic Critic" surveys the sources in Frazer and Jung, and the nature and dangers of the mythopoeic approach.

300. GREENBERG, Herbert. *Quest for the Necessary: W.H. Auden and the Dilemma of Divided Consciousness*. Cambridge, Mass.: Harvard University Press, 1968. viii,209 pp.

   The analysis of Auden's intellectual development takes the idea of divided consciousness as the central subject of his poetry. Auden's interest in modern psychology is illustrated by a brief discussion of the influence of Jung's *The Integration of the Personality* (1940) on his poem "New Year Letter" and the twenty "Quest" sonnets.

301. GREENBERG, Mark. "Blake's Vortex." *Colby Library Quarterly* 14:4 (1978) 198-212.

   The multiple meanings of Blake's symbol of the "vortex" are explored in his sources and in the occurrences of the term in his poetry. Blake's use of the vortex in *Milton* suggests the uroboros archetype, psychologically explained by Jung and Neumann as signifying a "positive process of self-annihilation" and reintegration.

302. GREENSPAN, Cory R. "Charles Olson: Language, Time and Person." *Boundary* 2:1-2 (1973-74) 340-357.

   Olson's use of time and history in the *Maximus Poems* (1953-1968) is related to the linguistic and thematic context of his "representation of person and process." The "labor of Maximus" is a process of individuation, "transformation of self and release from the object-world," expressed in archetypal poetic symbols that reveal Olson's interest in myth and in Jung's work.

303. GREIFF, Louis K. "Quest and Defeat in *The Natural*." *Thoth* 8:1 (1967) 23-34.

   Detailed analysis of Malamud's novel (1952) in terms of Roy's quest for psychological wholeness which is defeated because he cannot incorporate knowledge of death into his hero's journey. The infinite line of the long-ball hit that converts into the circular homerun along the points of the baseball diamond suggests the perfect mandala diagram which is part of the novel's pervasive symbolic theme of the failed union of opposites.

304. GRIMES, Mary Loftin. "The Archetype of the Great Mother in the Novels of William Golding." (Ph.D. 1976 University of Florida) 249 pp. *DAI* 37/10 A p.6496.

305. GUERARD, Albert J. *Conrad the Novelist*. Cambridge, Mass.: Harvard University Press, 1958. 322 pp.

   This study of tensions in Conrad's major works, though not otherwise specifically Jungian, makes use of Jung's notion of the archetypal night journey in analyzing the psychological symbolism of the descent into the unconscious and the meeting with the double (the shadow or outlaw figure) in *The Nigger of the Narcissus* (1897), *Heart of Darkness* (1899), *The Secret Sharer* (1912), and *The Shadow Line* (1917). It is suggested that the inner journey of the characters in these stories to achieve integration of the personality also expresses Conrad's own grappling with inward conflicts, such as the division in himself between the respectable rational seaman-self and the interior outlaw-self, between the man of action and the dreamer with a powerful introspective drive.

306. GUERIN, Wilfred L., et al. *A Handbook of Critical Approaches to Literature*. Second edition. New York: Harper and Row, 1979. xviii,350 pp.

This useful handbook for college students discusses at some length four major critical approaches to literature (traditional, formalistic, psychological, and mythical/archetypal). Each of these approaches is demonstrated by application to the same four literary texts: Shakespeare's *Hamlet*, Marvell's "To His Coy Mistress," Hawthorne's "Young Goodman Brown," and Twain's *Huckleberry Finn*. Jung's archetypes are discussed in relation to anthropolgy and mythological criticism, and there is a Jungian analysis of Hawthorne's story. The final chapter surveys briefly eleven other critical approaches, including structuralism, stylistics, the phenomenological approach, and feminist criticism.

307. GUERIN, Wilfred L., et al., eds. *Mandala: Literature for Critical Analysis*. New York: Harper and Row, 1970. xiv,766 pp. with Instructor's Manual.

An anthology of some of the best of (mostly) English and American short stories, poems, plays and short novels (selected for their "rich interpretative possibilities"), designed for college courses in literature. Life and the reading and teaching of literature are viewed as a search for wholeness. Jung and his archetypes are invoked in comments and questions. The editors believe that experiencing the psychological and archetypal depths of great literature helps the reader to achieve personal integration.

308. GUNN, Edward. "Myth and Style in Djuna Barnes' *Nightwood*." *Modern Fiction Studies* 19:4 (1973-74) 545-555.

Barnes's surrealist novel *Nightwood* (1936) "presents characters who act out their unconscious personal myth in terms of given cultural and religious myths." Personal experience has religious and psychological dimensions for which Jung's archetypes of Mother, Rebirth, Spirit, and Trickster provide parallels.

309. GUNSTEREN-VIERSEN, Julia van. "The Marriage of 'He' and 'She': Virginia Woolf's Androgynous Theory." *Dutch Quarterly Review* 6:3 (1976) 233-246.

The style and strong language of Woolf's feminist book *Three Guineas* (1938) was considered "cantankerous" and "neurotic" by contemporary critics. In a world where a woman was only supposed to talk "womanlike" it was her attempt to speak androgynously. Woolf's theory that the artist should harmonize in herself the masculine and feminine principles is briefly discussed in terms of Jung's anima-animus pair.

310. GUNTER, Garland. O. "The Archetypal Trickster Figure in James Still's *River of Earth*." *Appalachian Heritage* 7:4 (1979) 52-55.

The characters in James Still's novels about Appalachian rustics often have universal qualities that make them "archetypal in the Jungian sense." Uncle Jolly in *River of Earth* (1940) is an example of the "true Trickster" as analyzed by Jung and Radin.

311. GUNTER, Garland O. "Archetypal Patterns in the Poetry of Tennyson, 1823-1850." (Ph.D. 1966 University of Maryland) 267 pp. *DAI* 27/09 A p.3010.

312. *HAGENBüCHLE, Helen. *The Black Goddess: A Study of the Archetypal Feminine in the Poetry of Randall Jarrell*. Bern: Francke Verlag, 1975. 187 pp.

Randall Jarrell, who majored in psychology at Vanderbilt University and "was greatly influenced by his knowledge of Freudian and Jungian psychology," has been called "the most psychoanalytic oriented poet of his generation." Hagenbüchle examines the function and importance of the mother figure in his poetry, showing how behind the poet's ambiguous relation to the real parent there looms "the Great Mother, who represents the creative and destructive power behind all existence." This key theme is pursued throughout Jarrell's work by analysis of poems in which the archetypal woman embodies the poet's awe and fear of the unconscious. She symbolizes the struggle between "life and death, consciousness and the unconscious, the self or the loss of self," and is "the Muse who inspires the poet but also enslaves and kills him." The dangerous descent into the destructive unconscious, the realm of the Black Goddess, is at the same time the source of the poet's creativity.

The excellent Jungian archetypal explication of the themes and symbolic imagery of Jarrell's poetry adds a dimension to the more usual Freudian personalistic interpretations.

313. HALL, Marlene Laverne. "Consciousness and the Unconscious: Henry James and Jungian Psychology." (Ph.D. 1974 University of New Mexico) 157 pp. *DAI* 35/09 A p.6097.

314. HALLAB, Mary Y. *"The Turn of the Screw* Squared." *Southern Review* 13:3 (1977) 492-504.

In Henry James's ghost story *The Turn of the Screw* (1898) the fairy tale element of the prince and princess threatened by demons from another world, with the governess of the children as a hero to do battle with the forces of evil, is extended into an underlying mythical pattern of the youthful vegetation god or goddess abducted to the underworld. On this archetypal level Quint and Jessel resemble the witch and demon gods of the underworld, and the uncle and Mrs. Grose (less convincingly) the ideal counterparts of the beneficial deities of sky and earth. The governess then participates in an initiation into death followed by rebirth. If she is coupled with the other narrator, Douglas, as the conscious ego, the four male-female pairs represent a quaternity of aspects of the psyche, whose interaction suggests the pattern of a personality striving for integration, "in which all parts are balanced child, man, god, and devil." The frame narrator might than stand for the single psyche in which the story takes place. The story was written during a period in James's life in which he had to reorient his career after his failure as a playwright.

The parallels with fairy tale and myth are suggestive, but the archetypal patterning is too neat. The view that the children are merely innocent and that the governess, the ego figure, successfully overcomes and integrates the evil, disregards both the outcome of the story (death of the boy), the fiendish psychological ambiguity of James's tale, and its stark sexual elements.

315. HALLAM, Clifford B. "The Double as Incomplete Self: Studies in Poe, Melville, and Conrad." (Ph.D. 1979 Miami University) 180 pp. *DAI* 40/07 A p.4026.

316. HALLMAN, Ralph J. "The Archetypes in *Peter Pan." Journal of Analytical Psychology* 14:1 (1969) 65-73.

James Barrie's play (1904) is viewed as a regressive fantasy. The symbolic events enact "that crisis in the life of the child involving an exchange of the pleasure principle for the reality principle, wholeness of personality for a fragmentation of functions, and fantasy for usefulness." The characters all represent the child archetype, Peter Pan himself exemplifying the Eternal Child in its four components: abandonment, invincibility, hermaphroditism, and potentiality. Archetypal mother symbolism appears in the waters of

the lagoon, the cave and its tree, and the window through which the children enter and leave the Never Never Land. Peter Pan journeys into the darkness of the waters of the unconscious "in order to renew himself at the source of the all-creative power, the great mother."
Jungian theory is unsubtly applied while the author demonstrates how the story "follows in detail the blueprint which Jung has outlined."

317. HALPERN, Stefanie. "In Her Father's House: A View of Emily Dickinson." *Psychological Perspectives* 11:2 (1980) 188-207.
The "one-sided spiritual existence" of Emily Dickinson's life in the seclusion of her father's house was both the sacrifice of a larger personal life and the condition of her poetry. The father complex running in her family and the rigid puritanical ethic of her environment made this intensely emotional woman reject the conventional Christian God, yet she identified herself with the Puritan spirit of self-denial, living out "in its most extreme form, the Christian split between spirit and matter." In her poetry she suffers with Christ his pain and abandonment by the Father, and she records her struggle with the dark God, who gives and takes away. The imagery of whiteness in her early poetry points to an archetypal transformation of her dark experiences of loss, denial and personal frustrations through the fire of suffering into the immortality of her poetry.

318. HALPERN, Stefanie. "Theodore Dreiser's *An American Tragedy*: A Psychological Viewpoint." *Quadrant* 11:2 (1978) 86-103.
This specifically Jungian analysis of Dreiser's novel *An American Tragedy* (1925) emphasizes the archetypal drama of the young man who causes the death of the pregnant sweetheart who stands in the way of his ambitions. The outstanding themes of the story are discussed "from the tragic hero's point of view as though they were dream elements."

319. HALTRESHT, Michael. "Peter Benchley's *The Deep*: An Archetypal Analysis." *Journal of American Culture* 2:2 (1979) 231-234.
An interpretation of Benchley's novel (1976) as an initiation myth in which David is the hero, Treece is the wise old man and Cloche the shadow. Chosen because of its popularity as a film, *The Deep* is suggested for use with high school students as an introduction to Jungian archetypes and to teach them to appreciate the relevance of myths and literature in modern society. K.S.

320. *HALVERSON, John. "The Shadow in *Moby Dick*." *American Quarterly* 15:3 (1963) 436-446.

"Some rather perplexing events and relationships in *Moby Dick* become clear and significant," when seen in the light of Jung's theory of the meeting with the shadow as crucial to the development of psychic selfhood. Ishmael in the end is literally and symbolically saved through having accepted the "cannibal" Queequeg as his dark twin brother and helpful shadow. Ahab, hating everything not accessible to consciousness (symbolized in the white whale), is swallowed by the sea of the unconscious, irrevocably bound to his evil shadow, the mysterious "swart" Fedallah. The weak efforts of his helpful shadow, the negro boy Pip, are of no avail against his demonic obsession.

An admirable summary of archetypal shadow theory is applied with clarity and insight to the interpretation of the novel's symbolism.

321. HAMMOND, John F. "The Monomythic Quest: Visions of Heroism in Malamud, Bellow, Barth, and Percy." (Ph.D. 1979 Lehigh University) 224 pp. *DAI* 39/10 A p.6130.

322. HANDY, Patricia M. "The Woman as Hero in Twentieth Century Women's Fiction." (Ph.D. 1979 Bowling Green State University) 235 pp. *DAI* 40/04 A p.2055. (Wharton, Woolf, Plath, Welty, Gold, Sarton, Atwood)

323. HANNAH, Barbara. "All's Well That Ends Well." In *Studien zur analytischen Psychologie C.G. Jungs: Festschrift zum 80. Geburtstag von C.G. Jung*. Herausgegeben vom C.G. Jung-Institut Zürich Vol. 2. Zurich: Rascher Verlag, 1955. 344-363.
Rpt. in *Spring* (1956) 26-42.

Shakespeare's comedy is studied as an individuation process. Helena, functioning more as anima figure than as a human woman, liberates the ego (Bertram) from a state of complete possession by the shadow (Parolles) and establishes "a direct connection between the ego and the shadow." The King in Paris, symbol of the Self, summons Bertram from his mother's household and so causes a "separation between the Logos and Eros principles," the goal of the drama subsequently being the union of the opposites.

The discussion of the characters taken simply as interacting archetypes is mixed with speculations about Shakespeare's intentions and the lack of shadow integration in the collective psyche of his days.

324. HANNAH, Barbara. "The Animus in Charlotte Brontë's 'Strange Events'." *Harvest* 10 (1964) 1-12.

On the basis of her own experiences with the animus Hannah gives a speculative interpretation of one of Charlotte Brontë's Angria fantasies, written at the age of fourteen. This strange vision of herself and the world from a point of view outside herself is explained as that of the unintegrated animus showing her "two sparkling globes," symbolizing the state of separation of her inner and outer worlds, yet also affording her ego a glimpse of the archetypal Self in a figure "hundreds of feet high."

325. HANNAH, Barbara. *Striving towards Wholeness*. New York: Putnam, 1971. x,316 pp.

The works and lives of six nineteenth century artists are viewed under the aspect of their more or less successful archetypal journey towards individual psychic wholeness. The symbolic image of individuation Hannah particularly uses is that of man's expulsion from the Garden of Eden with its four rivers and four imaginary gates. She examines "the lives and the most pertinent novels of her exemplary artists," tracing their paths out of the paradise of childhood into the world and "the relative success with which they find - or fail to find - their way back to a more integrated 'four-square' condition of wholeness." In Robert Louis Stevenson the unresolved split between the opposites of good and evil (torn so widely apart in a Christian world that left "the dark side of God unrecognized") is projected into Dr. Jekyll and his murderous personal shadow Mr. Hyde. In the novels of Mary Webb and the Brontë sisters the authors' struggles with the psychological opposites are represented in the confrontations of their fictional characters with anima or, mostly, animus figures that embody the evil side of life. In how far ego demands and the self's "striving toward wholeness" are integrated in the novels is measured by the constellation of one of the ultimate symbols of psychological wholeness, the union of double marriages in the marriage *quaternio*. The quaternity symbol is strongly present in the greatest of these novels, *Wuthering Heights* (1847). This shows how Emily Brontë's unorthodox views joined the light and dark opposites that were kept apart in the lives and works of her brothers and sisters. The dark Heathcliff is "the principle of individuation" in this novel that is unique in its depiction of "an image of human wholeness in a feminine soul or psyche," and in being "one of the most complete *projected* processes of individuation."

Barbara Hannah started lecturing on the Brontës in Zürich in the early thirties. This book, published 40 years later, is still full of the pioneering spirit. The archetypes of Jung's individuation process are joyfully discovered at work in the lives and the novels of these Romantic authors. There is a good deal of acute psychological analysis of the works of Stevenson and Webb, of the lives of the Brontës and of their childhood myths and later fictional characters, especially in terms of the confrontation with evil.

From a literary-critical point of view there is much to be critical about. The works are too simply viewed as mere projections of the author's unconscious. The speculations about the authors' personal psychic developments at times become fanciful. The plots of the novels are often forced into quaternities. Jung's animus theories are dogmatically applied. And we hear how the archetypes of wholeness and of death "broke into" the Brontë family, but never how the consumptive illnesses wrecked their lives.

326. HANNAH, Barbara. "Victims of the Creative Spirit: A Contribution to the Psychology of the Brontës from the Jungian point of View." Guild Lecture No. 68. London: Guild of Pastoral Psychology, 1951. 24 pp.
Rpt. in *Spring* (1954) 65-82.

The creative impulse in the Brontë sisters is ascribed to Emily's ability to surrender to the images of her childhood world of the collective unconscious and to the demonic masculine genius of her animus, whereas Charlotte's relation to her creative spirit is more that of a struggle not to let herself be overwhelmed but to control the figures from the unconscious by establishing roots in the outside world. Their writings give us a "unique opportunity to study the collective unconscious as it appears in feminine psychology." *Wuthering Heights* (1847) is a "projected process of individuation," in which all the characters are taken as parts of a total personality. Heathcliff is the ruthless, destructive representation of the animus, without whom there would have been no transformation, however. The two Catherines are "more or less" the ego and Isabella Linton is the shadow. In the end a quaternity of two pairs of opposites is formed on the alchemist model: the royal pair, Heathcliff and the older Catherine, in the unconscious Beyond; Hareton and the younger Catherine, the human pair on earth in the conscious.

This early attempt at archetypal analysis of a Brontë novel carries little conviction. The characters are too simply viewed as personifications of archetypes, while their psychological interaction is only vaguely indicated.

327. HANSSON, Karin. *The Warped Universe: A Study of Imagery and Structure in Seven Novels by Patrick White*. Lund, Sweden: Gleerup, 1984. 271 pp.

In the section "In Search of Wholeness: Jung and White" (pp. 92-113) Hansonn analyzes in detail the affinities between White and Jung and claims that "it is obvious that Jungian patterns, terminology and moral designs support the structure of White's novels."

328. HARDING, D.W. "The Hinterland of Thought." In *Metaphor and Symbol*. Eds. L.C. Knights and Basil Cottle. London: Butterworths Scientific Publications, 1960. 10-23.

Rpt. in Harding, D.W. *Experience into Words: Essays on Poetry*. London: Chatto and Windus, 1963. 175-197.

An inquiry into the unconscious impulses and processes that precede and accompany the transformation of experience into images and words. Freud's theory of dream mechanisms works with the condensation and disguise of defined ideas; Jung's description of the archetypes seems to explain more satisfactorily how certain symbols suggest "the undifferentiated totalities out of which clear ideas may emerge." Harding feels, however, that Jung makes his archetypes more mysterious than need be, and he questions the application that the symbol arises from the depth of "the whole psychosomatic person," whereas it seems "most likely to have entered by way of the sensory surfaces."

Analysis of some strikingly complex poetic images in Shakespeare, Shelley and Wordsworth supports the subtle argument, which includes considered criticism of Jung's theory of archetypes.

329. HARDING, D.W. "The Theme of 'The Ancient Mariner'." In *Experience into Words: Essays on Poetry*. London: Chatto and Windus, 1963. 53-71.

After offering his own psychological reading of Coleridge's poem as centering in the human experience of "depression and the sense of isolation," Harding discusses a Freudian and a Jungian interpretation. Maud Bodkin is criticized for arguing (in *Archetypal Patterns in Poetry*, 1934) that "the poem revolves round the widespread and ancient theme of rebirth." Harding sees this as importing into the poem a "generalized Jungian idea of rebirth," while disregarding the mariner's return to a "guilt-haunted half-life."

330. HARDING, M. Esther. *Journey into Self*. New York: Longmans, Green, 1956. ix,301 pp.

John Bunyan's *Pilgrim's Progress* (1678), the allegorical narrative of Christian's religious life "under the similitude" of a dangerous dream journey from this world to the next is treated in this study as "a valuable psychological text illustrating the journey of the soul." Bunyan's story is more than a consciously contrived allegory. Harding explains each episode of Christian's progress, the landscapes through which he passes and the characters he meets, as expressions of psychological attitudes, as elements in the psyche of Christian, who is Bunyan's dream self.

In the light of Jungian psychology, the visions, the figures and the images come "from the deep level of the unconscious." This gives the story its universal character of the archetypal search for psychic wholeness common to all humanity. At the same time, Christian's quest expresses Bunyan's own inner journey and personal religious struggles. Harding shows how "the author draws freely on his own introverted and subjective experience, and makes use of the images of his own dreams and visions." Bunyan's own depressions and religious anxieties are reflected in Christian's burden, his adventures in the Slough of Despond and in the valleys of Humiliation and the Shadow of Death. Many of the characters he meets on the way are projections of the pilgrim's own shadow qualities. And the vision in the House of the Interpreter of a grave man (Christ) with female qualities, who is to be Christian's guide, may be seen, psychologically, as an intimation of the Self, the androgynous reconciliation of the psychic opposites.

Treating the story "as case material" for a psychological analysis of Bunyan's own spiritual journey, and constantly drawing comparisons with the experiences and dreams of patients in her own analytical practice, Harding demonstrates the remarkable similarities between Bunyan's story and the process of individuation in Jungian psychotherapy.

From a literary critical point of view the procedure has its drawbacks. There is a tendency to explain all symbolic details of Christian's journey as fitting unerringly into the analytic scheme. Harding sees strict Puritanism rightly as a belief that, psychologically speaking, keeps the opposites of good and evil too far apart, more concerned with punishment than with grace. Her moralizing on this score, however, leads occasionally to questionable interpretations. In the story Christian reaches his goal in the end, and with all the bells ringing is joyously received in the Celestial City, so how much point is there in arguing that Bunyan's restrictive Puritanism leaves Christian's individuation "incomplete"? Or in the comment that one of the chief defects of the story is the lack of an anima figure, a representative of the feminine principle? But even if the explanatory parallel is at times labored too hard, Harding's clear and very full exposition undoubtedly illuminates both the psychology of Bunyan's Pilgrim and the symbolism of the Jungian therapeutic process.

331. HARDING, M. Esther. "Some Afterthoughts on *The Pilgrim*." *Spring* (1957) 10-31.

Harding speculates on the absence of the anima figure in *The Pilgrim's Progress* and on Bunyan's own lack of an "adequate relation to the feminine principle of eros, as is evidenced by his exclusive concern with the masculine principles of authority and justice."

332. HARDING, M. Esther. "*She*: A Portrait of the Anima. A Critical Analysis of the Novel by Sir Henry Rider Haggard." *Spring* (1947) 59-93.

The novel, which Jung declared "the classic exponent of the anima motif," is summarized and explained "in psychological language." Accompanied by a young man with hero characteristics, who is the antithesis of his own inhibited personality, the protagonist goes in search of the mysterious, beautiful, cruel queen Ayesha, "She-who-must-be-obeyed," who for 2000 years has lived in the caverns of an extinct volcano in a remote part of Africa. Paradoxically the queen succumbs in her own life-renewing fire, while the men barely escape alive. The whole adventure is seen as an inconclusive individuation process.

The archetypal aspects of Rider Haggard's romance about a man who falls under the spell of an overpowering anima figure are simply outlined. This is one of the earliest attempts by a Jungian analyst to apply Jung's psychology to literature.

333. HARDING, M. Esther. *Woman's Mysteries: Ancient and Modern. A Psychological Interpretation of the Feminine Principle as Portrayed in Myth, Story, and Dreams*. London: Longmans, Green, 1935. Rpt. New York: Harper and Row, 1971. xvi,256 pp.

This pioneering Jungian study links the initiations of the ancient Near Eastern Moon Goddess religions and the moon mysteries of other early cults to the psychological problems of our modern world. In some perceptive pages it provides a starting-point for archetypal interpretation of T.S. Eliot's poem *The Waste Land* (1922). As in the Grail myths, which give the poem its underlying unity, the sterility in the life of the individual and the disruption and desolation of life in our culture can only be cured by a miraculous psychological transformation. In *The Waste Land* this is suggested in the commandments of the rain-bringing thunder that symbolize emotionally the need for a surrender of ego-control and the acceptance of feeling, of the feminine principle, which has been repressed in a world dominated by masculine and mechanical concepts.

334. HARE, Delmas E. "In This Land There Be Dragons: Carl G. Jung, Ursula K. Le Guin, and Narrative Prose Fantasy." (Ph.D. 1982 Emory University) 231 pp. *DAI* 43/01 A p.165.

335. HARLOW, Benjamin C. "Some Archetypal Motifs in *The Old Man and the Sea*." *McNeese Review* 17 (1966) 74-79.

Hemingway's novella (1952) is seen in Jungian terms as a "death and rebirth archetype" during which Santiago "passes from the death of social isolation to the primordial image of the sea-wanderer [...] When the fish is destroyed, the fisherman's symbolic death is completed. His rebirth is seen in his return to the land." K.S.

336. HARRIS, Charles B. "George's Illumination: Unity in *Giles Goat-Boy*." *Studies in the Novel* 8:2 (1976) 172-184.

George Giles, the hero of John Barth's very "self-consciously literary" novel (1966), "recapitulates [Joseph Campbell's] monomyth in modern times, becoming in the process a synthesis of man's endless quest for truth as well as an embodiment of the synthetic nature of that truth." "Jung's analysis of the fall into consciousness roughly parallels George's 'fall'[...] from a state of primal harmony with his environment into a world of differentiation and boundaries." George represents the concept of unity as he seeks the synthesis of the disparate aspects of "an apparently various universe." K.S.

337. HARRISON, Robert. "Symbolism of the Cyclical Myth in *Endymion*." *Texas Studies in Literature and Language* 1 (1960) 538-554. Rpt. in *Myth and Literature: Contemporary Theory and Practice*. Ed. John B. Vickery. Lincoln: University of Nebraska Press, 1966. 229-242.

With the help of Jung and Campbell, Keats's long poem is related to the "spiralling motion" of "the cyclical myth" in which the hero's descent is followed by an ascent to a higher level than the point of outset. The four books of *Endymion* (1818) correspond to the four stages of the myth: the call to adventure, descent and trials in the underworld, fulfillment of the quest, and return to society. The indecisiveness of the poem's unsatisfactory ending is explained by Keats's departure from the myth pattern.

-144-

338. HAWKINS, Anne O. "Archetypes in the Spiritual Autobiographies of St. Augustine, John Bunyan, and Thomas Merton." (Ph.D. 1978 University of Rochester) 423 pp. *DAI* 39/04 A p.2228.

339. HAYASHI, Susanne Campbell. "Dark Odyssey: Descent into the Underworld in Black American Fiction." (Ph.D. 1971 Indiana University) 143 pp. *DAI* 32/10 A p.5790. (James Baldwin, Ralph Ellison, Richard Wright, Jean Toomer, LeRoi Jones)

340. *HAYES, Dorsha. *"Heart of Darkness*: An Aspect of the Shadow." *Spring* (1956) 43-57.

This reading of Conrad's story (1899) explores the mood of uncanny mystery and the symbolic details in "this night-journey of the soul laid against the setting of dark, primeval Africa." Captain Marlow's "dream" and "nightmare" journey up the river Congo is a penetration into the primeval wilderness of the unconscious and a confrontation with the unrecognized shadow sides of his own personality, personified in the shadow figure of ivory trader Kurtz. However, Kurtz is not only Marlow's personal shadow, he is also "a symbol of collective guilt, applying to the whole of Western civilization." How thin the edge is on which civilized man walks, and how easily he can regress to savagery, is forcefully symbolized in Conrad's stressing of Kurtz's eloquence, the power of words, man's gift of expression, that may be "the bewildering, the illuminating, the most exalted and the most contemptible, the pulsating stream of light, or the deceitful flow from the heart of an impenetrable darkness."

A sensitive analysis of the shadow aspect, which skilfully addresses the moral and psychological implications of Conrad's novel.

341. HAYLES, Nancy K. "Sexual Disguise in *Cymbeline*." *Modern Language Quarterly* 41:3 (1980) 231-247.

After experiments with heroines disguised as boys in earlier plays, Shakespeare creates in *Twelfth Night* in Viola a female character for whom the male disguise assumes a relation to her identity. This "increase in the psychological complexities of the disguise" culminates in *Cymbeline*. In the irrational, archetypal atmosphere of this romance the problems of misleading appearances and disrupted family ties are mysteriously solved for the virtually mythical, androgynous heroine, Imogen. The dreams and intuitions associated with her disguised state suggest healing contact with the unconscious in the sense in which "commentators as various as Marsilio Ficino and C.G. Jung have interpreted the androgyne as a symbol of psychic wholeness."

Subtle discussion (based on a dissertation) of the psychological and moral implications of Shakespeare's use of sexual disguise.

342. HEILBRUN, Carolyn G. "*Toward a Recognition of Androgyny.*" New York: Knopf, 1973. English edition: *Towards Androgyny: Aspects of Male and Female in Literature.* London: Gollancz, 1973. xxi,192,v pp.

In the first of three original and provocative essays Carolyn Heilbrun (influenced by Joseph Campbell's books on mythology) offers an androgynous perspective of Western myth and literature, androgyny defined as the condition in which there is real "equality of the masculine and feminine impulses." She traces the androgynous vision in the English novel of the last three centuries, and in particular discusses the birth of the "Woman as Hero" who chooses her own destiny. This fictional female hero is found as "the embodiment of the male writer's artistic vision" in the work of Ibsen, James, Shaw, Forster, and Lawrence (perceptive analysis of *The Rainbow*). Finally there is a chapter on androgyny "as a way of life" among the writers of the Bloomsbury group (fine appraisal of Virginia Woolf's *To the Lighthouse*).

343. HELMICK, Evelyn. "The Mysteries of Antonia." *Midwest Quarterly* 17:2 (1976) 173-185.

The final part of Willa Cather's novel *My Antonia* (1918) parallels in both meaning and structure the Eleusinian mysteries. Antonia's mythical qualities make her in terms of Neumann and Jung a representative of Demeter: Great Mother, earth goddess, and man's anima.

344. HELMS, Randel. *Tolkien's World.* Boston: Houghton Mifflin, 1974. 167 pp.

In *The Lord of the Rings* (1954-55) Tolkien created a mythology for our times. This study analyzes the nature and the sources of Tolkien's myth. To explain the essential mythic theme, adumbrated in *The Hobbit* (1937), Jung's concept of the archetypal hero journey is discussed, as elaborated by Neumann and Campbell. Tolkien tells "a story about being born into a world of heroic necessities and having continually to descend into the dark depths of experience to confront the black elements of one's own self and the world and there to conquer them."

345. HELSON, Ravenna. "Fantasy and Self-Discovery." *Hornbook Magazine* 46:2 (1970) 121-134.

In the magazine founded "to publicize fine books for boys and girls" Helson reports on a study aimed at identifying types of fantasy in children's books that were selected and rated by a panel of judges. On the basis of Jung's theory of personality and of the changing relations between ego and unconscious during individuation, the fantasies are regarded as "chronicles of the development of the 'self'." It is found that the books written by male authors divide into three types of archetypal integration themes: Wish-Fulfillment and Humor, Heroism, Tender Feeling; those by female authors into three related but different types: Independence and Self-Expression, Transformation, Inner Mystery and Awe.

346. HELSON, Ravenna. "The Imaginative Process in Children's Literature: A Quantitative Approach." *Poetics* 7:2 (1978) 135-153.

A report on statistical research into the creative imagination as expressed in fantasy literature written for children. "Stylistic-motive patterns" (comic, heroic, tender) were extracted from some hundred nineteenth and twentieth century books, and questionnaires were sent to about one hundred authors and critics of children's literature. Relationships between story patterns, creativity and writer's personalities were studied, "how and why stories change from one historical period to another," and how society influences "the artist's 'feedback' from the unconscious for its own purposes."

The procedure followed in this essay yields few concrete results. Various psychological theories and methods are used. Helson's own "theoretical point of view as a psychologist is predominantly Jungian."

347. HENDERSON, Joseph L. "The Artist's Relation to the Unconscious." In *The Analytic Process: Aims, Analysis, Training.* Ed. Joseph B. Wheelwright. The Proceedings of the Fourth International Congress for Analytical Psychology. New York: Putnam, 1971. 309-316.

Jung's first concept of artistic creativity as a denial of reality was later changed into the view that art expresses the collective unconscious through archetypal imagery. Neumann carried this further in considering the artist as working in consonance with his cultural group or in compensatory opposition to it. Henderson emphasizes that the artist's own individuation involves an aesthetic attitude which does not make him merely a mouthpiece for the unconscious. Like Stephen Dedalus in Joyce's *A Portrait of the Artist as a Young Man* (1916) the artist finds his true creativity also on the personal level as a craftsman. The artificer experiences at the level of symbolic equivalence, but the creation of beauty is a conscious process.

348. *HENDERSON, Joseph L. "Stages of Psychological Development Exemplified in the Poetical Works of T.S. Eliot." *Journal of Analytical Psychology* 1:2 (1956) 133-144, 2:1 (1957) 33-50. Rpt. as "T.S. Eliot's Poetry and the Life of Man" in *Psychological Perspectives* 7:1 (1976) 23-51.

A paper exploring "an overall picture of psychological development in Eliot's evolution as a poet" by showing how his work presents an analogy to stages observed in patients undergoing Jungian analysis. In the early poetry psychic impotence is expressed through personae like Prufrock and Gerontion "waiting for rain" as well as by the speakers in *The Waste Land* (1922) and *The Hollow Men* (1925). Regeneration of their "paralysed force" may follow from confrontation with the shadow (personified in Apeneck Sweeney and abstractly in the Shadow thwarting the hollow men), and from the appearance of life-giving anima symbols like the Lady in *Ash Wednesday* (1930), just as in the dream images of patients in analysis. In *The Waste Land* the old ego's neurotic state of sterile hopelessness and its possible transformation by surrender to the forces of the unconscious is suggested in the archetypal symbolism of the dry desert, the initiation through psychic death and rebirth of the mystery religions and the Grail myth, the exposure to the sea of the unconscious through "death by water", and the promise of the life-enhancing rain. In analysis the development of the individuating consciousness involves a state of living out emotional family conflicts, in Eliot's work represented by the play *The Family Reunion* (1939). Finally the "agony of death and rebirth" is resolved in the "condition of complete simplicity" reached in *Four Quartets* (1943), where the ego symbols are replaced by that of the self which has its center in the "dance" and the "white light" at the "still point of the turning world." Illuminating discussion by a Jungian analyst of the process of individuation traced through Eliot's work.

349. HENDERSON, Joseph L. "Symbolism of the Unconscious in Two Plays of Shakespeare." In *The Well-Tended Tree: Essays into the Spirit of Our Time.* Ed. Hilde Kirsch. New York: Putnam, 1971. 284-299.

In *A Midsummer Night's Dream* the interactions of the four lovers as well as Puck's ministrations and Bottom's dream express the unconscious play of archetypal images. Imagination is the creative force which brings unconscious and conscious into "unexpected conjunction of opposites." This prefiguring of the process of individuation is not lifted to the conscious level in this play, because there is no thoroughly human participant. In *The Tempest*, another play of fantasy and symbol, Prospero is the fully

human character who matures from a power-inflated and vengeful
authoritarian into a forgiving philosopher who renounces his magic,
releases his prisoners and ultimately comes to terms with
weaknesses in himself. On various levels and through different
characters the play symbolizes individuation in the pervading
themes of death and rebirth and of "sea-change" transformations, in
Ferdinand's rite of initiation and confrontation with the feminine,
and in Prospero's relationship with the spirit and shadow figures of
Ariel and Caliban.

350. HENINGER, S.K., Jr. "A Jungian Reading of 'Kubla Khan'." *Journal
      of Aesthetics and Art Criticism* 18 (1959-60) 358-367.
      A Jungian analysis of Coleridge's dreamvision permits "the
correlation of a large number of diverse facts, biographical and
artistic as well as psychological." The poem was written during a
very turbulent period of Coleridge's life and its archetypal
symbolism expresses an attempt at psychological integration of
distracting conflicts. To escape these Coleridge withdrew to the
farmhouse. "He was seeking a protective mandala for meditation;
and his failure to find it is recorded in 'Kubla Khan'." In his
"sunny pleasure-dome with caves of ice" Kubla has clearly
constructed a mandala uniting a sun-world of the cultivated
consciousness and a moon-world of the savage unconscious with its
chasm, river and sunless sea. This attempt at interfusion fails,
however, when the river sinks again "in tumult to a lifeless sea."
In the epilogue the poet invokes the archetypes of anima and wise
old man in what is felt to be a despondent comment on the
meaning of his vision.
      The relevance of Jungian theory for the interpretation of
Coleridge's poem is convincingly established. However, the
symbolism of the "mighty fountain" is unjustly disregarded, while
the negative reading of the second part of the poem seems based
more on preconceptions than on the actual text.

351. HENKE, James T. *The Ego-King: An Archetypal Approach to
      Elizabethan Political Thought and Shakespeare's* Henry VI *Plays.*
      Salzburg: Institut für Englische Sprache und Literatur Universität
      Salzburg, 1977. 1-94.
      The political power struggle in Shakespeare's first trilogy of
historical plays is studied in Jungian terms as inner psychic drama.
If the state is viewed as the entire psyche and the king (equated
with ego-consciousness) according to the collective Tudor myth as
the "repository and the source of order," Shakespeare's
dramatization of disorder and rebellion in England has elements of
the chaotic manifestations of the unconscious in a schizophrenic

dissolution of the personality. This psychic fragmentation shows in the Ego-King's exposure to the multiple Shadow-intriguers and French Anima-temptresses, as well as in the proliferation of archetypal child figures in *3 Henry VI*.

Aware that the reductiveness of his archetypal approach produces a "limited vision," the critic offers an interesting psychological perspective of the plays that links the "collective political consciousness" of Shakespeare's age with the "social and political insanity" of fifteenth century English history.

352. HENNELLY, Mark M., Jr. "Games and Ritual in *Deliverance*." *Journal of Altered States of Consciousness* 3:4 (1977-78) 337-353.

A reading of James Dickey's novel *Deliverance* (1970) as Ed's mythic journey towards self-realization, in terms derived from Eliade and Campbell. While abandoning the civilized world and undergoing in the wilderness "three days of ritualistic testing, symbolizing life, death, and rebirth," Ed's successful quest allows him to reconcile the "splintered selves" of his three fellow-questers and of the mountain men, who all represent aspects of Ed.

353. *HENNELLY, Mark. "Hawthorne's *Opus Alchymicum*: 'Ethan Brand'." *ESQ: A Journal of the American Renaissance* 22:2 (1976) 96-106.

Hawthorne's knowledge of alchemy provides grounds for an alchemical reading of the story 'Ethan Brand' which clarifies many details that mystified earlier critics, such as "the meaning of Ethan's transformed marble heart, the roles of minor characters, the unpredictable rebirth of the Cosmos, and the final enigma of Ethan's personality." The story has mostly been read as Ethan's failure in life. In the light of Hawthorne's interest in psychological processes, however, the story is an allegory of the alchemical "opus", which Jung analyzed as a work of psychic integration. This explains why the "marvelous change that had been wrought upon" Ethan by his successful "search for the Unpardonable Sin" ends in an act of self-immolation, when Ethan throws himself into the fire of the lime-kiln. This is not a negative act, for both Ethan's final speech and the following description of sunrise, landscape and village suggest that Hawthorne is symbolizing the alchemist's final harmonization of "conscious with unconscious, society with the natural world, and heaven with earth."

With the help of Jung, Neumann and Eliade, the alchemical reading is pertinently pursued to bring out the positive side of Hawthorne's moral ambiguity.

354. HENNELLY, Mark M., Jr. "Oedipus and Orpheus in the Maelstrom: The Traumatic Rebirth of the Artist." *Poe Studies* 9:1 (1976) 6-11.

Although this is essentially a Freudian interpretation, Hennelly also draws on the work of Neumann, Jung and Campbell to show that Poe's tale "A Descent into the Maelstrom" "dramatizes the dynamics of the Oedipal tension, return-to-the-womb desires, and the resulting rebirth of the Orphic artist." K.S.

355. *HENNELLY, Mark M., Jr. "Stevenson's 'Silent Symbols' of the 'Fatal Cross Roads' in *Dr. Jekyll and Mr. Hyde.*" *Gothic* 1:1 (1979) 10-16.

A penetrating analysis of the symbolism in Robert Louis Stevenson's romance *The Strange Case of Dr. Jekyll and Mr. Hyde* (1886). The pervasive images of the meeting at the crossroads, and of Victorian London as a foggy wasteland function as archetypal symbols expressive of Stevenson's commentary on "the self-division of Victorian repression." In the life-denying surroundings, controlled by "Reason, Law, and Science," Dr. Jekyll's "dammed-up Self" splits off what should be his "balancing instincts" as Mr. Hyde, demonic figure who at the same time personifies the "life of natural renewal" in the wasteland. Crossroads and cross suggest the "unity of consciousness and life" in Jung's sense, embodied in the character of Gabriel Utterson, but out of reach for Jekyll-Hyde.

356. HERBERT, Wray C. "Conrad's Psychic Landscape: The Mythic Element in 'Karain'." *Conradiana* 8:3 (1976) 225-232.

Conrad's story "Karain, a Memory" (1898) is seen as a meeting of the white man's civilized conscious mind with the primitive Eastern mind not yet severed from its basis in the unconscious. In this symbolic reading Karain resembles the mythic archetypal hero who bridges the gap between the unconscious and the conscious and restores the original balance.

357. HERRING, Thelma. "Self and Shadow: The Quest for Totality in *The Solid Mandala.*" *Southerly* 26:3 (1966) 180-189.

Review essay of Patrick White's novel *The Solid Mandala* (1966). Herring sees Arthur as achieving "true totality" and so becoming "himself a mandala," unlike his egocentric brother Waldo.

A series of symbolic images of wholeness are discussed, including the four mandalic marbles, various flowers and allusions to androgynous figures in myth and religion.

358. HERRING, Thelma. "*The Solid Mandala*: A Note on Some Recurrent Images." *Southerly* 28:3 (1968) 218-222.

In a brief note Herring cites Jung several times while pointing out a number of mandala symbols in Patrick White's novel.

359. HERX, Mary Ellen. "The Monomyth in 'The Great Good Place'."
College English 24:6 (1963) 439-443.

In a dream, the hero of Henry James's story undergoes a
process of individuation. "In the lore of dreams, James presents a
fundamental monomyth, symbolic of the primordial experience of a
hero's departure from the physical world, his discovery of and
initiation into his spiritual realm, and his return, with his boon, to
his natural existence." Water is an important symbol in this story,
representing "embarkation on the spiritual sea of life," as well as
symbolic death and rebirth. K.S.

360. HINTON, Norman. "Anagogue and Archetype: The Phenomenology of
Medieval Literature." *Annuale Mediaevale* 7 (1966) 57-63.

The four-level structure of Biblical allegory (*littera*, *allegoria*,
moralia, *anagogia*) also underlies many multi-leveled medieval
literary texts. This means that the loose, episodic literal narrative
of so much medieval literature finds its real structuring in the
other levels: in the religious allegory of Christ and his church, in
the teaching of the moral system rising from the religious, and
ultimately in the eternal verities of the eschatological anagogues
(such as Death and Judgment, Heaven and Hell, God's love for the
Universe). The problems of form and structure that medieval texts
present to modern critics may be eased if it is observed that the
anagogues perform functions very similar to those of the archetypes
of Jung's psychological system. Both are timeless, goal-directed
organizing principles in symbolic structures. They "are always
present to the mind and lend their strength to the individual
artistic creation as they do to the progress of the individual soul."

Well-argued plea for combining insights from allegorical and
psychological criticism in medieval studies.

361. HINZ, Evelyn J. and John J. Teunissen. "Culture and the Humanities:
The Archetypal Approach." *par rapport* 1:1 (1978) 25-29.

C.S. Lewis claimed that his psychological dramatization of the
story of Cupid and Psyche in *Till We Have Faces* (1956) is closer to
the spirit of the myth than the first recorded version in Apuleius'
The Golden Ass. The authors use this example to recommend an
archetypal criticism that does not think in terms of relationships in
time and of the earlier version of a story as the source or literary
prototype. "What identifies a work of art as being informed by an
archetype is that it commands an emotional response which reflects
the numinous and mysterious nature of its source" in the collective
unconscious. Therefore, archetypal works of art from different
cultural periods may show different creative responses to the same
archetype, and the later writer may actually help to explicate the

earlier work. Such works should be viewed synchronically rather than in temporal sequence and the questions to be asked focus on "the understanding of how archetypes operate culturally." What is the relationship between archetype and form, style and historical context of the work of art? Why were writers in the first and in the twentieth century fascinated by the Cupid and Psyche myth, and why in the nineteenth century obsessed with the archetype of Prometheus and in the twentieth century with the Great Mother?

362. HINZ, Evelyn J. "Hierogamy versus Wedlock: Types of Marriage Plots and Their Relationship to Genres of Prose Fiction." *PMLA* 91:5 (1976) 900-913.

Convential marriage related to questions of social propriety and moral responsibility is the characteristic theme of the "great tradition" in the English novel, exemplified by Jane Austen, George Eliot and Henry James. In Emily Brontë's *Wuthering Heights* (1847), however, and later novelists like Lawrence, Lessing and Atwood we find the marriage theme in stories of violent passion in elemental surroundings between lovers of fundamentally different classes and types, who oppose conventional, social and moral values. These "mythic narratives" must be considered as a different genre of prose fiction. In the conventional novel the characters generally move "from romantic illusion to a novelistic sense of reality," and matrimony "in its social, ethical, and historical orientation" might be designated as "wedlock." In "mythic narrative" the conjunction of lovers has elements of the sacred marriage or hierogamy of ancient myth, which connects man and woman with the cosmos.

363. HINZ, Evelyn J. "Lorenzo Mythistoricus: Studies in the Archetypal Imagination of D.H. Lawrence." (Ph.D. 1973 University of Massachusetts) 405 pp. *DAI* 33/12 A p.6871.

364. *HINZ, Evelyn J. "The Masculine/Feminine Psychology of American/Canadian Primitivism: *Deliverance* and *Surfacing*." In *Other Voices, Other Views: An International Collection of Essays from the Bicentennial*. Ed. Robin Winks. Westport, Conn.: Greenwood Press, 1978. 150-171.

The phenomenal success of two return-to-the-wilds novels, published in the early 1970s, results from popular interest in primitive life, symptomatic of a decadence of modern urban society. In James Dickey's *Deliverance* (1970) and Margaret Atwood's *Surfacing* (1972), we find characters whose critical attitude to modern life motivates a return to nature, but with a "rational primitivism" that believes in man's capacity to control himself and his surroundings. These characters collapse in the wilderness and are contrasted with the protagonists who, though driven into irrational, destructive actions, finally survive. The confrontation disproves "the idea that nature is orderly according to a rationalistic concept of order and that the irrational is by definition a purely destructive force, antagonistic to all forms of civilization." Both novels may be read as "a plea for a recognition of the creative potential of the irrational and a veiled warning of the destructive form it would take if its determining role were not recognized." The primitivism of these novels, therefore, "goes beyond an ecological or a survivalist protest against technology" and is more than "a mere protest against excessive rationalism."

These "primitivist" novelists point to new universal religious symbols, which Hinz calls "prototypic" (avoiding the term "archetypal"). In *Surfacing* the ecological metaphor of a dead heron strung from a tree suggests the myth of the dying god, and in *Deliverance* Ed Gentry stalking the mountaineer becomes a new type of the God who requires the death of his son. The differences between the two novels are finally defined by recourse to Jung's theories of the bisexuality of both masculine and feminine psyche, and the logos-eros complementarity. James Dickey's male protagonist exemplifies the masculine and patriarchal character of the United States, man not in tune with his feminine side. Margaret Atwood's female narrator is equally "a victim of logos," and refuses to admit "her own animus or capability of taking control." Her passiveness and victim complex epitomize and criticize the Canadian mentality, which Hinz characterizes as essentially feminine.

An ambitious and ingenious essay on the contemporary cultures of Canada and the United States.

365. *HINZ, Evelyn J. and John P. Teunissen. "The Pietà as Icon in *The Golden Notebook*." *Contemporary Literature* 14:4 (1973) 457-470.

The climactic scene in Lessing's novel (1962), in which Anna tenderly cradles her lover in her arms, while seeing him gaze up at her with horror and hate, is symbolically related to Michelangelo's Pietà of the Madonna with her dead Son in her arms, here interpreted as the archetype of the Great Mother, including the darker, destructive side of maternal love. This final stage of Anna's therapeutic regression into seeming "madness" is analyzed in terms of Jung and Otto Rank as a positive surrender to the irrational.

366. HINZ, Evelyn J. "Rider Haggard's *She*: An Archetypal 'History of Adventure'." *Studies in the Novel* 4:3 (1972) 416-431.

This "reevaluation" of Rider Haggard's *She* (1887) explains the novel's lasting popular appeal as resulting from its archetypal pattern of the mythological return to the beginning. The various stages of the ritual of "eternal return" (as outlined by Mircea Eliade) are found in the novel, which makes Ayesha into "an avatar of Isis, the great goddess of vegetation and of the seasonal cycle." The details of Leo Vincey's journey into the heart of dark Africa conform to the stages of the mythical hero quest (described by Joseph Campbell) with its archetypal initiation and return. Unlike "the nostalgia of the historical romancer," this history of adventure uses "the past to evaluate the present" and its symbolism contains Haggard's criticism of the "cultural degeneracy of his times."

This cleverly argued analysis is an example of the "archetypal criticism" advocated by the author and John J. Teunissen (see their essay "Culture and the Humanities: The Archetypal Approach").

367. *HINZ, Evelyn J. and John J. Teunissen. *"Surfacing*: Margaret Atwood's 'Nymph Complaining'." *Contemporary Literature* 20:2 (1979) 221-236.

The success of Margaret Atwood's novel *Surfacing* (1972), hailed in Canada "as a significant nationalist and feminist work of art", is explained by its archetypal impact. The distraught young woman narrator, desperately trying to come to terms with her feelings of guilt and anxiety after aborting her first child, embodies the archetype of the Grieving Mother, who in classical and Christian mythology and iconography as "the Mater Dolorosa is firmly established within the collective unconscious of the race." Parallels from a variety of sources are adduced and a good deal of attention is paid to etymology and wordplay. The parallel and possible influence of Marvell's poem "A Nymph Complaining for the Death of her Fawn" is especially stressed, since "works of art informed by the same archetypal complex inter-interpret." "Maternal grief, its causes and effects, motivates Atwood's twentieth century heroine in much the same way that it motivated Marvell's nymph of an ahistorical pastoral age."

Pointed archetypal interpretation, clearly and persuasively argued, on a basis of close thematic and textual analysis.

368. HINZ, Evelyn J. and John J. Teunissen. "*Women in Love* and the Myth of Eros and Psyche." In *D.H. Lawrence: The Man Who Lived*. Eds. Robert B. Partlow, Jr. and Harry T. Moore. Carbondale: Southern Illinois University Press, 1980. 207-220 and 285.

In *Women in Love* (1920) Lawrence dramatizes experience that has its mythical parallel in the story of Eros and Psyche. "Psyche's refusal to be content with the terms which Eros has established for their love" is "a mythic precedent for Ursula's 'liberated' response to Burkin's male chauvinism." As it is for Psyche, love is impossible for Ursula without knowledge, but knowledge always in feminine form as a function of love and as a "passionate struggle into conscious being" (from Lawrence's Foreword to the novel). Not that Lawrence consciously used the mythical parallel, but since he dramatized similar archetypal experience, the novel has Eros and Psyche as an "informing myth." The crucial encounters between the characters show striking iconographical correspondences to Psyche, lamp in hand, discovering the identity of Eros. All the major motifs of the myth find expression in the novel.

Without forcing the parallel, the authors of this article illuminate the mythical aspects of the novel as well as the psychology of the characters.

369. HIRSCHBERG, Stuart. *Myth in the Poetry of Ted Hughes.* Portmarnock, Ireland: Wolfhound Press, 1981. 239 pp.

Makes extensive use of Jung's alchemical studies in analyzing Hughes's poems in *Cave Birds: An Alchemical Cave Drama* (1978).

370. HOFFMAN, Frederick J. *Freudianism and the Literary Mind.* Baton Rouge: Louisiana State University Press, 1945. Revised edition 1957. x,350 pp.

Summarizes Freudian theory and surveys its influence on many American and English novelists. The revised edition reprints as an appendix his essay on "Psychology and Literature" (q.v.) with its critique of the Jungian approach.

371. HOFFMAN, Frederick J. "Psychology and Literature." *Kenyon Review* 29:4 (1957) 605-619 and in the Freud Centenary Number of *Literature and Psychology* 6:4 (1956) 111-115. Rpt. in *Freudianism and the Literary Mind* (q.v.) Rpt. as "Literary Form and Psychic Tension" in *Hidden Patterns: Studies in Psychoanalytic Literary Criticism.* Eds. Leonard and Eleanor Manheim. New York: Macmillan, 1966. 50-65.

In an essay that has been frequently reprinted, Hoffman expounds his Freudian views and dismisses Jung's archetypal theory as "a quest of mythical surrogates for displaced symbols," although "the appeal to literature and literary criticism of Jung's archaic forms and residues is, of course, phenomenally great." Hoffman holds that the generalizing character of archetypes may be useful for "cataloguing and arranging," but that "the archetypal process, by enlarging and depersonalizing the expressive experience, threatens to destroy both its individuality and complexity." The inflexible forms of archetypes may "arrest the process of articulating psychic tensions and they may oversimplify the results."

It seems debatable in how far it is true that "once an experience is defined as 'shared archetype,' its particulars are threatened by dismissal," but a rather narrow view is taken of Jung's influence when seen as merely serving artists "by rescuing them from an unflattering Freudian diagnosis."

372. HOFFMAN, Steven K. "Individuation and Character Development in the Fiction of Shirley Jackson." *Hartford Studies in English Literature* 8:3 (1976) 190-208.

A plea for recognition of Shirley Jackson's novels and tales as more than a modern form of Gothic horror stories. They make "significant comments" on the struggle of the developing personality against the internal and external forces arresting growth. This "makes a comparison with Jung's process of individuation fruitful both as organizing technique, and as mark of the author's universality." The theme of the feminine character troubled by a confining persona or domineering "terrible mother" is traced in Jackson's fiction, the limiting life often symbolized in the image of "the enclosed house, room, or walled estate." The heroines confront shadow and animus figures, sometimes in the shape of alter-egos. In the end, however, "the large majority of the characters fail to establish a new center and either lapse into fantasy or the drudgery of the old life."

Jungian psychology may well be relevant to an understanding of Jackson's fiction, but the claims made for her work are hardly substantiated.

373. HOLLAND, Norman. *Psychoanalysis and Shakespeare.* New York: McGraw Hill, 1966. xi,412 pp.

Holland's book provides a thorough-going critical survey and extensive fifty-page bibliography of psychoanalytical and other psychological writings on Shakespeare from the beginnings in Freud up to 1964. Though hostile to the Jungian approach, his discussions of the various psychological interpretations of each of the plays contain many fair, brief summaries of the arguments in Jung-oriented articles and books.

374. HOLLIS, James R. "Convergent Patterns in Yeats and Jung." *Psychological Perspectives* 4:1 (1973) 60-68.

The similarity of fundamental concepts articulated by Jung and Yeats is noted in the principle of compensating oppositions as applied to Yeats's division of human personalities into primary and antithetical, corresponding to Jung's extraverted and introverted. Yeats's search for Unity of Being, expressed in the unifying symbols of his poetry, is also a personal process of individuation, in which Yeats is continually "remaking" himself, reconciling in himself Michael Robartes with Owen Aherne, the rigid mask of the public personality with the sensitivity of the inner man.

375.   HOLLOWAY, Karla and Stephanie Demetrakopoulos. *New Dimensions of Spirituality: A Biracial and Bicultural Reading of the Novels of Toni Morrison.* Westport, Conn.: Greenwood Press, 1987. 192 pp.
The portion of the book written by Demetrakopoulos is mostly Jungian criticism.

376.   HOLMAN, C. Hugh. "The Defense of Art: Criticism since 1930." In *The Development of American Literary Criticism.* Ed. Floyd Stovall. Chapel Hill: University of North Carolina Press, 1955. 216-225.
In the section "Psychological Criticism" Holman discusses the importance of the new psychology and anthropology for writers and critics in the twentieth century. It is mainly a brief survey of Freudian criticism (F.C. Prescott, Edmund Wilson, Frederick J. Hoffman singled out as the best to date). Myth criticism is represented by Richard Chase and Francis Fergusson, and Jungian influence by reference to Maud Bodkin.

377.   HOLMES, Stewart W. "Browning's *Sordello* and Jung: Browning's *Sordello* in the Light of Jung's Theory of Types." *PMLA* 56:3 (1941) 758-796.
In *Modern Man in Search of a Soul* (1933) Jung described the causes and the possible cure of the "spiritual malaise of the modern civilized world." A hundred years earlier Browning had "anticipated Jung in describing minutely, albeit poetically, the same illness and in prescribing a similar cure." In his first poem *Pauline* (1833) Browning may be said to have made an attempt at "auto-psychoanalysis" guided by the anima figure. The ideas expressed in *Sordello* (1840) give evidence that Browning had "a living experience of the unconscious." He pictures himself as an intuitive-introvert poet-prophet, who finds the saving symbol that will henceforth harmonize and give meaning to his life, when in Venice suffering presses itself upon him in the shape of a beggar-maid. Like Jung, Browning sees himself as a healer, and his unorthodox religious attitude finds expression in urging a Shelleyan ideal of humanitarianism.
The psychological implications of the ideas expressed in Browning's early poetry are interestingly developed by means of extensive parallel quotations from Jung and Browning, though the large claims made for Browning seem over-enthusiastic.

378. HOLSTEIN, Sandra J. "'The Windless Perpetual Morning': Archetypal Primitive Symbolism in the Poetry of Theodore Roethke." (Ph.D. 1978 University of Minnesota) 204 pp. *DAI* 39/12 A p.7341.

379. HO LUNG, Richard R. "'Life's Womb': A Jungian Archetypal Study of Five Novels by Joseph Conrad." (Ph.D. 1974 Syracuse University) 265 pp. *DAI* 35/11 A p.7256.

380. HOPPER, Stanley R. "Symbolic Reality and the Poet's Task." In *Eranos-Jahrbuch 1965*. Vol. 34. Ed. Adolf Portmann. Zurich: Rhein-Verlag, 1966. 167-218.

   This paper develops the theme that in our broken culture it is the poet's sense of mythic metaphors and symbolic forms that may lead the way to a reconciliation of opposites, to the recovery of the transcendental in the unconscious and of the numinous archetypal images in our "rationalistic ego-consciousness." Illustrations of the "new depth awareness" are adduced from philosophers since Kant, from the psychologists Jung and Neumann, and from poems by Hölderlin, Yeats, Eliot, and Stevens.

381. HORNE, M. "Portrait of the Artist as a Young Woman: The Dualism of Heroine and Anti-Heroine in *Villette*." *Dutch Quarterly Review* 6:3 (1976) 216-232.

   Traces in Charlotte Brontë's novel (1852) the process of self-discovery of the anti-heroine, Lucy Snow, as she comes to recognize her long-repressed jealousy of the self-fulfilled companion of her childhood, Paulina Home. In old age Lucy surveys her life and its frustrations. Her memoirs are analyzed as a therapeutic recalling of past events in terms of conscious confrontation with the shadow-side of her personality and the reconciliation of opposites through archetypal images of wholeness, rebirth and transcendence of inner division.

382. HOUGH, Graham. "Poetry and the Anima." *Spring* (1973) 85-96.

   The anima is one of the archetypal forms especially connected with poetry and imaginative literature. In love poetry the poet may be said to be "in a state of permanent anima projection," and the Muse invoked in so many traditional poems is clearly an embodiment of the anima as "the feminine inspiring principle." From Plato onwards this psychic content has been a source of fascination and fear, "because it upsets the conscious rationally adopted stance." Anima characters appear in clear, though schematic forms in popular literature, such as the novels of Rider Haggard and Pierre Benoit which Jung liked to quote as examples. But it is only in great literature, which involves spiritual conflict and the "confrontation between conscious and unconscious," that we find "the evidence of a real psychic development, which is itself a part of the individuation process."

This paper served as an introduction to a series of four lectures on "Anima Images and Moods in English Poetry," given at the C.G. Jung Institute Zurich in 1972, which remained unpublished.

383. HOUGH, Graham. "W.B. Yeats: A Study in Poetic Integration." In *Eranos Yearbook 1971*. Vol. 40. Eds. Adolf Portmann and Rudolf Ritsema. Leiden: Brill, 1973. 51-83.

In this Eranos lecture Hough compares Yeats's life and poetic career with traditional Western notions about a poet's development (early poetry of the senses followed by more contemplative themes in later life) and with Jung's stages of psychic growth (the outward direction of the first half of life and the inward turning, the spiritual journey of the second half). Although there are many "parallels between his version of the progress of the soul and Jung's account of the individuation process", it is typical for the "organized diversity of experience" in Yeats's poetry, and for his poetic vitality, that his life and work do not follow the standard patterns.

384. HOVET, Theodore R. "America's 'Lonely Country Child': The Theme of Separation in Sarah Orne Jewett's 'A White Heron'." *Colby Library Quarterly* 14:3 (1978) 166-171.

Quoting Freud and Campbell, Hovet shows that this short story portrays "the social enactment of the psychological drama of separation, the separation from bodily union with a nurturing environment which each individual must undergo in the process of maturation." Sylvia, still intimately bound to nature and therefore representing both childhood and man's primitive past, nearly breaks that connection with nature as a result of contact with the more adult, advanced, industrialized world represented by the hunter. She enacts the mythic trial by ordeal when she climbs the "tree of life", becomes initiated into the "unity of nature" and therefore cannot betray it to the hunter. But, "Sylvia's knowledge of vivification is useless if it is not connected to purposeful action; the young man's technical and scientific knowledge is destructive without Sylvia's insight into the heart of nature." K.S.

385. HOY, Christopher. "The Archetypal Transformation of Martiniano in *The Man Who Killed the Deer*." *South Dakota Review* 13:4 (1976) 43-56.

Martiniano, the Taos Indian protagonist of Frank Waters' novel (1942), educated into an "arrogant individuality" at a white boarding school, has to undergo a radical process of adaptation when he returns to the collective matriarchal pueblo life to settle there and find a wife. The article shows how Neumann's analysis of the Great Mother archetype provides a meaningful terminology to describe the psychological process. Having missed as a boy the initiation ritual, his transformation and rebirth into a new awareness takes place through his exposition to the archetypal feminine in his wife. She embodies for him both the elementary power of the Great Mother, whose magical life-force is symbolized for the Indians by the deer, and the transformational spiritual quality of the anima. When he watches her perform the central role of Deer Mother in the ritual Deer Dance, he feels her transpersonal power and experiences his spiritual growth as a participation in the instinctual wisdom and religious life of his tribe.

A clear demonstration of the relevance of Jung's archetypal theory for this classic evocation of Indian culture, written before Frank Waters became acquainted with Jung's work.

386. HUDSON, Suzanne H. "Night Journey Under the Sea: Theodore Roethke's Search for the Self." (Ph.D. 1972 Marquette University) 239 pp. *DAI* 33/10 A p.5681.

387. *HUGHES, Philip R. "Archetypal Patterns in *Edgar Huntly*." *Studies in the Novel* 5:2 (1973) 176-190.

Charles Brockden Brown's novel, published in 1799, is seen as "one of the most complex, compelling psychological works" before Hawthorne and Melville. To understand the novel one needs to appreciate the extent to which the characters exist for symbolic rather than realistic purposes, just as the description of the American wilderness through which they wander strongly suggests an "inner landscape." The main characters, Edgar Huntly and his "Dark Brother and alter ego" Clithero Edny, twinned in their rebellion against dominating parents, function as one mythic hero. Clithero provides the drama and psychological conflict of the early part of the novel. Edgar in his sleep-walking searches identifies with his father-murderer and continues the heroic struggle against the stifling mother in a flight toward masculine virtues. Beside the multiple hero there is a series of male characters representing aspects of the Good and Bad Father. Edgar's falling into a pit, where he kills a panther and eats his flesh, and his rescue of maidens from the Indians are further examples of the story's mythical "rebellion-and-initiation process."

A well-argued analysis that clarifies the complexities and obscurities of Brown's novel by bringing out the extensive "use of psychological projections" and "mythopoeic pattern."

388. HUGHES, Richard. "The Brangwen Inheritance: The Archetype in D.H. Lawrence's *The Rainbow*." *Greyfriar* 17 (1976) 33-40.
    Jungian theory is loosely used to argue that in the marriage of Tom and Lydia Brangwen there is "fusion of Anima and Animus, the wedding of the chthonic and the celestial." Their inheritance of creative wholeness, which involves integration of the "collective past," is spoiled by the following generations, but glimpsed again by their grandchild Ursula in her vision of the symbolic rainbow that concludes D.H. Lawrence's novel (1915).

389. HUGHES, Richard E. *The Lively Image: Four Myths in Literature*. Cambridge, Mass.: Winthrop Publishers, 1975. viii,227 pp.
    This book is an enthusiastic plea for the recovery of mythic consciousness in our rationalistic society. Contemporary emphasis on self-realization is related to the widespread interest in myths as means to explain and interpret human experience. Hughes retells the myths of Narcissus, Dionysus, Orpheus, and the life of Christ in St. Matthew's gospel. Taken in succession, they present the "gradual unfolding of *selfhood*" as envisaged by Jung in the different stages of personality development. Modern versions of these myths, so "rich in literary possibilities," are found by Hughes in a number of twentieth century novels. The myth of Narcissus, "the impulse to rediscover unity of being," is reflected in Richard Brautigan's *In Watermelon Sugar* (1968). The destructive and creative Dionysos rules Marlow's journey in Conrad's *Heart of Darkness* (1899). Orpheus' descent into the underworld finds an analogue in the river trip of James Dickey's *Deliverance* (1967) with its theme of the ego's immersion in the unconscious. Christ's life, for Jung the fulfillment of archetypal wholeness and the integrated self, sets the pattern of Flannery O'Connor's comic novel *Wise Blood* (1949) about "a man who expends himself entirely."
    Hughes offers imaginative readings of these myths and novels in the light of Jung's theory of individuation.

390. HUGHES, Ted. "Myth and Education." In *Writers, Critics and Children*: Articles from *Children's Literature in Education*. Ed. Geoff Fox, et al. London: Heinemann, 1976. 77-94.
    A complete rewriting of an essay under the same title in the first issue of the journal *Children's Literature in Education* (March 1970). Both essays show that Hughes is in broad agreement with Jung's ideas. Stories and myth are invaluable for developing the child's imagination, man's only faculty that embraces both the inner and the outer world. That the older myths were "the genuine projections of genuine understanding" has been "attested over and over again by the way in which the imaginative men of every

subsequent age have had recourse to their basic patterns and images."

391. HUMMER, T.R. "Robert Penn Warren: *Audubon* and the Moral Center." *Southern Review* (Baton Rouge) 16:4 (1980) 799-815.

In both his own work and that of others, Warren demands the presence of a moral center, that is "the deep engagement of the artist with human growth, in himself and in other men." This is discernable in *Audubon* (1969). Quoting from Jung and Campbell, Hummer demonstrates that this poem can be read as a monomyth in which both the hero and the artist come closer to the discovery of the self, and which challenges the reader to do the same. K.S.

392. HUNGERLAND, Isabel. *Poetic Discourse*. Berkeley: University of California Press, 1958. 177 pp.

In the chapter "Symbols in Poetry" there is a brief consideration of Jung's archetypal theory which gives a fair summary, but is critical of Jung's claim that speaking "in primordial images" is "the secret of the artistic effect."

393. HUNT, Bruce. "*Gormenghast*: Psychology of the *Bildungsroman*." *Mervyn Peake Review* 6:10 (1978) 10-17.

In brief compass a very plausible case is made out for Mervyn Peake's *Gormenghast* trilogy (1946-1950) as "a world of symbolic landscapes and characters." In *Bildungsroman* fashion the adventurous actions in this romance story suggest the growth of Titus from dependent childhood to individual identity. The psychological model of Jungian individuation illuminates the mythic qualities of Titus' heroic quest. The search for the mysterious Thing in the labyrinth of green and golden forest between the twin peaks of castle and mountain evolves into confrontation with the anima, while Steerpike, the demonic shadow, has to be destroyed and assimilated. In the third book further ordeals reduce the hero's over-confidence to a realization of his true self.

394. HUNT, George W., S.J. *John Updike and the Three Great Secret Things: Sex, Religion, and Art*. Grand Rapids: Eerdmans, 1980. 232 pp.

It is Hunt's contention that sex, religion and art form "the predominant subject matter, thematic concerns, and central questions" found in Updike's fiction. He explores Updike's repeated use of the Adam and Eve myth to show that Updike sees the human condition as being "mixed" and as "an on-going struggle between our impulses toward goodness and toward its opposite." Because Updike has been greatly influenced by Kierkegaard and

Karl Barth, their theologies are explained in detail and used to illuminate his work where applicable. When necessary, Hunt also calls on Jung, Freud, Campbell, de Rougemont, Frye, R.W.B. Lewis and John Bunyan.

Hunt offers Jungian interpretations of two novels, *Of the Farm* (1965) and *A Month of Sundays* (1975). The former may be seen as an archetypal quest involving "initiation, death and birth, sin, expiation and redemption." The protagonist returns to his mother's farm in search of psychic integration. To achieve it, he must free himself of the influence of his good/terrible mother. The women in the novel represent various aspects of the anima.

In *A Month of Sundays*, the Rev. Thomas Marshfield also achieves integration through encounters with the anima. Each of the women in his life corresponds to one of her four stages. Jane is an earth-mother of the stage Jung identifies with Eve; Alicia corresponds to the second stage, a romantic Helen of Troy; Frankie represents the virginal anima "who raises Eros to the heights of spiritual devotion"; and Ms. Prynne is the fourth stage, the Sophia. Hunt sees the circular imagery used in the story as mandalas representing psychic wholeness and symbolically uniting the themes relating to the "three great secrets." K.S.

395.　*HUNT, George W., S.J. "Updike's Omega-Shaped Shelter: Structure and Psyche in *A Month of Sundays*." *Critique* 19:3 (1978) 47-60.

Updike's novel (1975) of an over-sexed clergyman undergoing therapeutic treatment consists of the diary in which Marshfield reviews his past life and at the same time records his progressive discovery of himself as a writer. Updike's fascination with sex, religion and art is demonstrated as a "triple-layered simultaneity of interaction" in the treatment of such themes as generation and rebirth, seduction, fidelity and goodness, as well as in the use of symbolic imagery. The playful story is also "a radical psychological and religious exploration," in which Marshfield undergoes a process of psychic maturation. This process is illuminated when seen in Jungian terms as the conscious ego's aspiring toward integration with the unconscious self. The four women in his life represent successive stages in his meeting with the anima, and the final sexual encounter with the manageress of the therapeutic center "dramatizes in a single symbolic act the psychic, erotic, religious, and artistic resolution of the novel." The center's omega-shaped motel-building in the desert is shown to be a perfect structuring symbol and integrating image for this multi-layered experience.

A clever, witty and most satisfactory Jungian explication of a novel that "capsulizes humorously" the central themes of Updike's previous fiction. In slightly extended form this became a chapter in the book *John Updike and the Three Great Secret Things: Sex, Religion, and Art* (1980).

396. HYMAN, Stanley E. "Maud Bodkin and Psychological Criticism." In *The Armed Vision: A Study in the Methods of Modern Literary Criticism*. New York: Alfred A. Knopf, 1948. 142-167. Rpt. in *Art and Psychoanalysis*. Ed. William Phillips. New York: Criterion Books, 1957. 473-501.

Hyman's 1948 survey of modern British and American literary criticism makes enthusiastic claims for the work of Maud Bodkin and devotes a large part of the chapter on psychological criticism to *Archetypal Patterns in Poetry* (1934). Although the book "attracted almost no attention whatsoever," it is her "distinction to have made what is probably the best use to date of psychoanalysis in literary criticism." Her method entails two types of psychological analysis. In the detailed exploration of an archetype in a single work, such as that of rebirth in "The Ancient Mariner," Bodkin "not only has used the poem to illustrate her archetypal pattern, but has made the pattern illuminate the poem." The comparison of variants of an archetype in a number of works establishes the persistence of archetypal patterns, not only in great literature of the past, but as the organizing principle in much serious art of today. Bodkin draws not only on Jung, but on Freud, as well as philosophers, theologians, anthropologists and sociologists. Being a sensitive reader of poetry she "is saved from the excesses of psychoanalytical criticism by a constant wariness about overemphasizing the psychological factors in poetry." Hyman contrasts the limitations of traditional Freudian literary analysis with the hope that Bodkin's book offers for psychological literary criticism. "By focusing, not on the neurosis of the artist, not on the complexes concealed beneath the work, not on the art as a disguised fulfillment of repressed wishes, but on *how* a work of art is emotionally satisfying, what relationship its formal structure bears to the basic patterns and symbols of our psyches, she has furnished psychological criticism with endless vistas."

397. JACKAMAN, Rob. "Man and Mandala: Symbol as Structure in a Poem by Dylan Thomas." *Ariel: A Review of International English Literature* 7:4 (1976) 22-33.

The heavy use of symbols of life and death in Thomas' poetry is often controlled by his manipulation of archetypes. It is suggested that through friends or his own reading Thomas may have been acquainted with the main concepts of Jung's psychology. The early "I See the Boys of Summer" is an example of a poem in which an archetypal symbol mirrors and organizes the basic statement. In this poem the mandala's circle and quaternity are found in the fourfold structure, circular argument, and in much of the imagery and symbolism, such as the "deep of the womb" and its "quartered shades," or the "four-winded spinning" of the globe of earth.

398. JACKSON, Robert S. *John Donne's Vocation*. Evanston, Ill.: Northwestern University Press, 1970. viii,192 pp.

In this study of Donne's life and religious background Jung's "archetype" is loosely used as equivalent to Plato's "idea". Sexual and marital imagery in the religious poems is viewed as making up "a myth of the divine-human relationship," a "psychic marriage" that finds its final celebration in Donne's *Anniversaries* (1612). These meditations on the death of the fifteen-year-old Elizabeth Drury mourn the world's loss of its *anima mundi* and celebrate the rebirth in the "Next World" of the "idea of a woman" (Donne's Platonic explanation) as, in Jungian psychological terms, the reconciliation of "the most profound polarities" in Donne's own life.

399. JACOBS, Edward C. "Further Reflections on 'La Belle Dame Sans Merci' as Anima Archetype." *Journal of Altered States of Consciousness* 4:3 (1978-79) 291-297.

Jacobs suggests qualifications to Charles I. Patterson's Jungian reading of Keats's poem. "The world of normal humanity" and the "daemonic" are not antithetical, but compensatory. The meeting with the faery child is the knight's confrontation with his unconscious anima, which might have led to integration. The knight, however, fails to achieve psychic wholeness. He is seduced and lets his conscious Ego be assimilated by the Self. He becomes anima possessed, a captive in the dark world of the faery child.

400. JACOBS, Edward C. "Thoreau and Modern Psychology." *Thoreau Society Bulletin* 127 (1974) 4-5.

In "The Pond in Winter" section of *Walden* (1854), Thoreau anticipated Jung in the recognition of the existence of a collective unconscious with his comparison of Walden Pond to the human mind: "At one time each man's mind belonged to the larger body of water [...] But at birth man's mind begins to separate from that ocean in much the same way that a cove separates from the main pond." Like Jung, Thoreau saw the danger to the individual consciousness from both the collective unconscious and an overdependence on rationalism. K.S.

401. JACOBY, Mario. "The Analytical Psychology of C.G. Jung and the Problem of Literary Evaluation." In *Problems of Literary Evaluation*.

Yearbook of Comparative Criticism, Vol. 2. Ed. Joseph Strelka. University Park: Pennsylvania State University Press, 1969. 99-128. Discusses the difference between Freud and Jung in regard to art and the creative imagination, summarizes Jung's three essays which deal directly with literature, and considers the "value" archetype and the possibilities of a psychological contribution to the problem of literary evaluation.

402. JAFFé, Aniela. "Bilder und Symbole aus E.T.A. Hoffmanns Märchen 'Der Goldene Topf.'" In C.G. Jung: Gestaltungen des Unbewussten. Herausgegeben vom C.G. Jung-Institut Zürich. Zurich: Rascher Verlag, 1950. 239-253.

403. JAFFé, Aniela. "Hermann Broch: The Death of Virgil." Spring (1958) 65-120.
Translated from German: "Hermann Broch: Der Tod des Vergil." In Studien zur analytischen Psychologie C.G. Jungs: Festschrift zum 80. Geburtstag von C.G. Jung. Herausgegeben vom C.G. Jung-Institut Zürich. Vol. 2. Zurich: Rascher Verlag, 1955. 288-343.

404. JENKINS, E.S. "A Creative Force in John Donne's 'Holy Sonnets'." Psychological Perspectives 1:2 (1970) 139-151.
In Answer to Job Jung developed his paradoxical conception of Yahweh as partly unconscious of what He is doing, and therefore morally inferior to the man who is conscious of being persecuted by a God who embodies both good and evil. The idea that Job by his questioning contributes to the growth of consciousness in God is used to interpret several of Donne's "Holy Sonnets." The use of questions and paradoxes in Donne's confrontation with his God is seen as leading to catharsis and an insight into the nature of God that "shows what the moral superiority of conscious man can do to help God and his moral universe evolve toward consciousness."
The application of Jung's psychological view to Donne's sonnets leads to misinterpretation of theological content and the emotions expressed in the poems. Donne's paradoxes dramatize feelings of shame and sinful insufficiency. They emphasize a readiness to submit to the Christian God's just punishments that make Donne the opposite of an unjustly punished Job.

405. JESKE, Jeffrey M. "Macbeth, Ahab, and the Unconscious." American Transcendental Quarterly 31 (1976) 8-12.
Melville borrowed the device of the prophecies of the three witches in Macbeth for Fedallah's riddling warnings to Ahab in Moby-Dick. The supernatural shadow figures in both novel and play symbolize aspects of the protagonist's own unconscious. In both

cases there is an archetypal conflict between conscious and unconscious elements. "Each protagonist is overcome by that aspect of himself he had sought to deny, despite warnings from his own psyche."

Brief, but pointed discussion.

406. JOHNSTONE, Douglas B. "Myth and Psychology in the Novels of John Barth." (Ph.D. 1973 University of Oregon) 147 pp. *DAI* 34/09 A p.5973.

407. JONES, Joyce M. Meeks. "Jungian Concepts in the Poetry of T.S. Eliot." (Ed.D. 1975 East Texas State University) 123 pp. *DAI* 36/09 A p.6084.

408. JONES, Joyce Meeks. *Jungian Psychology in Literary Analysis: A Demonstration Using T.S. Eliot's Poetry.* Washington: University of America Press, 1979. 52 pp.

This pamphlet, written primarily for college students, attempts to demonstrate and systematize the application of Jungian concepts to a writer's work as a whole. After an introduction to basic terms, the relationship between the writer and his creations is examined by classifying the characters of Eliot's early poems according to Jung's typology. Then the psychological progression of "collective man" towards experiencing the unconscious and psychic harmony is traced in the later poems by means of "the individuational approach." Finally, the process of individuation is discussed and seven stages of a basic procedure for Jungian literary analysis are listed.

Elizabeth Drew's study of Eliot's work has shown how well his poetry lends itself to a Jungian approach. However, the complexities of Jung's ideas and of Eliot's poems are here reduced to such crude simplifications that this pamphlet is a very unsatisfactory model for Jungian literary analysis. The quality of the insights offered may be illustrated by a few of Jones's statements: Art is "an internal drive which forces an individual to become its instrument." Prufrock is classed as an extravert and Mr. Apollinax as an introvert. In *The Waste Land* the speaker regresses, though almost at the threshold of individuation; the rain does come and the Fisher King's virility is partly restored. The staircase in *Ash Wednesday* is seen as a mandala symbol. In "Burnt Norton" Eliot says that only the present gives meaning to existence.

409. JONES, William M. "Eudora Welty's Use of Myth in 'Death of a Traveling Salesman'." *Journal of American Folklore* 73:287 (1960) 18-23.

In her first published story Eudora Welty used what T.S. Eliot called "the mythical method," the conscious manipulation of a parallel with figures and symbols from ancient myth. It is "a principle of organization" found in much of Welty's later work. The worn-out Mississippi salesman R.J. Bowman, taken ill on the road, seeks help and comfort in the cabin of what he first takes for an old woman who reminds him of his grandmother, but who later turns out to be young and pregnant. As an archetypal earth-mother she is accompanied by the sun-fire symbolism of her husband Sonny.

Though the story certainly employs symbolism, the parallels with the deeds of the greatest bowman of antiquity, Hercules, seem strained. Unlike Hercules, the salesman is said by Jones to have rejected the archetypal symbols that might provide new psychic energy. But this is the story of the last hours of a dying man who is hardly in a state to accept or reject anything.

410.   JORDAN, John W. "An Examination of Eugene O'Neill's Plays in the Light of C.G. Jung's *Collected Works* and Recorded Conversations." (Ph.D. 1979 University of Houston) 602 pp. *DAI* 40/09 A p.5056.

411.   JUNG, Carl G. "Psychology and Literature." In *The Spirit in Man, Art and Literature. Collected Works*, vol. 15, 84-105. Bollingen Series XX. Princeton: Princeton University Press, 1966. (First published as "Psychologie und Dichtung" in *Philosophie der Literaturwissenschaft*. Ed. Emil Ermatinger. Berlin, 1930)

Although psychology will never be able to determine the nature of art and of the creative act, it can be applied to the study of literature. The psychologist should be able "on the one hand to explain the psychological structure of a work of art, and on the other to reveal the factors that make a person artistically creative."

Jung identifies two different modes of artistic creation. The "psychological" or "personalistic" mode derives its contents "from the sphere of conscious human experience - from the psychic foreground of life." In the "visionary" mode unfamiliar material "from the hinterland of man's mind" is expressed in symbols and mythical images. The psychological novel is a self-contained whole that explains itself and leaves the psychologist little work to do. The visionary work of art represents deep and impressive experiences that transcend the personal.

Among examples of visionary art expressing archetypal motifs Jung mentions works of Dante, Goethe, Blake and Melville, but also novels of "dubious merit" like Rider Haggard's *She* (1887) and *Ayesha* (1905). What is of importance for the study of literature is that "the manifestations of the collective unconscious are compensatory to the conscious attitude," not only of the artist himself, but also of his period. The artist is a "collective man" and "every great work of art is objective and impersonal." The impact of great art is due to the artist's tapping of archetypal images.

412. JUNG, Carl G. "On the Relation of Analytical Psychology to Poetry." In *The Spirit in Man, Art and Literature. Collected Works*, vol. 15, 65-83. Bollingen Series XX. Princeton: Princeton University Press, 1966. (First published as "Ueber die Beziehungen der analytischen Psychologie zum dichterischen Kunstwerk." *Wissen und Leben* (Zurich) XV:19-20 (1920))

After distinguishing his analytical psychology from the medical psychoanalysis of Freud, and the symbol as "an expression of an intuitive idea" from the Freudian reductive sign, Jung defines two types of art: the one created by the introverted artist who asserts his conscious aims upon his material, the other by the extraverted artist who submits to the demands of his subject. The two attitudes are illustrated by the differences between the first and second parts of Goethe's *Faust*. In both cases, however, the creative process must be considered as an "autonomous complex" that is largely or wholly guided by the unconscious. Works of the second class are more symbolic and have a "peculiar emotional intensity" that derives from the presence of images arising from the collective unconscious. The effect of great art is ascribed to the "unconscious activation" of archetypal images that have been elaborated and shaped into the finished work. "Whoever speaks in primordial images speaks with a thousand voices."

The social significance of art is found in its compensatory function. "Just as the one-sidedness of the individual's conscious attitude is corrected by reactions from the unconscious, so art represents a process of self-regulation in the life of nations and epochs."

413. JUNG, Carl G. *Symbols of Transformation. Collected Works*, vol. 5. Bollingen Series XX. Princeton: Princeton University Press, 1956. Second edition with corrections, 1967. xxx,557 pp.

This is the English translation of the German *Symbole der Wandlung* (Zurich: Rascher, 1952), the extensively revised version of the original *Wandlungen und Symbole der Libido* (Leipzig: Deuticke, 1912), which was first translated into English under the title *Psychology of the Unconscious* (New York: Moffat Yard, 1916).

Like Freud, Jung himself was the first to apply his new depth psychology to the interpretation of literary texts. Among the many amplifications drawn from the myths, religions and literatures of the world in Jung's *Symbols of Transformation*, the book that spells his break with Freud, there is an extended archetypal reading of the long narrative poem on North American Indian themes *The Song of Hiawatha* (1855) by Longfellow. Jung's book is an elaborate mythical and psychological explanation of the fantasies of a certain Miss Miller, who in her own comments related the hero of her dreamvisions to Hiawatha. In his chapter "The Dual Mother" Jung reads Longfellow's story of Hiawatha's struggles as the mythical sun-hero's fights with the dragon that symbolize the need for the young person to "sacrifice his childhood and his childish dependence on the physical parents, lest he remains caught body and soul in the bounds of unconscious incest." (par. 553)

414.   *JUNG, Carl G. "'Ulysses': A Monologue." In *The Spirit in Man, Art and Literature. Collected Works*, vol. 15, 109-134. Bollingen Series XX. Princeton: Princeton University Press, 1966. (First published in *Europäische Revue* (Berlin) VIII:2/9 (1929))

Jung's essay on *Ulysses* (1922) is not an attempt at scientific analysis of Joyce's novel, but a spirited "subjective confession" of his frustrations at reading seven hundred and thirty-five "unendurable pages" of monotonous and boring details of chaotic life, schizophrenically expressed with "little feeling" by "a completely detached observer." Yet "the very boredom and monotony of it attain an epic grandeur that makes the book a *Mahabharata* of the world's futility and squalor." In its "creative destruction" of the criteria of beauty and meaning that have held for so long in Western art, *Ulysses* may have positive psychological value as "a *document humain* of our time," a manifestation of the collective psyche that anticipates something new. There is no ego, no "human center" in the book, yet "Ulysses is the creator-god of Joyce" and "a symbol of what makes up the totality" of all the personages in *Ulysses*. In Molly Bloom's final soliloquy we hear "the masculine creative power turned into feminine acquiescence." Citing Goethe's "The Eternal Feminine still draws us on," Jung ends by hailing *Ulysses* as "truly a devotional book for the object-besotted, object-ridden white man!"

Jung's emotional and imaginative response to *Ulysses* conveys the psychologist's interest and may clarify the book's popular appeal.

415.   JUNKINS, Donald. "Hawthorne's *House of the Seven Gables*: A Prototype of the Human Mind." *Literature and Psychology* 17:4 (1967) 193-210.

The personality orientations of the main characters in Hawthorne's novel (1851) correspond closely to Jung's four psychological functions: Hepzibah (feeling), Clifford (sensation), Holgrave (intellect), Phoebe (intuition). Since the central symbol of the house is that of the house as a human head and living mind, the interaction of the four characters and their emergence from the house in unity and harmony at the end may be seen as symbolizing in general a "process of individuation as it occurs in the regenerative psyche." More in particular, the novel shows Clifford's gradual transformation from an emotionally and spiritually crippled child into psychological wholeness. This process parallels Hawthorne's own release from a personal "dungeon" of isolation into the flowering of his intellect and senses in his marriage with Sophia Peabody.

The analysis persuasively demonstrates on three different levels the psychological and symbolical depth of Hawthorne's character creations.

416. KAHN, Sy. "The Dainty Monsters." *Far Point* 1 (1968) 70-76.
The archetypal force of Michael Ondaatje's first book of poems *The Dainty Monsters* (1967) springs from the "hard-edged images" evoking the haunting shadows that "flit at the borders of consciousness." "Over the garden wall" of man's cultivated and controlled world he glimpses the bizarre creatures of half-remembered dreams, of living myth and symbol. "I think Jung might see in these poems the glittering evidence that the human mind recollects elements of racial consciousness and history."

417. KALLICH, Martin. "Swift and the Archetypes of Hate: *A Tale of a Tub*. In *Studies in Eighteenth Century Culture*. Vol. 4. Ed. Harold E. Pagliaro. Madison: University of Wisconsin Press, 1975. 43-67.
In his "typological satire" *A Tale of a Tub* (1704) Swift employed "archetypal symbols and images to communicate meaning and emotion." Kallich discusses the relationships between Swift's use of the word "type," the hermetic doctrine of correspondences, and Jung's typology. The psychological themes of madness and depravity find expression in such symbols as the mad hackwriter, Swift's own persona, and the ass, rat and goose, the repulsive animals used to satirize the fanatics and pseudocritics.

418. KAPACINSKAS, Thomas J. "*The Exorcist* and the Problem of Modern Women." *Psychological Perspectives* 6:2 (1975) 176-183.
William Peter Blatty's novel is seen as the story of a successful liberated woman who makes use of the "positive, creative side of the masculine within her" but who has not "become conscious of its dark, negative aspects." The latter appear as the "archetype of the dark side" which takes possession of her daughter. Father Merrin is

the "archetype of the spiritual father" and Father Karras the "archetype of the heroic redeemer." K.S.

419. KAPLAN, Morton and Robert Kloss. *The Unspoken Motive: A Guide to Psychoanalytical Literary Criticism.* New York: Free Press, 1973. xi,323 pp.

This outspoken guide, based strictly on Freudian psychology, opens with an introduction to the basics of psychoanalytic theory and the criteria which "make fruitful the application of this theory to literature," followed by six analyses of texts by Conrad, Melville, Kafka, Shakespeare, Sophocles and Mary Shelley. The emphasis is on "how characters are moved by unconscious fantasies," and the guiding principle for the critic is "analysis of the text as case history of the literary character." The third part surveys the development of psychological criticism through brief critiques of the major writers from Freud to Norman Holland. Among these Bodkin, Campbell, Fiedler, and in particular, "the dissenting schools" of Jung, Adler and Rank are lambasted for swerving from the straight Oedipal path. In the wake of Edward Glover's book *Freud or Jung* (1956) the psychology of Jung is declared totally deficient and Jungian criticism a "peril" for literary critics. Jung is accused, among other things, of having eliminated the unconscious and sex from psychoanalysis; Jungian criticism is reductive, a mere question of attaching archetypal labels. That any non-Freudian perspective should be able to shed light on a text is out of the question, and eclecticism is the worst of sins.

Whatever the analyses of individual texts may offer (see Richard Noland's critique in *Hartford Studies in Literature* 7:1 (1975) 48-58) the case of psychoanalytic criticism seems badly served by the authors' rigid assertiveness.

420. KAPLAN, Sydney J. "The Limits of Consciousness in the Novels of Doris Lessing." *Contemporary Literature* 14:4 (1973) 536-549.

Martha Quest, the heroine in Lessing's novel sequence *Children of Violence*, (1952-1969) moves from the limitations of self-concern through involvement in the political and social world to her vision of the need for an expansion of individual awareness into a communal consciousness. Martha represents what Lessing defined as "a study of the individual conscience in its relations with the collective." In *The Golden Notebook* (1962) Anna Wulf's psychoanalysis with a Jungian analyst suggests that only through contact with the collective unconscious can her own fragmented consciousness be healed. To penetrate into the deeper layers of the mind, Lessing attempts new novelistic structures in *The Golden Notebook* and abandons her exclusive concern with the feminine consciousness when evoking the inner experiences of the mentally ill Charles Watkins in *Briefing for a Descent into Hell* (1971). Insightful analysis that only briefly touches the Jungian framework.

421. KARIER, Clarence J. "Art in a Therapeutic Age." *Journal of Aesthetic Education.* Part 1, 13:3 (1979) 51-66; Part 2, 13:4 (1979) 65-79.

This essay explores the early use of psychoanalysis in America in the lives and work of the writer and journalist Waldo Frank, and of his wife Margaret Naumberg, founder of Walden School in New York, who applied the new theories of Freud, and in particular those of Jung, first in therapeutic education and later in the field of art therapy. Joining the young bohemians of Greenwich Village in rebellion against the values of bourgeois culture, Naumberg and Frank "adopted psychoanalysis as an instrumental philosophy of life." Naumberg was analyzed by Beatrice Hinkle, the first Jungian therapist in New York. While he underwent self-analysis, guided by his wife, Waldo Frank wrote a psychological novel, *The Dark Mother* (1920), which describes "the psychological rebirth of David Markand who suffers from an Oedipus complex." The "distinctive Jungian structure" of this expressionist novel is clear from its cast of archetypal characters that "are brought to the foreground of consciousness and played out" as part of the hero's personality.

422. KARRFALT, David H. "Anima in Hawthorne and Haggard." *American Notes and Queries* 2:10 (1964) 152-153.

Note on parallels in the archetypal symbolism of characters and situations in "Rappaccini's Daughter" and *She*.

423. *KARTIGANER, Donald M. "Process and Product: A Study of Modern Literary Form." *Massachusetts Review* 12:2 (1971) 297-328 and 12:4 (1971) 789-816.

Modern literary form may be seen as the outcome of a conflict between the opposed modes of movement and design, of process and product, a conflict between the artist's commitment to "the obviously impossible task of duplicating the constant movement of nature [and] of raw experience" and his attempt to create "the achieved form as conscious man's reply to chaotic life." The new depth psychology having strongly influenced modern literature, the nature of this tension may be illuminated by comparing the opposed methods of Freud and Jung in their approach to the unconscious. Their different methods in similar quests - Freud's for a personal unconscious, Jung's for the archetypes of a universal unconscious - "lead us to the polarity in literature of, on the one hand, commitment to human mind moving through a free-association method that renders 'plot' and 'superstructure' irrelevant or restraining, and, on the other, a commitment to the recovery of myth, of some key pattern or timeless event which provides the only justification for the individual art product."

Kartiganer's thesis is very convincingly illustrated by detailed discussions of four works by modern writers. W. C. Williams' long poem *Paterson* is an example of "process" operating in a comparatively pure form. The twin poles of process and product, in tension and "precariously fused," shape the considerably varying, "new and dynamic," mixed literary forms of some of the most representative twentieth-century works: Eliot's *Four Quartets*, Conrad's *Nostromo*, and Faulkner's *Absalom, Absalom!*.

424. KASPAREK, Carol A. "Ethan's Quest Within a Mythic Interpretation of John Steinbeck's *The Winter of Our Discontent.*" (Ph.D. 1983 Ball State University) 163 pp. *DAI* 44/09 A p.2766.

425. KATES, Bonnie R. "Novels of Individuation: Jungian Readings in Fiction." (Ph.D. 1978 University of Massachusetts) 353 pp. *DAI* 39/08 A p.4959. (Mary Shelley, E. Brontë, Hawthorne, Rider Haggard)

426. KATHE, Barbara A. "Self Realization: The Jungian Process of Individuation in the Novels of Saul Bellow." (Ph.D. 1979 Drew University) 269 pp. *DAI* 40/12 A p.6279.

427. KEITH, W. J. "*The Manticore*: Psychology and Fictional Technique." *Studies in Canadian Literature* 3 (1978) 133-136.

This is a just critique of Patricia Monk's article on the supposed ambivalence in Robertson Davies' evocation of a fictional Jungian analysis in his novel *The Manticore* (*Studies in Canadian Literature* 2:1 (1977) 69-81). Keith politely points out that far from ironically undercutting his own description, Davies is applying laws of sound fictional technique when in various ways he provides critical reflections and comic touches in order to achieve lively dramatization and artistic balance. K.S.

428. KELLY, Thomas L. "The Quest for Self in the Early Novels of Kingsley Amis." (Ph.D. 1975 University of Oklahoma) 129 pp. *DAI* 36/04 A p.2219.

429. *KENNEDY, Veronica M.S. "Mrs. Gamp as the Great Mother: A Dickensian Use of the Archetype." *Victorian Newsletter* 41 (1972) 1-5.

In his early life Dickens was influenced by a great variety of women. These experiences were "unique preparations for his role as an artist" and for his creation of archetypal figures like Mrs. Gamp in *Martin Chuzzlewit* (1843). Mother and midwife, layer-out and washer of the dead, this "monstrously comic personage" is a perfect embodiment of the Great Mother in all her mythical complexity of the nourishing, protecting and at the same time destructively devouring life force. Her speeches, her surroundings and the characters around her associate Mrs. Gamp with the multiple aspects of the great fertility goddesses of Greek and Oriental mythology.

The critic's liberal amplifications suggest the richness and mythical dimensions of Dickens' character creation.

430. *KEPPLER, Carl F. *The Literature of the Second Self*. Tucson: University of Arizona Press, 1972. xiii,241 pp.

A thorough and penetrating study of the figure of the *Double* or *Doppelgänger* in American and European literature since the end of the eighteenth century. The designation "the second self" is preferred to indicate that the relationship between the first and the second self is much more than that of physical and psychological duplication. The uncanny affinity with the shadow-self implies a complementary oppositeness of what is "excluded from the first self's self-conception." As a result there always exists a dramatic tension between them. With a wealth of pointedly analyzed examples from world literature and religion, this mostly evil (but sometimes good) second self is shown as twin brother, pursuer, tempter, vision of horror, savior and beloved. In the final chapter the meaning of the second self is not sought in what critics may have seen as its scapegoat quality, but in the fated self-meeting as part of a psychological growth. The paradox of the complementariness of first and second self, of "unity in duality," is considered in the light of two opposing theories that have the theme of man's self-realization in common: the philosopher Martin Buber's idea of the "true reciprocity" in the twofold entity I and Thou, and Jung's theory of the need for integration by the conscious ego of the ambivalent archetypes of the impersonal collective unconscious. Shadow, anima and wise old man correspond to the various aspects under which the second self appears in literature.

431. KERMAN Judith Berna. "Merwin's Journey: The Poems of W.S. Merwin as a Hero-Journey." (Ph.D. 1977 State University of New York, Buffalo) 242 pp. *DAI* 38/09 A p.5481.

432. KERMODE, Frank. *Shakespeare, Spenser, Donne: Renaissance Essays*. London: Routledge & Kegan Paul, 1971. 12-32.

In "Spenser and the Allegorists" Kermode considers the apocalyptic imagery in Book 1 of *The Faerie Queene* (1590-1596) in order to illustrate his thesis that the modern trend of discovering "radical myth-structures in works of literature" impoverishes the understanding of a poem in which the poet's imaginative effort is directed at conferring "upon archetypes complex interrelated meanings" and not at "the conversion of event into myth." The objection brought against the work of Northrop Frye and other archetypal critics (Bodkin and Wheelwright are mentioned) is that it results in a "fatal reduction of the work's actual complexity." Spenser does not sacrifice actuality and contemporaneity to the archetypes, but converts myth into event. His poem intricately celebrates the unique Elizabethan moment in history, "the event that transcends the archetype."

433. KESSLER, Edward. *Images of Wallace Stevens*. New Brunswick, N.J.: Rutgers University Press, 1972. 267 pp.

In various places brief use is made of Jung in this study of Stevens' "major or controlling images," particularly in clarifying the image of the sun "as a rational as well as an emotional symbol of creative power."

434. KESSLER, Jascha. "Descent in Darkness: The Myth of *The Plumed Serpent*." In *A D.H. Lawrence Miscellany*. Ed. Harry T. Moore. London: Heinemann, 1961. 239-261.

The real meaning of Lawrence's novel (1926) does not lie in the political religious myth of Don Ramón's revolution, but in the personal myth of Kate Leslie, whose life at forty has run dry. To be reborn she must die to her European life and descend into the darkness of her unconscious self. Viewed in terms of Joseph Campbell's myth of the hero her trip across a lake into a more primitive Mexico, where the old savage gods are being revived, becomes a development towards a new wholeness. Lawrence's descriptions evoke the various stages of the mythic journey from separation to initiation through trials and subsequent mystic marriage, though the sequence stops short of the heroine's symbolic return.

435. KEYES, Margaret F. "Art Processes Evoking Awareness of the Shadow Archetype." *Art Psychotherapy* 3:2 (1976) 77-80.

Some verbal and visual aspects of epic and mythic literature are discussed as ways of looking for the Jungian personal shadow.

436. KIRIK, Kathy L. "An Inquiry into Misogyny in *King Lear*: The Making of an Androgyny." *Journal of Evolutionary Psychology* 1:1 (1979) 13-28.

Citing the work of Campbell, Neumann, Frazer, and Jung, Kirik attempts to show that Lear's madness is a mythic descent into the underworld during which he learns to accept his anima (represented by Cordelia), thus achieving psychic wholeness. The misogyny arising from his "encounter with the dangerous sex" is purged through his suffering, and his "evolving selfhood" is "expressed in the making of a psychic androgyny" in his reunion with Cordelia. A pretentious and self-consciously psychological handling of Shakespeare's play. K.S.

437. KIRSCH, James. "The Birth of Evil in *Macbeth*." In *Spectrum Psychologiae: Eine Freundesgabe*. Ed. C.T. Frey-Wehrlin. Zurich: Rascher, 1965. 31-52.

The idea is developed that the motivating force in *Macbeth* is the archetype of evil from the collective unconscious. In a psychically disturbed Scotland, where the feminine in its "destructive aspect" (witches) is in the ascendency, the archetype is activated and tries "to contact some outstanding individual." Macbeth, an "impressionable man" with a weak ego, possessed by an uncontrollable fighting mood and under the influence of the negative anima (Lady Macbeth), is "used" by evil and must be seen more as "the victim than the criminal." *Macbeth* is "the classical drama of an unexpected meeting of man with the female archetype." This is part of Kirsch's book on Shakespeare. The weakness of the argument is discussed in my comments on the book (see No. 442).

438. KIRSCH, James. "The Enigma of Moby Dick." *Journal of Analytical Psychology* 3:2 (1958) 131-148.

This is a rewrite from a somewhat different angle of an earlier paper "Herman Melville in Search of the Self: Moby Dick."(q.v.)

439. KIRSCH, James. "*Hamlet*: A Drama of Haunted Man." *Harvest* 8 (1962) 24-47.

The key to solving the "mystery" of Hamlet's character is found in viewing his "inner process as an illness." The disease is caused by his "affects" about the incestuous marriage of his mother with Claudius. This has caused psychic "dissociation" in Hamlet which has "opened up" his unconscious for an invasion of the "autonomous complex" of his father's ghost. He regresses "to a more primitive state of mind" which stimulates his "rash unreflected deeds" and also "poisons" all the other characters, who may be seen as aspects of Hamlet's mind. Only at the end does Hamlet gain insight into his own mental condition.

This essay condenses the arguments in the lengthy chapter on Hamlet in Kirsch's book on Shakespeare. See for critical comment the annotation to the book (No. 442).

440. KIRSCH, James. "Herman Melville in Search of the Self: *Moby Dick*." In *Professional Reports*. First Annual Conference of Jungian Analysts. 1957. 20-55. Rpt. in *Psychological Perspectives* 7:1 (1976) 54-74.

The writing of *Moby-Dick* (1851) is seen as Melville's own confrontation with the forces of the collective unconscious, and Ahab's pursuit of the white whale as symbolizing Melville's own journey in search of the self. Melville's "conscious personality differentiates" into Ishmael, Captain Ahab and the three shipmates. Ishmael represents the ego and Queequeg the primitive unconscious, while Ahab (on one level modern man who identifies with God) is Ishmael's double, "the ego on a higher and more specific level," driven by traumatic experiences, which are related to events in Melville's own youth. The chase of Moby Dick ends in a collision of the ego and the self, and the book is said to express Melville's failure in individuation.

Characters and events in the novel are given archetypal significance, but their function in the psychological process is only perfunctorily indicated.

441. KIRSCH, James. "Jack London's Quest: "The Red One"." *Psychological Perspectives* 11:2 (1980) 137-154.

The story "The Red One" (1918) is interpreted as a symbolic expression of Jack London's own quest for the self. In his search for a wonderful sound heard on a jungle island inhabited by head-hunting savages, the ego representative in his story has negative meetings with archetypal figures representing shadow, anima and wise old man. His final vision of the mysterious red sphere, symbol of the self, that produces the sound leads at the same time to the hero's death. His inflated ego has all along identified too much with the forces of the unconscious without in any way coming to terms with them.

Kirsch sees the story not only as "a description of Jack London's psychology," but also very sweepingly as "an accurate picture of American psychology and of Western Man as a whole." Kirsch's argument is marred by disregard of the possibility that the tale's symbolism is based on London's reading of Jung. (See McClintock).

442. KIRSCH, James. "*King Lear* as a Play of Redemption." *Harvest* 7
      (1961) 25-45.

      King Lear is seen as a play of "transformation and redemption,"
      in which "the evil aspects, and the tremendous suffering are all
      necessary to show how King Lear passes from a state of utter
      unconsciousness to full consciousness," and how at the moment of
      death he experiences full redemption." In creating the problems
      with his daughters Lear causes "a break between ego and
      unconscious." But the introverted "flow of libido enriches and
      enlarges Lear's understanding of himself" so that "once the rage
      has run its course he can submit to his own true self." This is
      acted out and symbolized in his reunion with Cordelia, his positive
      anima. The last scene of the play is then read as the "coniunctio"
      of male and female that betokens the goal of individuation. Lear's
      final words express the vision in which "he perceives ultimate
      truth" and "achieves full consciousness."

      Kirsch, as a Jungian analyst, worries whether clinically
      speaking Lear can be called insane or not. Though diagnosing "his
      state of mind as a traumatic psychosis," he argues that he cannot
      really be called insane. Most "common" readers would see (with Dr.
      Johnson) in the second part of the play how the self-knowledge
      Lear has gained unsettles him to such an extent that all we can
      say (with Edgar) about his broken mind is that pathetically and
      paradoxically it gives glimpses of "reason in madness." For Kirsch,
      an individuation process is going on, and insight gained must lead
      to greater consciousness so that in the end Lear with the dead
      Cordelia in his arms symbolizes the "coniunctio" of complete
      individuation.

      Kirsch's readings contain misinterpretations of Shakespeare's
      text. His critical method is often not much more than the sticking
      on of Jungian labels that foster neither literary nor psychological
      insight: Lear is "the archetype of the Ego"; "the storm is a
      synchronistic event paralleling the storm in his unconscious"; in
      Lear's rage "the Anima, that is, the long-repressed emotionality,
      finds many opportunities to overwhelm the ego"; "the unconscious
      uses his hot affectivity and constellates terrible situations in order
      to bring [a division of personality] about." (In greatly extended
      form this essay became a chapter in Kirsch's book *Shakespeare's
      Royal Self*.)

443. KIRSCH, James. "The Problem of Dictatorship as Represented in
      Moby Dick." In *Current Trends in Analytical Psychology*.
      Proceedings of the First International Congress for Analytical
      Psychology. Ed. Gerhard Adler. London: Tavistock Publications,
      1961. 261-274.

Moby-Dick is not only "the personal myth of its author." Ahab as the dictator who tyrannizes his crew represents the "power-complex of the ego as it occurs in the nineteenth century" and gives us "insight into the collective psyche of our time." His monomaniacal pursuit of the white whale is a symbolic attempt "to destroy God himself," or at least that image of God which is the archetype of the self. The book depicts modern man's journey into the unconscious in the form of a battle between the inflated ego and the self, in which "the ego becomes a dictator, the self a destructive agent." " Individually this means psychosis, collectively a violent breakdown of the social order. Melville becomes the prophet of the modern dictator whose hybris results in catastrophe.

The idea of the self is rather loosely applied (Fedallah, too, represents the self). Sweeping statements and large cultural generalizations are supported by very little argument, and Melville's own psychological development is too easily identified with Ahab's.

444. KIRSCH, James. *Shakespeare's Royal Self*. New York: Putnam, 1966. xix,422 pp.

This book deals with three of Shakespeare's tragedies: *Hamlet, King Lear* and *Macbeth*. It offers scene by scene summaries with running psychological commentary, each play being analyzed "with the greatest possible detail to demonstrate the *whole* process of individuation." These three plays were chosen "out of the canon as significant steps in Shakespeare's inner development because in each of them the unconscious appears as a separate factor, as a dramatic figure (Ghosts, Witches), or because the consciousness of the hero is for a time concentrated on the unconscious and characteristically changed by it (King Lear)." In so far as any general view of the themes of the plays is developed all three main characters are pictured as having weak ego consciousness, easily invaded by "numinous" unconscious contents, which makes them into "divided personalities." The plays are treated "in the same way that a dream is analyzed," that is, the action is mostly seen as "a dramatization of inner events" taking place in the protagonist's mind. This means that the other characters are, psychologically speaking, aspects and projections of one mind (the protagonist's or Shakespeare's mind).

In Kirsch's view the all-important factor in these plays is the unconscious of Hamlet, Lear and Macbeth, in which the archetypes of the collective unconscious are "activated." Hamlet's consciousness is "overwhelmed and destroyed" by the "infiltration of the ghost complex," also described as the archetype of the King or "the Self returned in its most destructive aspect." The principal problem for Hamlet is "the conflict between his higher personality [or "royal self"] and the Ghost's demand for revenge." By contrast, in Lear, "subject to a daughter complex," Kirsch sees a development towards increasing consciousness so that in the end, with the dead Cordelia in his arms, "the coniunctio occurs" (the union of male and female opposites), and Lear "achieves full consciousness" and "has an otherworldly experience of eternal union." Kirsch believes that as the fruit of his suffering "Lear, in finding himself, experiences God," and even that, in this, the play "is truly a dramatization of Shakespeare's own process of individuation." Macbeth's weak ego, "never quite separated from the maternal unconscious," makes him an easy prey to the destructive feminine forces in the collective unconscious, personified in the witches and in Lady Macbeth, "the negative mother-anima type" whose own problem is "the repression of the unconscious." By murdering Duncan, Macbeth has "split the unconscious in two and deprived it of its healing capacity."

The above synopsis suggests more coherence in Kirsch's arguments than the book actually possesses. There is too much elaborate scene by scene summary, while the accompanying translation of plot and character into psychological terminology suffers from inconsistent, random and repetitive use of Jungian concepts. Shakespeare's plays in their dramatic complexity allow of many different interpretations. These blinkered Jungian readings, however, impress archetypal jargon and a preconceived individuation scheme upon the plays that often fit Shakespeare's text as badly as the royal robes sit on Macbeth.

The main characters are supposed to act and speak almost totally under the influence of forces from the unconscious. Kirsch insufficiently recognizes that Hamlet, and more particularly Macbeth, are from the beginning consciously struggling with their problems. This leads to serious misreadings of important scenes and speeches. And it would be hard to deduce from this book that Shakespeare brings to bear a great many other human factors, among which the moral implications of men's actions are at least as important as the psychological.

The quality of Kirsch's comments may be illustrated by a few examples from Macbeth. Of Lady Macbeth it is said that she intends "to stimulate his anima with her murderous impulses." Disregarding Macbeth's great soliloquies about the consequences of murdering Duncan, Kirsch maintains that what is missing in the play is "a real confrontation between ego and unconscious," a discussion about "a different course than that which the unconscious proposes." From Kirsch's analysis one would not realize how ambition, guilt and conscience plague and motivate Macbeth. In the prophecies of the witches "the images of the unconscious tried to show Macbeth a path to redemption, but his concretistic and literal thinking was a thick wall against any penetration of insight."

How much more subtle is Shakespeare's psychology than Kirsch's Jungian version of it. (See also the annotations to the separate articles extracted from the chapters of this book.)

445. KIRSCH, James. "The Sleepwalking Scene in Macbeth." *Harvest* 10 (1964) 80-91.

In the sleepwalking of Lady Macbeth "the repressed complex forced its way back to consciousness and manifested itself in symbolic actions." Overwhelmed by fragmented memory images her weakened ego commits suicide. The sleepwalking is also a "symbol for the twilight consciousness of Macbeth's anima." The disintegration of Lady Macbeth's mind reflects the deteriorating quality of Macbeth's soul. (This analysis of the scene is part of the chapter on Macbeth in Kirsch's book on Shakespeare. No. 442)

446. KIRSCH, James. "Some Comments about the Masque in Shakespeare's *Tempest*." In *The Shaman from Elko: Papers in Honor of Joseph L. Henderson on His Seventy-Fifth Birthday*. San Francisco: C.G. Jung Institute of San Francisco, 1978. 81-86.

It is suggested that the masque's ritual may be related through the classic goddesses and the dance of the reapers to the Eleusinian mysteries of death and rebirth. It is part of Ferdinand's initiation and of the play's general theme of reaching self-knowledge or individuation applied to Prospero and Shakespeare himself.

447. KISSANE, James D. *Alfred Tennyson*. New York: Twayne, 1970. Twayne's World Authors Series. 183 pp.

In this introduction to Tennyson Kissane works out the idea put forward by Lionel Stevenson (q.v.) that the "high-born maidens" in Tennyson's poems are anima figures. The developing love-relationship in *The Princess* (1847) lends itself very well to analysis in terms of Jung's anima/animus theory with Lady Psyche's little girl as symbol of the wholeness reached by the lovers "in taking possession of each other and of their true selves."

448. KITCHIN, Derek. "Matthew Arnold and the Scholar Gipsy." Guild Lecture No. 35. London: Guild of Pastoral Psychology, 1945. 27 pp.

In his poems "The Scholar Gipsy" (1853) and "Thyrsis" (1867) Matthew Arnold imagines a gypsy figure, "rebel against the intellect," wandering through the countryside around Oxford, who may be seen symbolically as the exact opposite of Arnold's own persona. He is for Arnold personal shadow and puer aeternus, functioning as a bridge between ego and collective unconscious, a source of spiritual energy.

449. KLEIMAN, E. "The Wizardry of Nathaniel Hawthorne: *Seven Gables* as Fairy Tale and Parable." *English Studies in Canada* 4:3 (1978) 289-304.

Kleiman traces the development of biblical and alchemical symbols to refute the criticism that Hawthorne's novel *The House of the Seven Gables* (1851) lacks structure. Jung's *Psychology and Alchemy* is cited to prove that such symbols as trees (the Pyncheon elm), fountains (Maule's Well) and the figure of Mercury (Judge Pyncheon with his cane) have their origin in alchemy. K.S.

450. KNAPP, Bettina L. *Archetype, Architecture, and the Writer.* Bloomington: Indiana University Press, 1985. 224 pp.

Probes the nature, meaning, and use of architectural metaphors and archetypes in literary works by Ibsen, Maeterlinck, Henry James, Ansky, Kafka, Borges, Fuentes, Wang Shih-Fu, Lorca, and Mishima.

451. KNAPP, Bettina L. *Archetype, Dance, and the Writer.* Troy, N.Y.: Bethel, 1983. 176 pp.

Explores archetypal imagery of dance in literary works of, among others, Melville, Oscar Wilde, and Yeats.

452. KNAPP, Bettina L. "Anaïs/Artaud - Alchemy." *Mosaic* 11:2 (1978) 65-74.

With the help of Jung's psychological interpretation of alchemy Anaïs Nin's *House of Incest* (1949) is read as "alchemical blendings which are the reflections and externalizations of her unconscious primordial dreams." The symbols used in Nin's book, like those of the alchemist, are in Jung's words "psychic transformers." They visualize the artistic process as a descent into the shadow world (the *nigredo* stage), then a rise through water imagery (the *albedo*) to the heating by fire (the *rubedo*). The artist's inchoate experiences are transformed into the transparent "crystal" of the Philosopher's Stone, the work of art that reflects the integrated cosmic pattern and generates "a sense of eternality and continuity."

A rapturous discussion, illuminating Anaïs Nin's rapturously lyrical work.

453. KNAPP, Bettina L. *Edgar Allan Poe.* New York: Frederick Ungar, 1984. 226 pp.

In the analysis of Poe's works Jung's archetypal theory and collective unconscious are extensively used.

454. KNAPP, Bettina L. *A Jungian Approach to Literature*. Carbondale:
Southern Illinois University Press, 1984. xvi,402 pp.

In ten essays on texts from world literature this ambitious
book purposes to demonstrate "the universality of Jungian or
archetypal analysis and criticism." Furthermore, the material is
"designed to enlarge the reader's views," for the Jungian approach
not only helps "develop one's own potential and spiritual élan," but
also broadens "the understanding of the individual's function and
role in society." The following texts are discussed in separate
chapters: Euripides' *The Bacchants*, Wolfram von Eschenbach's
Parzival, Montaigne's *Essays*, Corneille's *Horace* and *Rodogune*,
Goethe's *Elective Affinities*, Novalis' *Hymns to the Night*, Rabbi
Nachman's Kabbalistic tale "The Master of Prayer," Yeats's play *At
the Hawk's Well*, the Finnish epic *The Kalevala*, and the long
twelfth century Persian poem *The Conference of the Birds* by the
Sufi mystic Attar.

Each chapter has two sections: first the work is placed in its
historical period, in the author's life and background, and the
structure and nature of the work are explored; then follows a
lengthy archetypal analysis which amounts to a retelling ("fleshing
out" the author calls it) of the contents, with explication in terms
of Jungian concepts and amplifications from myth, religion, alchemy
and many other fields. The abstract lyrical style of parts of the
book may be illustrated by Knapp's comment on the lines "For the
wind, the salt wind, the sea wind Is beating a cloud through the
skies" from a song by the musicians in Yeats's play: "Turmoil, not
torpor, prevails in convoluted and convulsive force. Reminiscent of
the alchemist's *aqua permanens* which infiltrates the cosmos, so
here, too, liquids, gases, and solids interact. The psychological
picture has also changed; ego now flows into the Self, the
individual into the collective. Movement rather than stasis is now
encountered."

Professor Knapp's impressive erudition and enthusiasm will no
doubt have made the lectures on which this book was based a
stimulating course for students. The critical reader, however, soon
develops doubts about her method of large-scale archetypal
interpretation. My remarks are largely based on her treatment of
the Yeats play. Adequate critiques can only be written by
specialists in the widely different literatures Knapp has tackled.
For Yeats I refer to the review by Barbara Frieling in *Yeats: An
Annual of Critical and Textual Studies*. Ed. Richard J. Finneran.
Ann Arbor: U.M.I. Research Press, 1986. pp. 204-206. Frieling
questions the interpretation of Cuchulain as the hero who has
neglected the feminine, and of the Hawk Woman as the

"unintegrated anima," and she points out "several factual errors" and "fundamental misunderstandings" of the play and of Yeatsian concepts.

Knapp seems to be at her best in the more objective parts of her undertaking, where she writes fluently and informatively about the works in relation to the writers and their times. When in her archetypal interpretations she imposes her very broadly conceived Jungian notions and schemes upon the texts, she tends to lose sight not only of the details of the actual works but even of Jung's ideas. The longest chapter of the book expounds the Sufi's mystical experience in Attar's poem as a process of annihilation of ego and "reintegration into the Self: a dehumanizing process." One wonders what Jung would have made of his dehumanized Self! In sum, an interesting book that cannot be recommended for its Jungian approach to literature.

455. KNAPP, Bettina L. *Theater and Alchemy*. Detroit: Wayne State University Press, 1980. xiii,283 pp.

The Yeats chapter was published in slightly different form as "An Alchemical Brew: From *Separatio* to *Coagulatio* in Yeats's *The Only Jealousy of Emer*." *Educational Theatre Journal* 30 (1978) 447-465.

In this book Jung's psychological interpretation of the stages and operations of the alchemist's Great Work is applied to drama. The nine plays dealt with are all psychological or symbolical, and range from Strindberg's *A Dream Play* and Ansky's *The Dybbuk* to pieces from Japanese Noh (*Matsukaze*) and the Sanskrit theatre of India (*Shakuntala*). In the one English play discussed, Yeats's *The Only Jealousy of Emer* (1919), "the characters are put through two alchemical operations." They "begin as *prima materia* in the preformal stage of oneness," move through water and fire rituals into a *separatio* of the three anima figures, the feminine projections of Cuchulain's psyche, and they end up in the *coagulatio* of his choosing the superficial love of the mistress, which precludes the "*sublimatio* or evolution into a higher sphere of existence."

Interpretation of these plays is hardly helped by imposing such a general scheme. In the case of Yeats's play the alchemical symbolism positively distorts the dramatist's own symbol system.

456. KNAPP, Bettina L. *Word/Image/Psyche*. Tuscaloosa: University of Alabama Press, 1985. 224 pp.

With the help of Jungian psychology Knapp examines art criticism of Gautier, Baudelaire, the Goncourt brothers, Huysmans, Henry James, Rilke, Virginia Woolf, and Malraux.

457. KOPLIK, Irwin J. "Jung's Psychology in the Plays of O'Neill." (Ph.D. 1966 New York University) 276 pp. *DAI* 27/11 A p.3872.

458. KREKELER, Elisabeth M. "The Archetypal Dimensions of Joyce's Dedalian Novels." (Ph.D. 1972 Saint Louis University) 220 pp. *DAI* 33/03 A p.1173.

459. KROLL, Judith. *Chapters in a Mythology: The Poetry of Sylvia Plath.*" New York: Harper & Row, 1976. xvi,303 pp.
    This study of the thematic meaning of Plath's late poems understands her poetry "as constituting a system of symbols that expresses a unified mythic vision." In this "mythic biography" the images (of red, white and black, of the Moon-muse, of metamorphosis) become "emblems" of a myth whose central motifs are three sets of polarities with archetypal force: the male as god and devil, the false self and the true self, and death, rebirth and transcendence. The influence of Plath's reading of Jung, Frazer and Graves is considered.

460. KUBIS, Patricia L. "The Archetype of the Devil in Twentieth Century Literature." (Ph.D. 1976 University of California, Riverside) 522 pp. *DAI* 37/06 A p.3604. (C.S. Lewis, John Fowles, D.H. Lawrence)

461. KUGLER, Paul K. "Archetypal Linguistics: An Inquiry into the Relation between Phonetics and the Imagination." (Ph.D. 1980 State University of New York, Buffalo) 159 pp. *DAI* 41/01 A p.230. Became book *The Alchemy of Discourse: An Archetypal Approach to Language.* Lewisburg, Pa.: Bucknell University Press, 1982. 141 pp.

462. KUNITZ, Stanley. "Roethke: Poet of Transformations." *New Republic* 152 (1965) 23-29.
    Surveying the characteristic features of Roethke's poetry, Kunitz notes that in its associational method, "with frequent time shifts in and out of childhood," the style of this poet, "engaged in a quest for spiritual identity," points "straight to the door" of Jung and Maud Bodkin with whose work Roethke was familiar. "The monologues of Roethke follow the pattern of progression and regression [as discussed by Jung] and belong unmistakably to the rebirth archetype."

463. KUPPENS, Patricia F. "Patterns of Complementarity: Masculine and Feminine Relationships in *Othello, King Lear,* and *Macbeth*." (Ph.D. 1979 Yale University) *DAI* 40/06 A p.3317.

464. LA BELLE, Jenijoy. "Theodore Roethke's 'The Lost Son': From Archetypes to Literary History." *Modern Language Quarterly* 37:2 (1976) 179-195.

    Critics too easily take the influence of Maud Bodkin and Jung on Roethke's poetry for granted. He owed to them an archetypal perspective, but his imagination is stimulated mainly by the archetypal patterns transmitted through other poets. This is illustrated from the poem "The Lost Son", in which the theme of death and rebirth suggests a spiritual progress through temporary regression into the unconscious. The literary antecedents of its central images of "slime" and descent into a "pit" are traced to poems by Coleridge, T.S. Eliot and Blake to show that, rather than showing the influence of psychological theories, "Roethke's metaphors [are] based upon archetypal patterns rooted in the natural world and experienced through the poetry of his tradition."

465. LABOR, Earle. *Jack London.* New York: Twayne Publishers, 1974. 179 pp.

    London's "instinctive mythopoeic vision" is discussed in terms of what Jung called the visionary mode of artistic creation which derives its material from the collective unconscious. London's best work is seen as "the artistic modulation of universal dreams - i.e. of myths and archetypes." The archetypal wilderness of the White Silence in Northland is the landscape of myth that makes *The Call of the Wild* (1903) London's most forceful romance. In his dynamic career London himself lived the myth of the American folk-hero.

466. LACEY, Paul A. "The Inner War." In *Benchmark and Blaze: The Emergence of William Everson.* Ed. Lee Bartlett. Metuchen, N.J.: Scarecrow Press, 1979. 137-65.
    Rpt. from *The Inner War: Forms and Themes in Recent American Poetry.* Philadelphia: Fortress Press, 1972.

    Lacey objects to an ambiguity of form in Everson's poetry, arguing that the prefaces to his work "blanket and obscure the torment." Alongside Catholic theology, Jungian depth psychology acts as a "censor" shaping the poems. The woman of *The Rose of Solitude* falls short of her intended status as pure archetype. Throwing out the assumptions of Jungian psychology, Lacey insists that "symbols are built up by slow accretion" in literature, not by correspondence to universals of the collective unconscious. J.K.

467. LANE, Lauriat, Jr. "The Literary Archetype: Some Reconsiderations." *Journal of Aesthetics and Art Criticism* 13:2 (1954) 226-232.

    By combining Jung and Northrop Frye, Lane attempts "a redefinition and revaluation" of the term "archetype." A short history of its use is given from Samuel Johnson ("the first literary critic to use the term in its modern sense") to Gilbert Murray, whose paper on "Hamlet and Orestes" (q.v.) was "one of the first examples of directly archetypal criticism." The literary archetype is defined (from the point of view of the reader rather than that of the critic) by five major characteristics: relative universality, a traditional basis in literature, innate significance of form and content, subconscious elements in author, work and reader, and an emotional intensity at the moment of awareness.

468. LANGDON, Harry N. "Ritual Form: One Key to Albee's *Tiny Alice*." *Theatre Annual* 35 (1980) 57-72.

In *Tiny Alice* (1965) Albee "has designed an act of ritual which aids man in accepting, if not understanding his fate." In the course of the play Julian encounters the two sides of his nature (the rationalistic and the emotional, symbolized by the Lawyer and the Butler, respectively) in order to become united with truth (Alice). The mythical rebirth through a return to the womb, in Jung's terms, is symbolically achieved by Julian when he kneels before her womb, enveloped within her robes. K.S.

469. LAUREN, M., O.P. "Psychological Approaches to Literary Criticism." *Catholic School Journal* 68:2 (1968) 57-59.

Using Guerin's *Handbook of Critical Approaches* (q.v.) and its examples, Sister Lauren argues that high school teachers "can add new insights to literary works" by employing the Freudian and Jungian approaches to literary criticism.

470. *LAUTER, Estella. "Anne Sexton's 'Radical Discontent with the Awful Order of Things'." *Spring* (1979) 77-92.
Rpt. in *Women as Mythmakers: Poetry and Art by Twentieth Century Women*. Bloomington: Indiana University Press, 1984. 23-46.

The later poetry of Anne Sexton may be seen as her courageous quest for a viable relationship with the Christian God from whom she felt "exiled." This search is "an act of 'soul-making,' the effort to find connections between life and the fantasy images" of alternative forces and figures that arise abundantly in her volumes of poetry between 1970 and her suicide in 1974. Sexton's difficulties in accepting the fruits of her soul-making had much to do with her inability to name the feminine dimensions of the rich body of god-images that she produced. Lauter discusses the archetypal force of the dominant sea imagery in the poems and offers an interpretation of the sequence of "Jesus Papers" that illustrates how Sexton, while still acknowledging the worship of an inadequate Father-God, is ecstatically discovering an alternative attitude to the trials of female experience in Mary and to the traditional picture of an a-sexual Jesus. At the time of Sexton's death James Hillman and others were formulating new contexts for a re-conceptualization of God in terms of the recurring world-wide mythical god-images that might have led Anne Sexton to understand and believe in the feminine images of her poetic raids into the realm of the archetypal mother.

A lucid commentary and original interpretation.

471. LAUTER, Estella. *Women as Mythmakers: Poetry and Visual Art by Twentieth-Century Women*. Bloomington: Indiana University Press, 1984. xvii,267 pp.

A collection of essays on women writers with an introduction on "Steps toward a Feminist Archetypal Theory of Mythmaking" and a valuable bibliography.

472. LAVALLEY, Paul C. "The Visionary Art of Beckett's Drama: A Jungian View." (Ph.D. 1983 University of Toronto, Canada) *DAI* 44/10 A p.3061.

473. LECHNER, Emil T. "Experience of the Numinous in Yeats, Jung, and Bonhoeffer." (Ph.D. 1974 Rice University) 240 pp. *DAI* 35/04 A p.2280.

474. LEE, Grace Farrell. "The Quest of Arthur Gordon Pym". *Southern Literary Journal* 4:2 (1972) 22-33.

Poe's novel (1838) seen as myth, using the "structure of a sea-voyage, a familiar post-Jungian image of the collective unconscious," symbol of a journey into the human psyche "backward in time to the origins of creation." Far from lacking structure, the action in its symbolic details suggests the archetypal descent into the underworld, the "dream quest into the unknown where the terror of the universe and of man's confrontation with primal nature are reawakened." K.S.

475. *LEE, Ronald J. "Jungian Approach to Theater: Shaffer's *Equus*." *Psychological Perspectives* 8:1 (1977) 10-21.

This is an exercise in "applied Jungian aesthetics" that goes beyond the analysis of the fictional characters and into questions of form and content, dealing specifically with "the issue of how a theatricality is achieved which is appropriate to the fundamentally Jungian subject matter of the play." In Peter Shaffer's play *Equus* (1973) a child psychologist's investigation into a boy's apparently psychotic action of blinding six horses becomes the doctor's struggle of self-discovery. During the analysis he begins to see the religious vacuum of his own life through his recurring dream of being a priest in Homeric Greece officiating at a large ritual sacrifice of children. The boy's passionate worship of his mysterious god Equus, enacted in the ritual night-riding and mystical unification with his horse, is contrasted with the "normality" of his work in an appliance shop, the futile religion of his mother, and the atheism of his father. The repugnant outer world impinges on the boy's subjective inner life when he falls in love with a girl. Sexuality being a source of feelings of guilt and punishment, his attraction to the girl begins to contaminate the deep religious experience of his nighttime life with the horses, and when in the stable they watch the failure of his lovemaking with the girl his myth turns into a delusion that makes him destroy the omniscient eyes of the horses. "The success of Shaffer's play is that, while portraying through the subject matter the failure of accommodation between the inner and outer worlds, he finds an objective correlative in the action of the play for the feeling that accommodation is possible."

The audience experiences an actual encounter with the images of archetype and myth through the richly symbolic staging of the play. The actors wearing horse-head masks become "living symbolic images of the archetype of the unity of life." The action takes place in the realm of dream and memory as Doctor Dysart reconstructs his disturbing confrontation with the boy. The staging emphasizes the mythic, and Jungian, form of the play, the playing space being a raised, rotating square of wood set on a circle of wood that is never left by the actors during the performance. Although the destiny of boy and doctor is left open, "in the aesthetic event itself we are given a life-giving encounter with the rich interior life of myth and archetype."

Lucid analysis of the integration of symbolic form and psychological content in Shaffer's play.

476. LEE, Ronald J. "Pirsig's *Zen and the Art of Motorcycle Maintenance*: The Fusion of Form and Content. *Western American Literature* 14:3 (1979) 221-225.

The theme of Pirsig's novel (1974) is the narrator's discovery of meaning (the "quality" of life) through the romantic notion of immersion in experience. "The several strands of the plot [...] are carefully woven together with the philosophical digressions by means of establishing allegorical parallels to the inward search of the protagonist." We have the ancient archetypal pattern of the "romance narrative of the quest," which in line with other twentieth century works by, for instance, Eliot, Beckett, Ken Kesey

and Peter Shaffer, is, however, "laced with irony." The motorcycle journey of father and son is the search for the narrator's former "mad" self, from which he was divided by electro-shock treatment. It is a division between his conscious ego and his shadow figure, Phaedrus. Ironically, when at the end the whole quest seems to have led only to hopeless despair, it is the son who makes the father realize that psychic wholeness is possible through acceptance rather than rejection of the shadow.
Brief, but closely reasoned Jungian analysis.

477. LE GUIN, Ursula K. "The Child and the Shadow." *Quarterly Journal of the Library of Congress* 32:2 (1975) 139-148, and "Myth and Archetype in Science Fiction." *Parabola* 1:4 (1976) 42-47. Rpt. in *The Language of the Night: Essays on Fantasy and Science Fiction* by Ursula K. Le Guin. Ed. Susan Wood. New York: Putnam, 1979. 270 pp.
This collection of essays and talks contains critical discussions of Le Guin's own science fiction and of works of other writers in the field. In the two essays mentioned she describes the insights she derived from her discovery of Jung. She makes a plea for taking the best of science fiction as a serious form of art in which man's indispensable myth-making faculty comes to grips with our world of science and technology that "overvalues abstraction and extraversion." The reading and writing of fantasy and science fiction is an exercise of the imagination for which there is eminent need if society and the individual are to grow up facing their own hidden and repressed destructive energies.
The two essays provide popular explication of Jungian concepts, admirably written, playful and unpretentious, yet clear and imaginative.

478. LEVINE-KEATING, Helane. "Myth and Archetype from a Female Perspective: An Exploration of Twentieth Century North and South American Women Poets." (Ph.D. 1980 New York University) 346 pp. *DAI* 41/02 A p.664. (H.D., Margaret Atwood, Olga Broumas, Sylvia Plath, Denise Levertov, Diane Keating, Maxine Kumin)

479. LEWIS, Clifford L. "John Steinbeck: Architect of the Unconscious." (Ph.D. 1972 University of Texas, Austin) 317 pp. *DAI* 34/02 A p.781.

480. LEWIS, Clifford. "Jungian Psychology and the Artistic Design of John Steinbeck." *Steinbeck Quarterly* 10:3-4 (1977) 89-97.
Now that early Steinbeck letters and manuscripts have become available it is possible to see more clearly how much psychological theory he incorporated into his writings. The article considers

Steinbeck's knowledge of Jung's early work in the unpublished manuscript of "Murder at Full Moon," a not very successful parody of the detective story, in which the murderer is finally shown up as a case of "Dementia Praecox" or schizophrenia by a psychiatrist. "Steinbeck was influenced by various psychological schools of thought to the degree that his entire writing career can be interpreted as an effort to dramatize the conflict between unconscious and conscious reality."

481. LEWIS, C.S. "Psychoanalysis and Literary Criticism." In *Essays and Studies by Members of the English Association.* Vol. 27, 1941. Ed. Nowell C. Smith. Oxford: Clarendon Press, 1942. 7-21.

In a lighthearted paper the Freudian claim that all our enjoyment of literary images "can be explained in terms of infantile sexuality" is contrasted with Jung's views about the emotive power of the "primordial images." Lewis wishes to suspend judgment about the scientific value of Jung's theory of the archetypes of the collective unconscious, but admits that it helps to explain why certain images "have a strange power to excite the human mind."

482. LICHTMAN, Myla R. "Mythic Plot and Character Development in Euripides' *Hippolytus* and Eugene O'Neill's *Desire under the Elms*: A Jungian Analysis." (Ph.D. 1979 University of Southern California) *DAI* 40/04 A p.1750.

483. LILIENFELD, Jane. "'The Deceptiveness of Beauty': Mother Love and Mother Hate in *To the Lighthouse.*" *Twentieth Century Literature* 23:3 (1977) 345-376.

An examination in depth of the relations in Virginia Woolf's novel *To the Lighthouse* (1927) between overpowering Mrs. Ramsay and her "surrogate" daughter, the artist Lily Briscoe, who struggles to achieve her own independent "personhood." The analogy with Jung's and Neumann's description of the ambivalent Great Mother clarifies the mythic and psychological implications as well as the symbolism of Virginia Woolf's depiction of Mrs. Ramsay as the archetypal mother and housewife.

484. LISTER, Rota. "Alien Vision in Canadian Drama." *Canadian Literature* 85 (1980) 170-176.

The character of the outsider, frequently presented in Canadian drama as pathetic victim or benign redeemer, is viewed as archetypal scapegoat or mythical hero. Plays by Heavysege, Mair, Campbell, Davies, Scott, Denison, Peterson, Rygan, and Herbert are discussed.

485. LOCKERD, Benjamin G., Jr. "The Sacred Marriage in *The Faerie Queene*." (Ph.D. 1984 University of Connecticut) 361 pp. *DAI* 46/03 A p.708.

486. LONG, Charles H. "The Quest Dialectic: The Jungian and Kierkegaardian Quest for Unity in W.H. Auden's 'The Quest', 'New Year Letter', and 'For the Time Being'." (Ed.D. 1973 Ball State University) 210 pp. *DAI* 34/08 A p.5187.

487. LONGO, Joseph A. "Myth in *A Midsummer Night's Dream*." *Cahiers Elisabethains* 18 (1980) 17-27.
    This analysis of "the wholesome synthesis of the conscious and unconscious worlds" in Shakespeare's comedy views the play's mythical progress as a journey "from the Apollonian spirit of reason through the Dionysian release of frenzied energies to an Orphic re-creation." The characters move from the strictures of reason and law in the Athenian court into their night of illusion and irrational fantasy in the moonlit woods. From their immersion in a region of dream, primitive impulse and midsummer madness they awaken into a renewed and festively harmonious Athens. Bottom is the comic embodiment of the play's contraries. As frustrated lover and artist he is a delightful parody of the mythical singer and quester Orpheus, who transforms life's oppositions through the powers of his creative imagination. In the figure of Puck Shakespeare brings together the mythic materials of the play. Puck's final speech fuses and clarifies "the paradoxical relationship between reason and imagination, conscious and unconscious, reality and myth." It also gives us Shakespeare's own "observations about his art: trust in poetry and imagination, faith in myth as an instrument for self-understanding."
    Jung's views of myth and psychic oppositions inform Longo's essay. Though couched in too much abstract jargon, his discussion illuminates the mythical and psychological aspects, as well as the "poetic structure and dramatic argument" of Shakespeare's play.

488. LORD, George deForest. *Heroic Mockery: Variations on Epic Themes from Homer to Joyce*. Newark: University of Delaware Press, 1977. 162 pp.
    In his study of the foolish, festive and comic elements in some great epics and mock-epics of Western literary tradition Lord concludes that "the process of individuation [...] lies at the heart of Homeric epic," just as the Homeric vision of "survival and reconciliation" informs the transcendence of the comic and the tragic in the modifications of epic tradition in Milton and Joyce.

489. LORD, George deForest. *Trials of the Self: Heroic Ordeals in the Epic Tradition*. Hamden, Conn.: Archon Books, 1983. ix,249 pp.
Jung's individuation theory is used in discussions of the *Odyssey*, *Aeneid*, *Divine Comedy*, *Paradise Regained*, *The Prelude*, *Moby-Dick*, *Heart of Darkness*.

490. LORIMER, William L. "Ripples From a Single Stone: An Archetypal Study of Theodore Roethke's Poetry." (Ph.D. 1976 University of the Notre Dame) 161 pp. *DAI* 37/06 A p.3614.

491. LOWRY, E.D. "Chaos and Cosmos in *In Our Time*." *Literature and Psychology* 26:3 (1976) 108-117.
Applying the archetypal patterns of the Eternal Return (Eliade) and of "psychic balance and totality" (Jung, Campbell), Lowry discusses the mythic themes of death and rebirth in Hemingway's "collage" of short stories *In Our Time* (1925).

492. LUCAS, Peter D. "An Introduction to the Psychology of *Wuthering Heights*." Guild Lecture No. 25. London: Guild of Pastoral Psychology, 1958. 34 pp.
An analyst interprets *Wuthering Heights* (1847) "on the supposition that all the characters of the story are parts of the personality of one central character," Catherine the elder, and are, as it were, symbolic figures in her dream-life. This means that the characters project their shadow or anima or animus upon each other, that there are several marriages between shadow and animus figures, and so on. Catherine's problems develop to a psychotic climax and are solved in the last scene (the lovers, young Catherine and Hareton, entering the garden at the Heights) which corresponds to "the solution-dream of a successful analysis." Most of the novel's multiple oppositions fit fairly well into this therapeutic treatment of Catherine the elder and her problems. Little is gained, however, by simply attaching archetypal labels to the young lovers who in the end settle at the Grange and leave the Heights to Joseph and a boy. "Thus, the unconscious is left in charge of the Puer Aeternus and the Wise Old Man, while the reconciled Ego and Animus attain in harmony to the complete consciousness of the Grange."

493. LUCENTE, Gregory L. *The Narrative of Realism and Myth: Verga, Lawrence, Faulkner, Pavese*. Baltimore: Johns Hopkins University Press, 1981. x,189 pp.
In this study of the interaction of realism and myth in works of four novelists the chapter on "the origins of the mystic sign"

compares the symbol theories of Plato, Vico, Müller, Frazer, Jung and Freud.

494. *LUKE, Helen M. *Through Defeat to Joy: The Novels of Charles Williams in the Light of Jungian Thought.* Three Rivers, Mi.: Privately printed, 1977. vii,84 pp.

The seven fantastic novels of Charles Williams are read as stories "largely concerned with the relationships of men and women to the archetypal powers behind human life." Striking parallels with Jung's thought are found in the contributions of both writers to a "revitalizing of the Christian myth." "All Williams' novels celebrate the holiness of the flesh, the beauty of nature, and the essential values of feeling. Moreover, like Jung, he leaves us in no doubt about the reality of evil and of the part it must play in the process of redemption, or individuation," and he points clearly to the reconciliation of opposites in the image of God. In most of the novels power-seeking hubristic characters are opposed to those who strive for a free "exchange" of creative love relationships with people and with things. The state of "co-inherence" reached by the main character in *Descent into Hell* (1937) is expressed in the theme of "incarnation" and the experience of "joy" that accompanies the growing awareness of the complete pattern in the individual life.

This clear exposition of the archetypal and moral content of the novels goes directly to the heart of the human, psychological and religious insight allegorized in Williams' moral fables.

495. LUKE, Helen M. *The Way of Woman, Ancient and Modern.* Three Rivers, Mi.: Privately printed, no date. 60 pp.

Helen Luke finds in the work of three English authors "a symbolic and moving picture of the dilemma of modern woman" in search of a psychic wholeness that will encompass in Jung's sense both the feminine and masculine elements of the inner personality. The theme of woman's individuation is traced in the mythic stories of three women figures: Eowyn in Tolkien's *The Lord of the Rings* (1954-55), Psyche's sister Orual in C.S. Lewis' retelling of the myth of Psyche and Eros *Till We Have Faces* (1956), and Perceval's sister in two poems from Charles Williams' cycle of Arthurian poems, published in the volumes *Taliessin through Logres* (1938) and *The Region of the Summer Stars* (1944).

With imaginative insight Helen Luke brings out the "inner vision" of femininity in these works of three twentieth-century writers.

496. LYTLE, Andrew. "The Working Novelist and the Mythmaking Process." *Daedalus* 88 (1959) 326-338. Rpt. in *Myth and Mythmaking*. Ed. Henry A. Murray. New York: George Braziller, 1960. 141-156. Rpt. in *Myth and Literature: Contemporary Theory and Practice*. Ed. John B. Vickery. Lincoln: University of Nebraska Press, 1966. 99-108.

Creative writer Andrew Lytle describes how in the process of composing his novel *The Velvet Horn* (1957) the idea of writing about the life of older generations in the American South gradually centered on the theme of incest, and was infused with the archetype of the conflict and marriage of opposites in the union of brother and sister. As an act symbolic of man's straining toward a return to original innocence and wholeness, this gave the novel its informing myth, which found a controlling symbol in the deer horn with its velvet covering, combining the masculine and feminine aspects of being. The author names his reading of Frazer, Zimmer, Jung's *Psychology and Alchemy* and Neumann's *Origins and History of Consciousness* as influences in the shaping of his novel.

497. McALEER, Edward C. "Frank O'Connor's Oedipus Trilogy." *Hunter College Studies* 2 (1964) 33-40.

O'Connor's short stories "My Oedipus Complex," "The Man of the House" and "Judas" are analyzed as "literary treatments of the Oedipal situation" in the life of a boy, not so much in Freudian terms as illustrative of Jung's three stages of development: presexual, prepubertal, and maturity.

498. McCANN, Janet. "'Prologues to What is Possible': Wallace Stevens and Jung." *Ball State University Forum* 17:2 (1976) 46-50.

The explication of this late Stevens poem aims at showing his conscious use of archetypal imagery and his fascination with Jung's notion of metaphor and symbol. In his later work Stevens not only applies the concepts of self and collective unconscious, but the aesthetic he develops resembles a Jungian process of self-realization that reaches for wholeness through a recognition of likenesses between the individual mind and the world.

499. McCLINTICK, Michael L. "The Comic Hero: A Study of the Mythopoeic Imagination in the Novel." (Ph.D. 1974 Washington State University) 307 pp. *DAI* 35/01 A p.409. (Fielding, Dickens, Joyce, Cooke, Mailer, Cary)

500. McCLINTOCK, James I. "Jack London's Use of Carl Jung's
Psychology of the Unconscious." American Literature 42:3 (1970)
336-347.
After four years of potboilers Jack London wrote in the last
year of his life a series of impressive Alaskan and Hawaiian stories
which are clearly indebted to his reading of the 1916 English
edition of Jung's *Psychology of the Unconscious*. He finds in Jung a
"scientifically justifiable rationale" for expressing the major theme
of his work: "the conflict of modern scepticism, born of rationality,
with a primitive affirmation whose source is nonrational. Some of
the stories can be better understood by noting that their symbolism
and terminology are based on particular passages in Jung. The
stories deal imaginatively with the night journey of the sun-hero,
libido energy as the life force, oedipal attachment overcome
through "sacrifice," descent into the womb-cave of the unconscious
in search of treasure, and difficult rebirth. A pattern, recurrent in
London's life and fiction, of an excited sense of new revelation
changing into disillusionment, is discernible. Jungian concepts turn
from "a celebration of life's vitality to a final pessimistic
preoccupation with death."
A convincing demonstration of the extent to which London's
last stories are infused with Jungian psychology. The debt to Jung
is particularly clear in "Like Argus of Ancient Times" in *The Red
One* (1918) and in five stories in *On the Makaloa Mat* (1919).

501. McCLINTOCK, James I. "Jack London's Short Stories." (Ph.D. 1968
Michigan State University) 289 pp. *DAI* 29/06 A p.1902.
Became book *White Logic: Jack London's Short Stories* (1975).

502. McCLINTOCK, James I. *White Logic: Jack London's Short Stories*.
Cedar Springs, Mi.: Wolf House Books, 1976. xii,206 pp.
McClintock's last chapter is a revision of his 1970 article on
London's explicit use of Jung's *Psychology of the Unconscious*. It
extends the comparison of the late Hawaiian stories with the
earlier Alaskan ones, attempts an evaluation of the best of
London's short stories, and defines his main mythical theme as "the
search for salvation amidst hints of certain damnation."

503. McCULLY, Robert S. "'The Phoenix and the Turtle': An
Interpretation." *Harvest* 8 (1962) 50-56.
The poem, attributed to Shakespeare, usually read as an elegy
on the death of an ideally mated couple, continues to puzzle
commentators. It is here explained as an allegory of the mystical
union of immortal phoenix and mortal turtle dove, a *mysterium
coniunctionis* of female passion and (strangely!) male constancy.

Amplification of the symbolism of phoenix and turtle ranges from medieval bestiaries through references to Jung, Neumann and Corbin, among others, to parallels with Chinese and Hindu thought, and especially to a a Persian mystic bird epic which describes the merging of the individual soul into the collective cosmos, the Self enveloping the soul.

504. McCUNE, Marjorie W., Tucker Orbison, and Philip M. Withim, eds. *The Binding of Proteus: Perspectives on Myth and Literary Process.* Lewisburg, Pa.: Bucknell University Press, 1980. 350 pp.

A valuable collection of sixteen papers contributed to programs at Bucknell University on the relation between myth and literature "to see if myth criticism had progressed over the several years since Henry Murray's collection *Myth and Mythmaking* (1960) and John Vickery's *Myth and Literature* (1966)." (qq.v.) Both the limitations of myth criticism and its positive contributions to literary criticism are discussed. Most of the essays share the common ground that "myth and poetry are expressions of the same creative process, that creating and experiencing poetry always involve the mythic faculties." There is a wide variety of subjects, from medieval romances to authors like Blake, Whitman, Baudelaire, Rilke, LeRoi Jones, and Arrabal.

Jung's influence is pervasive in many essays, and the editors, surveying the current state of myth criticism, conclude that "there has been no abatement of interest in the archetype as a governing literary structure." The important opening essay by Joseph Campbell on "The Interpretation of Symbolic Form" and John Vickery's "The Scapegoat in Literature" have been extracted. (qq.v.) The extensive bibliography, covering works published between 1966 and 1976, supplements the earlier bibliography in John Vickery's *Myth and Literature*. (q.v.)

505. McGLASHAN, Alan. "Daily Paper Pantheon: A New Fantasia of the Unconscious." *The Lancet* 31 January 1953, 238-239.
Rpt. in *Savage and Beautiful Country.* London: Chatto and Windus, 1966.
Rpt. in *Journal of American Culture* 2:2 (1979) 217-219.

In this brief article (cited by Jung in *Collected Works*, Vol. 9.I, par. 465) the London psychiatrist McGlashan was the first to point out the remarkable archetypal analogies between the early gods and heroes of many cultures and the characters in certain comic strips then appearing in the London *Daily Mirror*: the beefy, long-suffering giant Garth, beautiful but virginal Jane, the shady Captain Reilly-Ffoull, and enigmatic young Jimpy, the *puer aeternus*.

506. McGUIRE, John F. "Thomas Hardy's Use of Fertility Archetypes in Four Novels of Character and Environment." (Ph.D. 1972 University of Utah) 154 pp. *DAI* 32/12 A p.6936.

507. McGUINNESS, Arthur E. "'Bright Quincunx Newly Risen': Thomas Kinsella's Inward 'I'." *Eire-Ireland* 15:4 (1980) 106-125.
   In the later poetry of the Irish poet Thomas Kinsella the exploration of self moves from the expression of an alienated modern self-consciousness to a quest into the unconscious. A new sense of order is suggested within the dominating landscape imagery through the "encountering of male and especially female archetypes" and the image of the quincunx, symbol of a Jungian creative tension of opposites.

508. McNEAL, Nancy. "Joseph Conrad's Voice in *Heart of Darkness*: A Jungian Approach." *Journal of Evolutionary Psychology* 1:1 (1979) 1-12.
   Marlow's experience is seen as an archetypal journey, the expression of Conrad's own quest for psychic wholeness. The jungle represents the unconscious, while Kurtz as his shadow personifies a disintegrating European civilization and is a warning of the primordial evil in man.
   This somewhat repetitive analysis attaches psychological labels, but adds little to our understanding of the novel. K.S.

509. McNELLY, Willis E. "Archetypal Patterns in Science Fiction." *CEA Critic* 35:4 (1973) 15-19.
   A brief review of several works of science fiction to illustrate the usefulness of applying Jungian archetypal criticism to the genre. Frank Herbert's *Dune* (1965) and Ursula K. Le Guin's *The Left Hand of Darkness* (1969) are discussed in most detail. The former is an expression of the hero-pattern and the latter a journey in search of the self, as well as a treatment of the anima-animus opposition. K.S.

510. *MAESER, Angelika. "Finding the Mother: The Individuation of Laurence's Heroines." *Journal of Canadian Fiction* 27 (1980) 151-166.
   The central female characters of Margaret Laurence's four Canadian novels - *The Stone Angel*, *A Jest of God*, *The Fire-Dwellers*, and *The Diviners* (1964-1974) - each engage in a struggle for wholeness and freedom that brings them into "acute conflict with the existing social forms and myths" of the dominant patriarchal culture. Only by integrating "the outcast feminine principle" within themselves - the maternal source of life,

mythically embodied in the archetype of the Great Mother - do these women discover their ground of being, "their own inner spiritual and creative depth." For the heroines in the novels this means opposition to, and escape from, the restricting social codes and structures of "civilized" city life, making contact with nature and with native Indians and social outcasts, relating to their repressed "instincts of nurturance and sexuality," and initiation into love and death.

Excellent exploration of the process of individuation in the women of Laurence's "quaternity" of novels. There is penetrating analysis, in general terms, of the psychological themes, including wide-ranging views of the religious and social implications. Morag Gunn's achievement (*The Diviners*) of "a creative resolution to the problems left unresolved by the previous novels" is illuminated by brief, but trenchant discussion of the novel's dominating symbols, and of the effect of the frequent allusions to Shakespeare's *The Tempest*.

511. *MAITRA, Sitansu. *Psychological Realism and Archetypes: The Trickster in Shakespeare*. Calcutta: Bookland, 1967. 159 pp.

Dismissing Freudian interpretations of Falstaff as the Oedipal father substitute that must be killed off, and finding the Frazerian mythical theme of the ritual slaying of the old king for the rejuvenation of the land equally unsatisfactory, Maitra points out that Shakespeare presents Prince Hal from his very first soliloquy as fully conscious of his relationship with the irresponsible fat knight. Falstaff is the "carnival spirit" in Hal himself, a weakness and "intemperance" for a future King of England, of which Hal promises his father: "I can purge myself" and "shall hereafter [...] be more myself." The necessity and the pain of the final rejection of Falstaff are best understood if we see him as the shadow side of Hal's character, the trickster in him that Hal has to work off and outgrow in order to become a fully rounded personality, who reaches a higher level of psychic integration in the Jungian sense.

As a projection and reincarnation of the ancient trickster archetype Falstaff is more than an individual character. "Sir John, as symbolizing the Renaissance zest for life, enjoyed life unrestrainedly and he set to naught the order of which Henry was the symbol." Maitra discusses the paradoxical nature of the trickster, and of archetypes in general, in the wider context of the one-sidedness of conscious psychic life in every historical period, and the great artist's compensatory function in giving "creative formulation" to unassimilated contents of the collective unconscious. He suggests that in becoming "the most popular figure of entertainment," Sir John Falstaff in certain ways compensated "an imbalance of the Renaissance mind" in its extraverted urge for power and fame, embodied in Hotspur.

Maitra's book is also an attempt to show that Shakespeare was "right in violating psychological realism for the sake of achieving greater truth to life," and he finds that "profitable use" may be made of the Jungian approach to solve the paradox. This is a most intelligent and satisfying application of Jungian notions to the interpretation of Shakespeare. There is a chapter of very able exposition of Jung's archetypal theory and its relevance for literary criticism. When explaining the idea of shadow projection, Maitra provides penetrating psychological analysis of Othello's projections, of *Antony and Cleopatra* as the portrayal of the hero's infatuation with the projected anima, and of Hamlet who projects his own shadow - "the archetype of original sin in man" - onto his mother, and onto Claudius and Ophelia in his fight against the evil in himself.

Maitra ranges widely and competently through Shakespeare criticism, Elizabethan culture, poetic theory, and Freudian and Jungian psychology, while basing his discussion in pointed readings of Shakespeare's texts and characters. He often illuminates points of Jungian or Shakespearean psychology by drawing instructive comparisons with conceptions from Indian aesthetics, Hindu philosophy or Buddhist religion.

512. MALEK, James S. "Persona, Shadow, and Society: A Reading of Forster's 'The Other Boat'." *Studies in Short Fiction* 14:1 (1977) 21-27.
    The pressure working in a British army officer against accepting his feelings for a colored boy are interpreted as the destructive conflict between his persona, buttressed by his fellow officers and his straight-laced mother, and his own "uncivilized" shadow qualities, embodied in the attractively unconventional childhood friend.

513. MALIN, Irving. *William Faulkner: An Interpretation.* Stanford, Ca.: Stanford University Press, 1957. ix,99 pp.
    The myth of the authoritarian father figure and the ambivalent son is central in the work of the novelist who is "an investigator of the psychological condition of his characters." In the chapter "Faulkner and Two Psycho-analysts" Malin considers the obvious similarities (with a spiritual difference) of Faulkner's father-son relationships with Freud's Oedipal struggle between ego and superego. He posits, however, that "the desire and need for self-realization" in Faulkner's characters brings them closer to Jung's individuation process than to Freud's determinism. The hero's

archetypal quest is expressed in Faulkner's novels in images of the hunt "to discover personal order," in his symbolic handling of primitivism, animals, flowers, and the elements, his use of opposing archetypal principles, and of symbols of fulfillment that "suggest the necessity of living cyclically or fully."

Suggestive outline for a fuller Jungian interpretation of Faulkner's characters and themes.

514. MALKOFF, Karl. *Theodore Roethke: An Introduction to the Poetry*. New York: Columbia University Press, 1966. viii,245 pp.

Contains discussion of Roethke's reading of Bodkin and Jung, and his use of archetypal imagery. In the long "developmental poems" the process of individuation is "at the heart of Roethke's search" for spiritual and psychological growth.

515. MANN, Betty Tucker. "Abyssinian Fount and Egyptian Plain: A Jungian Interpretation of Symbolism in *The Prelude*." In *Studies in the Romantics*. Ed. James Hogg. Salzburg: University of Salzburg, 1978. 3-28.

Mann suggests that the mountains in Wordsworth's poem represent the self and that rocks represent the ego, while plains, valleys, the Virgin Mary and the moon stand for the archetypal anima (the soul). Rivers, the means of uniting mountains and plains, the self and soul, in a sacred marriage, are the poet's personal anima, which, "being integrated into his conscious mind, acquired suitable masculine characteristics and came to symbolize for him the highest creative powers."

A goodly archetypal muddle. K.S.

516. MANN, Jeanette W. "Toward New Archetypal Forms: *Boston Adventure*." *Studies in the Novel* 8:3 (1976) 291-303.

The heroine of Jean Stafford's novel *Boston Adventure* (1944) seeks her identity, but her sex excludes her from the conventional archetypal pattern of the hero's journey. Sonia is trapped between the female principle, her mother, and the male principle, Miss Pride, neither of which offers satisfaction: the former means identification with the Terrible Mother and the latter represents "destruction and decay." The author suggests that new "psycho-mythological patterns" should be developed "with the intention not of disproving psychological theory, but of developing critical approaches appropriate to the study of women writers."

An original contribution to the debate about the applicability of the myth of the male hero to the female psychic journey toward consciousness. K.S.

517. MANNING, Stephen. "A Psychological Interpretation of *Sir Gawain and the Green Knight.*" *Criticism* 6:2 (1964) 165-177.
Rpt. in *Critical Studies of* Sir Gawain and the Green Knight. Eds. Donald R. Howard and Christian Zacher. Notre Dame, Ind.: University of Notre Dame Press, 1968.

Starting from the poet's emphasis on Gawain's feelings of guilt and shame, Manning studies the ego's encounter with the shadow. The poem, in its parallel structure of Arthur's court and Lord Bercilak's castle, shows how Morgan le Fey as the Terrible Mother, the dark side of the collective unconscious, tests Arthur's court, symbol of chivalric consciousness. Lady Bercilak, who challenges Gawain at the castle through his individual weaknesses, is the anima in her negative aspect, and Bercilak is the shadow. In the testing Gawain yields slightly to the unconscious and comes short of the ideal both as Arthurian knight and as individual, but self-knowledge is gained.

Informed Jungian analysis that links the psychological interpretation of Gawain's shaming with the moral view of his adventures as an exemplum of man's imperfection by chivalric and religious standards.

518. MARKS, W.S. "The Psychology of Regression in D.H.Lawrence's 'The Blind Man'." *Literature and Psychology* 17:4 (1967) 177-192.

In the light of a dream that was told in a letter recording the completion of this story, it is "understood as a regression fantasy of classic outline held under a strictly conscious [...] control." In the same year (1918) Lawrence had been reading Jung's recent book *The Psychology of the Unconscious* and this may have given him suggestions for the character types and "the psychodrama which runs as an undercurrent beneath the narrative's surface." The mythical and archetypal aspects of this "family romance" are worked out. In their meetings in the dark stable the scholar Bertie, and the blind Maurice and his pregnant wife perform a ritual that contains elements of the Bride of Darkness motif in the Dis-Persephone and Eros-Psyche myths. The congruence with the Paul Morel, Clara and Baxter Dawes triangle of the earlier *Sons and Lovers* (1913) points up the father-son polarity and mother-incest theme at the centre of both "the Jung book" and a great deal of Lawrence's writings. The essential bisexuality of all three characters and the connection of this fantasy with Lawrence's own problems in his relationship with John Middleton Murry are indicated.

An able introduction to the autobiographical psycho-symbolism of Lawrence's story.

519. MARSHALL, Roderick. *William Morris and His Earthly Paradises*. Tisbury, Wiltshire: Compton Press, 1979. xvii,317 pp.

Morris' prodigious activities in "half-a-dozen arts and crafts" cohere around his constant attempt to build a heaven on earth. In this sympathetic study of his inner life as reflected in the writings, drawings and in the houses he decorated, this search for the "Earthly Paradise" emerges as the unifying theme. His poems, stories, romances and art patterns are full of mandala designs - concentric squares and circles of forest, water, garden around sacred houses - whose beauty had in Jung's sense a psychologically healing and centering function in a life not untouched by troubles and frustrations.

520. MARTIN, Marjory. "Fitzgerald's Image of Women: Anima Projections in *Tender Is the Night*." *English Studies Collections* 1:6 (1976) 1-17.

Martin argues that the women in Fitzgerald's novel are anima projections of the hero. "Because they are projections, they lack an inner reality and doom Dick Diver to disillusionment and physical disintegration." The former occurs because these women cannot live up to his ideal and the latter because he has failed to integrate the anima into his personality. K.S.

521. MARTIN, Perceval W. *Experiment in Depth: A Study of the Work of Jung, Eliot and Toynbee*. London: Routledge & Kegan Paul, 1955. 275 pp.

The main concepts of Jung's psychology and the individuation process, with ample illustrations from the author's own dreams, are set next to the poetry and plays of T.S. Eliot. Arnold Toynbee's *A Study of History* (1934-54) forms the context within which Jung's discovery of the creative symbols of the unconscious is seen as providing "the constructive technique" for an "experiment in depth." In the present-day split of science and religion, and in the face of the challenging myths of the totalitarian systems, the free world is in need of what Toynbee calls "a different spiritual dimension." Toynbee's hypothesis in his study of the rise and fall of civilizations is that "in a time of troubles" a culture may find renewal when "a creative minority," through a process of withdrawal-and-return, finds new vitality in its contact with the inner world of the psyche. At the time when Toynbee was assembling his history and Jung was exploring the depth of his own psyche and working out his archetypal theory, T.S. Eliot was personally living the experiment in depth and expressing it in poetry.

Even if the reader finds it difficult to credit Jung's technique as the panacea for a divided world, one may appreciate Martin's claims for "transforming symbols" that may re-direct man's psychic energy. The emergence of these symbols in the work of T.S. Eliot forms the core of the chapter on the process of individuation.

522. MARTINDALE, Colin. "Archetype and Reality in 'The Fall of the House of Usher'." *Poe Studies* 5:1 (1972) 9-11.

Poe's story is interpreted in terms of myth and depth psychology as Usher's unsuccesful efforts "to escape from a regressive state of consciousness, to reach a more mature [...] level of ego development." If the decaying house is taken to symbolize "a psyche in the process of degeneration," the narrator functions as a sort of "proto-psychotherapist" and the internment of Madeline may be seen as the attempt of Usher's weak ego to master its threatening feminine components. "However, Usher's personality is too weak to support such a movement towards maturation, and the tale ends with the catastrophic breakdown of his repressions and the overwhelming of the ego by the unconscious." The tale of the "Mad Trist," which the narrator tells just before the final collapse, juxtaposes the ideal mythological-psychological pattern of the dragon-slaying hero (consciousness conquering the Terrible Mother of destructive unconsciousness) with the actual fall of Usher.

The analysis shows the narrator and the "Mad Trist" tale to be integral parts of Poe's story, essential for full understanding.

523. MARTINDALE, Colin. "The Night Journey: Trends in the Content of Narratives Symbolizing Alteration of Consciousness." *Journal of Altered States of Consciousness* 4:4 (1978-79) 321-343.

Jung's psychological interpretation of the hero's mythical night journey theme as symbolizing a regressive descent into the unconscious followed by rebirth is applied to a number of texts, among which parts of the *Aeneid*, *Divine Comedy* and Conrad's *Heart of Darkness*. In this narrative pattern an initial decrease of words indicating secondary process thinking (abstract, analytic) and increase of primary process content (concrete, free-associative) is to be expected, followed by the reverse trend. The author has conducted computerized word-counts on the basis of a Regressive Imagery Dictionary of words divided into "twenty-nine categories to measure primary process content." The scores of these counts are elaborately analyzed with the help of graphs and tables, and compared with apparently much more summarily conducted counts of words rated on "good-bad" and "active-passive" scales. The result is that the psychological interpretation is found to be more "widely applicable and fruitful" than the moral and action interpretation.

The computerized statistical word-counting on the one hand proves fairly self-evident points in a self-fulfilling procedure, on the other hand leads to very questionable claims for the superiority of psychological interpretation.

524. MARTINDALE, Colin. "A Quantitative Analysis of Diachronic Patterns in Some Narratives of Poe." *Semiotica* 22:3/4 (1978) 287-308.

The same "night journey" pattern analysis through word-counting as expounded in Martindale's article in the *Journal of Altered States of Consciousness* is applied to five Poe stories: three of unsuccessful burial ("The Fall of the House of Usher," "Berenice," "Ligeia") and two of successful burial ("The Cask of Amontillado," "Eleonora").

Statistical procedure and outcome are also the same: the psychological interpretation is found to be the most relevant. The same objections hold, and the claim that this "objective quantitative method" is superior to "the subjectivity of a qualitative approach" goes unproved.

525. MARTINDALE, Colin. "Transformation and Transfusion of Vitality in the Narratives of Poe." *Semiotica* 8:1 (1973) 46-59.

Structuralist analysis of a number of Poe's tales concerning the burial of corpses and their return from death discovers with the help of elaborate diagrams their "latent semiotic" pattern and "diachronic" narrative structure as: the original union of characters followed by "repulsion, maximal separation, attraction." This symbolic "translation" parallels Poe's own theoretical explanation in *Eureka* (1848) of the universe as a binary structure governed by the mediated forces of repulsion and attraction. In the light of Poe's interest in alchemy the pattern is also related to Jung's reading of the alchemist's sequence of steps in experimentation (*solve et coagula*) as the "separating and synthesizing of psychic opposites."

The tales are squeezed into such a very general narrative pattern that various details resist the "compelling nature" claimed for these "translations."

526. MATCHIE, Thomas F. "The Mythical Flannery O'Connor: A Psycho-Mythic Study of *A Good Man is Hard to Find*." (Ph.D. 1974 University of Wisconsin, Madison) 376 pp. *DAI* 36/01 A p.277.

527. MATTHEWS, Dorothy. "The Psychological Journey of Bilbo Baggins." In *A Tolkien Compass*. Ed. Jared Lobdell. La Salle, Ill.: Open Court, 1975. 29-42.

Tolkien's children's story *The Hobbit* (1937) has similarities with folk narratives and Bilbo's perilous journey is viewed as the mythical quest for psychological maturity. In general Jungian terms, the meeting with archetypal old man Gandalf, devouring-mother figures like Gollum and Sting, and the confrontation with treasure-guarding dragon Smaug form stages in the individuation process. The unheroic ending of Bilbo's adventures makes clear that he must not be seen as an epic culture hero, but as "a symbol of a very average individual" who has achieved, however, "self-reliance and self-knowledge."

The analysis would have gained if its point of view had included Tolkien's ironical treatment of Bilbo and his adventure.

528. MATTHEWS, Honor. *The Hard Journey: The Myth of Man's Rebirth*. London: Chatto and Windus, 1968. 208 pp.

The myth of the journey through darkness in search of psychological rebirth is studied in Sophocles' *Oedipus* plays and in Dante's *Divine Comedy*. In modern literature the theme persists as the "existentialist journey" towards a self that finds its center no longer in the divine but in the development of human self-knowledge. This is illustrated from the works of Ibsen, Sartre (Sartre's play *The Flies* is contrasted with T.S. Eliot's *The Family Reunion*), Camus, Kafka, Brecht and Beckett. Jung's view of the mythic journey and the hero's dependence on anima figures is in several places touched upon.

529. MATTHEWS, Marjorie Swanks. "Issues and Answers in the Book of Job and Joban Issues and Answers in Three Twentieth Century Writers: Carl Jung, Robert Frost, and Archibald Macleish." (Ph.D. 1976 Florida State University) 153 pp. *DAI* 37/12 A p.7800.

530. *MAUD, Ralph. "Archetypal Depth Criticism and Melville". *College English* 45:7 (1983) 695-704.

James Hillman's "re-visioning" of Jungian psychology in terms of "soul-making" ("the deepening of events into experience [...] through reflective speculation, dream, image, fantasy") constitutes "a psychology of image" that assumes "a poetic basis of mind" rooted in "the processes of the imagination." Maud proposes an "archetypal depth criticism" that will apply Hillman's "imaginal" psychology to literary interpretation, and he chooses Melville as "a remarkably good case for study" because of the psychological depth of both the author and his works. Hillman sees living with depressions as a condition for psychic development and the discovering of new, significant elements of "soul." Melville's "journey through depression" is powerfully expressed in the symbolism of his enigmatic works.

Applying Hillman's notion of "staying with" the dream image and amplifying it without converting it too quickly into concept, Maud develops the analogy "between written work and dream work." This process of "re-imagining the image" and intuiting the archetype behind it is demonstrated in Maud's "ruminations" over the images of the walls in *Bartleby* (1853), of the young whale in the maternal reticule in the Armada chapter of *Moby-Dick* (1851), and of the wounded *puer* in both Ahab and in *Billy Budd*. He suggests that *Symbols of Transformation* (1924), Jung's book on the deliverance of the hero from the mother, provides the perfect text for understanding the archetypal depth of Ahab's fixation on his mother-whale, just as Hillman's exposition of the puer-senex archetype gives us a key to Billy Budd's relationship to Captain Vere, as well as to Melville's own psychic development.

This outline and suggestive demonstration of an archetypal depth criticism based on Hillman's revision of Jung exemplifies a new and promising direction in Jungian literary criticism (see also Stewart, and Zonailo).

531. *MAY, Charles E. "Myth and Mystery in Steinbeck's 'The Snake': A Jungian View." *Criticism* 15:4 (1973) 322-335.
Rpt. in *The Practice of Psychoanalytic Criticism*. Ed. Leonard Tennenhouse. Detroit: Wayne State University Press, 1976. 237-251.

Steinbeck's puzzling story about a mysterious woman who visits a zoologist's laboratory and pays him to watch a rattlesnake swallow a rat has been read in terms of the woman's abnormal psychology. Charles May demonstrates that this short story does not so much present an individualized woman as a "mythically significant" archetype. The story is about the man's problem: the rational scientist's fear of the unconscious and of woman's sexuality. Analysis of significant details shows the dreamlike atmosphere and symbolic actions in the scientist's "tight little building" by the sea. Both the snake-like woman and the serpent itself become associated with the archetype of the "*vagina dentata* of the Terrible Mother, the voracious maw, the jaws of death."

The analysis brings essential aspects of the story into a meaningful interpretive framework. Though incorporating technical psychological language the essay is written with simple clarity. The argument makes excellent use of Jung on archetypal symbolism, of generic differences between the short story form and the novel, and of Steinbeck's own tentative pronouncements on the unconscious.

532. MAY, Keith M. *Out of the Maelstrom: Psychology and the Novel in the Twentieth Century*. London: Paul Elek, 1977. xvi,135 pp.

A study of the interactions and parallel developments between literature and psychology since 1890, in which the emergence of the concept of the unconscious and the growing awareness of problems of personal identity are traced both in the works of the great novelists and in the theories of Freud and Jung. In the chapter "The Living Self" Lawrence's novels are viewed as a search for integrating the personality, independent from, but remarkably similar to Jung's ideas. Lawrence's characters struggle for a balance between conscious and unconscious driving-forces, between spirit and flesh. The dark potent male characters and the sensual uninhibited women may be seen as Lawrence's attempts to come to terms with his own shadow-attributes and feminine side. They are confronted with both male and female figures living primarily from their consciousness and will-power. A figure like Birkin in *Women in Love* (1920), whose ego-consciousness is opposed to Ursula's anima qualities and Hermione's destructive over-consciousness, tries to achieve psychic integration. The later novels, especially *The Plumed Serpent* (1926) with its religious and psychological symbolism, give us essentially "this drama of inner forces, the main characters being embodiments of the author's most vital mental processes."

A suggestive beginning for a Jungian analysis of Lawrence's novels.

533. MAYNE, Isobel. "Emily Brontë and the Magna Mater." *Journal of Analytical Psychology* 7:1 (1962) 71-81.

The Gondal poems of Emily Brontë were written while the Brontë children engaged in a process of active imagination. The symbols of the archetypal mother in these poems are related to the early deaths of Emily's mother and elder sisters. The adventures of the Magna Mater figure of the great queen who tyrannizes and destroys her lovers on the imaginary island of Gondal show how difficult it was for Emily to develop her animus. When in the succession of poems ultimately a strong animus figure appears, who with a positive woman-friend defeats the cruel queen, a balance of male and female is established. It is at this time that Emily writes her great novel and her best lyrics.

534. MAZZARO, Jerome. "Theodore Roethke and the Failures of Language." *Modern Poetry Studies* 1:2 (1970) 73-96. Rpt. in Jerome Mazzaro, *Postmodern American Poetry*. Urbana: University of Illinois Press, 1980. 59-84.

This essay traces the influence of other poets on Roethke and the development of his own poetic voice before he achieved successful "self-expressions of the wholeness of the poet." This involved the merging of his childhood memories and his adult experiences into a symbolic language, a process Mazzaro relates to pronouncements by Jung about the importance of "the myths of childhood" for inner self-discovery, and of the artist's tapping of his archetypal roots in the collective unconscious.

535. MAZZARO, Jerome. *William Carlos Williams: The Later Poems*. Ithaca: Cornell University Press, 1973.

Jung is quoted to explain some general aspects of Williams' work and the "unstated, unconscious mythic" patterns underlying much of his poetry. Among these are the mythic descent into and rescue from hell (Orpheus, Kora), the figure of the wise old man (archetype of meaning), and the association of the unicorn and the virgin as anima.

536. MEAD, Philip L. "A Consideration of Some Archetypes in Malory's *Le Morte d'Arthur*." (Ph.D. 1969 University of New Mexico) 318 pp. *DAI* 31/04 A p.1765.

537. MEHROTA, R.R. "The Little Secret: Wordsworth's Relationship with Dorothy." *Samiksa* (Calcutta) 29:2 (1975) 62-79.

Rather than as an unconscious incestuous relationship, the intense affection between Wordsworth and his sister should be seen as largely spiritual, as a case of anima/animus projection of the "soul image."

538. MELENDREZ, Patricia M. "The Archetype in Nick Joaquin's *The Woman Who Had Two Navels*." *Saint Louis Quarterly* (Baguio City) 6:2 (1968) 171-192.

This 1961 novel by the Philippine writer Joaquin is an expression of the "dualism archetype." This archetype is embodied in Connie's living in both the real world and the world of her imagination (symbolized by her two navels), by the opposition of good and evil which Connie must come to terms with, and by the good and terrible aspects of the Great Mother as represented by Concha. In her search for psychic wholeness, Connie undergoes symbolic death, and rebirth into new life. K.S.

539. MELLARD, James M. "*Catch-22: Déjà vu* and the Labyrinth of Memory." *Bucknell Review* 16:2 (1968) 29-44.

In his novel *Catch-22* (1961) Joseph Heller uses a narrative technique, which Mellard calls *déjà vu*, that involves introducing characters and situations as if they had already been encountered, and waiting until they have been mentioned several times before telling the reader the whole story behind them. Citing Campbell,

Mellard claims that one can interpret Yossarian's flight to Sweden as an affirmation of both the values of American society and those of the individual by "seeing the rejection of society as a birth *from* rather than a denial of it." Yossarian's experience is seen as a "rite of initiation" in which Milo is said to be the shadow and Nately's whore the terrible mother.

An unclear, and therefore unconvincing analysis. K.S.

540. MELLARD, James. "Myth and Archetype in *Heart of Darkness*." *Tennessee Studies in Literature* 13 (1968) 1-15.

Symbolic interpretations of Conrad's (1899) story may be subsumed under Joseph Campbell's "monomyth." Not only the tripartite structure of the hero's journey (separation, initiation, return) applies to Marlow's adventure, but also Campbell's phases, "the call to adventure, the threshold crossing with the aid of helpers, the night-sea journey or wonder journey, underworld tests and helpers, father atonement, the elixer theft, flight, and threshold struggle, resurrection, and return with the possibility of granting the elixer." Conrad's ironic use of the mythic elements finally undermines the mythic pattern, for instead of the hero's return in triumph "the story actually reveals defeat and frustration," but "the mythic structure has given the story its form."

There are critical pitfalls inherent in Mellard's search for the monomyth. What strikes this reader are the differences rather than the correspondences with the mythic blueprint. In how far is Marlow's struggle with Kurz something of an "atonement with the father-creator of the world"? Can either Kurz or Marlow be seen as a "savior or redeemer," and Kurz's papers as the boon or elixer the hero carries back for the benefit of the world? Conrad's devastating irony and fundamental pessimism wither the monomyth's optimistic essence of renewal and redemption.

541. MELLOWN, Elgin W. *Edwin Muir*. Boston: Twayne Publishers, 1979. 181 pp.

Muir's life and literary work reveal a deep debt to Jung. Shortly after settling in London in 1919 as a professional writer Muir began a Jungian analysis with Dr. Maurice Nicoll. "While it was never completed and the Muirs discounted its influence, obviously Dr. Nicoll hastened and facilitated Muir's personal development, as well as teaching him enough Freudian and Jungian theory to make him one of the foremost psychological critics of literature in the 1920s." This can be seen in Muir's essay "A Plea for Psychology in Literary Criticism" (1921). Though few poems are discussed by Mellown in specifically Jungian terms, the archetypal quality of the images and symbols in much of Muir's poetry is brought out. Taught as he was by dreams and fantasies, Muir himself recognized that the vitality of his later poetry was partly due to his awareness of the powerful sources of his imagery in the "racial unconscious."

542. MERIVALE, Patricia. "The (Auto)-Biographical Compulsions of Dunstan Ramsay." In *Studies in Robertson Davies' Deptford Trilogy*. Eds. Robert Laurence and Samuel Macey. Victoria, B.C.: University of Victoria, 1980. 57-65.

Starting from similarities between "the stone of Ramsay's secret self" and Jung's childhood secret of the stone concealed in his attic, Merivale speculates on the ways in which the narrative structure of Robertson Davies' *Deptford Trilogy* (1970-1975), seen as Dunstan Ramsay's autobiography, corresponds to that of Jung's psychobiography, *Memories, Dreams, Reflections* (1962). Further parallels are drawn between Davies' "elegiac romance" and novels by the Canadian writer Hugh MacLennan and by Thomas Mann, Davies' favorite author.

543. MERRILL, Thomas F. *The Poetry of Charles Olson: A Primer*. Newark: University of Delaware Press, 1982. 228 pp.

Deals with the influence of Jung on Olson's ideas, especially in relation to the *Maximus Poems*.

544. MESSER, Richard. "Jeffers' Inhumanism: A Vision of the Self." In *Itinerary: Criticism*. Essays on California Writers. Ed. Charles E. Cross. Bowling Green, Ohio: Bowling Green University Press, 1978. 11-19.

Messer uses the poem "The Tower beyond Tragedy" to explain Jeffers' doctrine of Inhumanism, which "contends that man's misery stems mainly from his obsessive preoccupation with his own emotions." Man must therefore learn to look outside of himself, to Nature or God. In this poem, "what Jeffers has done in bringing Orestes completely through the tragedy of consciousness to his vision of nature is present a reconciliation of the real and idealized selves." Messer quotes Jung to show that Orestes has experienced a vision of the Self and learned to reconcile himself to the "union of opposites." He suggests that Jeffers' work forces the reader to explore the unconscious and that "the primitiveness and violence of his narratives brings us face to face with our own darker side." K.S.

545. *METMAN, Eva. "Reflections on Samuel Beckett's Plays." *Journal of Analytical Psychology* 5:1 (1960) 41-63.

Beckett is placed in the line of those European thinkers and artists who, beginning with Kierkegaard and Nietzsche, have expressed "the idea of man's self-estrangement" in a modern world in which the religious instinct is starved and life lacks meaning. *Waiting for Godot* (1952) offers the uncompromising image of the individual lost in a hostile and absurd world. "Beckett leads us into a deep regression from all civilized tradition." The four pauperized, lonely figures in the play may be understood as four components of contemporary man, the conscious personality dissolved into its more primitive components. This "dismemberment" is explored in terms of Jung's psychological reading of alchemy, the *nigredo* state of decomposition equivalent to the "increasingly unbearable contrast between conscious aims and unconscious needs" in modern man's cultural situation. In the later plays there are hints that the boredom of living may be replaced by "the suffering of being." In *Endgame* (1957) Hamm consciously accepts his suffering, and Clov in the final scene sees through his telescope a small boy, "potential procreator," sitting motionless on the ground. The symbolic child is a glimpsed image of the Self, promise of psychic wholeness. Beckett's plays, however, consistently picture man in a state of hopelessness and numb despair. The curtain falls on this moment of transition, when the old ego dies and the new is about to emerge.

A penetrating psychological analysis of Beckett's plays, convincingly supported by quotations from Jung and from Beckett's own early study of Proust.

546. MILLER, Bernice Berger. "William Faulkner's Thomas Sutpen, Quentin Compson, Joe Christmas: A Study of the Hero-Archetype." (Ph.D. 1977 University of Florida) 164 pp. *DAI* 38/11 A p.6728.

547. MILLER, James E., Jr. "Uncharted Interiors: The American Romantics Revisited." *Emerson Society Quarterly* 35 (1964) 34-39.

Quoting William James, Jung and Joseph Campbell, Miller argues that the American Romantics explored the unconscious mind in their work. Emerson recognized the existence of a conscious and an unconscious. Thoreau sensed the presence of the collective unconscious. Whitman seems to be preparing his mind for "the invading floods from the unconscious." Poe's work "represents [...] an exploration of hidden labyrinths of the interior." Hawthorne probes the "suppressed and unspeakable desires" of the personal unconscious. Melville "discovered complexities of motivation in the depths of the mind." K.S.

548. MILLER, R. Baxter. "'No Cristal Stair': Unity, Archetype and Symbol in Langston Hughes's Poems on Women." *Negro American Literature Forum* 9:4 (1975) 109-114.

A psychologically superficial discussion of the archetype of the Divine Mother in a number of "matriarchal portraits" of black women in well-known poems by Langston Hughes. The author takes his cue from a quotation in which Maud Bodkin defines "the function of the female image in literature." Hughes is said to combine "myth and pragmatism," while "his most captivating themes are heroic endurance, human mortality, marital desertion, and enduring art."

549. MILLER, Tracey R. "The Boy, the Bird and the Sea: An Archetypal Reading of 'Out of the Cradle'." *Walt Whitman Review* 9:3 (1973) 93-103.

Extending previous interpretations of Walt Whitman's poem, Miller, in the manner of Maud Bodkin, unravels the archetypal meanings of the key images, and in this way attempts to account for the poem's emotional impact. The identification of love and death in the mockingbird's lament suggests the May marriage of sacred king and goddess queen in ancient fertility rites. In sharing this ritual of life, love and death, expressed in the lyric images of bird, sea and word, the boy is reconciled "with the Eternal Mother" and awakened to his destiny as a poet-singer.

550. MILLS, Ralph J., Jr. "Donald Hall's Poetry." *Iowa Review* 2 (1971) 82-123.

Rpt. in *Cry of the Human: Essays on Contemporary American Poetry*. Urbana: University of Illinois Press, 1975. 1-47.

Lengthy review article prompted by the appearance of Hall's *The Alligator Bride* (1969), occasionally Jungian in its analysis of Hall's poetry. Mills points out an "integration of the self" and the well of the soul, the anima, and shadow, the regressive journey, the goal of renewal. J.K.

551. MILLS, Ralph J., Jr. "Theodore Roethke." In *American Writers: A Collection of Literary Biographies*. Ed. Leonard Unger. New York: Charles Scribner's Sons, 1974. Vol. 3, 527-550.

Within the frame of a literary biography of Roethke, the psychological dimension is stressed. In *Open House* (1941) Roethke fastens on "the correspondence between the poet's inner life and the life of nature." The poet undertakes a journey to the inner landscape in all his poetry, like a mythic hero. Eventually, after traversing the dark world, he encounters love in a woman "frankly physical and sexual" yet "a creature of spiritual and mythological proportions [...] the *Anima*." The terms of Jung's psychology are rarely used, the "organic" growth of the poetry and the man providing the critic with terms from their own language. J.K.

552. MILLS, Ralph J., Jr. "Theodore Roethke." In *Modern American Poetry: Essays in Criticism*. Ed. Guy Owen. Deland, Fl.: Everett/Edwards, 1972. 185-204. Rpt. in *Cry of the Human: Essays in Contemporary American Poetry*. Urbana: University of Illinois Press, 1975.

Implicitly this discussion of the basic themes of Roethke's work presents a Jungian view of his journey "into the hidden corners of the psyche." A representative poem like "The Lost Son," following the trials and advance of the self, "charts a process of individuation." In another poem, "In a Dark Time," Mills finds "an archetypal pattern of death and rebirth, of descent [...] to face [...] the shadow," while "The Rose" suggests "self-fulfillment in the mandala figure." J.K.

553. MIURA, Shoko Y. "The Trickster Archetype: His Function in Contemporary Fiction (Melville, Barth, Ellison, Nabokov, Mishima)." (Ph.D. 1982 University of California, Los Angeles) 339 pp. *DAI* 43/07 A p.2345.

554. MOLLINGER, Robert N. "Hero as Poetic Image." *Psychological Perspectives* 5:1 (1974) 60-66.

The Jungian approach may clarify the use of hero images in the poetry of Wallace Stevens. The hero appears as a compensatory symbol in his poetry of the later thirties and forties to counterbalance the pessimism arising from personal problems and the international crisis. Moreover, the general loss of belief in God makes the poet propose the heroic man as a humanistic ideal and symbol of psychic wholeness. The religious traits of Stevens' heroic figures relate them to the archetypal heroes of myth and the redeeming forces of the collective unconscious.

555. MOLLINGER, Robert N. *Psychoanalysis and Literature: An Introduction*. Chicago: Nelson-Hall, 1981. xiii,178 pp.

Provides an introduction to Freudian and post-Freudian psychoanalytic theory and its application to literature by way of analyses of works by Poe, Melville, Plath, and Dom Moraes. "Although Jungian theories have not been integrated into the commonly accepted framework of psychoanalysis (at some point they may be)," the Jungian approach has "particularly attracted literary critics," and therefore one chapter is devoted to demonstrating how Jung's concept of the archetypal hero elucidates the symbolism of

Wallace Stevens' image of the hero (originally published in *Psychological Perspectives* 5:1 (1974) 60-67).

556. MONAGHAN, David. "People in Prominent Positions: A Study of the Public Figure in the Deptford Trilogy." In *Studies in Robertson Davies' Deptford Trilogy*. Eds. Robert G. Laurence and Samuel L. Macey. Victoria B.C.: University of Victoria, 1980. 45-56.

Freud and Jung, who combined "a public role with exploration of the self," provided Davies with an ideal of personal maturity, of a synthesis of persona and self, that he embodied in the characters of Dunstan Ramsay and Magnus Eisengrim. It is argued that neither character is entirely convincing because "Davies is unable to integrate all the complex elements at work in their characters."

557. MONK, Patricia. "Beating the Bush: The Mandala and National Psychic Unity in *Riders in the Chariot* and *Fifth Business*." *English Studies in Canada* 5:3 (1979) 344-354.

The collision of cultures in the colonial experiences of Canada and Australia created a state of "fragmentation, confusion, schizophrenia" which is reflected in the novels of Robertson Davies and Patrick White. The quaternary of characters who "function as archetypes of the unconscious psyche of the protagonist" in Davies' *Fifth Business* (1970) is viewed as "producing the image of wholeness which is the completed Self of the Canadian collective psyche." The chariot as encompassing mandala symbol in White's *Riders in the Chariot* (1961) suggests a reconciling of the split consciousness and presents "a vision of a healed national psyche for Australia."

As applied to these novels, the sweeping thesis is fanciful and the discovery of mandalas rather forced. (See David Tacey for a critique of Jungian "psychic wholeness" readings of Patrick White)

558. *MONK, Patricia. "Engel's Bear: A Furry Tale." *Atlantis: A Women's Studies Journal* 5:1 (1979) 29-39.

The "strange and powerful effect" of Marian Engel's novel *Bear* (1976) about a woman who befriends a tame bear is explained by of the bear's symbolic ambivalence. In the "fierce and crucial psychological drama beneath the playful, tender and erotic pastoral idyll" of the overt narrative, the shabby old bear is the animus archetype, symbolizing "specifically the development of sexual activity and initiative" in the woman. Paradoxically, though the sex of the bear is male, its gender ("a symbolic attribute") is feminine, and in this story the bear also functions in Lou's psychic development as the generic archetype of the Sybil or Earth Mother.

The encounter with animus and mother-image leads to Lou's achievement of self-awareness.
The Jungian analysis elucidates the psycho-sexual symbolism of the story.

559. MONK, Patricia. "Psychology and Myth in *The Manticore*." *Studies in Canadian Literature* 2:1 (1977) 69-81.

In *The Manticore* (1972), the middle book of Robertson Davies' Deptford Trilogy, the novelist describes in realistic detail how the over-rational protagonist David Staunton undergoes a Jungian analysis in Zurich and is subsequently taught practical lessons in feeling by his friend Liesl. This essay argues that David's resistance to analysis, certain anomalies in the analyst's treatment, and the fact that it needs the "demonic" Liesl's help to scare David into real feeling, all imply that the novelist shows "a profound ambivalence" about the value of orthodox Jungian analysis "as a formula for meeting life," and that he is ironically undercutting this description of an individuation process.
The argument too easily identifies the novelist with his fictional character. David's critical responses to his treatment and the novelist's occasional humorous touches are essential aspects of Robertson Davies' narrative strategy to prevent the novel from becoming a psychological tract (see the critique of Monk's article by W.J. Keith).

560. MONK, Patricia. "Shadow Continent: The Image of Africa in Three Canadian Writers." *Ariel* 8:4 (1977) 3-25.

Characters struggling with unacknowledged shadow elements of "fertility, sexuality, violence, unreason and death" are traced in the African stories by three Canadian novelists who lived for some time in Africa: Dave Godfrey, *The New Ancestors* (1970); Audrey Thomas, *Mrs. Blood* (1970) and *Blown Figures* (1974); Margaret Laurence, *The Tomorrow-Tamer* (1963) and *The Diviners* (1974). It is claimed that, in Jungian archetypal perspective, for these artists, and thus for the Canadian collective experience, "Africa as the Shadow of Canada has developed as a part of the quest for a Canadian identity; and that the appearance of the Shadow Continent suggests that an integration of the scattered elements of this identity is imminent." In Margaret Laurence's Manawaka novels the "transmutation of the shadow archetype from the vision of Africa into Canadian terms" becomes apparent "in the steady bringing into focus of the Tonnerre family as an integral part of the community of Manawaka rather than as its outcasts."
A farfetched argument.

561. MONK, Patricia. *The Smaller Infinity: The Jungian Self in the Novels of Robertson Davies*. Toronto: University of Toronto Press, 1982. ix,214 pp.
This interpretive study, reworking a Ph.D. thesis, explores Davies' affinity with Jung, whose ideas of human personality can "be shown to inform all his work from the earliest journalism to the latest novel and collection of talks." Jungian psychology is used "as both a structural and a thematic device" in the novels.

562. MONROE, H. Keith. "Gatsby and the Gods." *Renascence* 31:1 (1978) 51-63.
The "mythic substructure" of Fitzgerald's *The Great Gatsby* (1925) leads beyond the often noted Gatsby-Christ comparison to older archetypal levels. The novel contains "allusions to vegetation myths with their dying gods and great mother goddesses" that find a parallel in a Gnostic version of the Christ story and link Daisy with the Earth Mother and Gatsby with "an Orphic or Gnostic Christ."

563. MONTELLA, Irene H. Zagorski. "'Images of Encounter': Maud Bodkin's Journal and Her Psychology of Literary Response." (Ph.D. 1978 Syracuse University) 474 pp. *DAI* 40/01 A p.273.

564. MOON, Samuel. "The Springs of Action: A Psychological Portrait of Robert Creeley." *Boundary 2* 6:3/7:1 (1978) 247-262.
This analysis of Creeley's poems of intense personal crisis in his volume *The Whip* makes use of both Freudian and Jungian concepts. Oedipal trauma as well as anima projection and the process of individuation find expression in Creeley's search for "an expansion of consciousness and a growing independence."

565. MOORE, Hastings. "Search for Self: Poetry of Emily Dickinson." *Dickinson Studies* 35 (1979) 35-51.
A description of a university course on Emily Dickinson's poetry. The class discussions were structured by focusing on selected poems in three categories: exploration of Nature, of the personal "self", and of the comprehensive "Self" of religious experience. In particular in the third category the poems were viewed "within a conceptual framework suggested by Jung" and by Albert Gelpi's book *Emily Dickinson: The Mind of the Poet*.

566. MOORE, Thomas V. "The Hound of Heaven." *Psychoanalytical Review* 5:4 (1918) 345-363.
Although Jung's more general libido theory is invoked, it is in terms of sublimation of the Freudian "lower libido" that Francis

Thompson's poem "The Hound of Heaven" is read as straight "autobiography of the author." The poet's flight from the divine voice becomes the wandering of the libido in its attempt to escape conscience. This transposition of the traditional interpretation into general psychological terms adds little to our understanding of the poem.

567. MOORE, Virginia. *The Unicorn: William Butler Yeats' Search for Reality.* New York: Macmillan, 1952. xix,519 pp.

In this book on the development of Yeats's religious and philosophical thinking the writer uses eight pages to summarize the remarkable correspondences in typology and symbolism between the system of Yeats's *A Vision* (1925) and Jung's theories, which are summarized from *The Integration of the Personality.* The resemblances are not due to knowledge of Jung's work, as the only Jung Yeats ever read was his commentary to Wilhelm's translation of *The Secret of the Golden Flower* (1929), and that some six years after the writing of *A Vision.*

These findings have been updated in James Olney's *The Rhizome and the Flower. (q.v.)*

568. MOORMAN, Charles. "Myth and Medieval Literature: *Sir Gawain and the Green Knight.*" *Medieval Studies* 18 (1956) 158-172. Rpt. in *Myth and Literature: Contemporary Theory and Practice.* Ed. John B. Vickery. Lincoln: University of Nebraska Press, 1966. 171-186.

A plea for the judicious use of myth in literary criticism. The Gawain poem may have as a mythical core "the pattern of the archetypal journey-initiation-quest," but a simple broad identification may miss or distort much of the poet's artistic use of myth. In Moorman's view the archetypal themes present the self-contained story of the trials of Gawain as "a semi-allegorical presentation of the whole history and meaning of the Round Table." The article starts with a critique of two myth critics who find a death-rebirth pattern in the poem and one-sidedly stress the initiation of the hero (Zimmer's Jungian interpretation) or the seasonal fertility ritual (John Speirs).

569. MOREY, Frederick L. "The Four Fundamental Archetypes in Mythology, as Examplified in Emily Dickinson's Poems." *Emily Dickinson Bulletin* 24 (1973) 196-206.

Dickinson's poems exemplify Frye's archetypes of birth, life, death, and immortality, which are equated with Jung's stages of consciousness.

570. MOREY, Frederick L. "Jungian Dickinson: The Hundred Best Poems of Emily Dickinson." *Emily Dickinson Bulletin* 27 (1975) 4-72.

Bizarre classifications and discussions of Emily Dickinson's poems under eleven themes and numerous subthemes, fitted into a mythological framework perfunctorily related to Jung's four "unconscious and conscious stages of life," to individuation through the seven ages of man, to Zen, the Tao, and to much else.

571. MORF, Gustav. *The Polish Heritage of Joseph Conrad.* London: Sampson, Low, Marston, 1930. Rpt. New York: Haskell House, 1965. 248 pp.

Basing himself on "the psychology of Freud and Jung," Morf studies Conrad's works as examples of "the compensatory function of artistic creation." In particular *Nostromo* (1904) and *Lord Jim* (1900), "a psychoanalytical novel before psychoanalysis was founded," are seen as symbolical expressions of "repressed Polish reminiscences, sentiments, aspirations and resentments, lying deep under the surface of the artist's conscious mind."

The thesis of this study is worked out in greater detail in the author's later and more Jungian book *The Polish Shades and Ghosts of Joseph Conrad* (1976).

572. MORF, Gustav. *The Polish Shades and Ghosts of Joseph Conrad.* New York: Astra Books, 1976. 334 pp.

After detailed description of Conrad's Polish youth and family background, the haunting quality and psychological depth of his best novels are explained in terms of their obsessive themes of betrayal, desertion, exile, anarchy and guilt, which are seen as issuing from Conrad's own struggle with the shades of his Polish heritage. The assumed personae, first of the wandering sea-captain and later of the respectably successful English author, have on their shadow-side very strong repressed feelings of guilt about his defection from his suffering Polish fatherland and the revolutionary ideals of his father. This made Conrad in his own words into a "duplex person." In the early novel *Lord Jim* (1900), the protagonist's struggle to come to terms with his cowardly jump from the ship is in a way the cathartic confession of Conrad's own break with his Polish past.

Conrad often puts his main characters in borderline situations in which their manhood is tested in the struggle between conscious personality and unconscious challenges. In their confrontation with shadow figures the crew in "The Nigger of the Narcissus" (1897), Marlow in "Heart of Darkness" (1899), the captain in "The Secret Sharer" (1912), and the skipper in "The Shadow Line" (1917) begin their individuation. At the same time, the sequence of these novels and stories is given a straightforward psychological reading as the process of maturation in Conrad himself.

573. MORLEY, Patricia. *The Mystery of Unity: Theme and Technique in the Novels of Patrick White*. Montreal: McGill-Queen's University Press, 1972. ix,251 pp.

White's novels are viewed as expressions of a vision "essentially religious, and belonging to the tradition of Christian mysticism." The basic theme of "man's eternal quest for meaning and value" in life is seen to issue in human relationships that bring spiritual fulfillment. Parallels with Jungian anima/animus theory, the marriage of feminine and masculine principles, and mandala and quaternity symbols are noted, but not really worked out. The term archetype is loosely used.

See David Tacey's book *Patrick White: Fiction and the Unconscious* (1988) for criticism of all interpretations that read White's novels in terms of psychic self-realization.

574. MORLEY, Patricia A. *Robertson Davies*. N.p.: Gage Educational Publishing, 1977. 74 pp.

A volume on Davies' plays in the series Profiles in Canadian Drama. The chapter "The Comedy Company of the Psyche" analyzes *General Confession* (1956) as "an ingenious dramatization of Jung's analytical psychology," with its four main characters representing the persona, the anima, the shadow and the self.

575. MORRIS, Benson. *Renaissance Archetypes: The Long Shadows*. London: Coleman, 1977. xxxx,180 pp.

The introduction to this collection of essays explains at some length Jung's theory of archetypes, bracketing them with the archetypal motifs and patterns of Wheelwright and Frye, but never defining precisely what must be considered typical Renaissance archetypes. It is left to the reader to find out for himself what is archetypal in the comparison between Chaucer's and Shakespeare's treatments of the Troilus and Cressida story, in the differences between Milton's and Pope's epics, and in the discussions of the "transchanged world of Ben Jonson," and of Congreve's *Love for Love* as a "comedy of reversal."

576. MORRISON, Claudia Christopherson. "Depth Psychology in American Literary Criticism, 1900-1926." (Ph.D. 1964 University of North Carolina, Chapel Hill) 308 pp. *DAI* 26/03 A p.1652.

Became book *Freud and the Critic* (1968).

577. MORRISON, Claudia C. *Freud and the Critic: The Early Use of Depth Psychology in Literary Criticism.* Chapel Hill: University of North Carolina Press, 1968. ix,248.

Excellent survey of the reception of the new psychoanalytic ideas by English and American literary critics in the period 1900-1926. "Depth psychology" not only covers Freud and his followers, but also dissidents like Jung and Adler. In fact, this is a study of "when and how Freudian and Jungian ideas entered the discipline of literary criticism, and the original impact these ideas had on the theory of literature." There are useful summaries and critical appreciations of all books and articles published before 1927, in which Jung's psychology is applied, such as the early essays of Herbert Read and Maud Bodkin, articles by Moore and Swisher, an extensive discussion of Thorburn's Jungian book *Art and the Unconscious* (1925), and appreciative pages on Taylor's essay "Shelley as Myth-Maker" ("one of the finest early Jungian studies of poetry"). In an appendix brief summaries are given of those publications of Freud, Jung and other psychologists that are particularly relevant to the application of depth psychology to literature.

578. MORTON, Beatrice K. "An Early Stage of Fisher's Journey to the East: *Passions Spin the Plot.*" *South Dakota Review* 18:1 (1980) 43-52.

Vardis Fisher's *Passions Spin the Plot* (1934), one of a tetralogy of autobiographical novels, is analyzed "in terms of the Jungian concept of individuation, expressed metaphorically as the journey to the East." Vridar's love for Nelox is a "complete and overwhelming" example of anima projection. The protagonist/ author never fully understands his fascination for this woman who is harlot and angel at the same time. This also explains why as an archetypal anima figure her character in the novel remains "shadowy, unsubstantial."

579. MOSIG, Dirk W. "The Four Faces of the Outsider." In *Essays Lovecraftian.* Ed. Darrell Schweitzer. Baltimore: T-K Graphics, 1976. 17-34.

Four different readings are offered of H.P. Lovecraft's horror tale "The Outsider" (1921). In the psychological explanation the story is analyzed as "an allegorical voyage through the Jungian conception of the unfolding human psyche and its fundamental conflicts." Although Mosig finds his own analytical reading attractive (particularly since Lovecraft had read Jung and may have incorporated Jungian symbols in his work), he ultimately dismisses it, together with the autobiographical and anti-metaphysical interpretations, because "too many assumptions are made which cannot be empirically verified." The philosophical reading is found to fit most satisfactorily Lovecraft's pessimistic view of a purposeless and mechanistic cosmos.

580. MOSIG, Dirk W. "Toward a Greater Appreciation of H.P. Lovecraft: The Analytical Approach." *Whispers* 1:1 (1973) 22-33. Rpt. in *First World Fantasy Awards*. Ed. Gahan Wilson. Garden City, N.Y.: Doubleday, 1977. 290-301.
   The disturbing emotional impact of the stories and novels of H.P. Lovecraft is ascribed to the fact that they seem to be built around archetypal symbols and images.

581. MOSIG, Dirk W. "'The White Ship': A Psychological Odyssey." In *H.P. Lovecraft: Four Decades of Criticism*. Ed. S.T. Joshi. Athens: Ohio University Press, 1980. 186-190.
   The protagonist of Lovecraft's story sails in a white ship ("archetype of the emergence of the Self") on the ocean of the unconscious to archetypal countries symbolizing aspects of the personal and collective unconscious, "Unlike Jung, the mystic," the sceptical materialist Lovecraft makes the search for ideal selfhood in the land of hope end in disaster, when the ship is carried down a monstrous cataract into "abysmal nothingness."

582. MOTYCKA, Ronda Nephew. "Beckett's Fiction: The Hero and the Quest." (Ph.D. 1979 State University of New York, Stony Brook) 261 pp. *DAI* 40/02 A p.844.

583. MOUNTFORD, Gwen. "Modern Fairy-Tale: Tolkien's *Lord of the Rings*." *Harvest* 7 (1961) 47-68.
   This is a summary retelling of the story of Tolkien's "romantic fantasy" with commentary pointing out the archetypal character of the dangerous journey, the landscape and its inhabitants. Though "the feminine element in this story is somewhat underplayed," psychologically, all characters in the story "are present somewhere in Men," and the struggle with Evil contributes to "the unfolding of human consciouness."

584. MOUNTFORD, Gwen. "Portrait of Animus." *Harvest* 25 (1979) 60-69.
   The androgynous protagonist of Virginia Woolf's *Orlando* (1928), who transforms from immature man to fulfilled woman in the course of the story, is discussed as a portrait of the animus. In this tale "of a woman's psychic journey [...] we are witnessing the birth of a woman's soul out of the male personality of long ago." Christina Rossetti's poem "Goblin Market" is said to offer "an animus-

situation." The girl pining away after having eaten of the luscious fruits sold by the goblins is an example of "animus taking over in the field of woman's sensuality."

An analyst discourses upon the qualities of the animus, but the arguments are not very adequately supported.

585. MOUNTFORD, Gwen. "The Shakespearian Dream." *Harvest* 2 (1955) 64-73.

A *Midsummer Night's Dream* seen as Shakespeare's own "big dream," in which a royal pair of anima-led men at odds with animus-driven women and a quaternity of mixed-up human lovers are brought into harmonious union. The king of fairies employs the help of trickster spirit Puck to resolve all conflicts arising from human shadow-projections, including the quarrel with his own fairy queen. The play's main theme of transformation centers in the changeling boy, symbol of the child archetype as reconciliation between conscious and unconscious, and also symbol of the poet's imagination that conjures the numinous totality of this dream of comic conflicts and happy harmony.

An engaging psychological interpretation of a play in which "the putting on and off of the magically induced eroticism is an adroit juggling with projections, rendering them conscious and finally overcoming their tyranny."

586. *MUELLER, Carl R. "Jungian Analysis" *Drama Review* 22:3 (1978) 73-86.

In this issue of *Drama Review* recent productions of contemporary plays are analyzed from various points of view. The Jungian analysis of *Cops*, a realistic drama by Terry Curtis Fox, and of *The Shaggy Dog Animation*, a sequence of dreamlike animated cartoons by Lee Breuer, brings out the theme shared by these two plays: their diagnosis of the illness of "a male chauvinist patriarchal society" that fears and represses the feminine.

In *Cops* the shoot-out caused by three macho policemen in an all-night Chicago coffee shop, with the verbally abused, passive waitress as the first victim, is a metaphor "for the state of much of Western society." If the play is seen as a kind of "societal dream," woman and male homosexuality serve as the anima factors and the scapegoats onto which the insecure and consequently violent males project their unrecognized and repressed femininity.

The succession of monologues in *The Shaggy Dog Animation* accompanies the manifestation of the dream of John Greed, the one-sided male character who denies the feminine within himself. The image of woman in our male-dominated society is here his shaggy dog, the bitch Rose, grovelling, abused and on the chain.

This rejection of the anima and her desertion of her master land her in an asylum for the insane and leave him a depleted puppet. The essay demonstrates how well the Jungian notions of psychic compensation and masculine-feminine complementarity clarify the symbolism of literature that deals with the problem of accepting the feminine in our patriarchal world. In his introductory exposition of Jung's theories the author claims that "the most unique aspect of Jungian psychology in its application to art in general is that it views the artist as the dreamer for the social collective of his time."

587. MUKHERJEE, Asim Kumar. "The 'Blissfully Unconscious' and the 'Careful Observer': A Jungian interpretation of *Othello*." *Literary Criterion* (University of Mysore) 13:1 (1978) 1-16.

Othello's "tragedy of extreme ego-consciousness" is studied in the light of Jung's observation that an unconscious complex may be clearly visible to a "careful observer [...], although the individual himself is blissfully unaware of the fact that he is exhibiting his most secret thoughts." Othello's unacknowledged egotism underneath his self-dramatizing "aesthetic attitude" turns his primitive passions into "insane ideas" that overpower his conscious mind. These passions occasionally break through the glamour of his noble rhetoric to become "poyson" and "dangerous conceits" when manipulated by the "careful observer" Iago.

Jung's idea of the overpowering unconscious complex applies well to Othello. To compare him to Lear, however, and complain of "Othello's intention to negate" the possibilities of self-knowledge seems less relevant to the dramatic character Shakespeare created.

588. MURRAY, Gilbert. "Hamlet and Orestes." British Academy Annual Shakespeare Lecture. London: Milford, 1914.
Rpt. in *The Classical Tradition in Poetry*. London: Milford, 1927. 205-240.

Murray's 1914 lecture is probably the first extended piece of directly archetypal literary criticism. The essay is remarkable for its conclusions, apparently reached independently of any preconcieved psychological theory, yet exactly matching the views Jung had formulated a few years earlier in *Symbols of Transformation* (German 1912, English translation 1916). In his careful literary analysis of the "sagas" of Orestes in Greek tragedy and of Hamlet in Shakespeare's tragedy and its Danish source, Murray identifies their stories as variations upon the myth of the death and rebirth of the Vegetation King, "the pre-historic and world-wide ritual battle of Summer and Winter, of Life and Death," which was the focus of Frazer's great comparative study of the world's folklore, magic and religion in *The Golden Bough* (original two-volume edition 1890, greatly enlarged and revised edition 1911).

In the literary "shaping and reshaping of a primitive folk-tale" Murray finds "a great unconscious solidarity and continuity, lasting from age to age, among all the children of the poets, both the makers and the callers-forth, both the artists and the audiences." His description of the mythical material of these stories and situations as "deeply implanted in the memory of the race, stamped, as it were, upon our physical organism" comes very close to Jung's early definition of the "primordial images" or archetypes as "the psychic residua" of "countless typical experiences of our ancestors."

589. MURRAY, Glenn. "Who Killed Boy Staunton: An Astrological Witness Report." *Studies in Canadian Literature* 2:1 (1977) 117-123.

A reading of the astrological charts of two fateful moments (Boy Staunton's throwing of the snowball and his drowning in Toronto harbor) in Robertson Davies' *Fifth Business* (1970) discovers many synchronicities or "meaningful coincidences" in the correspondences of the planetary positions with the events and characters in the novel.

590. *MURRAY, Henry A. "In Nomine Diaboli." *New England Quarterly* 24 (1951) 435-452.
Rpt. in various collections of critical essays on Melville.

In the centenary year of *Moby-Dick* (1851) Murray attempts a summary of the complex psychological meanings of Melville's "wicked book." Drawing on both Freud and Jung, and freely linking his interpretation of the novel with conjectures about the author's personal development, Murray advances a number of clearly formulated hypotheses. Ahab is an embodiment of the satanic Antichrist, who captains "the culturally repressed dispositions of human nature" (the Id) in their rebellion against the repressing Superego, the White Whale, "symbol of a sounding, breaching, white-dark, unconquerable New England conscience." Melville's target in *Moby-Dick* was "the upper-middle class culture of his time," inculcated by parents and ministers. Archetypally, Ahab is the protagonist of the Great Goddess of the oriental and primitive religions, of "the feminine principle as a spiritual force," dismissed by the first Biblical myth-makers and the whole Hebraic-Christian, and more particularly American Calvinistic tradition, "which conceived of a deity in whose eyes Eros was depravity." Although, just as Ahab in the novel's allegory, Melville in his personal life had to capitulate "in the face of overwhelming odds," in his art Melville, like a true poet, was "of the Devil's party."

The interpretation pertinently unites psychoanalytical, archetypal, religious and socio-cultural viewpoints.

591. *MURRAY, Henry A., ed. "Introduction" to *Pierre: or The Ambiguities* by Herman Melville. New York: Hendricks, Farrar, Strauss, 1949. xiii-ciii. Rpt. in *Endeavors in Psychology: Selections from the Personology of Henry A. Murray.* Ed. Edwin S. Shneidman. New York: Harper and Row, 1981. 413-481.

In the ninety-page introduction to his 1949 Hendricks House edition of Melville's *Pierre* (1852) Henry Murray undertakes a full psychological explanation of the "ambiguities" of this "spiritual autobiography in the form of a novel." In "writing the hushed story" of his inner life Melville incorporated "in the vocation of art, the function of a depth psychologist, of a moral philosopher, and of a religionist." "By placing his highest value (God) in the emotional forces of the unconscious [...] Melville made astounding discoveries in uncharted regions of the mind." The novel creates archetypal situations in the Lost Paradise of Pierre's life with his mother at Saddle Meadows, the unfolding of the Oedipus complex in his relations with his mother and half-sister Isabel, the underlying force of the incest motive, and in the enchantment of Isabel, the "dark anima" figure. Pierre's mental processes are penetratingly analyzed when Murray discusses "the invasion of his mind by the impersonal unconscious," or "his microscopic dissection of his mother's character," and "his descent into himself."

The novel's artistic failure is ascribed to the moral ambivalence of the author himself, who in his emotional search for ideal Truth came to see good in every evil, and evil in every good. The pervasive moral of the book is "that there is *no* moral." Melville's exhausted spiritual state after completing *Moby-Dick* is diagnosed as "an underlying will to wreck his self." His dilemma is that all the different Truths he brings up from his unparalleled exploration of the "mythological unconscious" are "culturally unacceptable" both for himself and for his society.

Murray was a "professing psychologist" of great literary sensitivity, widely read in 18th and 19th century literature. Making general use of both Freud and Jung, and writing in a refreshingly straightforward critical style, Murray gives an unusually thorough and perceptive analysis of the psychology of Melville's wildly uneven book. "Both the best and the worst features of this novel are consequences of [...] Melville's unconditional surrender to the forces of the unconscious."

592. MURRAY, Henry A., ed. *Myth and Mythmaking*. New York: George Braziller, 1960. 381 pp.
An important collection of seventeen essays on the study of myth from a variety of viewpoints. Contributions by Clyde Kluckhohn, Mircea Eliade, Northrop Frye, and many other well-known scholars. Opening essay on "The Historical Development of Mythology" by Joseph Campbell and concluding paper on "The Possible Nature of a 'Mythology' to Come" by Henry Murray. (See also McCune)

593. MUZINA, Matej. "Reverberations of Jung's *Psychological Types* in the Novels of Aldous Huxley." *Studia Romanica et Anglica Zagrabiensia* 33-36 (1972-1973) 305-334.
Huxley's interest in human typology and in Jung's theories shows in the character types which recur in his novels. "The hedonist, the man of action, the man of thought and the emotionally immature scientist" display different combinations of Jung's psychological attitudes of introversion or extraversion, with one of the four functions dominant and the others relatively undifferentiated or degenerated.
Lengthy descriptions of Jung's types and quotations from his work are used to support the discussions of the characters in this rather long-winded article. K.S.

594. MYERS, Karen Magee. "Female Archetypes in Selected Longer Poems of Shelley." (Ph.D. 1977 Northern Illinois University) 242 pp. *DAI* 38/08 A p.4850.

595. NANCE, William. " 'The Beast in the Jungle': Two versions of Oedipus." *Studies in Short Fiction* 13:4 (1976) 433-440.
Henry James's story "The Beast in the Jungle" (1903) about a man whose inhibitions and fear of life prevent him from marrying the woman who loves him is given a Freudian interpretation in terms of the unresolved Oedipal struggle with the father. The story's mythic overtones, however, as well as the man's ineffective search for the meaning of his life in a mythic past are related to the period in which James was writing the story. Only a few years later Jung broke with Freud over "such issues as Freud's kinship with the individualism of the nineteenth century and the reductive causalism of his whole outlook." Jung's description of a man living without a myth and James's man negating his human potential "are products of the same cultural matrix."

596. NATOLI Joseph. "Archetypal and Psychological Criticism." In *(Magill's) Critical Survey of Poetry*. Vol. 8. Essays and Index. Ed. Frank N. Magill. Englewood Cliffs, N.J.: Salem Press, 1982. 3414-3428.

Intelligent, very brief critical discussions of archetypal approaches to poetry (Jung, Frye), psychoanalytic approaches (Freud, Ego Psychology, Reader-Response, Object-Relations, Lacan) and the author's own Phenomenological Psychological approach. For practical demonstration each approach is applied to the same poem, "The Sick Rose" by William Blake.

597. NATOLI, Joseph and Frederick L. Rush. *Psychocriticism: An Annotated Bibliography*. Westport, Conn.: Greenwood Press, 1984. xxiii,267 pp.

A bibliography of critical and scholarly secondary works in the period 1969-1982. Coverage is restricted "to articles and books in which a fairly recognizable school or method of psychology is applied to literature." Included is psychocriticism based on the work of Freud, Jung, Adler, Reich, Fromm, Lacan, Horney, Holland, Schafer, Laing, as well as on cognitive, behavioral, and phenomenological psychology. The introductary essay "A Survey of Psychocriticism" contains succinct characterizations of these psychological approaches to literature, among which an appreciative section on Jungian criticism.

598. NATOLI, Joseph, ed. *Psychological Perspectives on Literature: Freudian Dissidents and Non-Freudians*. A Casebook. Hamden, Conn.: Shoe String Press, 1984. Archon Book. vii,288 pp.

Natoli has performed a very useful service by gathering this collection of "unorthodox" psychological perspectives on literature, unorthodox in the sense that they go beyond the orthodox Freudian viewpoint. Twelve literary critics contributed essays on the perspectives "dear to his or her heart" in chapters of similar format (exposition of the psychological approach and application to a literary text) "in the hope of expanding the literary world's sense of orthodoxy." Natoli's informative introduction places the various approaches in relation to each other and in the fields of post-Freudian psychology and of literary criticism after the New Criticism. In roughly chronological order the following perspectives are dealt with: Jung, Adler, Reich, Fromm, Jacques Lacan, Norman Holland, Roy Schafer, Third Force psychology, Laing, phenomenological psychology, cognitive psychology, and lastly, an empirical methodology based on the natural sciences.

Unfortunately, the chapter by Clifton Snider (q.v.) on Jungian theory and its literary application is not one of the more successful essays in this collection.

599. NATOLI, Joseph Ph. "A Study of Blake's Contraries With Reference to Jung's Theory of Individuation." (Ph.D. 1973 State University of New York, Albany) 159 pp. *DAI* 34/06 A p.3351.

600. NELSON, Howard. *Robert Bly: An Introduction to the Poetry.* New York: Columbia University Press, 1984. xi,261 pp.

Indicates Bly's reading of Jung in the "chronology" of his life and discusses Jung's influence in his poetry, especially in the volume *Sleepers Joining Hands.* (q.v.)

601. NELSON, Jane A. "Form and Image in the Fiction of Henry Miller." (Ph.D. 1966 University of Michigan) 270 pp. *DAI* 28/06 A p.2256. Became book in 1970.

602. *NELSON, Jane A. *Form and Image in the Fiction of Henry Miller.* Detroit: Wayne State University Press, 1970. 229 pp.

Miller's autobiographical fiction is examined in its "larger allegorical structure" as the narrator's progress from his early struggles with a threatening, yet fertile, unconscious to greater psychological integration and extended consciousness. In the "literary confessions" of *Tropic of Cancer* (1934), *Tropic of Capricorn* (1939) and the *Rosy Crucifixion* (1949-1960) trilogy we do not meet "characters from mimetic fiction." The hags and whores in the deadly cities of New York and Paris, and the phallic male companions of the narrator's endless erotic adventures are all projections of aspects of the I. The characters, the scenes, the lush imagery, the obsessive copulations are symbolic of the hero's inner development: his confrontation with destructive Terrible Mother and negative anima figures, manifestations of the archetypal feminine that is source of castrating dominance, but also of creative power.

If the negative aspects of the self are recognized and assimilated, the symbolic return to the womb may be prologue to psychic rebirth. This reversal (or enantiodromia in Jung's term) is traced in the symbolism of the recurrent images, motifs, and mythic themes of Miller's fiction. "Jung's exhaustive analysis of the manifestations of the [archetypes of the feminine and the self] provides a reading of Miller that is thoroughly substantiated by formal analysis of passage after passage" in the fiction. Jung's theory of the essential ambivalence of the archetype is illustrated in discussions of Miller's use of the symbols of "sacred centers," such as garden, city, child, wheel, androgyny, and "rosy crucifixion." They suggest at the same time the negative and transformative aspects of the search for the self in symbols of the reconciliation of opposites that function as "organizing principles" in Miller's allegories. His main theme is summarized as the movement toward inner realization in which "the experience of chaos and descent is necessary to the integration of the self."

Whatever literary value Miller's books may have, Nelson shows very persuasively that his sex-obsessed writings embody a vividly symbolic story of man's search for psychic self-realization. She elucidates Miller's mythical symbolism with a wealth of apt quotations from Jung and Neumann. This makes her book one of those outstanding Jungian literary studies which not only clarify the author's works, but also extend our understanding of the nature and implications of Jung's notions of the archetypes and the individuation process.

603. NETHERCOT, Arthur H. "The Psychoanalyzing of Eugene O'Neill." *Modern Drama* 3:3 (1960) 242-256 and 3:4 (1961) 357-372, "Postscript" 8:2 (1965) 150-155, "P.P.S." 16:1 (1973) 35-48.

Gathering all available evidence from within the plays and from the comments by contemporary critics and from O'Neill himself, Nethercot reviews in these four articles the discussions about the vexed "question of O'Neill's knowledge of psychoanalysis and the extent and degree of its influence on him." His conclusion is that O'Neill picked up a general knowledge of Freud, Jung and some of their followers from books and from hearsay, but that "certainly much of his psychological analysis of human beings, which to many of his critics has seemed psychoanalytical, came (as he always stoutly maintained, though perhaps somewhat disproportionately to the truth) from within himself and his own experiences."

604. NEWMAN, K.D. "A Study in Psychic Motion." *Psychological Perspectives* 10:2 (1979) 176-190.

Hemingway's novella *The Old Man and the Sea* (1952) is viewed as the "psycho-odyssey" of the old fisherman sailing out to catch his great fish, which is "like something new emerging out of the unconscious." The sharks that eat the fish lashed to the boat represent the "re-devouring tendency of the psyche." The old man's fantasies about having the boy with him and his dream about the young lions are symptomatic of the luck and strength he fails to recapture and of his "rigidity in trying to hold on to an old way of life."

Jungian concepts are applied with little discrimination. The interpretation does not make clear why the story should be read as a psychological "night-sea-journey", or why the brief appearance of a woman at the end should intimate that the sea has taken vengeance on a man who has denied the feminine aspect in his life.

605. NEWMAN, Robert D. "Light, Dark, and Shadow in Joyce's *Ulysses*." (Ph.D. 1982 University of North Carolina, Chapel Hill) 233 pp. *DAI* 43/11 A p.3592.

606. NIN, Anaïs. *The Novel of the Future*. New York: Macmillan, 1968. 214 pp.
The examples in Nin's book about the process of creation are mainly drawn from her own poetic novels and diaries. She gives Jung's phrase "Proceed from the dream outward" as the key to her work and the direct inspiration of her prose poem *House of Incest* (1949).

607. NOLAN, Patrick J. "*The Emperor Jones*: A Jungian View of the Origin of Fear in the Black Race." *Eugene O'Neill Newsletter* 4:1-2 (1980) 1-9.
The symbolism of O'Neill's play reflects Jung's theory of the collective unconscious. Nolan holds that black man Jones is reduced to fear since neither in the old tribal superstitions nor in their replacement by the white man's God of Money can he find the necessary religious release for his "collective unconscious instincts."

608. NORFORD, Don P. "The Devouring Father in *Paradise Lost*." *Hebrew University Studies in Literature* 8:1 (1980) 98-126.
Jungian notions about evil as the necessary shadow-side of God are brought to bear upon the continuing debate about Milton's picture of Satan. Seeing "Satan's rebellion as comparable to the father-son relationship among Uranus, Cronus and Zeus," which is that of devouring father and castrating son, relates Satan psychologically to Prometheus and to Jung's concept of individuation. Individual consciousness can only realize itself as "disobedience and rebellion," and at the expense of the "pure unmixed life" of unconscious harmony. "Evil, then, [...] originates in God's very decision to create; that is, evil is an inevitable part of *becoming*."
Although Jung's final thoughts about the problem of evil in his *Answer to Job* would have been relevant, Norford makes good use of Jung's ideas as expressed in *Alchemical Studies*, and as elaborated by Neumann, Campbell, Werblowsky (q.v.), Kluger, and Murray Stein.

609. NORTON, Henry R. "The Archetypal Feminine in the Poetry of Percy Bysshe Shelley." (Ph.D. 1976 Syracuse University) 311 pp. *DAI* 37/11 A p.7145.

610. NORVIG, Gerda S. "Images of Wonder, Images of Truth: Blake's Illustrations to *The Pilgrim's Progress*." (Ph.D. 1979 Brandeis University) 465 pp. *DAI* 39/12 A p.7360.
"Effectively incorporates the subtle interrelationships between Blake and Jung." (Bickman, *The Unsounded Centre*, p. 156)

611. OBLER, Paul C. "Psychology and Literary Criticism: A Summary and Critique." *Literature and Psychology* 8:4 (1958) 50-59.
In this balanced and well-documented survey of the state of psychological criticism Obler, besides reviewing the landmarks of Freudian literary criticism, also writes some appreciative pages on the promise of the Jungian approach. Whereas Freudian criticism has particularly focused on psychoanalyzing the artist through his writings, "Jung supplies an excellent psychological rationale for concentrating attention on the work." Obler notes the parallels between the findings of the Cambridge school of Classical Anthropology and Jung's theory of archetypes. He summarizes Jung's two essays on literature and psychology, and his theory that great works of art embody the archetypes of the collective unconscious. And although Maud Bodkin's 1934 pioneer work had no direct follow-up, he finds evidence in the writings of Herbert Read, the early work of Northrop Frye, and in the criticism of Auden, Burke, Fiedler, Troy and Campbell that in the 1950s a re-valuation is taking place of "Jung as an independent thinker of profound significance." Discussing the pros and cons of applying Jung's concepts in literary interpretation he concludes that "by and large the possibilities Jung suggests for psychoanalytic criticism are great."

612. O'FLAHERTY, Gerald V. "In Search of the Self: The Quest for Spiritual Identity in Five Nineteenth Century Religious Novels." (Ph.D. 1973 University of Pennsylvania) 203 pp. *DAI* 34/12 A p.7717. (Campbell's Monomyth in: James A. Froude, *The Nemesis of Faith*; Charlotte M. Yonge, *The Heir of Redclyffe*; Joseph H. Shorthouse, *John Inglesant*; Walter Pater, *Marius, the Epicurean*; Mrs. Humphrey Ward, *Robert Elsmere*)

613. *OLNEY, James. "The Esoteric Flower: Yeats and Jung." In *Yeats and the Occult*. Ed. George Mills Harper. Toronto: Macmillan of Canada, 1975. 27-54.

With excellent command of the writings of both Yeats and Jung (and of the ancient philosophers), Olney traces the roots of their thinking back to common sources in the tradition of Western philosophy. The esoteric flowering of the Pre-Socratic/Platonic tradition in the works of the Gnostics, Hermetists, Neo-Platonists and alchemists issued for Jung in his interest in alchemy, for Yeats in magic and the occult. The voices and the visions they both heard and saw taught them that the ultimate reality is form, displayed in a series of perfect, formal correspondences, symbolized in the images of gyre, cyle, circle, sphere. "Yeats' poetry and his Tower, like Jung's Collected Works and his Tower," are symbolic artifacts, embodiments and images of "the Living Creature and the Collective Unconscious of the Universal Psyche" as outlined in Plato's *Timaeus*.

Admirably clear exposition of similarities in the synchronous thinking of Yeats and Jung.

614. OLNEY, James. *Metaphors of Self: The Meaning of Autobiography*. Princeton: Princeton University Press, 1972. xiii,342 pp.

For Olney a theory of metaphor ("to grasp the unknown through the known") goes with his theory of autobiography ("the emotional configuration," the metaphoric creation of "an awareness of 'self' as a life coming into being then and now"). He is interested in "the philosophy and psychology of autobiography." Fox, Darwin, Neumann, and Mill are discussed as examples of "simpler" autobiographers under the influence of one dominating faculty. The *Essays* (1580-1588) of Montaigne, Jung's *Memories, Dreams and Reflections* (1962), and Eliot's *Four Quartets* (1943) were written by authors who created complex "symbolic images" of their lives, in which "the self is meditating on its own nature." It is their art that makes these autobiographies into symbolic lives of more than individual meaning that speak to us readers as metaphors for our own selves.

In describing Jung's creation of his "personal myth," as well as in analyzing Montaigne's book "consubstantial with its author" and Eliot's poems of "significant emotion," Olney's views naturally imply the theories of Jung, "who is largely responsible for developing the concept [of selfhood] in modern psychology." *Four Quartets* is a portrait of "the whole psyche and self," and its symbols for the soul's center are "much like God and the self in Jung."

615. *OLNEY, James. *The Rhizome and the Flower: The Perennial Philosophy - Yeats and Jung*. Berkeley: University of California Press, 1980. xv,379 pp.

The "astonishing" similarities in the thinking and the systems of Yeats and Jung are traced back through the Platonic and Hermetic traditions of Western philosophy and occultism to their roots (*rhizomata*) in the writings of the four pre-Socratic philosophers. In separate chapters on Pythagoras, Heraclitus, Parmenides, and Empedocles it is argued that the basic components of Yeat's poetics and of Jung's psychology are to be found in the cosmic philosophies of these four thinkers with their implied views of human history and human psychology. Plato, "the synthesizer and systematizer of what went before him," also "takes up the question of myth and the whole man" that is at the heart of Yeats's idea of Unity of Being and Jung's concept of individuation. Among the other "ideas, images, figures, and expressions that the poet and the psychologist shared" are the collective unconscious, archetypal symbolism, synchronicity, and the reality of psychic phenomena, the belief in "the daimon," the division and unification of human types, the balancing of conflicting opposites, the cycles of history, and the schematic representations of antinomies, circles, and quaternities.

The admirably thorough expositions of the philosophies of the pre-Socratics and of Platonism are linked in much detail to the systems of Yeats and Jung as typical expressions of Western thought and the Western psyche. The parallels between Yeats and Jung issuing from their common roots in Greek philosophy are very convincingly, if at times overelaborately, worked out.

616.   *O'NEILL, Timothy R. *The Individuated Hobbit: Jung, Tolkien and the Archetypes of Middle-earth.* Boston: Houghton Mifflin, 1979. xv,200 pp.

This thoroughly Jungian interpretation of Tolkien's three-volume fantasy *The Lord of the Rings* (1954-55) first surveys personality theory and Jungian psychology. Tolkien's fairy-tale world and its Hobbits, Elves, Orcs, Wizards and Men is charted for "a relatively few repetitive themes: the transforming archetypes of Self-realization and the personifying archetypes of the various characters in the psyche. The symbols of the Self - crystal, mandala, quaternion - and the map of the human psyche provided by a complex series of star-sun-moon metaphors, the recurrent union of opposites, and a variety of battling creatures of the unconscious provide one of the most fertile sources of archetype in human expression to be found in modern literature."

With Tolkienian drawings as helpful illustrations, Middle-earth's neurosis (lopsided consciousness) is analyzed. Resolution is achieved when the Hobbit Frodo Baggins gets rid of the dangerous Ring of Absolute Power. His testing journey is the pivotal event in this dramatization of a "great collective psyche at war with itself." A healing individuation process is at work in the strife of Frodo and the wizard Gandalf against the shadow forces of the Dark Lord of Mordor. The struggle for Self-realization is the central theme of both Jung's and Tolkien's work. The striking parallels between Jung's theory of the collective unconscious and Tolkien's mythology of Middle-earth are firmly established. In view of these similarities the possibility of Tolkien being directly influenced by Jung is considered, and rejected. The source of the tremendous appeal of Tolkien's work must be that "the direct kinship [with Jung] through the universality of mythical themes remains as evidence of archetypes, their existence and their effect on human mentality."

This searching, informed, and often witty study provides a convincing archetypal reading of Tolkien's great mythical entertainment. The extensive glossary of succinctly defined key-terms adds to O'Neill's lucid exposition.

617. ORBISON, Tucker. "'This Distracted Globe': Self in *Hamlet*." In *Perspectives on Hamlet*. Eds. William G. Holzberger and Peter B. Waldeck. Lewisburg, Pa.: Bucknell University Press, 1975. 112-141.

Invoking Jung and Laing, the author argues that the ghost and Claudius are aspects of Hamlet's "divided self" and represent "the unconscious impulse to violence" in his psyche. The difficult integration of these shadow sides of his personality, and the attainment of self-knowledge in dialogue with the alter egos Fortinbras, Horatio and Laertes form an important pattern in the "internal drama" of Hamlet. Shakespeare has dramatized and resolved deep-seated anxieties and fears in his audience by creating "what may be called the myth of the civilized man, the man who is able to throw off the psychic chains that tie him to the past and to his inferior impulses."

Although this interpretation overstates a development that Shakespeare only lightly sketched in, it interestingly highlights one strain in the play's complex psychology.

618. OREOVICZ, Cheryl Z. "Edward Taylor and the Alchemy of Grace." *Seventeenth Century Studies* 34:2-3 (1976) 33-36.

Jung's writings on alchemy are adduced to argue that in his *Meditations* the poet Edward Taylor frequently employs alchemical metaphors in elaborating his religious themes.

619. OVERSTREET, Linda K. "'This Globe, Full of Figures': An Archetypal Study of Virginia Woolf's *The Waves*." (Ph.D. 1982 University of Arkansas) 358 pp. *DAI* 43/10 A p.3316.

620. PANKAKE, Jon A. "The Broken Myths of Jack London: Civilization, Nature, and the Self in the Major Works." (Ph.D. 1975 University of Minnesota) 268 pp. *DAI* 36/08 A p.5301.

621. PARKS, Kae I. "Faulkner's Women: Archetype and Metaphor." (Ph.D. 1980 University of Pennsylvania) 158 pp. *DAI* 41/03 A p.1054.

622. PARSONS, David. "H.G. Wells and the Psychology of Utopianism." *Stand* 22:1 (1980) 40-47.
    The utopianism of Wells' *A Modern Utopia* (1905) is echoed by Edith Nesbit's *The Story of the Amulet* (1906). Both stories are analyzed in Jungian terms.

623. PATTERSON, Charles I., Jr. *The Daemonic in the Poetry of John Keats*. Urbana: University of Illinois Press, 1970. xi,257 pp.
    A study of the daemonic element in Keats's poetry viewed as nonmalicious, neither good nor evil, and giving access to "a realm of superior joy beyond mortality." Patterson uses Jung's concept of the anima's ambiguity to explain Keats's pictures of fascinating amoral female figures that relate to "the dark mysterious side of his mind." They give him creative "possession of subconscious materials," though he remains aware of their engulfing, destructive power.

624. PATTERSON, Nancy-Lou. "Archetypes of the Mother in the Fantasies of George MacDonald." *Mythcon* I. Proceedings of the Mythopoeic Society. Ed. G. Goodnight. Los Angeles, 1975. 14-20.

625. PATTERSON, Nancy-Lou. "'Guardaci Ben': The Visionary Woman in C.S. Lewis' Chronicles of Narnia and *That Hideous Strength*." *Mythlore* 6:3 (1979) 6-10 and 6:4 (1979) 20-24.
    The visionary woman is vividly evoked in C.S. Lewis' fantasy novels *That Hideous Strength* (1945) and the seven books of the Narnian Chronicles (1950-1956). With particular reference to Emma Jung's *Animus and Anima* (1957) the books are explicated in terms of heroines gifted with vision who make others see the divine light in archetypal form after meetings with shadow and animus figures.

626. PATTERSON, Nancy-Lou. "Homo Monstrosus: Lloyd Alexander's Gurgi and Other Shadow Figures of Fantastic Literature." *Mythlore* 11 (1976) 24-28.
    The companion-monster Gurgi of the hero Taran in Lloyd Alexander's five-volume fantasy cycle of Prydain - *The Book of Three, The Black Cauldron, The Castle of Llyr, Taran Wanderer*, and *The High King* (1969) - is amplified with shadow figures from

myths, folktales and literary works to show that he embodies Taran's self-emasculating fear and his hunger for self-knowledge and identity.

627. PATTERSON, Robert G. "Death on the Mississippi: Mark Twain's *Huckleberry Finn.*" *Psychological Perspectives* 7:1 (1976) 9-22.

Some of the many actual and metaphorical deaths in the novel are related to the mythical theme of initiation through ritual death and rebirth. The pig-killing, the axe, the canoe and its store of grain and liquids are compared to details of the Eleusinian mysteries, such as the use of the sacred fertility vessel. Huck's waking in the canoe then becomes a spiritual rebirth during his journey to manhood. Similarly, Buck Grangerford's death at the riverford contributes to the archetypal thematic unity and universal appeal of the novel.

The article does not demonstrate sufficiently in terms of the actual narrative that the alleged ritual parallels illuminate the undoubted archetypal aspects of the novel.

628. PAUL, Sherman. *Olson's Push: Origin, Black Mountain, and Recent American Poetry.* Baton Rouge: Louisiana State University Press, 1978. xx,291 pp.

A study of Olson's work, its sources, mythology and importance for American poetry. In his chapter on *The Maximus Poems* (1953-1968), Sherman Paul considers, among many other things, the influence of Olson's reading of Jung and Neumann, especially of *Psychology and Alchemy* and *The Great Mother.*

629. PAULSEN, Lola. "The Shadow: This Thing of Darkness I Acknowledge Mine." *Harvest* 5 (1959) 3-15.

Jung's concept of the shadow is illustrated from Hans Andersen's tale "The Shadow" and Shakespeare's play *The Tempest.* Prospero owes his banishment partly to his own addiction to magic and neglect of state affairs. The events and characters on the island may be seen as symbolically acting out a psychological process in Prospero himself. Prospero's rough treatment of his alter-ego Ferdinand, and of shadow aspects in himself in Antonio, Caliban and Ariel are ways of coming to grips with "the internal traitor and the internal Caliban." Even Gonzalo's unworldly idealism and Stephano's drunkenness represent subtle forms of evading the reality of power struggle and conflict in human existence. By actively using his power and working his revenge, yet in the end forgiving all his enemies, Prospero achieves integration of his shadow.

A valuable Jungian perspective on Shakespeare's play.

630. PAYNE, Michael. "Origins and Prospects of Myth Criticism." *Journal of General Education*. 26:1 (1974) 37-44.
Connects Northrop Frye's theory of literature as myth with the views of Jung and Neumann on the psychological origin of myth, and with the mythical approach to philosophy, language and aesthetics of Cassirer and Langer. Mythical thinking being man's attempt to grasp the totality of concrete experience, myth criticism aims "to achieve a vision of the organic unity of life and thought, experience and literature."

631. PEARSON, Carol and Katherine Pope. *The Female Hero in American and British Literature*. New York: Bowker, 1981. ix,314 pp.
A study of female heroes in traditional literature along the lines of Joseph Campbell's hero quest, reinterpreted in the light of feminist analysis. The hero's journey is seen with Carl Jung "as dramatizing the human being's inner development toward maturity and psychological wholeness."

632. PEARSON, Carol. "The Shadow Knows: Jung, Pynchon, and *The Crying of Lot 49*." *Higginson Journal* 20:2 (1978). 29-45.
Pearson believes that "Pynchon is not simply using archetypal material, but is consciously employing Jungian principles as a source" for his novel *The Crying of Lot 49* (1966). "She cites his use of the concepts of synchronicity, entropy, the trickster (Pierce Inverarity, as well as the comic elements of the novel itself) and the shadow (Trystero). Oedipa must come to terms with the shadow in order to achieve psychic wholeness. Whether or not she succeeds is never made clear. K.S.

633. PEARSON, Theresa Lee. "The Sound and the Fury: An Archetypal Reading." (Ph.D. 1976 University of New Mexico) 175 pp. *DAI* 37/10 A p.6487.

634. PETERNEL, Joan. "Doubling the Hero and the Bride: Four Modern Quest Novels." (Ph.D. 1981 Indiana University) 165 pp. *DAI* 42/07 A p.3156. (Fielding, Joyce, Djuna Barnes, Virginia Woolf, Faulkner)

635. PETRIE, Neil H. "Psychic Disintegration in the Early Poetry of Tennyson." (Ph.D. 1969 Kent State University) 209 pp. *DAI* 30/10 A p.4423.

636. PETTY, Anne Cotton. "The Creative Mythology of J.R.R. Tolkien: A Study of the Mythic Impuls." (Ph.D. 1972 Florida State University) 151 pp. *DAI* 33/05 A p.2390.
Became book *One Ring to Bind Them All* (1979).

637. PETTY, Anne C. *One Ring to Bind Them All: Tolkien's Mythology.* Alabama: University of Alabama Press, 1979. ii,122 pp.

The folkloristic and mythic structures of Tolkien's trilogy *The Lord of the Rings* (1954-55) are studied with the help of Vladimir Propp's analysis of the morphological elements in fairy tales, of Lévi-Strauss's theory of binary oppositions and mediation in the deep structure of myths, and of Joseph Campbell's perspective of the "patterns of the deep structure" when the story is viewed as the mythic three-stage hero quest. The journeys of the heroes in Tolkien's "dizzyingly complex" fantasy are analyzed in terms of these linear, paradigmatic and mythical-psychological patterns as expressions of man's "mythic impulse." Each of the three heroes, initiated through his trials into "total knowledge of good and evil, pleasure and pain, active and passive, yin and yang," becomes "knower, guide and saviour": Frodo the sacrificial savior, Gandalf "the hero-saint, or world redeemer," and Aragorn the conquering warrior and ideal king.

Petty's exposition anchors abstract structuralist analysis firmly in narrative detail and frequent quotations, while she admirably achieves her overall aim of exploring the "humanistic implications" of Tolkien's work. For twentieth century man in need of mythologies Tolkien is an artist-mythmaker who brings back from his own spiritual quest the "ultimate boon" of a dramatized vision of moral and psychological order achieved amidst the chaos of experience, and so offers "stimulus to the creative imagination in each of us."

638. *PHILIPSON, Morris. *Outline of a Jungian Aesthetics.* Evanston, Ill.: Northwestern University Press, 1963. x,214 pp.

This critical inquiry into the nature of Jung's "thought relevant to aesthetics" begins by reviewing the Jungian "image of man" in which the Self rather than ego-consciousness is the center of psychic life. Then Jung's writings on symbolism are examined with their emphasis on "the living symbol" that reconciles the tensions between the conscious and the unconscious mind. Freud's theory that art has its causes in the earlier life history of the artist is contrasted with Jung's view that the psychological significance of art lies in its final causation. Just as "private" symbols may foster wholeness in the individual psyche, visionary art by animating archetypes functions in a purposive and compensatory manner directed at restoring equilibrium in a whole culture's one-sided psychic state.

Jung's concepts of the "archetypes" and the "collective unconscious" are critically questioned and compared with the theories of other scholars concerning "cultural universals." Here a trenchant critique is inserted of the "dogmatic and vitriolic attack" on Jung by the Freudian psychoanalyst Edward Glover in his book *Freud or Jung?* (1957). Citing a number of early Jungian critical studies, mostly literary, Philipson weighs Freudian "reductive art criticism" against the possibilities offered by applying analytical psychology to art. If the function of criticism is to further new knowledge of "the progressive re-organization of psychic life" in art, the value assigned by Jungian psychology to intuition offers "the critics justification for a truer, fuller, more accurate and adequate interpretation of symbolic works."

This lucid and systematical study provides a useful perspective of both Jungian and Freudian aesthetics.

639. PHILLIPS, Robert. *The Confessional Poets.* Carbondale: Southern Illinois University Press, 1973. xvi,173 pp.

In this crisp introduction to the work of the "confessional" poets Lowell, Snodgrass, Sexton, Berryman, Roethke, and Plath the insights of Freud and Jung are matter-of-factly used to explain poems that often express mental illnesses and serve as "self-therapy." In the case of Sylvia Plath, for instance, her father complex and unconscious incest feelings are analyzed from both Freudian and Jungian viewpoints.

640. PHILLIPS, Robert. *Denton Welch.* New York: Twayne, 1974. 189 pp.

Some of the novels by Denton Welch "warrant a Jungian perspective," in particular the mythic implications of *Maiden Voyage* (1943) with its "symbolic conflict of Eastern versus Western cultures."

641. PHILLIPS, Robert S. *William Goyen.* Boston: Twayne, 1979. 157 pp.

The method of this critical introduction to Goyen's fiction "has been a close textual reading and, wherever applicable, a Jungian mythic perspective." In a few places it is pointed out that the stories often record a struggle for psychic growth, while an archetypal child or a vision of light may function as a symbol of wholeness.

642. PICKERING, Jean. "Marxism and Madness: The Two Faces of Doris Lessing's Myth." *Modern Fiction Studies* 26:1 (1980) 17-30.

Pickering examines the connections between Lessing's "politics of the left" and "politics of madness" by tracing the process of individuation undergone by Martha Quest in the *Children of Violence* series (1952-1969). She argues that both of these themes "have their roots in a vision of Jerusalem, the archetypal city," a symbol which appears repeatedly in Lessing's work. At the individual level, this city represents psychic wholeness and an acceptance of the shadow, goals toward which many of her protagonists struggle. K.S.

643. PIEHLER, Paul. *The Visionary Landscape: A Study in Medieval Allegory*. London: Edward Arnold, 1971. 170 pp.

This lucid and methodical study of medieval allegory from Boethius to Dante and the *Pearl* poet has two main aims: to trace its central imagery and intellectual structure back to their sources in ancient myth and classical culture, and to interpret the allegorical visions "as a profound and far-reaching exploration of the human psyche, sustained and developed for over a thousand years." It makes use of Jung in defining the terms myth and symbol, and in the first of its nine propositions: "Medieval allegory offers its readers participation in a process of psychic redemption closely resembling, though wider in scope than, modern psychotherapy. This process typically includes the phases of crisis, confession, comprehension and transformation." In the discussion of the symbol of the maiden in the English *Pearl* poem, Jung's essay on the child-archetype is used to argue that in harmonizing the claims of reason and the non-rational the pearl-maiden (together with Dante's Beatrice) represents "something of a peak in the development of medieval allegory as a genre." In the constant transformations of the maiden as pearl, flower, jewel and deceased daughter, the dream vision fuses allegory and Biblical image in a process of healing and maturing for the dreamer that has striking parallels with Jung's description of individuation.

644. POLAND, Peter D. "'The Christ that Is to Be': A Study of Tennyson's Religious Thought." (Ph.D. 1979 State University of New York, Stony Brook) 234 pp. *DAI* 40/04 A p.2078.

645. POPS, Martin L. *The Melville Archetype*. Kent, Ohio: Kent State University Press, 1970. xi,287 pp.

Melville's art and life are examined as "a quest for the Sacred, for the realization of soul." Approaching Melville as a religious artist, Pops elaborates ideas of James Baird, Mircea Eliade, Jung and Neumann. The "cultural failure" (Baird) of Protestantism's impoverishment of sacramental symbolism leads Melville on the romantic quest for the Sacred Center beyond the barriers of Secular Reality (Eliade). For most of Melville's quester-protagonists this means the total commitment to a search for the Ideal in nature or primitive life, from Tommo's adoption of Polynesian primitivism in *Typee* (1846) to Ahab's monomaniacal pursuit of the white whale in *Moby-Dick* (1851). In this mythological quest the primitively sacred and the sexual are intimately related (Eliade). Pops, therefore, views Melville's questers under two aspects: one, the "personal or ontogenetic," which allows their "quest for sexual gratification" to be analyzed through the sexual symbolism of Freud's dream interpretation; the other, the "transpersonal or phylogenetic," which links the "psychological and spiritual evolution" of all questers to the "thirst for self-realization" of the one archetypal Quester.

The stages of the transpersonal quester's individuation process are traced from captivity by the unconscious Great Mother in the early novels and stories to confrontation with the personal shadow (Ahab's Fedallah, and Pip), and assimilation of the shadow in Ishmael's relation with Queequeg, to Pierre's meeting with the anima in Isabel. The emergence of Self-symbols ranges from Ishmael's vision of the Sacred Center in the whale armada to the Dansker as wise old man in *Billy Budd* (1924). "Baby" Billy is the hermaphroditic Divine Child, who in his Christ-like character symbolizes the union of opposites in the individuated psyche that is Melville's intimation of "the paradox of divine reality."

Pops's archetypal thesis provides a valuable perspective of the all-pervasive symbolism in Melville's fiction. His scheme, however, is too neat and the theory is ridden too hard, while the argumentation suffers from the tendency to flourish large abstractions. Archetypal symbols are too easily ascribed, just as the Freudian game of reading sexual meanings everywhere is played too insistently by Pops. Sexual metaphors are lurking in every harpoon on board the *Pequod* and in every use of the word "erect." Ahab's pursuit of Moby-Dick is the attempt to slay the phallic Father as well as the wish to commit incest with the Great Mother. The wedding of Freud and Jung produces some glib off-spring. "It is Melville's great triumph that as he made the symbolic elements of the whale coextensive with one another - the realm of God and Sexual Energy one - so he made Ahab's quests seamlessly coincide and both depend on the hurling of one harpoon in an ultimately definitive act."

646. POPS, Martin L. "The Winding Quest: A Study of Herman Melville." (Ph.D. 1965 Columbia University) 402 pp. *DAI* 28/10 A p.4141. Became book *The Melville Archetype* (1970).

647. PORAT, Zephyra. "The Madonna and the Cat: Transcendental Idealism and Tragic Realism in Henry James's *The Portrait of a Lady*." *Hebrew University Studies in Literature* 5:1 (1977) 67-101.
A penetrating analysis of Isabel Archer's psychology in terms of Emerson's idealism and Jungian views of the masculine and

feminine within the individual psyche. Seeing Isabel's inner conflict as the tension between rigid persona and repressed anima involves a significant revision of Jung's theory, for, "unlike Jung, James believes women have anima-problems too, when they repress their femininity and overdevelop their masculine qualities."

648. PORESKY, Louise A. *The Elusive Self: Psyche and Spirit in Virginia Woolf's Novels*. Newark: University of Delaware Press, 1981. 283 pp.

Deals with each of the nine novels seen as a part of a search for spiritual wholeness. Makes extensive use of Jung and Jungians, such as Neumann, Eliade, and June Singer on androgyny.

649. PORTER, Lawrence M. "Do Literary Dreams Have a 'Latent Content'?: A Jungian View." *Journal of Altered States of Consciousness* 4:1 (1978-79) 37-42.

Although using Freudian dream terminology, Porter advocates Jungian interpretation of literary dreams, because this may disclose latent meaning in a literary text in a non-reductive way, not tied to universal dream symbols. "The Jungian critic will tend to focus on the undetermined elements, seeing them as the artist's intentional solutions to the problem of implying, rather than stating, his characters' drive towards self-realization."

650. PORTER, Roger J. "Edwin Muir and Autobiography: Archetype of a Redemptive Memory." *South Atlantic Quarterly* 77:4 (1978) 504-523.

This sensitive examination of Muir's autobiographical writings, in particular of the earlier *The Story and The Fable* (1940), brings out the special character of his "reflective literary art" by comparing it with Jung's similar effort in autobiography. Each writer attempted to discover the fable, the personal myth of his life "as a way of retracing the roots and reestablishing bonds with the primal sources of his own early experience."

651. PRATT, Annis. "Archetypal Approaches to the New Feminist Criticism." *Bucknell Review* 21:1 (1973) 3-14.

After a critical review of Jung's reading in *Symbols of Transformation* of Miss Miller's fantasies, which in 1912 he used to outline his archetypal theory of the myth of the hero, Pratt proposes a revision of Jung's onesidedly male anima/animus theory. The Miller fantasies are reinterpreted as symbolizing her feminine quest for the fully integrated self through a positively experienced erotic hero figure. If Jung's animus theory is refocused in this way, the Jungian archetypal mode need not be rejected as invalid for women's literature, as some feminist critics have urged, but may be "helpful in the elucidation of the psycho-mythical development of the female hero." To illustrate this thesis the quest of the female hero is briefly traced in Ann Radcliffe's *The Mysteries of Udolpho* (1794), Virginia Woolf's *To the Lighthouse* (1927), and Doris Lessing's Martha Quest novels (1952-1969).

652. PRATT, Annis. *Archetypal Patterns in Women's Fiction.* With Barbara White, Andrea Loewenstein, and Mary Wyer. Bloomington: Indiana University Press, 1981. x,211 pp.

Annis Pratt's examination of more than three hundred novels by English and American women writers of the past three centuries has made her see women's fiction as a distinctive field of narrative and symbolic structures "reflecting feminine archetypes that are signals of a repressed tradition in conflict with patriarchal culture." The recurring themes of "the green-world lover, the rape trauma, enclosure, and rebirth" find their counterparts in three sets of interrelated systems of feminine archetypes: "the Demeter/Kore and Ishtar/Tammuz rebirth myths, Arthurian grail narratives, and the Craft of the Wise (or witchcraft)." These manifest themselves in four categories: novels of development, novels of domestic enclosure (marriage), novels of Eros, and novels of rebirth and transformation.

A pioneering study and admirable example of imaginative and insightful archetypal criticism.

653. PRATT, Annis. "Aunt Jennifer's Tigers: Notes toward a Preliterary History of Women's Archetypes." *Feminist Studies* 4:1 (1978) 163-194.

In this extensively researched essay four traditional needlework patterns are interestingly linked to their archetypal expression in images of modern feminist poets. These figures, worked into medieval tapestries - Medusa's mask, Philomela's nightingale, the Lady and the Unicorn, and genitalic flower patterns - are placed in their mythical and historical contexts and found to be important themes in poems by Louise Bogan, May Sarton, Denise Levertov, among others.

654. PRATT, Annis. *Dylan Thomas' Early Prose: A Study in Creative Mythology.* Pittsburgh: University of Pittsburgh Press, 1970. xiii,226 pp.

In her excellent study of the religious, literary, psychological and personal sources of the "creative mythology" of Thomas' early prose tales, Pratt considers the relevance of "the archetypal categories explored by Jung and Frye," when used as "the flexible critical tools for which they are useful." The way in which "feminine characters spring from within the heroes" of the tales and become anima figures is linked with Thomas' reading of the Paris magazine *transition* and its boosting of "psycho-myth" as evinced by its publication of Jung's essay "Psychology and Poetry" in the 1930 issue. The narrative patterns of Thomas' tales are informed by a vision that gives familiar and personal imagery "the characteristics of a myth or a dream."

655. PRATT, Annis. "The New Feminist Criticisms: Exploring the History of the New Space." In *Beyond Intellectual Sexism: A New Woman, a New Reality.* Ed. Joan I. Roberts. New York: David McKay, 1976. 175-195.

A report on the author's findings in her research into the British and American women novelists of the last two hundred years, largely neglected by literary critics so far, and, if dealt with, viewed from stereotyped male points of view. (see Annis Pratt *Archetypal Patterns in Women's Fiction*, 1981). For a feminist perspective Pratt found traditional textual, contextual and archetypal criticism useful, provided the existence of typical female patterns is recognized. By way of example she discusses the need for a revised Jungian archetypal "myth of the heroine" with positive anima encounter.

656. *PRATT, Annis. "Sexual Imagery in *To the Lighthouse*: A New Feminist Approach." *Modern Fiction Studies* 18:3 (1972) 417-432.

This analysis of the psychosexual symbolism in a key passage of Virginia Woolf's novel *To the Lighthouse* (1927) attempts a more balanced interpretation of the character of Mrs. Ramsay than the readings of earlier critics who range between the extremes of viewing her as a typical Victorian mothering female or as the victim of paternal abuse. The strongly erotic imagery of "erection and life-giving powers," used to describe Mrs. Ramsay's feelings, reverses the conventional male-female patterns. It suggests that in response to her husband's "infantile asexuality" she can only achieve psychic integration through androgynous self-experience.

In Jungian light, Mrs. Ramsay's solitary ecstasy is seen as the fusion of her phallic animus qualities with her encircling femininity (both symbolized in the figure of the lighthouse), or, as Virginia Woolf bluntly puts it, "a woman must have intercourse with the man in her."

Pratt's new feminist approach to the female hero in women's fiction offers an original and very pertinent perspective on the characters and the symbolism in Virginia Woolf's novels. This essay was worked into the chapter "Novels of Rebirth and Transformation" in Pratt's book *Archetypal Patterns in Women's Fiction* (1981).

657. PREDMORE, Richard L., Jr. "The Defeated: The Archetypal Hero in Hawthorne's Tales." (Ph.D. 1974 University of Florida) 191 pp. *DAI* 36/03 A p.1508.

658. PREDMORE, Richard. "'Young Goodman Brown': Night Journey into the Forest." *Journal of Analytical Psychology* 22:3 (1977) 250-257.
   The hero of Hawthorne's short story undergoes a descent into the unconscious during which he encounters the Terrible Mother (witches), his anima (his wife, Faith) and the shadow (Satan). "The task for Brown is to 'incorporate' the shadow into the conscious side of the psyche; ultimately, however, Brown's Puritan consciousness is too weak to recognize its own opposite." As a result, he becomes a desperate and suspicious man, seeing in others the evil he cannot accept in himself. K.S.

659. PRESTON, Kerrison. *Blake and Rossetti*. London: Alexander Moring, 1944. 111 pp.
   In what David Erdman (*Romantic Movement Bibliography 1936-1970*) calls "a rambling, inconsequential essay," Preston is the first to note that "*Four Zoas* is a book about the four functions of the mind [...] almost identical with Dr. Jung's four basic functions of psychic activity."

660. PRIESTLEY, John B. *Literature and Western Man*. London: Heinemann, 1960. xi,512 pp.
   In Priestley's bold and very readable panorama of the literature and thinking of Western Man since the Renaissance, he often presents his views in Jungian terms and freely acknowledges his debt to Jung, "one of the great liberating thinkers of the century." In his conclusion he says, for instance: "The greatest writers [of the Renaissance] are nicely balanced between their conscious and their unconscious life, [...] neither extroverted nor obviously introverted." His ideal for the writer of genius in our own "schizophrenic" age is that of one who "cannot help becoming, through his own relation to his unconscious, [...] an instrument of whatever there is in the general deep unconscious, the inner world of the whole age, that is trying to compensate for some failure in consciousness, to restore a balance destroyed by one-sidedness."

661. PRINGLE, Mary Beth. "From Richmond to a Home Where the Whooping Cranes Roam: Sissy Hankshaw's Quest in *Even Cowgirls Get the Blues*." *Journal of Altered States of Consciousness* 4:3 (1978-79) 237-252.
   Author's abstract: "Tom Robbins' *Even Cowgirls Get the Blues* (1976) may be the first American novel for adults dominated by the

literal, initiatory quest of a female. Sissy Hankshaw's journey corresponds closely to the male quest monomyth described by Joseph Campbell in *The Hero With a Thousand Faces*. Although Campbell insists that at the end of their journey female questers must be "rescued from without," Sissy successfully completes the quest by herself. Despite Erich Neumann's claim (in *Amor and Psyche; The Psychic Development of the Feminine*) that women quest only for love, Sissy Hankshaw seeks to understand the complexities and contradictions of the universe. She also decides how she wants to live. Sissy's quest is represented in distinctly American terms. Sissy is depicted as a twentieth-century cowgirl (a hitchhiker of cars instead of horses). Her quest takes her to the four corners of the nation and, in particular, to the American West. Ultimately, Sissy's quest and initiation represent not what American women are, but what we can become."

The mythic dimension of this humorous quest novel is brought out with gusto.

662. RADFORD, F.L. "The Apprentice Sorcerer: Davies' Salterton Trilogy." In *Studies in Robertson Davies' Deptford Trilogy*. Eds. Robert G. Laurence and Samuel L. Macey. Victoria B.C.: University of Victoria, 1980. 13-21.

The three novels of Davies' Salterton trilogy *Tempest-Tost* (1951), *Leaven of Malice* (1954), *A Mixture of Frailties* (1958) are viewed as "preliminary exercises in the development of certain themes and motifs that are brought to mature expression" in *Fifth Business* (1970), the first novel of the Deptford trilogy. Among the themes prefigured in the earlier trilogy are some distinctly Jungian ones: the "revenge of the unlived life," the psychological after-effects of negative possessive mothers or positively comforting mothers, and the characters' search for self-realization. The most developed Jungian character pattern is found in Monica Gall's progress towards individuation in *A Mixture of Frailties*, but on the whole the characters of the earlier novels still "tend to be one-dimensional figures carrying out individual functions of plot."

A concise, but penetrating scrutiny of Robertson Davies' first three novels.

663. *RADFORD, F.L. "The Great Mother and the Boy: Jung, Davies, and *Fifth Business*." In *Studies in Robertson Davies' Deptford Trilogy*. Eds. Robert G. Laurence and Samuel L. Macey. Victoria, B.C.: University of Victoria, 1980. 66-81.

Acknowledging the influence that Robertson Davies' extensive reading of Jung had on the conception of his Deptford trilogy - *Fifth Business* (1970), *The Manticore* (1972), *World of Wonders*

(1975) - Radford shows how its "Jungian pattern is centred on the theme of individuation typified in the myth of the Hero and the Mother." Detailed examination of the relations of the three main characters with the women in their lives reveals the ambivalent protective and demonic influence of both the natural mothers and other female figures. Fulfilling the men's emotional needs, the women carry the male's personal projections of the dual life-giving and destructive aspects of the archetypal Great Mother. Of the three men, it is only Dunstan Ramsay who achieves a considerable measure of psychic wholeness. "In his true role as Jung's hero of the psyche, his journey begins with flight from the demon-mother and ends with the 'healing tenderness' of the embrace of the demon-mistress."

Astute psychological analysis of the characters in Davies' novels and subtle application of Jungian concepts.

664. *RADFORD, F.L. "Heinrich Heine, the Virgin, and the Hummingbird: *Fifth Business* - A Novel and Its Subconscious." *English Studies in Canada* 4:1 (1978) 95-110.

The intricate use of the Faust legend in Robertson Davies' first (and in Radford's opinion much the best) part of the *Deptford Trilogy* (1970-1975) is surprisingly traced to playfully concealed poems by Heinrich Heine. The central character, narrator Dunstan Ramsay, develops along lines that run back to the once-mentioned "old fantastical duke of dark corners, C.G. Jung." The complex argument reveals "a careful structure of mythic analogues" underneath the seemingly "limpid surface" of the novel. Ramsay, as an inverted Faust, "draws together many dualities of the novel," the oppositions of angelic and demonic forces embodied in the men and women he meets.

His life journey is meaningfully interpreted in terms of Joseph Campbell's pattern of the hero-myth as "the desired and feared adventure of the discovery of the self." Unlike the other principal male characters, business tycoon Boy Staunton and magician Paul Dempster, Ramsay "resolves the need for a developed Anima," and "finally appears as the synthesizing psyche." Main agent of his individuation is Liselotte Vitzipützli, whose name is traced back to the Aztec God of War, Huitzilopochtli, through the Heine poems (one of which is set in Mexico) so that she becomes a "link between the mythologies of the old and the new worlds." The mythical allusions of the novel relate the three male characters to the three Great Gods of the Aztecs. There is , moreover, a pattern of Arthurian legend, in which Ramsay figures as the bard Taliesin and Liesl as Caridwen, Welsh goddess of nature and poetry. The mythical gods and demons function as aspects of the human psyche itself and suggest the odyssey of psychological growth within the individual "hero," successfully achieved by Ramsay.

An excellent essay and revealing interpretation, thoroughly researched and brilliantly argued.

665. *RADFORD, F.L. and R.R. Wilson. "Some Phases of the Jungian Moon: Jung's Influence on Modern Literature." *English Studies in Canada* 8:3 (1982) 311-332.

This excellent essay considers the "wide and diverse" influence of Jung on modern literature in general and on the characterization of three novelists in particular. Building on a number of earlier Jungian studies of D.H. Lawrence, Patrick White, and Robertson Davies, Radford and Wilson show how the acquaintance of these authors with the theories of Jung lends archetypal significance and psychological depth to the characters in Lawrence's *Women in Love* (1920) and in White's novels, and how it informs the patterning of the novels of Robertson Davies, who is in a direct line of descent from the Jung-influenced German authors Hermann Hesse and Thomas Mann. There is also very sensible discussion of the limitations and possibilities inherent in the application of Jungian psychological theory to the interpretation of literary texts.

666. RAINE, Kathleen. *Blake and the New Age*. London: Allen and Unwin, 1979. 179 pp.

A collection of essays and lectures on the theme that Blake's thought has an immediate bearing on social changes taking place at the present time. Though writing at the beginning of our age of materialism, Blake was the prophet of a New Age to come in which spirit (or mind, imagination) will challenge the primacy of matter. Now that the twentieth century has progressed into the Age of Aquarius, the reversal Blake was foreseeing becomes manifest in the growing emphasis on facts of the mind and matters of the spirit.

In this stimulating introduction to Blake's thinking, written for the common reader, the correspondences between Blake's system and many of Jung's fundamental notions are taken for granted.

667. RAINE, Kathleen. "Blake's Job and Jung's Job." *Harvest* 27 (1981) 14-37.
Rpt. in *The Human Face of God: William Blake and the Book of Job*. London: Thames and Hudson, 1982. 320 pp., 130 ill.
Comparative study of Blake's and Jung's interpretations of Job.

668. RAINE, Kathleen. "The Inner Journey of the Poet." *Harvest* 22 (1976) 61-77.

Rpt. in *In the Wake of Jung: A Selection from Harvest.* Ed. Molly Tuby. London: Harvest, 1983.

In a lecture given for a group of analytical psychologists Kathleen Raine discusses her debt to Jung. Though she does not consider herself a Jungian she has read "most of Jung's published writings with pleasure and profit." The poet's inner journey of self-discovery is a confrontation with symbolic figures representing the psyche's archetypes. This is demonstrated from Dante's encounter with wise old man, shadow and anima in the *Divina Commedia,* and from a discussion of Plato's cosmic memory or universal mind, which has been known by many names: Christian Logos, Indian Self, and Jungian collective unconscious. The cosmic order of the omniscient timeless mind that upholds the world speaks to the poet through his muse or daimon, and through his Platonic recollections of this "other" mind. The terms of modern psychology are misleading, for the inspired poet is awakened from the unconscious "sleep" of normal life to the consciousness of this greater knowledge. References to Blake, a poem by Raine herself and an analysis of Yeats's "Sailing to Byzantium" are used to illustrate this.

669. RAINE, Kathleen. "Yeats, the Tarot and the Golden Dawn." *Sewanee Review* 77:3 (1969) 112-148.

In this study of Yeats's use of the symbolism of magic, acquired through his association with the Hermetic Society of the Golden Dawn, Kathleen Raine points several times in passing to parallels with Jung's theory of the archetypes and the collective unconscious, which is viewed as springing from the same "perennial philosophy" of the Western esoteric tradition.

670. *RAPER, Julius R. "Invisible Things: The Short Stories of Ellen Glasgow." *Southern Literary Journal* 9:2 (1977) 66-90.

Raper's analysis of the short stories Ellen Glasgow wrote between 1916 and 1924 shows how she consciously uses the new psychological theories, especially those of Jung. The main themes of the stories, "the projection of the masks of the self and the spontaneity of compensatory phantasies are both central" to Jungian psychology. In the earliest of these stories, "The Professional Instinct," the protagonist is even conceived of as an "analytical psychologist," and Jung's anima theory, "according to which men project the unacknowledged feminine side of their personality [...] upon women [...] explains the dynamics of the story." Glasgow's stories "provide a record of the ways one well-established American novelist came to terms with the psychological knowledge that

began, after 1910 or so, to be more and more the central concern of fiction."
Interesting discussion of the psychological aspects of these stories, written during a low period in Glasgow's creative career, and of their importance, as "a series of experiments in characterizations," for the psychological insight that distinguishes her later novels. K.S.

671. *RAPER, Julius R. "Running Contrary Ways: Saul Bellow's *Seize the Day.*" *Southern Humanities Review* 10:2 (1979) 157-168.
The downhill course of Tommy Wilhelm's day is seen in Jungian perspective as leading to emotional catharsis and to enantiodromia, a running contrary ways into the opposite psychological attitude. In the final scene Tommy's crying bout at the sight of a dead stranger takes him "toward the consummation of his heart's ultimate need" and this clarifies the role of confidence-man Tamkin. Ironically, the extraverted Tamkin, who fleeces him of his last money, speaks for the repressed sensitive side of introverted Tommy, who all his life has tried to act the part of the hard-boiled businessman imposed upon him by his father. This is Tamkin's "compensatory" psychological attraction. Bellow has studded the novel with mythical fragments that imply Tommy's gradual immersion in the collective unconscious and the breakthrough to his "real soul." It is proposed that the novel's theme applies to American society as a whole and that "the influence of psychoanalysis, especially the Jungian school, appears central" in Bellow's long-standing preoccupation with the hidden self.
Perceptive analysis of the archetypal aspects of Bellow's subtle psychological novel. One gladly overlooks a slight tendency sometimes to carry amplification too far (e.g. Tommy as Tammuz).

672. READ, Herbert. "Charlotte and Emily Brontë." In *Reason and Romanticism.* London: Faber and Gwyer, 1926. 159-185. Rpt. in *Collected Essays in Literary Criticism.* London: Faber and Faber, 1938. 280-298.
In an essay centering on the relation between art and neurosis, the early writings of the Brontë sisters are traced to "the one cause: the early rupture of the maternal bond of affection and protection, the intolerance of a stern, impassive father, the formation of inferiority complexes in the children, and the consequent compensations by phantasy." But "art is a triumph over neurosis," and in his discussion of the novels Read emphasizes Charlotte's imaginative transformation of her experiences and the depth of her "psychological observation and analysis." If "emotion

in subjection" (Charlotte's phrase) is the characteristic quality of their art, Jane Austen may be seen as "antitype" to the Brontës. Rather than by the outworn contrast between the classical and romantic temperaments, the difference between Austen and the Brontës might be defined, according to Read, by Jung's distinction between extraverted and introverted characters.

673. READ, Herbert. "The Nature of Criticism." In *Collected Essays in Literary Criticism*. London: Faber and Faber, 1938. 124-146. American edition entitled *The Nature of Literature*. New York: Horizon Press, 1956.

In the introduction to this collection of his essays Read declares his interest in "a psychological type of literary criticism." The essay on "The Nature of Criticism" discusses in cautious generalizations how Freud and Adler help to explain the process of poetic creation in its individual aspect, while Jung's theories of psychological types and collective ideas relate the poetic imagination to the "root-images of the community."

674. READ, Herbert. "The Poet and His Muse." In *Eranos-Jahrbuch 1962*. Vol. 31. Ed. Adolf Portmann. Zurich: Rhein-Verlag, 1963. 217-248.

In this lecture Read intends "to show how the myth or image of the Muse in art personifies certain stratagems of the creative imagination that enable the artist to endow his work with universal significance." From the idea of the poet inspired by a personified feminine Muse in the classical tradition, the emphasis shifts in the nineteenth century to poetic inspiration working from the unconscious within the poet's mind. The "energy proper to the poet," Coleridge's "shaping spirit of imagination," is explained with the help of William James's theory of the stream of consciousness, and with Jung's concepts of self, anima, and mana-personality. (Read pays tribute to Jung's influence on his own life and writings in two essays about Jung in *The Tenth Muse*, London, 1957, and in *The Cult of Sincerity*, New York, 1969.)

675. READ, Herbert. "Poetic Consciousness and Creative Experience." In *Eranos-Jahrbuch 1956*. Vol. 25. Ed. Olga Fröbe-Kapteyn. Zurich: Rhein-Verlag, 1957. 357-389.

Herbert Read philosophizes with Giambattista Vico about the myth-making poetic consciousness and examines Coleridge's "Dejection: An Ode" as an example of the specifically modern (post-Renaissance) form of poetry as self-revelation. To support his arguments about the "immediacy which was the original characteristic of poetic utterance" he calls upon Jung's theory of archetypal patterns deriving from the collective unconscious. The discussion of Coleridge's "shaping spirit of imagination" is based on Maud Bodkin's statement that the "archetypal pattern in poetry" is always one of conflict, of creative tension resolved in poetry.

676. READ, Herbert. "Psychoanalysis and the Critic." *Criterion* 3 (1925) 214-230.
Rpt. in *Reason and Romanticism*. London: Faber and Gwyer, 1926. 83-106.

Herbert Read was one of the first art critics who made use of the new depth psychology. In this early essay he draws more on Jung and Adler than on Freud, suggesting in particular that certain concepts from Jung's book *Psychological Types* (English translation 1923) apply to the problem of literary evaluation. Jung's distinction between introversion and extraversion sheds light on the conflict between romanticism and classicism. The difference between abnormal and artistic fantasies may be explained through Jung's idea of "active fantasy," of the poet as "one who is capable of creating fantasies [...] of universal appeal," and of "the social validity of the symbol." Psychology can help the critic to discriminate between the "real" and the "neurotic" in art, because it "finds in art a system of symbols, representing a hidden reality, and by analysis it can testify to the purposive genuineness of the symbols; it can also testify to the faithfulness, the richness, and the range of the mind behind the symbol." (Read's early essays are analyzed by Claudia Morrison, q.v.)

677. REED, Toni. "The Projection of Evil: An Analysis of Nineteenth- and Twentieth-Century British Fiction Influenced by 'The Demon Lover' Ballad." (Ph.D. 1986 Ohio State University) 233 pp. *DAI* 48/04 A p.929.(Emily Brontë, Hardy, Lawrence, Elizabeth Bowen)

678. REEDER, Roberta. "'The Black Cat' as a Study in Repression." *Poe Studies* 7:1 (1974) 20-22.

The unbridled aggressiveness of the narrator in Poe's tale is ascribed to his total identification with his reason and his repression of instinctual psychic energy. In this story of self-delusion and moral and psychological disintegration the black cat functions as the anima, personification of the unconscious, felt and feared as the "spirit of Perverseness," expressing the dark forces of irrational impulses which have to be destroyed.

679. REGAN, Robert A. "Updike's Symbol of the Center." *Modern Fiction Studies* 20:1 (1974) 77-96.

"Updike's ubiquitous symbol of the center" is related to the circular form of his stories, in which the artist's "eye/I" surveys and transcribes a circle of existence from a geographical "midpoint" in empirical reality. Jung's notions of mandala circle and centering Self illuminate what critics of Updike's "absurd art" have too often overlooked: the religious force of his ordering of chaotic experience through the symbolism of circle and center, which he sees as "the seal of the divine" upon the organic world. An analysis of the story "Pigeon Feathers" illustrates how many of Updike's stories are integrated around these archetypal symbols.

Though in sometimes gratuitously baroque style grand claims are made for the "incredible organic harmony of substance and form in Updike's work," perceptive things are said about Updike's symbolism and his "usufruction of Jung."

680. REINGOLD, Gail M. "The Masks of Eugene O'Neill." In *A Well of Living Waters: A Festschrift for Hilde Kirsch.* Ed. Rhoda Head, et al. Los Angeles: C.G. Jung Institute, 1977. 61-72.

A discussion of the play *A Touch of the Poet* (1957) as a heroic fairy tale fantasy in which the protagonist, the pompously proud Irish innkeeper Con, enacts the psychological problem of O'Neill himself. Childhood circumstances had led to the spiritual isolation of the grown-up with his unconscious power complex and false mask of the gentleman. The hero's deliverance from self-delusion is achieved through the feminine, the unselfish love of his wife and the opposition of his daughter. Con's shooting of his mare, in Jungian terms the mother symbol, is the heroic sacrifice of his animal nature that sets him free.

This interpretation of the play, though somewhat sketchily worked out, also suggests what it was that afflicted "the tragic O'Neill."

681. RICE, Julian C. "*Equus* and the Jungian 'True' Symbol." *International Journal of Symbology* 7:2 (1976) 60-65.

The article is preceded by the critic's own abstract: "*Equus*, the play by Peter Shaffer, communicates the numinous symbolic experience, which Jung found necessary for individuation. At the same time, the play is about the difficulty of discovering such experience in a society which places mechanistic conformity before the religious need of the individual. While society at large attempts to literalize all experience into a sign system, so as to make "crucifixion," or objectification, permanent, religion and art communicate through symbols, which ritually incarnate in order to liberate, rather than confine, experience. In *Equus* (1973), representation is able to exceed itself, and the incarnate central symbol of the horse points, in the Jungian sense, toward an ineffable God-within-the-Self."

The psychological force of the figure of Equus, the numinous archetypal symbol that mediates between consciousness and unconsciousness, is well explained. The critic notes Shaffer's public acknowledgement of his debt to Jung, whom he praised in an interview (*Vogue*, February, 1975) as one of the "greatest" and "most accessible" minds of the twentieth century.

682. RICE, Julian C. "Male Sexuality in *Moby-Dick*." *American Transcendental Quarterly* 39 (1978) 237-244.

In this ingenious essay Rice combines Freudian and Jungian psychology to argue that "Ishmael learns from Ahab the consequences of acknowledging only the male impulse in the psyche, but in Queequeg he observes a hero who balances male and female principles." The dives of several characters into the sea are symbolical sexual acts. "Ahab's death, when he 'gives up the spear' is a sacrifice in which he begets upon the feminine Moby-Dick, a 'new man' or 'son', who is Ishmael." Ahab's archetypal maleness and Moby-Dick's symbolic femininity "represent the basic psychic opposites, while Ishmael is the individuated center."

683. RIDGWAY, Jeanette Fuller. "Prospero's Alchemy: The Metaphor of Psychological Change in William Shakespeare's *The Tempest*." (Ph.D. 1984 University of California, Los Angeles) 303 pp. *DAI* 46/05 A p.1289.

684. RIEMER, A.P. "Visions of the Mandala in *The Tree of Man*." *Southerly* 27:1 (1967) 3-19.

The explicit mandala symbolism in Patrick White's novel *The Solid Mandala* (1966) is interpreted in the light of passages from Jung's lectures on *Psychology and Religion*. Riemer argues that White's conscious employment of Jungian material also shows in the earlier novel *The Tree of Man* (1955). Jung's description of modern mandala's lacking a god in the centre is reflected in the alienated, stunted characters of White's novels. They can only glimpse the wholeness of man within themselves, but are unable to project the divine image.

Other scholars and White himself have since disputed the alleged use of Jung in the early novels. (See David Tacey)

685. RIKLIN, Franz. "Shakespeare's *A Midsummer Night's Dream*: A Contribution to the Process of Individuation." In *The Reality of the Psyche*. Proceedings of the Third International Congress for Analytical Psychology. Ed. Joseph B. Wheelwright. New York: Putnam, 1968. In German pp. 262-277, in English pp. 278-291.

In *A Midsummer Night's Dream* mandala symbolism, one of the prerequisites of the process of individuation, "is depicted by the characters themselves in an extremely differentiated manner." In the contrasting settings the city of Athens represents the principle of Logos, the world of human consciousness, but serving at the same time as the womb of real life it also "corresponds to the feminine-spiritual aspect of the collective unconsciousness" (the Duke's palace, symbol of wholeness, represents London, and Queen Elizabeth and her court). The wood near Athens stands for the world of instinct, where the quaternio of lovers, under the influence of the king and queen of fairies, dwarf-god figures of the Self, find harmonious "coniunctio". What the play depicts is "the integration of the anima into the masculine world of collective consciousness or into the animus world of the woman."

While translating Skakespeare's light-footed comedy into Jungian jargon, Riklin overlooks the literary conventions of Elizabethan allegory. The unconscious is given credit for the entertainments that Shakespeare and his audience very knowingly enjoyed.

686. RINGEL, Faye J. "Patterns of the Hero and the Quest: Epic, Romance, Fantasy." (Ph.D. 1979 Brown University) 248 pp. *DAI* 40/11 A p.5854. (William Morris, Lord Dunsany, Tolkien, *Beowulf, Sir Gawain and the Green Knight*)

687. ROBERTS, Mary. "Androgyny and Imperfect Love in the Works of Carson McCullers." *Harvest* 25 (1979) 46-59 and *University of Hartford Studies in Literature* 12:2 (1980) 73-98.

In this subtle analysis of the main characters in the novels of Carson McCullers, studies of androgyny by Carolyn Heilbrun (*Towards Androgyny: Aspects of Male and Female in Literature*, 1973) and by the Jungian analyst June Singer (*Androgyny: Towards a New Theory of Sexuality*, 1976) are used to argue that McCullers always portrays the "incomplete androgyny," the person who is neither the sexual hermaphrodite nor the true androgyne of psychic wholeness. The characters possess "an ambiguous sexuality," and "attempt in desperation or frustration to achieve an androgynous self by imagining a beloved who can make him or her whole. Love thus becomes a power-based phenomenon in which narcissism is the impetus."

688. RODI, Dolores S. Bissell. "A Study of the Contributions of Carl Jung and James Frazer and their Followers to the Hero Archetype with Suggestions for Teaching Literature." (Ph.D. 1977 University of Texas, Austin) 304 pp. *DAI* 38/07 A p.3920.

689. ROGERS, Howard E. "Irish Myth and the Plot of *Ulysses*." *ELH* 15:4 (1948) 306-327.

Rather than the overt Homeric parallels, it is the numerous allusions to Finn and other figures of traditional Irish myth, "casually scattered throughout *Ulysses*," that give Joyce's book its functional inner structure. "An undercurrent of Jungian symbology" accompanies this inner plot. References to Finn and Morgan, for instance, make Stephen "a Jungian hero" in his search for "entelechy," while Bloom and Stephen together may be seen as "opposing factors of a single personality in search of integration."

690. ROPER, Gordon. "Robertson Davies' *Fifth Business* and 'That old Fantastical Duke of Dark Corners, C. G. Jung'." *Journal of Canadian Fiction* 1:1 (1972) 33-39.

Citing statements about his interest in Jung from an unpublished talk Davies gave to students in 1968, Roper shows how Jung's concepts of the shadow and of the anima helped to shape the characters and their interactions in *Fifth Business* (1970), and how its structure is determined by Jung's views about the growth of the personality. The novel is analyzed as a modern myth of individuation with "a structure enriched by many archetypal images, ideas, and situations, and enhanced by interwoven signs."

One of the earliest essays about Jung's influence on the Canadian novelist.

691. ROSE, Charles. "*Romance* and the Maiden Archetype." *Conradiana* 6:3 (1974) 183-188.

The artistic failure of the novel *Romance* (1903), written in collaboration by Joseph Conrad and the young Ford Madox Ford, is ascribed to their idealization of its heroine Seraphina. Her role as static anima figure ignores the dark side of the archetype, as she is primarily a sublimation of "the masculine dynamics of a symbiotic relationship" between the two authors, neither of whom was, at the time, willing to come to terms with the anima within himself. Ford's "feeble sense of identity" made him want to share the suffering hero in Conrad and neutralize the anima, while Conrad, who needed the younger man to project his vision of himself as heroic tormented genius, tended to lend her an inflated identity.

692. *ROSE, Ellen C. "The End of the Game: New Directions in Doris Lessing's Fiction." *Journal of Narrative Techniques* 6:1 (1976) 66-75.

Dissatisfied with the conventional novel because it falsifies the reality of chaotic experience when imposing the order of artistic form, Doris Lessing in some of her later novels attempts to find new fictional structures. Envisaged, though never actually written by the writer-protagonist of *The Golden Notebook* (1962), this unconventional novel will contrast a surface story of comparatively pointless life with a counterpointed motif of developing meaning related to each other like the conscious rational ego and the collective unconscious in Jung's model of the psyche. The novel's pattern is then based in the process of psychic integration of the main character. Lessing works out this idea in the dream sequence of Kate Brown's mid-life crisis in *The Summer before the Dark* (1973), and in the access to a fantastic parallel world through the dissolving walls of the narrator's flat in *The Memoirs of a Survivor* (1975).

Cogently argued examination of the "Jungian fictional structure" of Lessing's later novels.

693. ROSE, William. "The Psychological Approach to the Study of Literature." In *German Studies Presented to Leonard Ashley Willoughby*. Oxford: Basil Blackwell, 1952. 171-190.

A discussion of the ways in which the psychological study of literature and the creative process might be further developed. The Jungian approach is briefly considered and dismissed on the strength of Rose's misunderstanding of archetype as "image".

694. ROSEN, Ellen I. "Martha's 'Quest' in Lessing's *Children of Violence*." *Frontiers: A Journal of Women Studies*. 3:2 (1978) 54-59.

The mother-daughter relationship is a unifying theme in the five novels of the *Children of Violence* series (1952-1969). Doris Lessing "brings a background in both Jungian and socialist theories to the exploration of the tensions" experienced by the woman who attempts to break through the traditional maternal role in search of personal autonomy and wholeness. After several marriages Martha Quest finds in her affair with the femininely sensitive Thomas the freedom that "completes the transformation of the Jungian myth of the mother and the son into Lessing's parable" of the daughter who comes to understand and transcend the "psychic ambivalence" of her mother's position.

695. ROSENFIELD, Claire. "Paradise of Snakes: Archetypal Patterns in Two Novels by Conrad." (Ph.D. 1960 Radcliffe College) 123 pp. No abstract in *DAI*.

Became book *Paradise of Snakes* (1968).

696. ROSENFIELD, Claire. *Paradise of Snakes: An Archetypal Analysis of Conrad's Political Novels*. Chicago: University of Chicago Press, 1967. 187 pp.

After a wide-ranging introductory chapter on the nature of myth, readings are offered of *Nostromo* (1904), *The Secret Agent* (1907) and *Under Western Eyes* (1911) in which recurrent motifs and archetypal patterns are traced, especially that of the night-journey of the questing hero. This brings out the ironic effects of the mythic suggestions often present in Conrad's metaphoric style and in the symbolism of his novels. Viewed on this mythic level, the despair, anguish and failure of his anti-heroic protagonists express the impotence and frustration of the lonely individual in a chaotic world. In the tainted Sulaco of silver-mine and material interests the "heroic" lives of Nostromo and Decoud, who undertake an actual night-sea journey, end in tragic failure. In *Under Western Eyes* Razumov's quest for self-knowledge, under the influence of his irrational second self Haldin, leads to his destruction, though he achieves a measure of personal illumination through his confession and consequent suffering.

The mythic perspectives applied by Rosenfield are Jungian, "filtered through the unifying intelligence" of Joseph Campbell and Northrop Frye's synoptic view. *The Secret Agent* is presented (quoting Frye) as a "world of total metaphor in which everything is identifiable with everything else." Both Winnie and London become the demonic, destructive feminine principle, the devouring mother. Ossipon, possessed by the negative anima, equates with a perverse sun-god. We see Stevie as the composite figure of myth, traditional scapegoat and social victim, resembling the child-god Christ, his death paralleling the ritual mutilation of the suffering god-hero.

Though Rosenfield's main thesis about the ironic effects of the mystic symbolism yields valuable insights, the lavish attribution of general archetypal themes obscures the subtle psychological and moral discriminations attaching to the individuality of Conrad's character creations.

697. ROSENFIELD, Claire. "The Shadow Within: The Conscious and Unconscious Use of the Double." *Daedalus* 92:2 (1963) 326-344. Rpt. in the anthology *Stories of the Double*. Ed. Albert J. Guerard. Philadelphia, Pa.: Lippincott, 1967. 311-331.

Beginning with Otto Rank's classic study "The Double as Immortal Self" and relating the duality theme to the Jungian concept of the irrational, anti-social shadow personality, Rosenfield pursues the motif of the psychological Double in novels by nineteenth and twentieth century authors.

698. ROSENTHAL, Lynne. "The Development of Consciousness in Lucy Boston's *The Children of Green Knowe*." *Children's Literature* 8 (1980) 53-67.

A Jungian reading of the *Green Knowe* novels (1954-1976) reveals Boston's intention to provide children with a knowledge in which consciousness and time are seen as rounded and whole.

699. ROSENUS, A.H. "Joaquin Miller and His 'Shadow'." *Western American Literature* 11:1 (1976) 51-59.

Miller's *Unwritten History: Life among the Modocs* (1873) reflects the author's own guilt about his treatment of the Indians he once befriended. Through his experiences in California, the narrator is faced with the shadow side of his psyche. There is no psychic renewal, however, because "he never acknowledges his destructive side - and since there is no recognition of its dangers, there is no effort at reform." K.S.

700. ROSS, Catherine Sheldrick. "Nancy Drew as Shaman: Atwood's *Surfacing*." *Canadian Literature* 84 (1980) 7-17.

Margaret Atwood's novel (1972) is read in terms of myth and ritual as the narrator's quest, involving spiritual dismemberment, descent into a watery underworld, and "penetration into some source of power, and a life-enhancing return" (Joseph Campbell). The dead ritual of Christianity and the "evil grail" of technological and rational Americanization are rejected in favour of a shamanistic initiation into the sources of natural life-power, when during her dive into the lake the discovery of the Indian rock-paintings induces an experience of "complete renewal, a mystical rebirth" (Mircea Eliade).

701. ROWE, Karen E. "Feminism and Fairy Tales." *Women's Studies* 6:3 (1979) 237-257.

Argues the thesis that "fairy tales perpetuate the patriarchal *status quo* by making female subordination seem a romantically desirable, indeed an inescapable fate." Good bibliographical notes about everything related to fairy tales: early collections, later editions, histories of the genre, and among the psychological interpretations details of the standard works by Max Lüthi, Bruno Bettelheim (Freudian), and by Marie-Louise von Franz and Hedwig von Beit (both Jungian).

702. ROWLEY, Brian A. "Psychology and Literary Criticism." *Psychoanalysis and the Social Sciences* 5 (1958) 200-218.

A survey of three ways in which psychology may be used in literary criticism. The creative process, the psychology of fictional characters and the aesthetic effect may be studied. "The psychology of appreciation" may especially contribute to a more adequate theory of interpretation and evaluation. Here the theory of archetypes, "introduced by Freud" and "restated by Jung", goes a long way toward explaining the gripping intensity of certain works of art. The critic should guard against reducing literature to a lowest common factor, such as the Oedipus complex, and against the fallacy of the single factor, such as Jung's claim that animation of the archetypes is "*the* secret of aesthetic effect." Excellence of the autonomous poetic work is a function of the total meaning of form and content for readers as a whole.

703. RUBENSTEIN, Roberta. *The Novelistic Vision of Doris Lessing: Breaking the Forms of Consciousness*. Urbana: University of Illinois Press, 1979. 271 pp.

The first eleven novels of Doris Lessing, through *The Memoirs of a Survivor* (1975), are seen as mythic-psychological fiction which develops from realistic narration to an increasingly symbolic exploration. From *The Golden Notebook* (1962) onwards, Lessing attempts "to break certain forms of consciousness and go beyond them." Unconventional narrative structures help to suggest "altered states of consciousness" within the protagonist. The individual in conflict with convential values is forced into fragmentation, mental breakdown and self-examination, expressed through dream symbols, hallucination, madness or mystical vision. The Jungian bent of Lessing's dramatization of this process is traced in the thematic and formal structure of the novels, which are seen as combining linear and circular patterns. Rubenstein shows that already in the first novel *The Grass is Singing* (1950) Lessing's awareness of the polarities within the personality corresponds with Jung's model of the psyche and his theory of the possibility and necessity of a synthesis of conscious and unconscious elements in the individuating totality of the self. "Images of wholeness, archetypal structures awaiting realization, and psychic integration" permeate the later novels and "reveal their Jungian basis most explicitly in the 'centering' activities" of the main character in *The Memoirs of a Survivor*.

An intelligent and accessible book on a novelist whose mentors are said to have been Hegel, Marx and Jung.

704. *RUBENSTEIN, Roberta. "*Surfacing*: Margaret Atwood's Journey to the Interior." *Modern Fiction Studies* 22:3 (1976) 387-399.

A very full exegesis of Atwood's novel that stresses its "continuity of ideas, images, and concerns" with her six volumes of poetry and the critical study *Survival: A Thematic Guide to Canadian Literature*, published in the same year as *Surfacing* (1972). The novel's mythic and symbolic force is demonstrated in the handling of the key motif of drowning and surviving that pervades the description of the narrator's search for the father and descent into her personal past, as well as her plunge into the lake and "symbolic regression into the collective unconscious." Her self-division and spiritual malaise suggest the self-destructive diseases and the incomplete psychic development in contemporary society, whereas her "journey towards wholeness involves a Jungian rejoining of the radically severed halves of the narrator's self."

705. RUDE, Roland V. "A Consideration of Jung's Concept of the Self as an Aid to the Understanding of Character in Prose Fiction." (Ph.D. 1960 Northwestern University) 457 pp. *DAI* 21/10 A p.3195.

706. RUDERMAN, Judith G. "'The Fox' and the 'Devouring Mother'." *D.H. Lawrence Review* 10:3 (1977) 251-269.

Lawrence's novella depicts the child's struggle against the devouring mother. The various relationships among Banford, March and Grenfel are "oral and nutritional rather than genital and sexual," and recreate the bonds of dependency and the child's fear of the dominating mother. "The need for mothering, together with the fear and hatred of the mother, runs like a *leitmotiv*" through the novels and stories of Lawrence's middle period. At the time he was writing "The Fox" in 1918, Lawrence read Jung's *Psychology of the Unconcious* with its theme of the child's perception of the mother figure in her dual capacity as sustainer and destroyer. In a letter Lawrence said that the book made him aware of the devouring-mother aspects in his own relationships with his mother and his wife Frieda. As a reaction to this Lawrence advocates in his later works the need for male leadership. K.S.

707. RUNNELS, James A. "Mother, Wife, and Lover: Symbolic Women in the Work of W.B. Yeats." (Ph.D. 1973 Rutgers University, New Brunswick) 277 pp. *DAI* 34/01 A p.336.

708. RYALS, Clyde de L. "The 'Fatal Woman' Symbol in Tennyson." *PMLA* 74 (1959) 438-443.

In addition to the high-born, suffering maidens there are also strong, enigmatic "Fatal Women" can also be found in Tennyson's poetry. Both are "soul images" of the poet, the former representing the side of his nature which "advocated the development of moral purpose," and the latter his taste for sensual indulgence and the morbid side of romanticism. These symbols "followed the pattern of development of the *anima*, and once the conflict had been resolved they merged into a new figure, the stock literary female who was representative of the poet's confident orientation." K.S.

709. RYALS, Clyde de L. "D.H. Lawrence's 'The Horse Dealer's Daughter': An Interpretation." *Literature and Psychology* 12:2 (1962) 39-43.

What Lawrence asks the reader to respond to in this story is not so much the realistic surface as the archetypal symbolism of death and rebirth evoking the inner life of the characters. Mabel's attempt to drown herself and her rescue by Dr. Fergusson are described as a descent into slimy, watery darkness, a return to the maternal depths followed by actual rebirth under the hands of the doctor. For both of them the experience brings the germs of new life and love into a state of stunted psychic existence.

710. SADOFF, Diane F. "Mythopoiea, the Moon, and Contemporary Women's Poetry." *Massachusetts Review* 19:1 (1978) 93-110. Rpt. in *Feminist Criticism: Essays on Theory, Poetry and Prose*. Eds. Cheryl L. Brown and Karen Olson. Metuchen, N.J.: Scarecrow Press, 1978. 142-160.

Jung's "problematic" archetypes, the anima and animus, are examined critically. In his last book, *Mysterium Coniunctionis* (1956), Jung modifies his warnings against animus-ridden women by conceiving of a distinct "lunar consciousness" for women, which merges things together rather than separates them as in man's solar consciousness. The traditional moon myths, Sadoff argues, are "gender-based stereotypes" of the ambivalent Moon Goddess as virgin and prostitute, life-giver and life-destroyer. Moon poems by Denise Levertov, Nancy Willard and Diane Wakoski are shown to re-imagine the moon as archetypal image from a feminine perspective, the goddess seen not only in her lunacy and duality, but as a source of spiritual inspiration and transformation.

711. *ST. ARMAND, Barton L. "The Dragon and the Uroboros: Themes of Metamorphosis in *Arthur Gordon Pym*." *American Transcendental Quarterly* 37 (1978) 57-71.

Poe's *Narrative of Arthur Gordon Pym* (1838), even if it is a conscious hoax, may well be viewed as a mythical tale of "monstrosities and grotesqueries" in a world of metamorphosis, where there is "continual creation of anomalies and mutations." Poe's documented knowledge of the philosophy of alchemy makes a parallel of Pym's journey with the stages of alchemical transmutations meaningful. The alchemical symbols of the Dragon and the Uroboros are a convenient "means of exploring imagistic clusters that appear to define two opposite poles of archetypal metamorphosis in Poe's art." The story's corpses, carcasses and monsters, in Jung's interpretation of alchemical symbolism, are manifestations of the Dragon of earth-bound disorder that has to be killed off "that it may rise again in the higher form of the Uroboros." In the light of Neumann's chapter on the maternal womb-like Uroboros in *The Origins and History of Consciousness*, Pym's struggles are seen as an attempt to free himself "from the slumber of unconscious envelopment." Womb-symbols, expressive of the metamorphoses of this undeveloped embryonic ego-consciousness, pervade the story, as with the dreamlike states, premature burial and resurrection of Pym, as well as much else that is puzzling in Poe's *Narrative*. The mysterious final encounter with the shrouded human figure behind the gigantic curtain of white water then becomes the grand finale of this "psycho-drama of consciousness," the piercing of the veil of Isis, and the meeting with the Great Mother herself.

St. Armand's amplifications afford a very satisfactory archetypal reading of Poe's enigmatic tale.

712. *ST. ARMAND, Barton L. "Hawthorne's 'Haunted Mind': A Subterranean Drama of the Self." *Criticism* 13 (1971) 1-25.

In his early sketch "The Haunted Mind" Hawthorne, like Poe, explored the shifting "fancies" that flood the mind in the hypnagogic state between sleeping and waking. Whereas Poe in his stories abandons himself to his dream visions, Hawthorne shies away from the spectres "affrighting this actual life with secrets that perchance belong to a deeper one." Instead of fully facing the dark spirits and integrating the "light" and "dark" sides of his personality in an individuation process as outlined by Jung, Hawthorne banishes his psychological demons and replaces them by the sentimental images of conventionally idealized American life.

A revealing parallel is drawn with Jung's description of "active imagination" in *Mysterium Coniunctionis*. Hawthorne's failure to integrate the "shadow" of his guilt is seen as a unifying rhythm in his work. "In some way each piece of his fiction was an attempt to renew the journey into his own haunted mind and confront once again those phantoms on whom he slammed the doors of the tomb and the dungeon so peremptorily."

713. ST. ARMAND, Barton L. "Poe's Emblematic Raven: A Pictorial Approach." *ESQ: A Journal of the American Renaissance* 22:4 (1976) 191-210.

The Raven of Poe's poem is learnedly interpreted as a type image in the emblem tradition, more especially in Renaissance books on alchemy, with fixed meanings of "darkness, death, and melancholy." Ambivalent archetypal symbol of "mortification," the alchemical raven, in Jungian terms, is for the student's dark imagination the expression of his own black shadow self. His dangerous search for forbidden knowledge leaves him in a state of never-ending mournful remembrance, "without any hope of rescue by the good anima, his lost Lenore."

714. ST. ARMAND, Barton L. "Poe's 'Sober Mystification': The Uses of Alchemy in 'The Gold-Bug'." *Poe Studies* 4:1 (1971) 1-7.

An ingenious interpretation of Poe's tale "The Gold-Bug" that brings out his "clever manipulation of traditional alchemical signs and symbols." Jung, among other writers on alchemy, is adduced to show that "The Gold-Bug" is "the story of Legrand's gathering of the diverse ingredients which will ensure completion of the alchemist's *opus magnum*, the great work, and it records his deciphering of the hermetic formula which details the secret of the process." The tulip tree in the tale becomes the *arbor philosophorum* and the gold-bug itself "an avatar of the philosopher's stone."

Martin Bickman, in his book *The Unsounded Centre* (q.v.), claims that ST. Armand's essays on Poe make "accessible to the critic formerly unsuspected sources and approaches to American texts." (p. 152, note 20)

715. *ST. ARMAND, Barton L. *The Roots of Horror in the Fiction of H.P. Lovecraft.* Elizabethtown, N.Y.: Dragon Press, 1977. viii,102 pp.

This essay offers a close reading of Lovecraft's horror tale "The Rats in the Walls" (1923) "as a means of isolating fictional elements contributing to the creation of horror." The psychological interpretation is based on Jung and uses for its intellectual framework Darwin's theory of evolution, American puritanism, Rudolf Otto's investigation into numinous religious feelings, and Frazer's anthropology. The power of Lovecraft's tales resides in his fusion of Gothic horror with cosmic terror. A striking parallel with "The Rats in the Walls" is found in Jung's dream of the psyche as a house with various levels from eighteenth century topfloor to Roman cellar and pre-historic cave under it. The last descendant of the Delapores, obsessed with the family secret, explores the rat-invested cellars of the mansion built on the foundations of a ruined abbey, and in the lowest grotto succumbs to his own atavistic shadow tendencies, man's animal nature in the springs of the collective unconscious.

Comparison with Poe's tale "The Black Cat" shows how Lovecraft invests "Gothic machinery" with "new, archetypal meaning." The numinous symbols of Lovecraft's "constant dream-quest of the dreadful" (houses, cellars, rats, blood, viscosity) are analyzed as paradoxical and archetypal elements that fuse contrary emotional states of "fear and desire, attraction and repulsion, horror and terror." Delapore ultimately undergoes an "instantaneous devolution of the species." In this early tale horror is uppermost, but in his later stories Lovecraft occasionally manages to "synthesize Gothic romance and science fiction," to express "awe as well as nausea, majesty as well as trembling, sublime dread as well as panic fear."

A brilliant analysis and model of Jung's method of amplification that demonstrates "not only that Jung is uncannily relevant to an understanding of the place and meaning of horror in Lovecraft's fiction, but also that Lovecraft may provide some evidence for the powerful working of Jung's notions of archetypes and the collective unconscious."

716. ST. ARMAND, Barton L. "Usher Unveiled: Poe and the Metaphysics of Gnosticism." *Poe Studies* 5:1 (1972) 1-8.

Poe is not the puerile thinker and writer of shallow Gothic tales, as implied by Christian orthodoxy. His work is imbued with the unorthodox metaphysic of Hermeticism and the philosophy of alchemy, both deriving from the doctrines of Gnosticism. Significant images and incidents in "The Fall of the House of Usher" are related to the occult symbolism of "classic" alchemical treatises. Jung's psychological reading of the alchemical opus as an allegory of individuation provides the key to the climax of the story. Symbolically, Roderick Usher is "the successful alchemist" who, locked in the embrace of his self-surrected sister-bride as in a mystic marriage, has freed himself completely from the crumbling house of matter, has liberated his soul and "achieved gnosis."

The flaw in this intriguing argument is that a "positive" symbolic meaning accords ill with the spirit and atmosphere of Poe's sensationally sombre view of "the melancholy House of Usher," even were one prepared to believe that a conventionally-minded narrator ironically misses the "metaphysical" significance of what he has witnessed.

717. SALIBA, David R. "Nightmare in Miniature: 'Ligeia'." *American Transcendental Quarterly* 40 (1978) 367-378.
Became a chapter in his book *A Psychology of Fear* (1980).

718. SALIBA, David R. *A Psychology of Fear: The Nightmare Formula of Edgar Allan Poe*. Lanham, MD: University Press of America, 1980.
In his Gothic tales Poe aimed at "unity of effect" by deliberately applying a formula of terror and horror "for eliciting the response of fear in his reader" which can be shown to follow exactly the development of a nightmare according to present-day psychiatry. How closely Poe's insights into the workings of the

unconscious parallel Jung's theories of dream psychology is illustrated by analysis of a number of Poe's tales, in particular of the women in "Ligeia" as anima figures, and of the characters in "The Fall of the House of Usher" as aspects of the mind encountered in anxiety dreams. It is claimed that "Poe was able to craft literary nightmares and come up with a world view [in *Eureka*] that anticipates Jung's pronouncements about the integrated psyche."

719. SANZO, Eileen. "Blake and the Great Mother Archetype." *Nassau Review* 3:4 (1978) 105-116.

The Great Mother archetype in its duality provides "a key to the understanding of William Blake's images of women." As the negative Terrible Mother we see her in Vala, Rahab, Tirzah, and the cruel daughters of Albion, all symbolic of fallen nature. In Ololon, Milton's anima, the duality of the feminine shows in the metamorphosis of the beneficent figure, corresponding to nature's goodness, into "dreadful mother, priestess of religious sacrifice." Jerusalem, the maternal city, is the Good Mother symbol in Blake. When Albion awakens his Emanation (or anima) at the end of *Jerusalem*, this represents Blake's vision of society's attainment of "a new level of consciousness and maturity."

720. SARCONE, Elisabeth F. "Andrew Lytle and the Mythmaking Process." (Ph.D. 1977 Vanderbilt University) 352 pp. *DAI* 38/03 A p.1395.

721. SAUTTER, Diana. "Dylan Thomas and Archetypal Domination." *American Imago* 31:4 (1974) 335-359.

Sautter aims at eliciting mythical resonances in the metaphoric density of Dylan Thomas' poetry. The images in a number of his short poems are found to embody the various stages or "gestalt patterns" of the *Urmythos* of human life as presented by Edward Whitmont in his systematic survey of Jungian psychology in *The Symbolic Quest* (1969). The poems are dominated by "the particular antinomies between the Eros of the archetype and the Death of separation in the imagery of the One crucified." Thomas' symbolism is unique in that these mythical elements are "directly precipitated into words without the intervention of characters or contemporary situation."

The interesting, if rather vague, thesis is not substantiated by sufficiently detailed analysis of the poems.

722. SCHAFER, William J. "Ralph Ellison and the Birth of the Anti-Hero." *Critique: Studies in Modern Fiction* 10:2 (1967-1968) 81-93.

The Invisible Man (1947) is "basically a quest for identity" describing "along mythic lines" the essential Black experience in twentieth century America. Ellison structures his novel around the birth and life of the hero as explicated by Lord Raglan and Joseph Campbell. On the personal level the nameless hero's journey from the rural South to Harlem is an "internal quest" for self-knowledge during which he undergoes a series of trials, experiences a symbolic death in an explosion and goes underground in the New York subway to await rebirth. K.S.

723. SCHECHTER, Harold. *The Bosom Serpent: Folklore and Popular Art.* Iowa City: University of Iowa Press, 1988.
Generally archetypal. Updates in the last chapter the earlier essay on the "myth of the eternal child" in America. (q.v.)

724. SCHECHTER, Harold. "Deep Meaning Comix: The Archetypal World of R. Crumb." *San José Studies* 3:3 (1977) 6-21.
The comic strips of the underground cartoonist Robert Crumb derive their force not only from their outrageous social satire, but even more from the richness of their archetypal symbolism. The mythopoeic bent of Crumb's imagination is illustrated from the appearance of shadow, trickster and great mother figures as well as from rebirth and night sea journey archetypes in his work. The material of this article was worked into the wider context of Schechter's book *The New Gods* (q.v.).

725. SCHECHTER, Harold, and Jonna Gormely Semeiks, eds. *Discoveries: 50 Stories of the Quest.* Indianapolis, Ind.: Bobbs-Merril, 1983. xxxvii,562 pp.
An anthology of short stories by nineteenth- and twentieth-century American and English writers, including some "important new talents," and such international authors as Gustave Flaubert, Alberto Moravia, Hermann Hesse, Isaac Babel, Julio Cortázar, and Gabriel García Márquez. The book is intended as material for an introductory fiction course to teach students how to explicate a text, and is provided with a discussion of "The Elements of Fiction," questions and a glossary of critical terms. The fifty stories are grouped in six chapters (The Call, The Other, The Journey, Helpers and Guides, The Treasure, Transformation), corresponding to the main stages of the quest narrative as set out in Joseph Campbell's classic study of world mythology *The Hero with a Thousand Faces* (1949).

726. SCHECHTER, Harold. "The Eye and the Nerve: A Psychological Reading of James Dickey's *Deliverance.*" In *Seasoned Authors for a*

New Season: The Search for Standards in Popular Writing. Ed. L. Filler. Bowling Green, Ohio: Bowling Green University Popular Press, 1980. 4-19.

Dickey's best-selling novel (1970) is placed in the tradition of American Gothic romances that runs from Charles Brockden Brown through Hawthorne and Melville to Faulkner. It is an example of what Jung calls "visionary literature" which derives its special power from the richness of its archetypal imagery. The novel's "mythic substructure" is that of the hero's adventurous quest or "night sea journey" to achieve spiritual illumination. The canoeing expedition undertaken by a middle-aged businessman suffering from a mid-life crisis turns into a "perilous journey of self-exploration." His encounter with a couple of murderous backwoodsmen forces him to confront the evil beast in himself and to descend into the depth of his own "dark psyche." His deliverance follows the mythical pattern, complete with ritual death and rebirth.

This convincing Jungian analysis of the novel's psychological and mythical aspects (with introduction added) forms a chapter in Schechter's book *The New Gods* (q.v.).

727. SCHECHTER, Harold. "Kali on Main Street: The Rise of the Terrible Mother in America." *Journal of Popular Culture* 7:2 (1973) 251-263.

Signals the shift from the popular image of the big-breasted Good Mother of the fifties to the archetypal Terrible Mother, the equivalent of the Eastern devouring goddess Kali, in America's counterculture of the sixties. Illustrated from films, comics, pop songs and poems by Robert Bly and Sylvia Plath.

728. SCHECHTER, Harold G. "The Mysterious Way: Individuation in American Literature." (Ph.D. 1975 University of New York, Buffalo) 201 pp. *DAI* 36/10 A p.6691. (Cooke, Brown, Hawthorne, Twain, Dickey)

729. SCHECHTER, Harold. "The Myth of the Eternal Child in Sixties America." In *The Popular Culture Reader*. Eds. Jack Nachbar, et al. Bowling Green, Ohio: Bowling Green University Popular Press,1978. 64-78.

Rpt. as an appendix in Schechter's book *The New Gods* (q.v.).

730. SCHECHTER, Harold. *The New Gods: Psyche and Symbol in Popular Art*. Bowling Green, Ohio: Bowling Green University Popular Press, 1980. 172 pp.

The popular art of our period is full of archetypal symbols. The comic strips, TV series, films and bestsellers are as much projections of the collective unconscious as the myths and "high" works of art of the past. Religion may have lost its meaning for many people in our culture, but the spiritual quest for individuation (basic also to Christianity) continues to express itself in the adventures of such "new gods" as Captain Marvel, Superman, the Star Trek team or the quaternity of the Beatles and their songs. The popular hero encounters the shadow in its personal form or in its collective manifestation of trickster or helpful animal, and he meets with anima figures in both life-affirming and destructive guises. Schechter applies this Jungian perspective to many well-known figures from American cartoons, TV shows, films and from the world's myths, fairy tales and great works of "visionary" literature. He analyzes the comic strips by the underground cartoonist Robert Crumb, James Dickey's best-selling novel *Deliverance* (1970), and the film version of Jules Verne's *Journey to the Center of the Earth.* Jung holds that mythic symbols surface in the collective fantasies of a whole culture as compensation for psychic one-sidedness. In the final chapter this notion is provokingly applied to America's aggressively competitive technological society in the 1960s and to flower-power counterculture activating the archetype of the *puer aeternus*, the eternal child, as the living symbol of "an attempt (ironically) to set American society straight."

Thoroughly researched, clearly written and persuasively argued study. The author is not only well read in the essential texts of Jung himself, but also in the best Jung scholars. One difficulty is left unconsidered. The work of Crumb and Dickey seems so obviously archetypal that one wonders if these writers did not apply Jungian notions deliberately.

731. *SCHECHTER, Harold and Jonna Gormely Semeiks. *Patterns in Popular Culture: A Sourcebook for Writers.* xix,476 pp. With teacher's handbook *Popular Culture in the Classroom.* 69 pp. New York: Harper & Row, 1980.

This unusual reader for composition courses reproduces selections from comic books, popular novels, science fiction, newspaper strips, rock and country-western songs and other forms of popular art, as well as from more traditional material, such as myths, folktales and literary clasics. These are grouped in eight chapters devoted to the major archetypes, arranged roughly in the order in which they appear in the individuation process: Shadow, Trickster, Temptress, Mother, Wise Old Man, Helpful Animal and Holy Fool, Quest, Rebirth. Each chapter opens with a description of the archetype and discusses the appearance of the archetypal character in popular and classical art. The selections include (e.g. in the case of the Rebirth archetype) an Ovid story, a Grimm fairy tale, James Dean and John Denver songs, a Will Eisner comic strip, an advertisement, the short story on which the film *2001: A Space Odyssey* was based and an extract from the Henry James novel *The American*. Each piece is followed by questions on language and content, and suggestions for writing; each chapter concludes with additional writing suggestions, many of the questions appealing to the student's own experiences. There is an appendix containing seminal critical essays on the subject of myths, fairy tales and popular art, among others by Bettelheim, Le Guin and McGlashan. A separate teacher's handbook with suggestions for using the coursebook in class gives brief analyses of all the selections, drawing on the authors' own teaching experiences, together with a brief introduction to Jung's psychology and a selected bibliography.

The highest praise should go to the authors of this most stimulating sourcebook for classroom discussion and writing assignments, which is at the same time an excellent popularization of Jung's archetypal theory.

732. SCHECHTER, Harold. "The Return of Demeter: The Poetry of Daniela Gioseffi." *Psychocultural Review* 1:4 (1977) 452-458.

The re-appearance in the late 1960s of the archetype of the Terrible Mother, in the popular art of the counterculture as well as in individual works of serious literature, may be seen as a compensatory adjustment for an age-long devaluation of the feminine in our Western patriarchal society. The Indian cannibal goddess, Kali the Devourer, is found with mouth agape and tongue rolling as the trademark of the Rolling Stones, as the man-eater in the poetry of Robert Bly and Sylvia Plath, and in underground comics. The next phase in the evolution of a possible new collective consciousness is the return of the corn goddess Demeter, visible in our back-to-nature movement as well as in the "vaginal vegetal world" which pervades the work of the poet-dancer Daniela Gioseffi. The theme of woman as creative life-bearer dominates her poetry and she stresses the need for uniting "the male intellectual consciousness with the matriarchal world of the psyche" within each individual and in society.

733. SCHECHTER, Harold. "The Sot-Weed Factor in Hell." *Higginson Journal* 20:2 (1978) 4-20.

"The Sot-Weed Factor," a little-known poem by the colonial American poet Ebenezer Cooke, is analyzed in Jungian terms as "a mythological quest, an archetypal descent into the realm of the deep unconscious." The male figures in the book, particularly the sot-weed (tobacco) planters and Indians, are personifications of the shadow archetype, while the female characters are "bad animas."

The factor undergoes a series of trials in order to achieve individuation. Unable to persevere, he flees back to Europe, thus failing in the attempt. K.S.

734. SCHEICK, William J. "The Geometric Structure of Poe's 'The Oval Portrait'." *Poe Studies* 11:1 (1978) 6-8.
The "fictive space" of Poe's short story is geometrically shaped as "a series of more or less circular layers," narrowing the reader's attention toward the portrait, and, in the portrait, toward the young woman's eye and "life-likeness of expression." In simultaneous patterns of dilation from and contraction toward a center, Poe suggests that the process of art reflects the "ambiguous cyclic" nature of phenomenal life "by artistically reproducing those rhythms in the mandala-like structure of "The Oval Portrait." K.S.

735. SCHLEPPENBACH, Barbara Aschemann. "Irony and beyond: The Mythic Method in Conrad, Eliot, and Pound." (Ph.D. 1977 Stanford University) 383 pp. *DAI* 38/09 A p.5467.

736. SCHNEIDER, Daniel J. *D.H. Lawrence: The Artist as Psychologist*. Lawrence: University Press of Kansas, 1984. xix,313 pp.
In analyzing Lawrence's psychology, Schneider discusses the influence of Freud, Jung and Fromm on Lawrence's theory of the unconscious.

737. SCHOTZ, Myra Glazer. "For the Sexes: Blake's Hermaphrodite in *Lady Chatterley's Lover*." *Bucknell Review* 24:1 (1978) 17-26.
In Blake's "sexualized world" the androgynous Albion is "the male who has accepted the female within him, the male at peace with his anima," while the hermaphrodite is the negative being who is neither wholly male nor wholly female. Lawrence's "very Blakean novel" *Lady Chatterley's Lover* (1928) is seen as "a portrayal of hermaphroditic characters" entering into sterile relationships until Mellors redeems the masculine principle and conquers his fear of the devouring feminine by taming Connie and incorporating "the female in the male."

738. SCIGAJ, Leonard M. "Myth and Psychology in the Poetry of Ted Hughes." (Ph.D. 1977 University of Wisconsin, Madison) 471 pp. *DAI* 38/08 A p.4819.

739. SCOGGAN, John. "Charles Olson: Acts of the Soul: Chapter Four." Ladner, B.C.: Iron Magazine, 1976. 107 pp.
Provides a wealth of reference to Olson's use of Jung and Jungian material.

740. *SCOTT, W.I.D. *Shakespeare's Melancholics*. London: Mills and Boon, 1962. 192 pp.

After synopses of the theories of melancholy in Elizabethan days and of neuroses and psychoses in modern medical psychology, eight characters from Shakespeare's plays are analyzed as examples of the melancholic man: Antonio, Don John, Orsino, Jaques, Hamlet, Timon, Pericles, and Leontes. In considering these dramatic characters in relation to their psychological types, Scott makes use of Freud and Adler but, in the first place, applies the "more complicated and more comprehensive theories" of Jung.

Hamlet, for instance, is seen as a "real manic depressive" whose actions do not so much result from an Oedipus complex as from the reactions of a "morally oriented introverted intuitive" to a dominating extraverted father. In the case of Antonio, an "endogenous depressive," Jungian interpretation goes beyond the Freudian diagnosis of repressed homosexuality by being able to explain Antonio's outbursts against Shylock as caused by the suppression of feeling in this introverted feeling type, which may lead in Jung's terms to "an extravagant eruption" influenced by his inferior extraverted thinking function.

These two clinical summaries give no indication of the subtlety of Scott's analysis and his sensitivity to the complexity of Shakespeare's characterization. Moreover, he is fully alive to the literary and dramatic qualities of the plays. He attempts, for instance, to explain certain plot developments where Shakespeare deviated from his sources. It is part of his thesis that "Shakespeare assimilated the persons in his plays to types which he observed around him, and that, intuitively, he let them control his plots according to a complexity in their nature of which he himself was only partly aware." From this angle interesting things are said about the plot and structure of *The Merchant of Venice*.

Scott has "as much concern for the psychological atmosphere of the plays as a whole - reflective of the mind of the author - as for the individual analysis of the character under review." In the final chapter he considers the "relationships of Shakespeare's characters to himself." He sees Shakespeare as an introverted intuitive and is "certain that most of his own self has gone into his introverted characters, of which a majority of my melancholics are examples."

This is an excellent study of the psychology of Shakespeare's characters with highly illuminating illustrations from Jung's *Psychological Types*.

741. SEMEIKS, Jonna Gormely. "The Summoned Spirit: The Quest Motif in D.H. Lawrence." (Ph.D. 1981 Rutgers University, New Brunswick) 248 pp. *DAI* 42/09 A p.3995.

742. SEVIER, Marcus W. "Adventures of the Ego in the Unconscious: A Jungian Analysis of the Unspelling Group of Sir Gawain Poems in Middle English." (Ph.D. 1978 University of Texas, Austin) 209 pp. *DAI* 40/03 A p.1456.

743. SEWELL, Ernestine P. "The Jungian Process of Individuation as Structure in *The Painted Bird*." *South Central Bulletin* 38:4 (1978) 160-163.
        Jerzy Kosinski's "holocaustic chronicle" *The Painted Bird* (1965) of a young boy's horrifying experiences in a primitive peasant community is read as a German *Märchen*, for which the Jungian process of individuation offers the "most complete interpretative scheme." The bizarre details of the folkloristic narrative are interpreted as archetypal motifs and traced to the lists in Stith-Thompson's *Motif Index of Folk Literature*. The anonymous boy's "picaresque progress moves from wholeness of the psyche to dissociation of the three levels of consciousness, to psychic deformity, and eventually back to wholeness." Development of persona, shadow obsession, and meetings with the anima and wise old man are pointed out. The discovery of the Self occurs at the point where the boy, made mute by all the horrors he has witnessed, regains his speech.
        No doubt the Jungian analogue illuminates Kosinski's brutal "folktale." Little is gained, however, by labelling all the folk motifs as archetypes, and by using Jung's theory of the four psychic functions simply to describe how the boy assimilates his experiences.

744. SHARMA, Radhe Shyam. "The Symbol as Archetype: A Study of Symbolic Mode in D.H. Lawrence's *Women in Love*." *Osmania Journal of English Studies* 8:2 (1971) 31-53.
        The thesis of this essay that "the nature of the symbolic mode in Lawrence is archetypal in the Jungian sense" seems perfectly arguable, but the woolly abstractions in which the argument is couched make it virtually unreadable. *Women in Love* (1920) is shown to be "a myth of failed polarities."

745. *SHARP, Sister M. Corona. "The Archetypal Feminine: *Our Mutual Friend*." *University of Kansas City Review* 27:4 (1961) 307-311 and 28:1 (1962) 74-80.

Unlike critics who consider Dickens' last completed novel "the darkest and bitterest " of his works, Sister Sharp reads in its "mythical themes of initiation and rebirth, fertility and death [...] his literary testament of hope." She shows how many contrasting symbols of fertility and barrenness in the novel "find their ultimate meaning in the duality of the Great Mother," whose life-giving and death-dealing aspects are embodied in a whole range of vividly portrayed women characters. The most powerful amongst these are the good Lizzie and the dwarf Jenny Wren. In helping to throttle the life of her own father but preserving that of Eugene, Jenny fully represents the Great Mother in her good and bad aspects. "The archetypal feminine is the dominant figure" in *Our Mutual Friend* (1865), not only through the pervading mother-child imagery, but also through related ocean-river images. The pure river, polluted in filthy London, runs into the sea from which it is reborn, its water a source of perpetual regeneration informing the symbolic meaning of the novel.

This lucid exposition of the mythical overtones in the characters of *Our Mutual Friend* makes excellent use of insights from Mircea Eliade and Erich Neumann, and argues very plausibly that "Dickens has created a complex structure of clashing values which in the end are harmonized."

746. SHEARER, Mark S. "The Poetics of the Self: A Study of the Process of Individuation in T.S. Eliot's *Four Quartets*." (Ph.D. 1985 University of South Carolina) 416 pp. *DAI* 46/06 A p.1637.

747. SHMIEFSKY, Marvel. "*In Memoriam*: Its Seasonal Imagery Reconsidered." *Studies in English Literature* 7 (1967) 721-739.

Following Maud Bodkin's discussion of the archetypes of Heaven-and-Hell and of Rebirth in Virgil and Dante (in *Archetypal Patterns in Poetry*), Shmiefsky reviews the imagery of the seasons in Tennyson's *In Memoriam* (1850). "Heaven is mainly a garden in spring, Hell the scape of winter or the desert, and Rebirth an April violet." On the symbolical, natural and personal levels the image of the violet functions as an embodiment of the rebirth archetype and as "a unifying agent" in the sequence of poems. "The violet is to Tennyson what the golden bough is to Virgil": mythical symbol of the unity of all life in its subjection to death and its power of self-renewal.

748. SHOWALTER, Eliane. "Guilt, Authority, and the Shadows in *Little Dorrit*." *Nineteenth-Century Fiction* 34:1 (1979) 20-40.

Dickens' use of shadows and shadow figures emphasizes the importance of the prison and the hero's guilt in *Little Dorrit*

(1857). As the shadow, in Jungian terms, represents the violent and the sexual, meeting the shadow may result in strong feelings of guilt.

749. SIGAL, Lillian F. "Matthew Arnold's Search for Wholeness: A Jungian Study." (Ph.D. 1982 University of Pittsburgh) 185 pp. *DAI* 44/05 A p.1463.

750. *SIGMAN, Joseph. "Death's Ecstasies: Transformation and Rebirth in George MacDonald's *Phantastes*." *English Studies in Canada* 2:2 (1976) 203-226.

Phantastes: A Faerie Romance for Men and Women (1858) is the depiction of a young man's "psychological crisis and the resulting process of transformation and rebirth." The hero's journey through fairyland symbolizes his confrontation with his suppressed and neglected inner life. The first part of the book centers in the realm of the feminine, where the hero meets archetypal good and bad mothers, muse and temptress. Unlike similar German Romantic tales like Novalis' *Heinrich von Ofterdingen* (1802) the emphasis is less on belief, wonder and imagination than on the dangers the unconscious holds for consciousness. After a first symbolic death in the sea, the hero is reborn on the island of the Wise Woman. His departure from her "re-enacts a key moment in Romantic myth: the primal loss of union with the unconscious and instinctive processes of nature and the fall into separate conscious existence." In the second part of the story we are in the realm of the father. The hero achieves masculine independence as a warrior with male companions. He fights with giants, a dragon and a wolf, until an act of self-sacrifice brings on his death and final rebirth. In his quest the hero conquers "the negative aspects of both the father and the mother."

This is an illuminating explication of MacDonald's strongly archetypal fantasy, as well as a valuable demonstration of the relevance of Jung's theory (as expanded by Neumann) of the psychological ambivalence of anima, mother and incest images. One possible reason for the fact that Jung's ideas "fit" this story so well "may be that the roots of Jung's work, like those of MacDonald's, lie deep in German Romanticism." Sigman discusses parallels with a wide variety of European Romantic writers and with the myths of Pygmalion, Orpheus and Narcissus.

751. SILVA, Nancy Neufield. "Doris Lessing's Ideal Reconciliation." *Anonymous* 1:1 (1974) 72-81.

Using three short stories, "A Sunrise in the Veld," "The Eye of God in Paradise" and "Dialogue," Silva argues that "the recurrence

-

of antithesis needing reconciliation is evidence of Lessing's concern that people integrate themselves including their conscious minds and their shadows."
A poorly written article that garbles Jungian theory. K.S.

752. SINGER, June K. "Creativity in Blake and Jung." *Harvest* 20 (1974) 71-87.
A paper developing free-flowing thoughts on creativity, larded with choice quotations from Jung as psychologist and observer of the creative process, and from Blake, the active participant in the creative act.

753. SINGER, June K. *The Unholy Bible: A Psychological Interpretation of William Blake.* New York: Putnam, 1970. 270 pp.
Blake's life and work are linked in this thoroughly Jungian study, the author's diploma thesis for the Zurich Jung Institute expanded into a book. The symbolism of the poems and the prophetic books is viewed "primarily as a projection of unconscious factors in Blake upon mythological characters which arise from transpersonal or archetypal foundations." Singer concentrates on detailed psychological explications of the texts and the drawings of all the plates in the "extremely personal volume" *The Marriage of Heaven and Hell* (1790). These provide a key to Blake's "spiritual transformation and creative development," which is further traced in brief chapters on all the prophetic books. Blake's unconscious desires, fueled by his "need to become aware of the other side of God" and "the darker area of man's life," together with the "unsatisfactory marital relationship" with his wife Catherine, are seen as the driving forces behind his radical questioning of orthodox Christian morality.
Singer views Blake's journey through hell as a descent into the personal and collective unconscious, although Blake also relates his experiences to the wider social and political issues of his time. The "personal struggle for liberation from a paralyzing tension of opposites" is projected into the paradoxical Contraries: Angel and Devil, limiting Reason and free-flowing Energy, passive Good and active Evil, devouring female and inspiring anima, the restrictive dogmatic God of orthodox Christianity and the creative Divine in the human being. Blake's mythical view with its central psychological tenet "without contraries there is no progression" is full of striking resemblances to Jung's notions of the union of opposites, of the life force, and of the individuation process. And Jung's theory of the balancing quaternity finds its analogy in Blake's development from his early stress on dualism to the

"fourfold image of Man" that is also the God image in the later prophetic books.

As we know very little about Blake's personal life, Singer's psychobiographical procedure may be too naïve in its readiness to read Blake's poems in the light of speculations about the unconscious desires and drives that he projected into the poems. Yet this Jungian reading offers many insights into the undoubted archetypal contents of Blake's mythical poetry, if the reader does not insist on academic prejudices about scholarly sources and causal argument, but is prepared to go along with Singer's imaginative method of amplification and treatment of dream material. Holding up the "Proverbs of Hell" against Jungian psychological notions is often illuminating, and the "Memorable Fancies" are clarified when understood as dreams and instances of active imagination.

754. SINGLETON, Mary A. *The City and the Veld: The Fiction of Doris Lessing*. Lewisburg, Pa.: Bucknell University Press, 1977. 243 pp.

In this clear-headed study of Lessing's main themes, narrative techniques, and imagery, Singleton finds "many parallels with the psychology of Carl Jung." The central concern of Lessing's fiction is the development in the individual and in society of a unified consciousness to overcome the fragmentation of modern life. In *The Golden Notebook* (1962) Anna's development bears a strong resemblance to Jung's process of individuation, complete with mandala and uroboros symbolism. The Jungian search for psychic wholeness, informs Lessing's use of alchemy, dream symbolism, mythic parallels, and the concept of the collective mind. In all her work Lessing stresses the need for society and its individuals to come to terms with the personal and the mass shadows. Only then will mankind ever approach the ideal of a socially responsible life in a more "ideal city."

755. SMITH, Evans Lansing. "The Descent to the Underworld: Towards an Archetypal Poetics of Modernism." (Ph.D. 1986 Claremont Graduate School) 273 pp. *DAI* 47/05 A p.1736. (Yeats, Conrad, Mann, Eliot, Lawrence, Lowry, Broch, Hillman)

756. SMITHSON, Isaiah. "Iris Murdoch's *A Severed Head*: The Evolution of Human Consciousness." *Southern Review* (Adelaide) 11:2 (1978) 133-153.

The symbolism of Iris Murdoch's novel *A Severed Head* (1961) is explained in terms of the mythic patterns used by Erich Neumann to describe the ego's emergence from the unconscious. The childishly passive protagonist, mothered by a number of characters with Great Mother traits, develops active self-definition in his "dragon fights" with the Medusa-like Terrible Mother figure of Honor Klein. Martin's love for Honor involves the mythic motifs of the captive maiden and of incest. Murdoch's novel may be seen as "a symbolic representation of the evolution of human consciousness." This supports the view that the modern novel is "an extension of myth."

757. SNIDER, Clifton. "C.G. Jung's Analytical Psychology and Literary Criticism." *Psychocultural Review* 1:1 (1977) 96-108 and "Jung's Psychology of the Conscious and the Unconscious." *Psychocultural Review* 1:2 (1977) 216-242.

These two articles offer a summary of Jung's theories and definitions of Jungian concepts with a view to applying them as tools of literary criticism. The discussion of Jung's psychology draws very usefully on Jung's own works and on studies of well-known Jungian scholars, while all along examples are adduced from literary works in the major genres of all periods. These illustrations are of necessity so brief that the literary application sometimes appears over-simplified. However, in a third article an extensive Jungian analysis is presented of Swinburne's poetic romance *Tristram of Lyonesse* (1881).

758. SNIDER, Clifton. "The Archetypal Self in Swinburne's *Tristram of Lyonesse.*" *Psychocultural Review* 1:3 (1977) 371-390.

As an example of the thesis that, in general, "the analysis of literature from the Jungian point of view explores the stages in the process of individuation" Swinburne's longest poem is analyzed as showing the ascending stages of Tristram's and Iseult's achievement of psychological wholeness. The poem belongs to what Jung called "visionary" art; it compensated for Victorian prudery and offered an alternative for the loss of faith in traditional religion. "Because of all Swinburne's verse *Tristram of Lyonesse* is the finest and most complete example of the successful completion of individuation, it is his best and most 'religious' poem."

Though Swinburne's copious use of oppositions, paradoxes and oxymorons lends itself to analysis in terms of psychological opposites and complementaries, this essay is an over-enthusiastic Jungian reading. Every fight of Tristram is a slaying of the archetypal shadow; every love-meeting with the Irish Iseult a *coniunctio oppositorum* and *syzygy* of anima and animus, as well as an immediate achievement of selfhood and symbolic death in the unconscious from which they are reborn into expanded consciousness. There is confusion of symbolic levels and distortion of Jungian theory when the lovers' final union in death is said to be "the ultimate achievement of the archetypal self" through "their return to an undifferentiated state of unity" and "loss of individual identity." "Individuation is a process of differentiation" (Jung, Collected Works 6, par. 757) and the achieving of Self can hardly be a return to "undifferentiated nature".

759. SNIDER, Clifton. "Jungian Theory, Its Literary Application, and a Discussion of *The Member of the Wedding.*" In *Psychological Perspectives on Literature: Freudian Dissidents and Non-Freudians. A Casebook.* Ed. Joseph Natoli. Hamden, Conn.: Shoe String Press, 1984. 13-42.

For Natoli's collection of psychological approaches to literature (q.v.) Snider rewrote his earlier articles (q.v.) in *Psychocultural Review* and here presents an extensive summary of Jungian theories related to literature. As an example of literary application he gives a "Jungian examination" of Carson McCullers' novel *The Member of the Wedding* (1946), written during World War II, seen as "an unconscious attempt - an attempt, indeed, from the collective unconscious - to compensate" for a collectively split world. The lonely androgynous main character, Frankie, "in need of psychic wholeness and growth," attempts to live her "personal myth" that she will go off with her brother and his bride, because she has become "possessed by the archetype of the *hieros gamos*, or 'sacred wedding,' [...] symbolizing the union of opposites."

Although Jungian theory is competently summarized, Snider is inclined to dogmatize Jung's flexible concepts. This shows particularly in the literary applications. In spite of his own warnings, Snider often succumbs to the dangers of reductive psychological interpretation. Instead of providing literary insight, the archetypal overlay, in Snider's hands, too often results in unconvincing simplifications and insensitive readings of the texts. Two examples must suffice: "Shakespeare's Caliban, who fits Jung's definition of the shadow exactly, projects his own shadow onto Prospero and thus remains oblivious of his true self." The twelve-year old Frankie, in Carson McCullers' novel, is "not at all prepared psychologically or physically, I suspect, for a 'date' with a grown man. Archetypally this means she is not ready for an encounter with the animus, the archetype of the male in the female."

760. SNIDER, Clifton. "'A Single Self': A Jungian Interpretation of Virginia Woolf's *Orlando.*" *Modern Fiction Studies* 25:2 (1979) 263-268.

An analysis of Virginia Woolf's "fantasy-biography" from a Jungian point of view, "because the writing of *Orlando* and the book itself illustrate a number of Jungian theories. The composition of the book is a fine example of Jung's theory of creativity. The book itself shows the individuation of the character Orlando, how the character is able to develop each of Jung's four functions of consciousness and then to achieve an integrated personality through the joining of the anima and the animus." The androgynous Orlando, who changes sexes halfway through the story, unites the contrasexual opposites, just as in the dominating symbols of the house and the oak tree the unconscious and conscious are joined.

Though a Jungian reading of *Orlando* (1928) seems very well possible, the archetypal ascriptions are hardly argued and this slight article does not substantiate its sweeping claims.

761. SNIDER, Clifton M. "The Struggle For the Self: A Jungian Interpretation of Swinburne's *Tristram of Lyonesse*." (Ph.D. 1974 University of New Mexico) 174 pp. *DAI* 36/10 A p.6716.

762. SNYDER, Cecil Kane. "Mandala: A Proposed Schema for Literary Criticism." (Ph.D. 1968 Pennsylvania State University) 470 pp. *DAI* 29/10 A p.3588. (Hawthorne)

763. SOILE, 'Sola. "The Myth of the Archetypal Hero in Two African Novelists: Chinua Achebe and James Ngugi." (Ph.D. 1973 Duke University) 239 pp. *DAI* 34/03 A p.1296. (Also African novels by Rider Haggard, Joseph Conrad, Graham Greene)

764. SOUBLY, Diana M. "The Sun and Stars Nearer Roll: Jungian Individuation and the Archetypal Feminine in the Epics of William Blake and James Joyce." (Ph.D. 1981 Wayne State University) 577 pp. *DAI* 42/02 A p.716.

765. SPENCER, Sharon. *Collage of Dreams: The Writings of Anaïs Nin.* Chicago: Swallow Press, 1977. 188 pp.

This discerning study of the writings and personality of Anaïs Nin considers the influence of Jungian ideas on her thinking about women. The books of Esther Harding opened her eyes to qualities which her background of Spanish Catholicism had repressed: sexuality, independence and self-assertiveness. Therapy with a Jungian analyst helped her to bring into consciousness the undeveloped masculine powers of her animus and to achieve greater self-sufficiency and psychic wholeness, which gave her "a sure sense of her identity as an artist."

766. SPENCER, Sharon. "'Femininity' and the Woman Writer: Doris Lessing's *The Golden Notebook* and the *Diary* of Anais Nin." *Women's Studies* 1:3 (1973) 247-257.

Lessing's *The Golden Notebook* (1962) and Nin's *Diary* (1966-1976) "follow the process through which two women writers (the one fictional) gradually come to recognize and accept the animus or the male principle within themselves." Such acceptance is important, for an artist must develop abilities usually associated with the opposite sex, must become a "unified being." This is especially difficult for women who fear being considered masculine and who would therefore "deny and penalize the larger component of being, the self, in order to satisfy the ego's need for approval." K.S.

767. SPENCER, Sharon. "The Novelist's Dance of Numbers." *par rapport* 1:1 (1978) 41-45.

Jung's ideas about archetypal number symbolism, as developed by Marie-Louise von Franz in *Number and Time* (1955), are applied to novels by Marguerite Duras, *The Square* (1955), and Malcolm Lowry, *Under the Volcano* (1947).

768. SPERO, Richard H. "The Jungian World of Tennessee Williams." (Ph.D. 1970 University of Wisconsin) 294 pp. *DAI* 31/11 A p.6205.

769. SPICE, Wilma H. "A Jungian View of Tolkien's 'Gandalf': An Investigation of Enabling and Exploitative Power in Counseling and Psychotherapy from the Viewpoint of Analytical Psychology." (Ph.D. 1976 University of Pittsburgh) 329 pp. *DAI* 37/03 B p.1417.

770. SPIVACK, Charlotte K. "The Journey to Hell: Satan, the Shadow, and the Self." *Centennial Review* 9:4 (1965) 420-437.

The archetype of the journey to the underworld or to hell is a prominent theme in literature. Dante's descent in the *Inferno* shows evil as "the enslaving loss of choice." This moral and theological concept finds its equivalent in modern psychology in the possessive quality of the unrecognized shadow sides of the human personality. Carl Jung may be said to have "translated the theological journey to hell in search of spiritual salvation into the psychological journey to hell in search of self-integration." The centrality of the theme in modern literature is demonstrated by brief analysis of Dostoevski's *Notes from the Underground* (1866) and *Crime and Punishment* (1866), Conrad's *Heart of Darkness* (1899), Hesse's *Der Steppenwolf* (1927) and Golding's *Lord of the Flies* (1954).

771. SPIVEY, Ted. R. "Archetypal Symbolism in the Major Poetry of T. S. Eliot and Conrad Aiken." *International Journal of Symbology* 2:3 (1971) 16-26.

Aims to show how a systematic application of archetypal concepts will reveal similar mythic patterns in Eliot's *Four Quartets*

(1943) and Aiken's *Preludes* (1966) and *Ushant* (1952). The main works of both poets have the same circular structure, beginning and ending with mandalas and moving through the experience of chaos towards the quester's affirmation of the self or cosmic man in the center of his soul, a vision of harmony symbolized in images of dance and music.

Superficial article with over-simplified notions both of the archetypes and of the works of the poets.

772. SPIVEY, Ted R. "Conrad Aiken's Fusion of Freud and Jung." *Studies in the Literary Imagination* 13:2 (1980) 99-112.

Aiken said that "Freud was in every thing I did," but Spivey argues that, since he was "one of the most mythopoeic men of letters in our time," Aiken must also have been deeply influenced by Jung. In his work "the self-knowledge gained from Freudian psychology was the beginning of the journey that would end eventually in religious affirmation of the Self at the center of man's being." To illustrate this thesis Spivey traces in several of Aiken's poems the symbolism of the hero's pilgrimage to the mandalic center of an archetypal paradise.

773. SPIVEY, Ted R. *The Journey beyond Tragedy: A Study of Myth and Modern Fiction.* Gainesville: University Presses of Florida, 1980. xi,190 pp.

In sweeping generalizations the author expounds the optimistic thesis that certain modern artists pointed the way out of the "sterile wasteland" of our present tragic age. Literary critics have largely missed the visionary powers of writers who expressed in their art the great archetypal symbols of the mythic hero's journey and the mandala of totality, the image that sums up the "inner essential, creative center that many call the true self." Spivey analyzes works by eleven "modern" novelists from George Eliot to Walker Percy, who affirm the harmony "basic to a spiritual tradition," and he claims that we are moving into a postmodern period that will be "an age of high comedy." Jung, Campbell and Eliade are used to pursue images of the quester, the shadow, the anima/animus, and the cosmic man in novels by Thomas Mann, James Joyce, Hermann Hesse and others.

774. STACK, Frank. "The Experience of a Poem: Jung and Wallace Stevens." Guild Lecture No. 224. London: Guild of Pastoral Psychology, 1986. 16 pp.

Applies Jung's statements about the creative process, made in his essay "On the Relation of Analytical Psychology to Poetry," to an interpretation of Stevens' "The poem is the cry of its occasion," poem no. XII in the sequence "An Ordinary Evening in New Haven."

775. STALKER, Jacqueline W. "The Anima-Animus in Four Faulkner Novels." (Ph.D. 1983 Michigan State University) 275 pp. *DAI* 44/12 A p.3688.

776. STAPE, John H. "Dr. Jung at the Site of Blood: A Note on *Blown Figures*." *Studies in Canadian Literature* 2 (1977) 124-126.

This brief note on the novel *Blown Figures* (1974) by the Canadian author Audrey Thomas points out that the main character Isobel is based on the historical American woman, whose fantasies and visions, published under the pseudonym of Frank Miller, formed the inspiration of Jung's *Symbols of Transformation* (q.v.). Isobel's dreams and fantasies show parallels with those of Miss Miller, and the novel traces Isobel's descent into madness, just as Miss Miller's visions turned out to be "the Prelude to a Case of Schizophrenia," as Jung subtitled the second version of his book.

777. *STEELE, Robert S. and Susan W. Swinney. "Zane Grey, Carl Jung and the Journey of the Hero." *Journal of Analytical Psychology* 23:1 (1978) 63-89.

The wide appeal of Zane Grey's popular Western novels is ascribed to their archetypal appeal. *Wandered in the Wasteland* (1919) in particular "displays, in the unfolding of the hero's story, a striking similarity in structure and content" to the archetypal journey of the hero. Shuttling between Jung's work and the text of the novel, the authors demonstrate how the protagonist's journey in the desert, his struggle with his shadow brother, his meetings with various anima figures and wise old men, as well as many details of the imagery, tell the story of the hero who achieves significant psychic growth.

A fine discussion of the importance that writing the novel had for Grey himself is included. It is highly unlikely that he had any knowledge of Jung's early work. The strikingly Jungian character of the novel must be seen as an "expression of unconscious contents of Grey's mind," and as proof of Jung's contention that especially in popular literature we find the "visible manifestations" of the archetypes of the collective unconscious.

778. STEIN, Charles F. "The Secret of the Black Chrysanthemum: Charles Olson's Use of the Writings of C.G. Jung." (Ph.D. 1979 University of Connecticut) 285 pp. *DAI* 41/02 A p.675.

Became book *The Secret of the Black Chrysanthemum* (1987).

779. STEIN, Charles. *The Secret of the Black Chrysanthemum: The Poetic Cosmolology of Charles Olson and His Use of the Writings of C.G. Jung.* Barrytown, N.Y.: Station Hill Press, 1987. 232 pp.

Stein explores Olson's extensive reading of Jung "with the hope of bringing to light the complex and varying significance of the poet's attention to the psychologist." He neither offers a Jungian interpretation of Olson's thought and poetry, nor claims that Olson himself was a "Jungian".

780. STEIN, William B. *Hawthorne's Faust: A Study of the Devil Archetype.* Gainesville: University of Florida Press, 1953. vii,172 pp.

In this study of Hawthorne's fiction the confrontations with human evil in "the mythic substructure" of the tales are viewed as dramatizations of the devil archetype used as a symbolic image in the Jungian sense. The characters attain or fail to attain moral self-awareness through a Faustian pact with the devil and their ensuing "ordeal by sin."

781. STEIN, William B. "Melville's Poetry: Its Symbols of Individuation." *Literature and Psychology* 7:2 (1957) 21-26.

The poetry of Melville's old age is analyzed as expressing metaphorically his overcoming of personal anxiety and insecurity, "the monsters of his own imaginative deeps." In a culture losing its organizing religious myth, the fear of death may turn, as in Ahab, into a deep-seated destructive death urge. Melville's poetic imagination transfigured it into an acceptance of the natural cycle of life and death through realization that the psychic struggle may be resolved by forces within man himself. Though Jung is not explicitly mentioned, this discussion of the poems views Melville's psychological development in terms of the individuating consciousness that reaches a new balance of the psyche, which "admits the basic function of the law of opposites."

In somewhat different form this became chapter 4, "The Gorgons of the Underworld," in *The Poetry of Melville's Late Years* (q.v.).

782. STEIN, William B. "The Old Man and the Triple Goddess: Melville's 'The Haglets'." *ELH* 25:1 (1958) 43-59.

"The Haglets" (about 1888) is Melville's rewriting, a few years before his death, of an earlier poem about the ironical wrecking on its homeward journey of the ship and crew of a victorious English admiral. The malignant force of fate that dooms the sailors becomes in the revised poem a "sacred law of nature administered by the Great Mother in her role of Triple Goddess, at once creator, preserver, and destroyer," symbolized by the three haglets (seabirds) that preside over the violent death of the sailors as over a ritual. This reflects the profound changes in Melville's outlook on life in his later years. "The triple Goddess of Fate metamorphoses into the compassionate Great Mother." Denying the primacy of logos and intellect, and accepting the eternal feminine in nature, Melville sees time and death as transfigured in the endless regeneration of the eternal circle of life, death and rebirth. The "real" becomes an archetypal sacred marriage of life and death.

A slightly condensed version of this article became chapter 3, "The Triple Goddess," of Stein's book on *The Poetry of Melville's Late Years* (q.v.).

783. *STEIN, William B. *The Poetry of Melville's Late Years: Time, History, Myth, and Religion*. Albany: State University of New York Press, 1970. xii,275 pp.

In these readings of Melville's later poetry, written after "a tormenting psychological and spiritual crisis" had been resolved, Stein frequently undertakes "psychoanalytical interpretations, Freudian, Jungian, and sometimes plainly Steinian." In rebellion against nineteenth century idealism, traditional theology and romantic subjectivity, Melville writes verse of startling metrical irregularity in which he presents with ironic detachment harsh and unconventional pictures of life, often relating "the basic insecurity of experience to unsuspected psychosexual anxieties and disturbances." For him truth is not to be found in "the linear timetable of Christian salvation," but it is "the unchanging cycle of the year in its rhythm of birth, death, and rebirth" that "attests the continuity of existence." These insights of Melville's old age are expressed in patterns of mythic imagery and metaphors that work deep beneath the realistic surface of his poems. Close analyses of recurrent metaphors employed by Melville "to organize the activities of his sensibility, like the rose, the Great Mother, the redeemer figure, and the sea," demonstrate that he had "a keen understanding of the archetypal symbols of the unconscious."

Stein makes out a case for a reappraisal of Melville's neglected poetry by taking "his manipulated clumsiness for granted" and "focusing primarily on his strategies of imagery and wordplay." He puts Jungian archetypal theory to good use in these original readings of the later poetry and provides a new perspective on Melville's psychological and spiritual development in the later part of his life. Several chapters of this study were previously published as articles (see separate annotations).

784. STERNLICHT, Irwin R. "Shakespeare and the Feminine." In *A Well of Living Waters: A Festschrift for Hilde Kirsch*. Ed. Rhoda Head, et al. Los Angelos: C.G. Jung Institute, 1977. 189-203.
A paper on the theme that in Shakespeare's plays we often find a very sensitive portrayal of the feminine role "in the eventual development of greater wholeness in men." The weakness of one-sided rational attitudes is illustrated from Brutus' failure in *Julius Caesar*, and in particular from the collapse of Angelo's self-righteous coldness in *Measure For Measure*. Angelo's harsh treatment of Claudio (as threatening shadow figure) breaks down when he is confronted with the image of "a prodding anima - an authoritative mother" in the person of Isabella, who forces him to face the repressed feelings within himself.

785. STEVENSON, Lionel. "The 'High-Born Maiden' Symbol in Tennyson." *PMLA* 63:1 (1948) 234-243. Rpt. in *Critical Essays on the Poetry of Tennyson*. Ed. John Killham. London: Routledge & Kegan Paul, 1960.
The "high-born maiden," originally borrowed from Shelley, is a recurring anima symbol which went through three distinct phases during Tennyson's career. Because "a poet [...] keeps an unintentional diary of his psychological evolution in his poems," one can trace Tennyson's struggle with his own anima in the changes he makes in the nature of his maidens. K.S.

786. *STEWART, Allegra. *Gertrude Stein and the Present*. Cambridge, Mass.: Harvard University Press, 1967. xii,223 pp.
The art and thought of Gertrude Stein are placed in the context of the intellectual and artistic avant-garde of early 20th century Europe, and meaningfully related to the philosophies of Santayana, James, Bergson, Whitehead and Wittgenstein, as well as to the art of Picasso, Kandinski and Klee, many of whom Stein knew personally. The prose style she developed, with its baffling dislocations and repetitions, serves to express a meditative vision committed to "the search for meaning," for "sacred experience" in a world becoming ever more secular. Through ingenious linguistic and metaphorical analysis of its key words "carafe" and "fountain" it is argued that, if read in depth "downward to root meanings," the series of prose poems *Tender Buttons* (1914) is a significant attempt to use words vibrantly and creatively for the purpose of the "deracination of consciousness" (Jung's words) and the subsequent integration of mind as "being existing" (Stein's terms). *Tender Buttons* as a whole may be regarded as a work of "self-exploration and self-organization," a verbal mandala "enclosure for the unconscious mind."

The later opera libretto *Doctor Faustus Light the Lights* (1938), "dream vision and drama of individuation," is given a thoroughly Jungian interpretation as a significant version of the one genuine myth produced by modern Western man. The archetypal characters and events of this enigmatic "psychic monodrama" with its ballet of electric lights "symbolize a neurotic crisis of self-division and self-confrontation" in civilized man's shadow figure, Faustus. The outcome of the drama (Mephisto carrying Faustus to hell, and "the man from overseas standing with the anima figure in his arms") suggests the surrender of the ego and the reconciliation of the opposites that constitutes the Self.

This lucidly written, intelligent study of Gertrud Stein is marked by its comprehensive grasp of the literary, linguistic, philosophical, psychological and cultural aspects of its subject. It is at the same time a model of Jungian interpretation in depth of two literary works. In passing we are given in less than eight pages one of the best brief summaries of Jungian concepts and theory available. With an open eye for "the elements of triviality and frivolity in much of her writing," Allegra Stewart convincingly argues that Gertrude Stein's life and work make her "one of the more authentic voices of the human spirit in the twentieth century," representative of our own times precisely because she was not a person of genius.

787. *STEWART, Mary Zeiss. "'The Book of Thel': Amplifying Text as Dream." *Dragonflies* 2:2 (1980) 140-162.

Following the lead of writings on dream and image by James Hillman and Patricia Berry, the author reads Blake's mythical poem as a dream. The approach is by way of "amplification" of the poem as a sequence of dream-images. Unlike the intellectual method of critical discrimination and of generalization from particular facets of the image, amplification attempts to stay imaginatively close to the image, to feel its way into the archetypal essence by elaborating patterns, mythic allusions and associations. Blake's picture of the evasive lovely maiden who identifies with the beauty of vanishing shadows, clouds, dewdrops and blooms in "the eternal vales of Har," and who flees the realities of sensual life, is in the "amplificatory exercise" related to a handful of analogues from Greek mythology. Thel, like Ariadne, leads us on "a continuous circuit of advance and retreat," while we follow her through the labyrinth of parallels and patterns. "Untouched and untouchable," she "could be the image of the opus of amplification itself," leading us "back to the beginning of the round, back to a deeper involvement." This method, which disallows the move in the direction of conceptualization," gives "the personal factor" its due, for as Hillman says, "we are always ourselves in the image and unconscious because of it."

What emerges from the mythological parallels in this imaginative reading of Blake's poem may in the end not differ much from what another sensitive, but more logically ordered interpretation could offer. Yet the conceptualizing academic critic could do worse than ponder this meditation on the method of amplification for the light it sheds on Blake's poem, and for its claim that "approaching the text as dream means maintaining the integrity of the image."

788. STOLL, John E. *W.H. Auden: A Reading.* Muncie, Ind.: Ball State University Press, 1970. 35 pp.

Auden's poetry expresses the split in modern man between the intellect and feeling. This pamphlet argues the view that after "the Freudian preoccupation of the early work" Auden embarks on a "Jungian quest for psychic integration," which ultimately takes him to God in a "quite unorthodox way." Only after fully recognizing "his own incapacity to reconcile the opposites within himself does he take the religious leap." God's grace as the final hope for men is the religious analogue "for the entire integrative process through which all dualities are reconciled."

The influence of Blake, Lawrence and Jung is discussed in the successive phases of Auden's poetic career, but only in a very general way.

789. STOLL, John E. *The Novels of D.H. Lawrence: A Search for Integration.* Columbia: University of Missouri Press, 1971. vii,263 pp.

This psychological study of the "aesthetic imbalance" in Lawrence's work argues that for him consciousness is a social product imposed from without which poisons "the spontaneous wellsprings" of the unconscious (the vital self). The novels are seen as a continued search for psychic integration, which can only be achieved by destroying our "white mental consciousness" and obeying the dark "blood-self" (Lawrence's terms). In his introductory chapter Stoll defines Lawrence's agreements and disagreements with Freud and Jung. By dismissing the id as a principle of the unconscious, Lawrence differs radically from Freud. His view of the unconscious as healthy and creative aligns him with Jung, but there is this crucial difference that Lawrence rejects the reconciliation of the opposites as a means of overcoming psychic duality.

790. STONE, Donal. "Steinbeck, Jung, and *The Winter of Our Discontent.*" *Steinbeck Quarterly* 11:3-4 (1978) 87-96.

In his novel *The Winter of Our Discontent* (1961) Steinbeck, consciously or unconsciously, describes the process of individuation of the hero, Ethan, during which he encounters the shadow (the grey cat), helpful animas (the fortune-teller and his daughter Ellen), and the wise old man (his grandfather). Other archetypal symbols are introduced in the form of Ethan's talisman: a round, translucent stone, four inches in diameter, carved with a circular snake. K.S.

791. STONE-BLACKBURN, Susan. *Robertson Davies, Playwright: A Search for the Self on the Canadian Stage.* Vancouver: University of British Columbia Press, 1985. 249 pp.

Considers Jung's influence on Davies.

792. STREATFEILD, D. *A Study of Two Worlds: Persephone.* London: Routledge & Kegan Paul, 1959. 367 pp.

The success of Hadley Chase's best-selling novel *No Orchids for Miss Blandish* (1939) is ascribed to its mythical and archetypal qualities. The story of a millionaire's daughter, abducted by a young gangster, closely parallels the myth of Persephone carried off by Pluto to the underworld. Part of the book is a philosophical disquisition on the nature of their "two worlds": consciousness and order over against unconscious and rebellious but vital life forces. It becomes a plea for a Jungian integration of our outer world of scientific "facts" with the equally important inner world of dreams and intuitions.

Half of this book is an enthusiastic, elaborate exposition of Jung's theory of archetypes and individuation supplemented by elucidations from biology. The discussion of *No Orchids for Miss Blandish* aims at illustrating the mythical and psychological theme rather than at literary analysis.

793. STRELKA, Joseph. "Comparative Criticism and Literary Symbolism." In *Perspectives in Literary Symbolism.* Yearbook of Comparative Criticism, Vol. 1. Ed. Joseph Strelka. University Park: Pennsylvania State University Press, 1968. 1-28.

In this first essay in the prestigious series of Yearbooks of Comparative Criticism, Strelka outlines his aims for comparative criticism as "a field of experimentation [...] for comparative methods, ideas, and conceptions in the area of literary criticism and literary theory." This implies consideration of literary evaluation, as well as related fields. Symbolism being "the common feature and mutual problem" of many of these disciplines, the study of mythical and esoteric symbols is singled out as particularly meaningful for comparative criticism, and least explored. When discussing "the esoteric traditions from which Western literature has drawn throughout the centuries," Strelka argues (from the example of James Baird's Melville study) that "critics who hold and represent Jung's views would generally have good insight into the relation between literary symbolism and esoteric tradition."

794. STRICKLAND, Edward. "Metamorphoses of the Muse in Romantic Poesis: *Christabel.*" *ELH* 44:4 (1977) 641-658.

The meeting of Christabel with the lady Geraldine in Coleridge's poem is explained archetypally as the confrontation of the "poet-surrogate" with the ambivalent anima, both demon and angel, seductress and madonna. Geraldine's self-contradictions as ambivalent Muse-figure "mirror the ambiguities of the unconscious and its exploration" by Coleridge. This may be seen as "the cause of his inability to complete the poem." Reading the poem "in terms of the dialectics of vision rather than sexual neurosis," the essay shows the "appositeness of Jungian theory" to the theme of "preternatural females in Romantic poetry."

795. STRONG, Paul. "James Dickey's Arrow of Deliverance." *South Carolina Review* 11:1 (1978) 108-116.

Ed Gentry's wounding himself with an arrow in Dickey's novel *Deliverance* (1970) is related to Jungian and Zen theories. "Inner harmony is metaphorically achieved when the archer is impaled on his own arrow."

796. STROUD, Joanne Herbert. "Archetypal Symbols in the Poetry of W.B. Yeats." (Ph.D. 1975 University of Dallas) 218 pp. *DAI* 37/01 A p.302.

797. STULL, William L. "The Quest and the Question: Cosmology and Myth in the Work of William S. Burroughs, 1953-1960." *Twentieth Century Literature* 24:2 (1978) 225-242.

The basic pattern of adventure in the early novels of William Burroughs from *Junkie* (1953) to *Naked Lunch* (1959) makes them a modern version of the mythic hero quest as described by Joseph Campbell. Trailing across the Americas in his campaign against the "junk" of "chaotic, self-consuming power," the evil virus that blights life in the modern waste land, the protagonist undergoes a maturing process that has its parallel in the stages of Campbell's "monomyth." The "boon" brought back from this quest is the hero's insight that only a "program of anarchic individualism" can revitalize the junk universe.

798. SUGG, Richard P. *Robert Bly*. Boston: G.K. Hall, 1986. 160 pp. Treats the poetry of Bly from a Jungian viewpoint.

799. SULLIVAN, G. Brian. "The Alchemy of Art: A Study in the Evolution of the Creative Mind of John Keats." (Ph.D. 1967 University of Nebraska, Lincoln) 270 pp. *DAI* 28/07 A p.2698.

800. SULLIVAN, Rosemary. *Theodore Roethke: The Garden Master*. Seattle: University of Washington Press, 1975. xv,220 pp.

This study of Roethke's work in its development considers, among other things, the influence of "his intense reading of Maud Bodkin's *Archetypal Patterns of Poetry*. The archetypal character of his symbolic images is specifically analyzed in "The Lost Son" series of poems, written at the time of Roethke's breakdown in 1945, which is seen as an interior journey, a plunging into and return from the depths of the unconscious. It is argued that critics have misread his later "North American Sequence" as a collection of "random sensational images," because they failed to appreciate "the hierarchical and moral values" implied in his nature symbols.

801. SUTTON, Max K. "Selving as Individuation in Hopkins: A Jungian Reading." *Hopkins Quarterly* 2:3 (1975) 119-129.

Hopkins' complex notions of "selving" and "unselving" may be compared with Jung's process of individuation. "Both men hold the view that the self is to be discovered, not invented, and the stages of selving in Hopkins' poetry are marked by figures who correspond to the psychic archetypes - the anima, the shadow, and the goal of individuation, the realized Self. Seen chronologically, the poems reveal a questing movement toward this goal." Already in his earliest poems Hopkins sees selving as a transforming process that brings pain and suffering, and must be achieved through sacrifice and struggle with rebellious sensual shadows. In his mature poems anima figures like the tall nun in "The Wreck of the Deutschland" and the captive maiden in "Andromeda" lead the poet in psychological terms to the crucified Christ as the perfect image of the Self. Taking bitterness and despair as "God's most deep decrees," Hopkins, in the final sonnets, tries to accept all of himself and finds his "poor Jackself" to be "immortal diamond," an "image of his fulfilled being." Though the diamond is also one of Jung's symbols for the Self, Sutton believes the analogue ends here. For Jung, God is "contained within" the psyche, whereas for Hopkins God is "an independent reality, a self beyond the Jungian Self."

802. SUTTON, Walter. *Modern American Criticism*. Englewood Cliffs, N.J.: Prentice Hall, 1963. 175-218.

The chapter "Psychological and Myth Criticism" gives a balanced survey of the work of the main Jungian and Freudian literary critics until 1960. Sutton appreciates Maud Bodkin's three books and her modification of the archetype into the type-image. The myth critics Wheelwright and Frye, the Freudians Wilson, Trilling and Lesser are reviewed, as well as the eclectics Burke and Fiedler. Sutton points out the strengths and the weaknesses of much general Jungian ("merely a search for archetypes" and the monomyth) and Freudian criticism (the tendency to reduce literature to wish-fulfillment and self-expression).

803. SWEET, Charles A., Jr. "Bernard Malamud and the Use of Myth." (Ph.D. 1970 Florida State University) 160 pp. *DAI* 31/09 A p.4797.

804. SWISHER, Walter S. "A Psychoanalysis of Browning's 'Pauline'." *Psychoanalytic Review* 7:2 (1920) 115-133.

Browning's poem "Pauline" (1833) is psychoanalyzed with the help of Freud, Adler and Jung as the expression of Browning's father-complex, its projection upon Shelley, the abreaction in the poem, and, "possibly, sublimation through religion." At the same time symbolic images and two dreams in the poem suggest that Browning identifies with gods and heroes of mythology to express the ego's struggle to free itself from Jung's "terrible mother" imago and attain independence.

An interesting early application of the new depth psychology to a literary text, though the poem is considered in the first place for its therapeutic effect on Browning, and the symbols are seen as merely "typical," since "we lack the subjective material for the personal analysis we should like."

805. TACEY, David J. "'It's Happening Inside': The Individual and Changing Consciousness in White's Fiction." In *Patrick White: A Critical Symposium*. Eds. Ronald Shepherd and Kirpal Singh. Adelaide: Centre for Research in the New Literatures in English, 1978. 34-40.

The external "reality" of Patrick White's novels is an expression of the characters' psycho-spiritual inner drama. In this essay Tacey looks at the novels from the perspective of their "mandala" symbolism taken as suggesting that characters achieve a form of psychic wholeness. This view was abandoned when Tacey came to see the devouring mother myth as the central psychological theme in all of White's fiction (see his essay in *Journal of Analytical Psychology* 28:2 (1983) 165-183).

806. TACEY, David J. "In the Lap of the Land: Misogyny and Earth-Mother Worthship in *The Tree of Man*." In *Mapped But Not Known: The Australian Landscape of the Imagination*. Eds. P.R. Eaden and F. H. Mares. Adelaide: Wakefield Press, 1986. 192-209.

807. TACEY, David J. *Patrick White: Fiction and the Unconscious*. Melbourne: Oxford University Press, 1988. xxiii,269 pp.

See for a summary of the argument of this unorthodox Jungian study of White and his fiction the annotation to Tacey's essay in the *Journal of Analytical Psychology* (see following entry).

808. *TACEY, David J. "Patrick White: The Great Mother and Her Son." *Journal of Analytical Psychology* 28:2 (1983) 165-183.

Tacey's radically original views about the mythical and psychological symbolism in White's novels will be mostly given in his own words abstracted from an article that summarizes the arguments worked out in his book *Patrick White: Fiction and the Unconscious* (1988).

"White's novels seem Jungian because the writer has in his own way drawn upon the deep unconscious and its archetypes. It is precisely this fact that makes the novels so powerful and that accounts for their genuine visionary quality. They are not the products of his conscious mind but spring up, as it were, from the creative unconscious." White himself claims that he did not read Jung until the time of writing *The Solid Mandala* (1966). The symbolism of the circular form which is evident in all the earlier novels is "never a true mandala, a symbol of the integration of the personality, but rather a representation of the uroboros, the womb-like image of the unconscious. The crucial distinction between the uroboros (circle-as-beginning) and the mandala (circle-as-end) is not recognized by the novelist ... White's characters merge into the oceanic oneness of the uroboros and, by a systematic misapplication of the individuation paradigm, the author translates this movement toward disintegration into terms of self-realization and wholeness. The end result is that White and his critics talk about psychological and spiritual triumphs which bear no relation to the actual *regressions* which take place in the fiction."

Tacey argues that White's novels are all variations upon the matriarchal myth of the great mother and her eternal youth. The fatal marriage of mother and son is one of the earliest mythical themes in Western culture. In White's stories "the masculine spirit constantly succumbs" to the strength of the devouring mother, "the son does not mature psychologically beyond adolescence." White himself, however, "presents the mother myth in a wholly positive light; in fact he (mis)represents it as Christianity. Just as the maternal round is viewed as a 'mandala', so the *puer*'s longing to return to the mother is seen in the context of man's desire for unity with God. The protagonist is extinguished in the source-situation and the author assumes he is becoming 'at one' with the divine. It appears that the ecstasy of dissolution (i.e. loss of ego and its limitations) is confused with the heightened feeling of religious integration and spiritual endeavour. White chooses to ignore completely the nihilistic character of uroboric regression. But while the teller focuses upon the ecstatic aspect of dissolution, the tale itself tends to emphasize the destructive and devouring nature of the process."

To illustrate his thesis Tacey demonstrates how in the earlier novels the protagonist's craving for self-annihilation is constantly reduced by "terrible mother" figures. In White's best-known novels *Voss* (1957) and *Riders in the Chariot* (1961) his "Christian misrepresentation of this central theme" reaches its most advanced stage "in terms of Christian sacrifice and the redemptive mystery of 'man returning into God'." In *The Solid Mandala* (1966) "the unconscious rises up in reaction to the author's misreading of the myth." The inner life takes on a personified form in the figure of Waldo's retarded "shadow-brother who rejects the Christian frame." In his detailed analysis of this novel Tacey shows that the disintegration of Waldo's ego-personality is due to the "psychologically incestuous" fusion of the brothers, and to Waldo's refusal to accept responsibility for his own urgent need for transformation.

In the novels of the 1970s the male characters evermore sink into the oblivion of the mother-world. Archetypal females, on the other hand, pursue "a vigorous and extraordinarily productive course of self-development," most evident in the "vastly inclusive" figure of the dying Mrs. Hunter in *The Eye of the Storm* (1973)

Tacey finally suggests that the Great Mother *mytheme* dominates Australian art and forms the mythic background of many Australian novelists, because "the mother rules the interior life of this country." Patrick White must be seen as "a pioneer who [...] journeyed into the lower realm [...] risked the descent and was strangely absorbed into the archetypal field of the goddess."

To a non-specialist in White, Tacey's bold but cogently argued readings of the psycho-symbolism in White's novels appear most convincing. It is clear that he penetrates to the psychological roots of the themes and characters of the novels, as well as to those of White's personality and his creative process. Tacey's style is lucid and direct. His full understanding of Jung's psychology is subtly and brilliantly applied to the entangling of intricate knots in the web of conscious and unconscious elements in Patrick White's art.

809. TACEY, David J. "Patrick White: Misconceptions about Jung's Influence." *Australian Literary Studies* 9:2 (1979) 245-246.

810. TACEY, David J. "Patrick White's *Voss*: The Teller and the Tale." *Southern Review* (Adelaide) 18:3 (1985) 251-271.

811. TACEY, David J. "The Reign of the Mother Goddess: A Jungian Study of the Novels of Patrick White." (Ph.D. 1981 University of Adelaide, Australia). *DAI* 44/06 A p.1788.
Became book *Patrick White: Fiction and the Unconscious* (1988).

812. TACEY, David J. "A Search for a New Ethic: White's *A Fringe of Leaves*." In *South Pacific Images*. Ed. Chris Tiffin. Brisbane: South Pacific Association for Commonwealth Literature and Language Studies, 1978. 186-195.
By confronting the shadow side of her own life Ellen Roxburgh, the protagonist of Patrick White's novel *A Fringe of Leaves* (1967), achieves the self-knowledge that makes her into a representative of the new humanity that has learned to integrate its own evil, envisaged in Erich Neumann's book *Depth Psychology and a New Ethic* (1948).

813. TANENHAUS, Beverley. "Politics of Suicide and Survival: The Poetry of Anne Sexton and Adrienne Rich." *Bucknell Review* 24:1 (1978) 106-118.
Anne Sexton's expression of female helplessness in the face of patriarchal oppression is contrasted with Adrienne Rich's struggle for a poetical language that attempts to break down cultural barriers. Rich develops in her poetry a radical feminist "redefinition of the patriarchal woman" who is merely selfless wife and mother, when she claims "in a Jungian context" the superior male as a strong, vitalizing element within her own personality.

814. TAORMINA, Agatha. "The Hero, the Double, and the Outsider: Images of Three Archetypes in Science Fiction." (D.A. 1980 Carnegie-Mellon University) 221 pp. *DAI* 42/02 A p.693. (Isaac Asimov, Arthur C. Clarke, Robert A. Heinlein, Ursula K. Le Guin)

815. TATHAM, Cam. "Anima Rising: Notes toward a Mediating Fiction." *Higginson Journal* 20:2 (1978) 46-61.
Demonstrates the influence of Jung and Campbell on John Barth's *Chimera* (1972). In this novel, "the central conflict between the masculine and the feminine is unresolved, undifferentiated, the potential balance frustrated [...] Logos [is] exalted to the detriment of Eros." A difficult and rather opaque analysis. K.S.

816. TATHAM, Peter. "Beowulf, and the Renewal of the Old King."
Harvest 26 (1980) 21-36.

The Old English epic *Beowulf* with its many digressions
(considered as a "dream sequence") is seen as focusing on the
mythic theme of the need to replace the Old King by a young
virile one. If the poem is taken as "a model of psychic totality,"
there is also a movement from one-sided ego-consciousness towards
integration of unconscious contents (symbolized in the underwater
fight with Grendel's mother) and greater realization of the Self.
Beowulf, who is described as "eager for fame" but also "the mildest
and gentlest of men," is the archetypal "bear" hero who combines
in his nature contradictory elements that include the feminine
aspect of his illogical self-sacrifice in the final dragon fight.

This paper is based on the author's diploma thesis for the C.G.
Jung Institute, Zurich. Both the renewal myth and the optimistic
Jungian individuation scheme are imposed upon the epic in very
general terms which seem at odds with the sternly tragic mood of
the Anglo-Saxon narrative.

817. TAYLOR, John F. "A Search for Eden: Thoreau's Heroic Quest."
(Ph.D. 1971 University of Maryland) 137 pp. *DAI* 32/06 A p.3334.

818. TAYLOR, Eugene C. "Shelley as Myth-Maker." *Journal of Abnormal
Psychology* 14 (1919-1920) 64-90.

In this early "application of the general principles of
psychoanalysis" in a study of Shelley's longer poems, Taylor blends
Freud's notions of repression, sublimation, and the Oedipus complex
with Jung's ideas of compensation and the spiritualization of the
incest theme in the myth of the hero's quest. The "repressed
portion of Shelley's libido" finds expression in the sexualized
landscape of caves, water, wind and moving boats. The dream of
the hero's impassioned union with veiled maidens suggests in
psychological terms the search for the lost childhood and the
mother. In an early poem like *Alastor* (1816) this symbolic quest for
the ideal woman ultimately fails, and, blocked by the incest
prohibition, the hero ends in death.

In the later poems, where incest is stressed, the women are
more clearly "mother-surrogates" and the theme becomes the
renewal of life through symbolical union with the mother and
consequent spiritual rebirth. Love "must be sacrificed and
spiritualized before it can escape from the toils of the incest
bond." *Prometheus Unbound* (1819) successfully mythologizes the
repression and release of the "forward-striving libido," in what
Taylor analyzes as a "drama of emancipation." Through self-
sacrifice Prometheus conquers the tyrant Jupiter ("the incest

barrier"), his beloved Asia descends into the underworld of the unconscious to face the Demogorgon of "the repressed incest wish" and "receive confirmation of her motherhood." She returns transfigured as the eternal mother. Jupiter and Demogorgon fall, and in the final apotheosis Shelley's "spirits of the human mind" announce the new dispensation of universal love. Thus Taylor traces "the unconscious development of the religious myth" in Shelley's poetry and at the same time shows how "the poet's psychic growth followed the evolution of the human mind in general, as it is outlined by Dr. Jung."

In what is probably the earliest piece of Jungian literary criticism following the English translation of Jung's *Psychology of the Unconscious* (1916), Taylor still happily combines Freud and Jung, as well as the artist's work and his personal life, while he demonstrates the possibilities of the new psychology for the understanding and interpretation of literature.

819. TERRY, Phyllis Ch. "Female Individuation in the Twentieth Century as Seen through Contemporary Fiction." (Ph.D. 1977 California School of Professional Psychology, San Diego) 213 pp. *DAI* 38/08 B p.3860. (Atwood, Penelope Mortimer, Lessing, C.S. Lewis)

820. TEUNISSEN, John J. and Evelyn J. Hinz. "The Attack on the *Pietà*: An Archetypal Analysis." *Journal of Aesthetics and Art Criticism* 33 (1974-75) 43-50.

The attack by a disturbed man with a hammer on Michelangelo's *Pietà*, the famous sculpture of the Virgin Mother cradling the body of her dead Son in her lap, is taken as the starting-point for a discussion of the negative valuation in our culture of the irrational and unconscious. In contrast with the ancient religions of the dying and reborn god that celebrate the life-preserving cycle of the natural year, the Christian belief in a resurrected god involves a concept of spiritual rebirth that is essentially life-denying. The Virgin Mother with her dead Son may be seen as an image of the archetype of the anima and mother imago in their negative, destructive aspects, while the iconoclast's action paradoxically represents the rebellious living out of irrational impulses necessary for the perpetuation of human life in a world losing its natural human values. This at any rate was the view embodied in essays and novels of that other iconoclast D.H. Lawrence. His quarrel with Christianity is often expressed in images of the all-loving mother, "this infernal self-conscious Madonna starving our living guts and bullying us to death with her love" (*Fantasia of the Unconscious*). Examples from several novels, such as the relationship of Clifford Chatterley to his nurse, and the return in the flesh of Jesus in "The Man Who Died" illustrate Lawrence's concern with the archetype of the Magna Mater.

821. TEUNISSEN, John J. *"For Whom the Bell Tolls* as Mythic Narrative." *Dalhousie Review* 56:1 (1976) 52-69.

Hemingway's novel should be read as mythical narrative, not as a realistic novel. Robert Jordan's actions, his blowing up of the bridge, his heroic last stand and his love affair, are related by Hemingway to archetypal events in the history of the young American's forefathers and their fights against the Indians. In the perspective of Jung's archetypes and Eliade's myth of ritual renewal, the novel's characters and events acquire iconographic significance.

822. THERIOT, Ibry Glyn-Francis. "The Dark Night of the Soul: The Archetype and Its Occurrence in Modern Fiction." (Ph.D 1973 Louisiana State University) 333 pp. *DAI* 35/02 A p.1125. (Conrad, Julien Green, Charles Williams, Beckett)

823. THOMPSON, Phyllis J. "Archetypal Elements in *The Faerie Queene* with Special Reference to Book Six." (Ph.D. 1965 University of North Carolina, Chapel Hill) 263 pp. *DAI* 26/07 A p.3964.

824. THOMSON, George H. *The Fiction of E.M. Forster*. Detroit, Mi.: Wayne State University Press, 1967. 304 pp.

Thomson studies the visionary element in Forster's fiction, which he sees "as romance rather than novel," by focusing on the ecstatic experience as its central theme. Already in the early stories "the eternal moment" of ecstatic feeling is a mystical experience of identity with nature, with something outside the self. Forster conveys to the reader this "sense of a living totality" by the use of archetypal symbols that function not through associations with traditional myths, but as freshly created myth (the wisp of hay in *Howards End* (1910), the Marabar caves in *A Passage to India*). The archetypal qualities of Forster's fiction are explored in, for instance, the Great Mother aspects of Mrs. Wilcox and the Schlegel sisters, and in Adela's vision during the trial scene in *A Passage to India* (1924), the "archetypal novel" in which the moments of ecstasy make characters "participate in this mystery of oneness and so apprehend [man's] own divinity." Thomson emphasizes the similarities between Forster's art and Jung's theories: "his intuitive grasp of whole experience, his firm acknowledgement of the unconscious, and his intense commitment to life and its individuality." For both Forster and Jung the cultivation of individual personality was in the end directed towards a spiritual goal.

Though Thomson's argument has its vaguenesses and critics have complained that the complexity of Forster's vision is unduly simplified, this is a very readable discussion of the mythic and symbolic aspects of Forster's fiction.

825. THORBURN, John M. *Art and the Unconscious: A Psychological Approach to a Problem of Philosophy*. London: Kegan Paul, 1925. xii,242 pp.

The philosopher Thorburn is one of the first to apply Jung's theories to problems of aesthetics. In his analysis of the psychology of the creative process in art he concentrates on the analogy and the difference between art and dream, but he rejects the Freudian "negative attitude towards the imagination." Jung's views of the collective nature of the unconscious and the dream image as symbol are basic to Thorburn's formulation of his theory that art is a symbolic expression of positive values in a particular artistic medium. Illustrations are drawn mainly from sculpture, music and literature. His ideas were developed for literature by Maud Bodkin (see Claudia Morrison for extensive summary and critical discussion of Thorburn's book).

826. THORNBURG, Thomas R. "The Quester and the Castle: The Gothic Novel as Myth with Special Reference to Bram Stoker's *Dracula*." (Ed.D. 1970 Ball State University) 179 pp. *DAI* 31/09 A p.4752.

827. TIMPE, Eugene F. "*Ulysses* and the Archetypal Feminine." In *Perspectives in Literary Symbolism*. Yearbook of Comparative Criticism, No. 1. Ed. Joseph Strelka. University Park: Pennsylvania State University Press, 1968. 199-212.

With Jung's concept of symbolism and Neumann's elaboration of the archetypal feminine as basis, the manifestations of the Great Mother are traced in the eighteen books of Joyce's *Ulysses* (1922). The transformations of the wayward, contradictory and all-powerful feminine run from the Good Mother symbolism of birth and rebirth in the opening books, Molly Bloom as anima embodiment in the "Calypso" and "Nausicaa" chapters, via women with devouring Terrible Mother aspects in, among others, the "Wandering Rocks" and "Circe" books, to end in the "Penelope" chapter with Molly as the Earth Mother, "basic figure of containment, protection and nourishment."

828. TINDALL, William York. *Forces in Modern British Literature 1885-1946*. New York: Alfred Knopf, 1947. xiii,386 pp.

In the chapter "The Unconscious" of Tindall's survey of developments in British literature between 1885 and 1946 he indicates briefly the influence of Jung on Joyce, Lawrence, Read and Graves.

829. TINDALL, William Y. *A Reader's Guide to James Joyce*. New York: Noonday Press, 1959. 304 pp.
Tindall's lively guide to the intricacies of Joyce's meanings often points to "characters and relationships that seem archetypal," particularly Molly Bloom as anima and Great Mother, image of Woman, "central among Joyce's archetypes."

830. TODD, Robert E. "The Magna Mater Archetype in *The Pardoner's Tale*." *Literature and Psychology* 15:1 (1965) 32-40.
An archetypal interpretation of Chaucer's tale is proposed in terms of Erich Neumann's study of the Great Mother, the terrible goddess that feeds and destroys man. Womb-tomb imagery is used to describe the mysterious old man who directs the three revelers in their search for Death, the man's wish to enter mother earth, and the use of the tree under which the deadly treasure and poisoned wine are found.
The interpretation does not get far beyond the simple attribution of the archetype.

831. TODD, Robert E. "The Magna Mater Archetype in *The Scarlet Letter*." *New England Quarterly* 45:3 (1972) 421-429.
The duality of Hester Prynne, saint and sinner, is explained as an embodiment of the Magna Mater archetype, who in her double role of "good" and "terrible" mother, causes her lover's psychical rebirth in the forest scene, as well as his ultimate death.
Though Hawthorne's ambivalence and overt symbolizing certainly give full range to archetypal interpretations, the unsubtle handling of Jungian notions makes for an unconvincing essay. Psychological confusion rather than clarification is achieved by treating anima and great mother archetypes as identical and by picturing the permanently flawed Arthur Dimmesdale as a character who reaches full individuation.

832. TUCKER, Betty J. "An Archetypal Imagery Study of the Fall of the Family in the Nineteenth-Century English Novel." (Ph.D. 1970 University of Alabama) 568 pp. *DAI* 31/10 A p.5430.

833. TURNER, Dixie M. *A Jungian Psychoanalytic Interpretation of William Faulkner's As I Lay Dying*. Washington: University Press of America, 1981.

Examines each member of the Bundren family in relation to a Jungian archetype as "an image of mind process and primordial inheritance."

834. TYRRELL, William B. "Dionysus in Sendak's Night Kitchen." *Psychocultural Review* 1:4 (1977) 459-466.

An archetypal interpretation of Maurice Sendak's children's book *In the Night Kitchen* (1970). Mickey's adventures in the bakery are related to the quest into darkness and confrontation with the feminine of so many Greek mythical heroes. "The motifs of his story, especially the prominence of milk and the complex of eating, sensual experience, and power evoke the mystery of Dionysus." The bisexual bakers and their kitchen suggest the Jungian union of opposites in the unconscious, well-spring of creativity and destruction. Mickey's flight over the top of the Milky Way is the supreme ordeal of the heroic journey, which in its festive ending embodies the exuberance of life.

The psychological/mythical dimension of this children's story is ably and wittily explained.

835. VAN DE VYVERE, James. "Psychological Naturalism: The Jungian Myths of John Steinbeck." (Ph.D. 1979 University of Ottawa, Canada) No abstract in *DAI*.

836. VAN EENWIJK, John R. "Individuation in Graham Greene: *Brighton Rock* and *The End of the Affair*. Viewed from the Perspective of Analytical Psychology with Special Reference to the Role of Religious Images in Psychological Development." (Ph.D. 1981 University of Chicago) 303 pp. No abstract in *DAI*.

An account of the role of religious images in psychological development, with reference to Jung's theory of the mana-personality, utilizing two novels by Graham Greene.

837. VAN GHENT, Dorothy. "Keats's Myth of the Hero." *Keats-Shelley Journal* 3 (1954) 7-25.

Keats's poetry is pervaded by the theme of the mythical quest of "a hero who is afflicted with a feverish strive of opposites," undertakes a journey for an otherworldly love, is tested, and finally wins immortality or "identity." In various forms, expanded in the epics and adumbrated in the longer poems and lyrics, we find "the familiar archaic motifs of the underground journey, death and symbolic burial, the foetal sleep-healing, the rebirth, and the mystic marriage" of hero and earth-goddess figure. The essay examines the poems in terms of the transformation of the Dionysian hero into his Apollonian counterpart, and of the hero's movement "from emotional ravage and temporal death to healing in marble and immortality." Even if Keats's ideal of human progress is sometimes at odds with the narrative form of the myth, the psychological aims of "the one mythologizing impulse" is unmistakable: the object of the hero's quest is "homogeneous selfhood, permanent oneness of feeling."

This subtle analysis of the psychological implications of Keats's use of mythological themes is obviously indebted to the writings of Jung and Campbell, although in this early essay their names are not mentioned. Van Ghent expanded her treatise into a book published in 1983 after her death.

838. VAN GHENT, Dorothy. *Keats: The Myth of the Hero.* Revised and edited by Jeffrey C. Robinson. Princeton: Princeton University Press, 1983. ix,277 pp.

Archetypal study of Keats's poetry in which Jung and Campbell are extensively used. (In the *Year's Work in English Studies*, 1983, p. 340, noticed as one of the "few really good books on Keats in recent years.)

839. VANN, Barbara. "A Psychological Interpretation of *Daisy Miller.*" In *A Festschrift for Professor Marguerite Roberts.* Ed. Frieda E. Penninger. Richmond: Richmond University Press, 1976. 205-208.

This slight piece offers a Jungian view of Henry James's story. "Randolph and Daisy can be viewed as aspects of Winterbourne's personality, which he needs to integrate to achieve self-actualization."

840. VICKERY, John B. "T.S. Eliot and the Golden Bough: The Archetype of the Dying God." (Ph.D. 1955 University of Wisconsin) 930 pp. No abstract in *DAI*.

841. VICKERY, John B., ed. *Myth and Literature: Contemporary Theory and Practice.* Lincoln: University of Nebraska Press, 1966. xii,391 pp.

These thirty-four essays by different hands survey the development, theory, practice and problems of "myth criticism" in the 1960s. Well-known American critics provide discriminations and practical applications. There are three sections: the Nature of Myth, Myth and Literature, Myth and Criticism. The third section of twenty-one articles ranges over texts from Homer to Milton, Melville, Zola, Faulkner, Kafka and Mann, to name a few. Vickery's introduction and interspersed commentary explain how archetype, myth and ritual entered the explication of literature. The seminal influence of Frazer, Freud and Jung is stressed. Although only a few specifically cite Jung, many of the essays resonate with his archetypes. (See Blotner, Harrison and Moorman)

842. VICKERY, John B. "The Scapegoat in Literature: Some Kinds and Uses." *The Binding of Proteus: Perspectives on Myth and the Literary Process.* Eds. Marjorie W. McCune, Tucker Orbison and Philip Withim. Lewisburg, Pa.: Bucknell University Press, 1980. 264-278.

A survey of the scapegoat theme in literature with examples from Euripides, Hawthorne, Melville, Ibsen, Strindberg, Lawrence and Faulkner, that takes its starting-point from Jung's concept of the shadow qualities of the individual or the group projected onto stranger or enemy as personifications of evil. The ritual expulsion of the scapegoat to discharge the group's repressed negative impulses and eliminate guilt feelings results in society's self-degradation or the victim's heroism. Three basic types of scapegoats are distinguished: the king/hero, the criminal/knave, and the fool/clown, who in literature may all suffer ironic reversals.

843. VICKERY, John B. and J'nan M. Sellery, eds. *The Scapegoat: Ritual and Literature.* Boston: Houghton Mifflin, 1972. viii,386.

Excellent anthology with some theoretical pieces on the cultural phenomenon of the scapegoat by scholars of anthropology, comparitive religion and psychology (Erich Neumann), and eight literary texts embodying the scapegoat pattern. Short stories by Hawthorne, Faulkner, Pritchett, Jackson and Baldwin, a novella by Strindberg, and Euripides' play *The Bacchae* are followed by critical material, issues for discussion and suggestions for further study.

844. VIJN, Jacob P. *Carlyle and Jean Paul: Their Spiritual Optics.* (Ph.D. 1982 University of Utrecht) Amsterdam: John Benjamins, 1982. xii,284 pp.

The basic ideas of Carlyle's philosophy are linked to depth psychology and shown to be analogous to the fundamental concepts of analytical psychology.

845. VINCENT, Howard P. "And Still They Fall from the Masthead." In *Melville and Hawthorne in the Berkshires.* Melville-Hawthorne Conference. A Symposium. Ed. Henry A. Murray. Kent, Ohio: Kent State University Press, 1968. 144-155.

White-Jacket's plunge into the sea at the end of Melville's novel *White-Jacket* (1850) symbolizes the moment of the writer's self-discovery in his artistic development. Jung's suggestive account of the libido's descent into its own depths and consequent rebirth into creative fruitfulness is quoted as the appropriate comment.

Metaphorically, the passage not only announces Melville's emergence as a serious artist, but it is possibly "the first time in American letters that the unconscious and its special significance to man has been described."

846. VITOUX, Pierre. "Aldous Huxley and D.H. Lawrence: An Attempt at Intellectual Sympathy." *Modern Language Review* 69:3 (1974) 501-522.

Vitoux examines the influence on Huxley of Lawrence's philosophy and Jung's system of psychological types. The latter was "useful to Huxley for the purpose of analysing more clearly his experience of himself and of others; and, naturally, it became an important element in the counterpoint which underlies his most important novel." However, the characters in *Point Counter Point* (1928) were not constructed solely on the basis of Jung's typology. Rather, it provided a new perspective on the problem of passion versus reason, something which Huxley had already had in mind before he became familiar with Jung. K.S.

847. VIVAS, Eliseo. *D.H. Lawrence: The Failure and the Triumph of Art.* Evanston: Northwestern University Press, 1960. xvii,302 pp.

Vivas sees Lawrence as one of the "constitutive" (i.e. genuinely creative) writers of his generation, whose vision of life influences others. After tracing the constitutive symbol at work in Lawrence's best novels, he considers in an appendix the similarity between his term "constitutive symbol" and Jung's concept of the symbolic archetype.

848. VIVAS, Eliseo. "On Aesthetics and Jung." *Modern Age* 18:3 (1974) 246-251.

In this essay Vivas sketches a general aesthetic theory that is in agreement with Jung's ideas on the relation of psychology to art.

849. VON FRANZ, Marie-Louise. "Analytical Psychology and Literary Criticism." *New Literary History* 12:1 (1980) 119-126.

Summarizing Jung's views, von Franz discusses the role of the collective unconscious in literature and the use of analytical psychology for understanding "visionary" literature, i.e. art that is fairly directly dictated from the unconscious in a "puzzling and mysterious" dreamlike form. The interpretations of the psychologist and the psychological literary critic can never be definitive, as art is ever symbolic and, according to Jung, a symbol "is the best possible expression for what is still unknown." But with the help of Jung's theory of archetypal compensation and his method of amplification the critic/psychologist may extract from the literary work "*new meaning*, a formulation or translation of the imagery into specific, knowable, psychological terms."

850. VYVYAN, John. *The Shakespearean Ethic*. London: Chatto and Windus, 1959. 208 pp.

The true dynamic of Shakespearean drama lies in the "spiritual progress or degeneration" of his protagonists. Dramatic structure may be viewed as the stages in a sequence that leads the noble hero "with a weakness" through temptations and inner conflicts to his "deed of darkness", the realization of its horror and to tragic death; or conversely, to a reversal of the tragic act, regeneration, harmony and rebirth. These contrasting patterns are traced in *Hamlet* ("a study in degeneration from first to last") and *Measure for Measure* (tragedy averted by creative mercy), in *Othello* ("the replacement of love by hate") and *The Winter's Tale* (the force of repentance). *The Tempest* is almost wholly given to the resolution of the tragic conflict through Prospero's regeneration. From the archetypal viewpoint the hero's choice is always "between the Anima at her fairest and the Shadow at his worst" with "the aged counsellor symbolizing Fidelity" as the Wise Old Man in the background. Shakespeare's ethic emerges as a blending of "the philosophia perennis and the higher morality of the Gospels," its moral essence being "truth to one's Self, fidelity to Love, and creative mercy."

Vyvyan's awareness of Jung adds to the depth of this excellent moral, aesthetic and psychological study of the plays. The interpretative scheme is seldom allowed to constrict the sensitive analysis of detail, while it continually supports challenging insights and interpretations.

851. WADLINGTON, Warwick. *The Confidence Game in American Literature*. Princeton: Princeton University Press, 1975. xii,331 pp.

A study in depth of the "mode of fictive experience" in reading the works of Herman Melville, Mark Twain, and Nathanael West. The "transactions of confidence" that "establish imaginative authority and renew individual identity, in both the world the writer imagines and the relationship he fashions with his reader," are viewed in the light of the confidence game associated with the archetypal trickster figure. Paul Radin's book on the North American Indian trickster with Jung's psychological commentary forms part of the groundwork for this study.

852. WALCOTT, William. "Notes by a Jungian Analyst on the Dreams in *Ulysses*." *James Joyce Quarterly* 9:1 (1971) 37-49.

Dreams of Stephen and Bloom together with a number of synchronicities foreshadowing their meeting in the Circe episode of Joyce's *Ulysses* (1922) are given a Jungian interpretation in terms of Stephen's individuation. He descends into the unconscious when in the streets of harlots he confronts Bella, the archetypal witch. But guided by the dream figure of Haroen al Raschid as psychopomp and the talisman of earth mother Molly, as well as by the "participation mystique" with his "consubstantial father and spiritual redeemer" Bloom, Stephen achieves "new creative consciousness."

853. *WALCOTT, William. "The Paternity of James Joyce's Stephen Dedalus." *Journal of Analytical Psychology* 10:1 (1965) 77-95.

The history of Stephen Dedalus, as it emerges from Joyce's novels *Portrait of the Artist as a Young Man* (1916) and *Ulysses* (1922), is examined "from the standpoint of the masculine development of consciousness." The various stages in the hero's relation with the father, as outlined by Jung, are traced in Stephen's life: early identification, disenchantment, and attempts to break with the personal and with the archetypal father projected upon teachers, nation and church. After his visionary encounter with the anima girl on the beach Stephen discovers his own "creative, artistic, poetic resources." In the final stage Stephen becomes the creative individual and mythological hero who searches for "a spiritual father, consciousness of which is essential to masculine individuation."

"Through the use of dreams, fantasies, synchronicities, and meaningful encounters," Joyce reveals by "acausal rather than causal links" unconscious processes, which finally result in the conscious relationship of Stephen and Bloom. Stephen's smashing of the chandelier in Bella Cohen's whorehouse in the Circe episode is seen as symbolizing his breaking with the anima as Siren and the overcoming of his fascination with the one-sided "old-world consciousness" of brilliant intellectual reason without genuine feeling. In the sensitive and warm-hearted Bloom and his sensual wife Molly, Stephen finds the spiritual elements and "the compensating feminine-creative unconscious" needed for the fuller "new consciousness" of modern man.

Walcott demonstrates very well how in Joyce's partly autobiographical and very personal novels the characterization of Stephen Dedalus makes him into a "contemporary hero in an archetypal struggle with the father."

854. WALL, Richard J. and Roger Fitzgerald. "Yeats and Jung: An

Ideological Comparison." *Literature and Psychology* 13:2 (1963) 44-52.

With the help of well-chosen quotations from both writers the resemblances between Yeats's concepts of Spiritus Mundi, the Mask and the play of opposites, and Jung's notions of the collective unconscious, the persona and enantiodromia are examined. Their greatest similarity is found in their optimistic view of man's capacity to reconcile the opposing forces in the individual personality and realize the "whole man" or "Self".

855.   WALLACH, Judith D. Lowenthal. "The Quest for Selfhood in Saul Bellow's Novels: A Jungian Interpretation." (Ph.D. 1975 University of Victoria, Canada) *DAI* 36/05 A p.2829.

856.   WALTON, James. "Tennyson's Patrimony: From 'The Outcast' to 'Maud'." *Texas Studies in Literature and Language* 11:1 (1969) 733-759.

An aggressive, self-indulgent father and an adored mother determined the oedipal patterns in Tennyson's poetry. The fear of sexuality, the Victorian conflict between art and the moral life are projected into erotic gardens, violent females, isolated maidens and maternal muses. In discussing the feminine mask often adopted by Tennyson, Jungian theory is invoked to explain the masculine will to power shown by female personae like Oenone and the Princess.

An interesting essay on the psychology of Tennyson and his heroines. Jungian concepts are rather unorthodoxly used when the rebelliousness of certain anima figures is ascribed to their animus qualities as "another convulsion in [Tennyson's] personality."

857.   *WARD, Theodora. *The Capsule of the Mind: Chapters in the Life of Emily Dickinson.* Cambridge, Mass.: Harvard University Press, 1961. x,205 pp.

"This small book" attempts to trace Emily Dickinson's inner development "through the self-revelation to be found in her poems and letters," and "by following the main stream of the emotional life" to come close to the creative sources of her art. As one of the editors of the poems and letters (editions of 1955 and 1958 respectively) Ward was well placed to trace "the conditions that led to the years of crisis and the subsequent development of Emily's inner life," and to explore her relations with three of her male friends through the letters that have survived. Ward sees the agonizing inner conflicts as "the effect on a sensitive personality of slowly accumulated pressures, both within and without, working against forces for growth and fulfillment."

In this light Emily's dream-encounter with the "King, who does not speak" and the letters to the mysterious "Master" become confrontations with symbolic personifications of the "power within herself of the masculine principle," of the need of "a mediator between her struggling consciousness and the unplumbed depths of her own nature to bring her being into focus and enable her to experience wholeness in life." Projected into the distant lover, he became "the consciousness of the hidden self" that set her mind free and enabled her to translate "into art the varied emotional states that had swept through her being." Emily's seven-year struggle was an "intense experience of spiritual death and rebirth," from which resulted "an inner integrity of soul" and a capacity for further growth in the often painful experiences of later life, as well as in her happy relations with her brother's child Gilbert and in the fulfillment of the spiritual love relationship with the widowed judge Otis Lord, friend of her father. In reviewing the many paradoxes of her character and her life Ward remarks that "she lived so close to her own center that she maintained a tension between the opposites that left her free from domination of either side."

This very sensitive study of Emily Dickinson's inner life is full of illuminating readings of the poems. Though Jung is quoted only once, Ward's whole view of the poet's psychological and spiritual development is clearly fed by Jung's theory of the critical stages and the growth towards wholeness in the individuation process. One of the happy effects of Ward's deep understanding of the powerful symbolism of the poems is that she treads very delicately in the mysterious forest of Emily Dickinson's feelings for her male friends.

858. WASSERMAN, Earl R. "*The Natural*: Malamud's World Ceres." *Centennial Review of Arts and Sciences* 9:4 (1965) 438-460.
Rpt. in *Bernard Malamud and the Critics*. Ed. Leslie A. Field and Joyce W. Field. New York: New York University Press, 1970. 45-65.
In his first novel *The Natural* (1952) Malamud drew on real events and figures to write a distillation of baseball history which raises the game to a ritual that "expresses the psychological nature of American life and its moral predicament." At the same time Roy Hobb's baseball career has its parallel in the chivalric tourneys and archetypal quest of young Sir Percival, the Grail knight in search of the "sources of life." "By drawing his material from actual baseball and yet fusing it with the Arthurian legend, Malamud sets and sustains his novel in a region that is both real and mythic, particular and universal, ludicrous melodrama and spiritual probing - Ring Lardner and Jung."

The detailed Jungian analysis makes clear why critics have found Malamud's ambitious project of writing an essential American myth too obtrusively symbolical and therefore less successful.

859. WATSKY, Paul. "The Human Figures in Wallace Stevens." (Ph.D. 1974 State University of New York, Buffalo) 213 pp. *DAI* 35/07 A p.4568.

860. WEBSTER, David. "Uncanny Correspondences: Synchronicity in *Fifth Business* and *The Manticore*." *Journal of Canadian Fiction* 3:3 (1974) 52-56.
    Discusses meaningful coincidences in two novels of Robertson Davies' Deptford Trilogy (1970-1975) in the light of Jung's theory of synchronicity.

861. WEBSTER, Peter D. "Arrested Individuation or the Problem of Joseph K. and Hamlet." *American Imago* 5:3 (1948) 225-245.
    The problems of Hamlet and Joseph K. are analyzed as anxiety neuroses arising from unadmitted guilt over unconscious incest feelings and rejection of the father. Trapped in rationalizations of the conscious mind their individuation is arrested by "the inhibiting patterns derived from childhood orientations." Acceptance and release into consciousness of their personal guilt might lead to redeeming image-formation in the form of a personal God or integrating mandala symbol. They both lack the humility which would bring healing self-knowledge or religious grace, as illustrated in the parable of the Prodigal Son.
    Though the main thesis of this somewhat repetitive article provides a valuable perspective, it does not do justice to the psychological subtlety of *Hamlet* and Kafka's *The Trial*.

862. WEBSTER, William B. "Meaning and Significance: The Limits of Archetypal Interpretation." (Ph.D. 1972 Stanford University) 255 pp. *DAI* 33/08 A p.4370.

863. WEISS, Timothy. *Fairy Tale and Romance in Works of Ford Madox Ford*. Lanham, MD.: University Press of America, 1984. 160 pp.
    Investigates Ford's fiction as romance whose special theme is "the transformative power of the feminine principle of anima."

864. WELDON, Roberta F. "Wakefield's Second Journey." *Studies in Short Fiction* 14:1 (1977) 69-74.
    Hawthorne's bizarre tale of the man who "in the meridian of life" for no apparent reason suddenly leaves his wife and friends to stay away for twenty years is read as an unsuccessful attempt to

seek mental maturity. Seeing Wakefield as a sort of mythic quester, who in his late middle years sets out on a "journey into the Self," explains some enigmatic details of the story as well as its powerful archetypal appeal to the reader.

865.   WELDON, Suzanne K. *Color Symbolism in Hopkins' Poetry.* Montreal: privately printed, 1971. 69 pp.

This study of the color symbolism in Hopkins' poems supports a reading of his poetry as a search for self-integration. Color expresses rhythm and feeling and is thus intimately related with the human psyche. With the help of Cirlot's *Dictionary of Symbols* and Jung's individuation theory Weldon traces in the poems "the search for the father." The search progresses from the sacred "crimson/blue/purple chord of ecstasy" in "The Wreck of the Deutschland" through Hopkins' preference for blue as "the deepest expression of color" to the dark sonnets, where the triad of colors develops into the quaternary of blue/red/yellow/green, which in Jung's alchemical analogy symbolizes wholeness. The "full complement" of these four colors is for the first time present in the late sonnet on Patience, which is explained as expressing "the successful reintegration of the poet's psyche."

Hopkins' intense use of, and sensitiveness to, colors makes this combination of color symbolism and psychology a valuable approach to the poetry.

866.   WERBLOWSKY, Raphael J. Zwi. *Lucifer and Prometheus: A Study of Milton's Satan.* London: Routledge & Kegan Paul, 1952. xix,120 pp. With an Introduction by Professor C.G. Jung.

Milton's ambivalent picture of Satan in *Paradise Lost* forcefully expresses the human dilemma that *hubris* is "a psychic necessity on the way of individuation and differentiation towards higher levels of consciousness." It is argued that Milton's Satan has much of the archetypal culture-hero Prometheus, who is at the same time bringer of civilization and sinner against the divine order. The tension between the heroic and "foolish" in Satan, which is the tension between Greek and Hebraic inheritances in Milton, accounts both for the devilish vitality and for the ultimate failure of Milton's treatment of his great Christian theme.

This searching inquiry into "the fatal split" in Milton's presentation of Satan utilizes Jung's theory that mythical figures are projections of the human psyche, the archetypes of the collective unconscious being "expressive of various stages and levels of psychic development." The term archetype is not used in a strictly Jungian sense, however. It indicates the "Kulturtypische" rather than the "Archetypische". The book has an introduction by

Jung himself, in which he outlines the psychological development of the figure of Satan in pre-Christian and Christian times.

867. WESTON, Susan B. *Wallace Stevens: An Introduction to the Poetry.* New York: Columbia University Press, 1974. xix,151 pp.

In this introduction to Stevens' work the "archetypal dimensions" of his poetry are emphasized. The symbolic woman in the early poetry, now fecund mother, now virginal beloved, has "all the earmarks of a Jungian archetype." His favorite theme - the struggle between imagination and reality - emerges again in the hero of his later poetry, the representative man of "highest imagination," who exemplifies Jung's dictum that it is psychic, imaginative reality that makes up "existence itself."

868. WHALLEY, George. *Poetic Process.* London: Routledge & Kegan Paul, 1953. xxxix,256 pp.

This imaginative inquiry into "the facts of artistic experience" and the nature of critical judgments draws in particular on Coleridge, Yeats and Jung to clarify the "poetic character" of image-making, symbol and myth.

869. WHAN, Michael W. "'Don Juan,' Trickster, and Hermeneutic Understanding." *Spring* (1978) 17-27.

Jung's essays on the Trickster and on the spirit or Wise Old Man (C.W., vol 9.i) are used to explain why the Indian sorcerer in Carlos Castaneda's Don Juan novels must be seen as an archetypal senex-trickster figure who "contains the ambiguity of wisdom and deception." "Meaning" in Don Juan's world is not literal but equivocal, as psychological realities are "phenomenological and imaginal" and every kind of knowledge is "interpretative understanding."

870. WHEELWRIGHT, Philip. "The Archetypal Symbol." In *Perspectives in Literary Symbolism,* Yearbook of Comparative Criticism, Vol. I. Ed. Joseph Strelka. University Park: Pennsylvania State University Press, 1968. 214-243.

After defining "symbol" and "archetype" ("universally found symbol") Wheelwright considers three groups of archetypal symbols: those concerned with sky divinities, with chthonic counter-divinities, and with pilgrimage. As he does in the section "Archetypal Imagining" in his book *The Burning Fountain* (1954), Wheelwright stresses that his "study of archetypes is altogether independent of Jung's special theories," and he distinguishes his use of archetype as a concrete universal from Jung's concept of inherited archetypes.

Wheelwright mistakes Jung, however, in criticizing him for the idea that "primordial images are transmitted by inheritance." He fastens on Jung's early term "primordial image" and disregards the clear distinction Jung later made between the "archetype as such," the structuring disposition in the unconscious psyche inherited with the brain structure, and its conscious actualization and representation as a perceptible "archetypal image."

871. WHITAKER, Thomas R. *Swan and Shadow: Yeats's Dialogue with History*. Chapel Hill: University of North Carolina Press, 1964. 340 pp.

Yeats's subjective dialogue with history is seen as "sometimes a bright reflection of the poet's self, sometimes a shadowy force opposed to the self." His willingness to explore and assimilate the "dark part of the mind," to "enter into the abyss of himself" in his search for wisdom and wholeness of being, is related to Jungian, gnostic and alchemical views of the reconciliation of opposites. Whitaker points to, but does not work out in detail, many correlations between Yeats's thought and Jung's psychology.

872. WHITE, Virginia L. "Bright the Hawk's Flight: The Journey of the Hero in Ursula Le Guin's Earthsea Trilogy." *Ball State University Forum* 20:4 (1979) 34-45.

The three volumes of the trilogy exemplify the three successive stages of departure, initiation and rebirth in the hero's journey as described by Joseph Campbell.

873. WICKERT, Max A. "Form and Archetype in William Morris, 1855-1870." (Ph.D. 1965 Yale University) 263 pp. *DAI* 27/02 A p.489.

874. WIENS, Esther R. "Archetypal Patterns in a Selection of Plays by William Robertson Davies." (Ph.D. 1984 Northwestern University) 307 pp. *DAI* 45/12 A p.3484.

875. WILLEFORD, William. *The Fool and His Scepter: A Study in Clowns and Jesters and Their Audience*. Evanston, Ill.: Northwestern University Press, 1969. xxii,265 pp.

A scholarly study of the character of fools and folly, and "the psychological source of our response to fools" by a Jungian analyst who is also a teacher of literature. Willeford draws his examples from medieval and Renaissance jesters, the fools in Shakespeare's plays, the clowns in modern circus, stage and films, and applies insights from Freud and Jung. He focuses on the psychological and symbolical significance of the archetypal "pattern of folly" and the fool's position on the borderline of good and evil, order and chaos.

876. WILLEFORD, William. "Jung, Carl Gustav." In *Encyclopedia of World Literature in the 20th Century* in four volumes. Eds. Frederick Ungar and Lina Mainiero. New York: Ungar, 1975. Vol 4, 179-184.

The six-page entry on Jung gives a succinct, informative survey of Jung's life, works, theories, and influence, as well as a discussion of the elements that characterize his attitude to literature: focus on its archaic elements, interpretation on the subjective level, compensatory function in the development of individual and collective consciousness, distrust of aestheticism, and admiration of visionary literature.

877. WILLEFORD, William. "The Mouse in the Model." *Modern Drama* 12:2 (1969) 135-145.

A sensible reading of possible religious and mythical contents of Edward Albee's "mystery play" *Tiny Alice* (1965). Miss Alice, "numinous female presence," is Julian's anima or feminine soul-image. As "erotic temptress" fused with the Christian God into a curious kind of hermaphroditic divinity, she also symbolizes how in our patriarchal culture (in line with Jung's view) there is "increased penetration of woman [...] into the image of God."

878. WILLIAMS, Donald L. *Border Crossings: A Psychological Perspective on Carlos Castaneda's Path of Knowledge.* Toronto: Inner City Books, 1981. 153 pp.

A Jungian interpretation of Castaneda's novels.

879. WILLIAMS, David. *Faulkner's Women: The Myth and the Muse.* Montreal: McGill-Queen's University Press, 1977. xviii,268 pp.

James Baird's theory of Melville's "authentic primitivism" in reaction to rationalism's "cultural failure" and the impoverishment of Christian symbolism is applied to the work of William Faulkner. Williams sees Faulkner's despairing Christ-like male victims as examples of the psychic debility of a desacramentalized culture that has lost its life-giving symbols, whereas the women stand as embodiments of the archetypal feminine, atavistic symbols of the powerful doubleness of the divine life-force in its creative and destructive aspects. The process of symbolization in the novels is examined through Faulkner's use of imagery, diction, tone, structure and character. Williams argues that Faulkner's art is at its most powerful when in his four central novels, *The Sound and the Fury*, *As I Lay Dying*, *Sanctuary*, and *Light in August*, he creates women as anima figures whose mythical dimensions make them incarnations of the Great Goddess, who appears in the guise of the mother of life and death.

Williams feels that "to help a new age into being" it is the function of literary criticism to develop a new kind of "matriarchal mode" that will give the feminine its due. In how far this archetypal analysis of Faulkner's women sheds light on the characters in the novels and on Faulkner's artistic development must be left for the Faulkner specialists to judge. Williams makes informed use of Jung and Neumann. His style is one of easy-flowing rhetoric and many large generalizations and abstractions.

880. WILLIAMS, Lyle T. "Journeys to the Center of the Earth: Descent and Initiation in Selected Science Fiction." (Ph.D. 1983 Indiana University) 329 pp. *DAI* 44/03 A p.746.

881. WILLIAMS, Mary E. "John Donne's 'Orbe of Man ... Inexplicable Mistery': A Study of Donne's Use of Archetypal Images in the Round." (Ph.D. 1964 University of Wisconsin) 402 pp. *DAI* 24/10 p.4203.

882. WILLIAMS, Philip. "The Birth and Death of Falstaff Reconsidered." *Shakespeare Quarterly* 8:3 (1957) 359-365.

In discussing a debate between Shakespeare critics as to whether Prince Hal's rejection of Falstaff may or may not be seen as also having elements of the symbolic sacrifice of a father-substitute, it is argued that Jung's concept of the collective unconscious provides the needed perspective. As already prefigured in the tavern scene in *I Henry IV*, where Falstaff as father-king is deposed by his prince-son, Shakespeare is in the parallels between Falstaff and King Henry drawing upon the archetypal image of the ritually slain king, well-known from anthropology, whose death regenerates a wasted land.

883. WILSON, F.A.C. *W.B. Yeats and Tradition*. London: Gollancz, 1958. 286 pp.

This is the less Jungian of Wilson's two studies of Yeats. It focuses on the late poems and plays, and discusses in general terms the archetypal character of the poetry and the parallels between the ideas of Yeats and Jung.

884. WILSON, F.A.C. *Yeats' Iconography*. London: Gollancz, 1960. 349 pp.

This learned study interprets the symbolism of five plays and a number of related poems by studying Yeats's sources and intellectual background. Yeats attached archetypal meaning to his plays. The analysis of the *Four Plays for Dancers* and *The Cat and the Moon* (1926), all inspired by the Japanese Noh drama, shows that Yeats's "great symbols will tend to derive from one or other of the world religions," and in his view were preserved in the Anima Mundi that is comparable to Jung's collective unconscious. The correspondence with Jungian theory is particularly noted in the discussion of *At the Hawk's Well* (1917), the play that embodies the archetypal "journey to integration" and its stages in Yeats's "religion of the Self."

But Yeats developed his own metaphysical and psychological systems quite independently from Jung and the differences with Jung are important, according to Wilson. The "dark anima" figures in *At the Hawk's Well* and *The Only Jealousy of Emer* (1919) must not be interpreted as the "terrible woman" to be overcome but as the "ideal" beauty to which the lover should dedicate himself.

885. WILSON, G.R., Jr. "Incarnation and Redemption in *The Old Man and the Sea*." *Studies in Short Fiction* 14:4 (1979) 369-373.

Hemingway's *The Old Man and the Sea* (1952) can be interpreted in terms of Joseph Campbell's monomyth: Santiago is the hero who undergoes a series of trials before he returns with the boon, "the knowledge that man, who can be destroyed, cannot be defeated." The fisherman's heroic role is emphasized by the Christ symbolism found in the story. K.S.

886. *WILSON, Katharine M. *The Nightingale and the Hawk: A Psychological Study of Keats' Ode*. London: Allen & Unwin, 1964. 157 pp.

This study of Keats culminates in a reading of the "Ode to a Nightingale," but in fact it attempts to trace his "inner biography" throughout his poems and letters. Wilson shows how Keats's impulse to creation came from "the inward experience of his developing psyche." She finds that the psychology of Jung offers the key to a full understanding of the process that Keats in his famous phrase described as "soul-making." Keats's longer poems have often been considered vague and incoherent allegories. If their mythic symbolism is recognized for what it is, however, they move to their "goal with a sure instinct." Without knowing all the implications beforehand, in *Endymion* Keats deliberately set out on a journey of self-discovery "to make clear to himself his own inner processes." In Jungian terms this is the quest for the Self, for wholeness in the individual psyche. Endymion (Keats) begins by seeking the essence of Beauty while dedicating himself to the Moon Goddess, then finds that what he really wants is Love. Thereupon the Self is found by descent into the archetypal world, but in the end Endymion realizes that the significance of the archetypal can only be found in everyday life.

Explicating passages that show the numinous force of Keats's imagery, and clarifying symbolic images that suggest his awareness of the Self, Wilson discusses Keats's surprising ability to express and reflect on the workings of his own mind. Keats lived by his imaginative vision and inward experiences. He was in terms of Jungian typology an introverted intuitive feeling-type. Sensation being his inferior function (i.e. inferior in consciousness!), his unconscious sensations were strongly feeling-toned. This helps to explain Keats's term "beauty" (its use "neither sentimental nor muddleheaded"), by which he means "imagery from the senses felt to have a numinous quality involving great depth of feeling."

The unfinished *Hyperion* tells how the older gods of power are superseded by the new gods of beauty and of knowledge, the latter being for Keats much more than merely "knowing with the intelligence." Knowledge is wisdom "felt upon the pulse" with intuition and intensity. The theme of *Hyperion* is "increase in consciousness." Wilson interprets the poem in a wider context as the symbolic expression of a Romantic "new consciousness" that will bring a new sense of values to our Western power-obsessed civilization. It is "part of Jung's psychology that the creative artist is the first man to intuit the new consciousness of mankind." Keats's quest for beauty and wisdom is essentially "the search for the self as modern man's goal."

Wilson demonstrates that along with the growing self-awareness in Keats's poetry there is a personal maturing, expressed in the commentary of his letters and in his human relationships. Further self-knowledge is reached in the discovery that disinterestedness may be a high good, but that it is an "agony of ignorance" not to realize that the selfishness of desire and love, and even the Hawk of "fierce destructiveness," are inevitably natural and human. The insights of the sonnet "Why did I laugh tonight" ("Verse, Fame and Beauty are intense indeed, But Death intenser") involve an acceptance of death as fundamental in all nature. At the end of this process of self-discovery Keats expresses in his great odes and in some of his letters "the sense of peace, a feeling of calm sanity," based on the realization of his own identity and psychic wholeness. The Self that up till then "had been hidden within poetry as a goal" is addressed as the goddess herself in the "Ode to Psyche". And Wilson explains the "Ode to a Nightingale" as a meeting with the Self, "not in imagination, or by means of intuitive imagery, but as an overwhelming experience."

One reviewer dismissed this study as one that "is unlikely to satisfy anyone other than the author's fellow-Jungians" (Miriam Alliott, *Modern Language Review* 61 (1966) 114). It is true that the Jungian terms retain a certain unavoidable vagueness, though they are clearly and carefully explained by Wilson. And it must be conceded that the "Self" is worked rather hard in this book. But a little patience with the terminology and a certain measure of the "willing suspension of disbelief" urged by Coleridge should make clear that this is a subtle and imaginative exploration of the psychological depth of Keats's poetry which elucidates the complexity of image, theme and symbol in his poetry.

Wilson's understanding of the essence of Jung's psychology is profound. Not only does she make good use of Jung to explain Keats, her analysis of Keats's grasp of his inner processes in its turn sheds light on aspects of Jungian psychology. What is equally remarkable, she even illuminates the "re-visioning" of Jung's theories in the imaginal and archetypal "post-Jungian" psychology of James Hillman, who borrowed his key concept of "soul-making" from Keats. In fact, Wilson's study, written before 1964, may well be read as an admirable essay in Hillmanian psychology *avant la lettre*.

887. WIMSATT, William K., Jr. and Cleanth Brooks. *Literary Criticism: A Short History*. New York: Knopf, 1957. xviii,755,xxii pp.

In the chapter "Myth and Archetype" Jung's influence upon modern literary criticism is discussed, and demonstrated in the applications of myth study to literature by Maud Bodkin (*Archetypal Patterns of Poetry*, 1934) and by W.H. Auden (*The Enchafed Flood*, 1950). Jung's conception of "purposive" myths and dreams is explained, as well as his views on the similarities and differences between the dream and the work of art. The literary critic who interprets what Jung calls "visionary" literature will profit from what Jung has "added to our knowledge about man's processes of symbolization and the great immemorial symbols - the archetypes - in which man tends to express himself."

888. WITCUTT, W.P. *Blake: A Psychological Study*. London: Hollis & Carter, 1946. 127 pp.

Developing the suggestion of Kerrison Preston (q.v.) that the four Zoas are equivalent to Jung's four psychic functions, Witcutt aims at clearing a path through the "veritable jungle of symbols" in the "mythological maze" of Blake's Prophetic Books with the help of Jungian psychology. Blake is analyzed as an intuitive introvert with thinking (Urizen) as his secondary function, and sensation (Tharmas) as his repressed function. Together the poems provide "a kind of outline of the unconscious mind" in general, and they dramatize the working of Blake's own psyche in particular. The conflicts between the four Zoas, placed by Blake in crosswise opposition in the mind of Albion, the Universal Man, follow upon the usurpation of the place of Urizen by Luvah/Orc, who represents feeling and passion. Blake's epics deal with "the story of the soul, its disintegration through sin and ultimate reintegration." Witcutt identifies the "Fall" in Blake's own psychology with the adolescent's loss of innocence ("the narcissistic delight in the beauty of his own body") in his fourteenth year, the age at which in the poems Luvah rebels against Urizen and is repressed. This personal "Trauma" and the consequent disintegration of the personality is symbolized by a complex series of conflicts between the Zoas (in other words, the repressions and displacements of psychic functions). They are separated from their accompanying Emanations (the Jungian animae) which must be reintegrated with the help of their Spectres (the Jungian shadows). The final reintegration is symbolized by the building of Golgonooza, when Urizen and the other functions are reborn as children of Los.

There are no doubt striking resemblances between aspects of Blake's myths and Jung's picture of the psyche, and some of the details in Witcutt's briskly argued book make sense. However, the rigid Jungian schema imposed upon Blake's complex and flexible mythology, the often arbitrary identifications of mythical figures with various psychological qualities, and the over-confident links between mythical events and speculation about Blake's own psychology make this a very questionable interpretation of Blake's poetry. A good deal of Witcutt's argumentation about the four Zoas is based on the mistaken equation of Jung's feeling function with desire and passion. And can any interpretation of Blake's myth leave the religious, social and political dimensions completely out of account? If Blake's mythology is already confusing, Witcutt's reading makes it more so.

889. WITCUTT, W. P. "The Structure of the Psyche: A Psychological Examination of the Poetry of Blake." *The Wind and the Rain* 3:1 (1945) 14-21.

Witcutt previews the argument of his book on Blake. "Under the appearance of cosmic happenings" the prophetic books give "a history and description of Blake's own psyche." The fourfold division of the Zoas, corresponding to Jung's four psychic functions, is also found in the emblems of Ancient Egyptian mythology and Ezechiel's vision in the Bible.

890. WITCUTT, P. W. "Wm. Blake and Modern Psychology." *John O'London's Weekly* 61 (1947) 317-318.

In this popularizing summary of his book *Blake: A Psychological Study*, Witcutt explains how Jungian psychology provides the key to Blake's mythology. The theme of his epic poetry is the conflict between the four Zoas who stand for Jung's four psychic functions:

"Urizen is thought, Luvah or Orc is feeling, passion or love, Los is intuition, 'prophecy', the poetical imagination, and Tharmas is the body, sensation." As an intuitive introvert Blake saw in his imagination the archetypal symbols of the unconscious and named them long before Jung. Albion is the Self, his Emanation is the Jungian anima, and the Spectre, the archetype of evil, Jung calls the shadow.

891. WOLFINGER, W.O. "The Seven Deaths in *Hamlet.*" *Cresset* (Valparaiso, Ind.) 28:7 (1965) 7-12.

With a good deal of unreason, a far-fetched allegorical interpretation is offered of *Hamlet* as a redemptive "drama of initiation," in which through "the struggle of man against his own attributes" (worldly wisdom, illusion, pride and conceit, ambition, emotion and intellect, as embodied in the other characters) the protagonist achieves "the liberation or identification with the Higher Self." Parallels are found in Gnosticism and Jung's psychology.

892. WOODMAN, Ross. "Literature and the Unconscious: Coleridge and Jung." *Journal of Analytical Psychology* 25:4 (1980) 363-375.

A parallel is drawn between Jung's descent into the collective unconscious during his psychological crisis at the time of the First World War and similar plunges into "the mind's abyss" in the work of the major English Romantic poets. Coleridge's "The Rime of the Ancient Mariner" exemplifies the artist's radical encounter with his anima muse, "who by ensnaring the poet in the labyrinth of the unconscious, robbed him of his soul." It is "the tendency of the creative process to capture psychic energy and reduce the ego" to a primitive and inferior level. Jung rescued himself from the temptation to submit to the alien personality within himself and to take his fantasies for works of art by using his reason and will, employing empirical methods to come to a conscious understanding of his "Nightmare LIFE-IN-DEATH." In the process he developed the new science of psychology. It is suggested that in a similar way the poets Coleridge and Matthew Arnold turned from their personal life-and-death struggles with a fatal muse to conscious analysis of the creative imagination in their philosophical and critical writings.

Although the comparison between Coleridge and Jung underplays the positive achievements of Romantic art and overlooks Coleridge's own tragic sense of the loss of his "shaping spirit of imagination," it provides an interesting perspective on how Jung carried forward a movement which had its "immediate origins in the psychic revolution of Romanticism."

893. WOODMAN, Ross. "Shaman, Poet, and Failed Initiate: Reflections on Romanticism and Jungian Psychology." *Studies in Romanticism* 19:1 (1980) 51-82.

From "observations on the similarities between Coleridge's "The Rime of the Ancient Mariner" and the healing rites of the Shaman" Woodman proposes a view of English Romanticism that links it with the attempt of Jung's analytical psychology to raise the level of consciousness at which mankind is functioning. The 19th-century Romantic poets, followed by the 20th-century psychologists and artists, unveiled dark and chaotic aspects of the psyche. If the Shaman is seen as the embodiment of the healer archetype, the person who from initiation into the unconscious has gained a hard-won control over the psychic forces and the spiritual realm, the Romantic poets ("with the possible exception of Blake") must be viewed as failed Shamans. They see themselves as prophets of the future, "unacknowledged legislators of the World," but their explorations of the creative imagination, as in the case of Shelley, lead to suicidal visions rather than mastery over the unconscious. Keats's "Odes", Shelley's "Adonais" and especially Coleridge's "Ancient Mariner" illustrate the Romantic poets' evocation of and struggle with the dark forces. The Ancient Mariner in his journey and his treatment of the Wedding Guest is a type of the failed Shaman, and Romanticism is seen as "on the whole the record of a failed initiation." Jung's own "journey into the collective unconscious was quintessentially the Romantic trip." The conscious understanding he brought back from his confrontation with shadow and anima in both their dangerous and positive aspects makes his analytical psychology into a "scientific tool of objective insight" that in a sense brings the visionary work of the Romantic poets to its completion.

The thesis of this ambitious paper carries more conviction than some of the discussions of literary examples.

894. WORTHINGTON, Anne Poole. "The Triadic Archetype in Keats' Poetry." (Ph.D. 1976 University of Maryland) 269 pp. *DAI* 38/06 A p.3525.

895. WRIGHT, R. Glenn. "Science Fiction, Archetypes, and the Future." In *Clarion III*. Ed. Robin Scott Wilson. New York: New American Library, 1973. 174-181.

A plea for the world to heed science fiction (with Frank Herbert's *Dune* as an example), since it both dramatizes dangerous tendencies in our technological society and proposes radical solutions for the problems. In their visions science fiction writers often combine expert scientific knowledge with a deeply felt imaginative response to the vital archetypal drives of the collective unconscious.

896. WRIGHT, Elizabeth. *Psychoanalytic Criticism: Theory in Practice*. London: Methuen, 1984. xii,208 pp.

Brief discussions of psychoanalytic theories and of the various schools of psychological literary criticism, Freudian and post-Freudian. The chapter on archetypal criticism is very critical of Jung and Bodkin; Frye finds favor.

897. WYATT, David M. *Prodigal Sons: A Study in Authorship and Authority*. Baltimore: John Hopkins University Press, 1980. Chapter 7: "Davies and the Middle Journey", 129-149.

In a series of essays on the moment in a career "when an author makes his accommodation with authority and ceases wrestling with his role as a son," the chapter on Robertson Davies argues that in his *Deptford Trilogy* (1970-1975) he weathers the crisis of middle life by making it the subject of his novel. The secret of the fateful stone that the novel's hero Dunstan Ramsay (like Jung in his boyhood) keeps hidden may be read retroactively in its Freudian aspects as expressing an unresolved Oedipus conflict, but also in Jungian fashion as a symbol of future developments. Davies' "deceptively reticent style misdirects" the reader's attention away from the questions of origins, and in "playing Jung (life as *telos*) against Freud (life as *arche*), Davies suggests that the shape of any career" (including his own) "may be a function of the interpretative strategies we bring to bear upon it."

898. WYLDER, Edith. "The Speaker of Emily Dickinson's 'My Life Had Stood - A Loaded Gun'." *Rocky Mountain MLA Bulletin* 23:1 (1969) 3-8.

The riddle of Emily Dickinson's poem, and particularly of the "live-kill-die" paradoxes of its last stanza, are explained "by reading the speaker of the poem as the poem itself and the owner as the poet." The poems power to kill the "dream-foe" of the poet's night world suggests its power to control the dark fearful side of "the archetypal workings of the creative imagination," the act of poetic creation functioning as psychological self-preservation. (Compare Albert Gelpi's very different Jungian interpretation of this poem in his essay "Emily Dickinson and the Deerslayer.")

899. YOUNG, Gloria L. "'The Fountainhead of All Forms': Poetry and the Unconscious in Emerson and Howard Nemerov." In *Artful Thunder: Versions of the Romantic Tradition in American Literature*. Robert

J. DeMott and Sanford E. Marovitz, eds. Kent, Ohio: Kent State University Press, 1975. 241-267.

Young shows that "Emerson's ideas of the unconscious anticipate certain psychological, linguistic, and aesthetic theories of Carl Jung, depth psychologist, and Howard Nemerov, poet, critic, and theorist." All three use images of water and light to describe the unconscious, believe it to be a potentially dangerous force that is accessible only indirectly in uncontrollable flashes, and see it as the source of the creative powers of the artist. "Both Emerson and Nemerov (like Jung) view poetry as uniting the me and the not-me through the psyche's participation in a creative process manifested by symbolic language." K.S.

900. YOUNG, James H. "The Child Archetype." *Quadrant* 10:2 (1977) 64-72.

The romantic idealism of Wordsworth's portraits of children features what Jung called the child archetype: image of ethereal fragility and unearthly radiance, bringer of redemptive grace, an innocent attuned to nature. These qualities are especially visible in the "divine child" of the "Immortality Ode." The poem is read as affirming a unity that transcends the duality of the child's rapture and man's "philosophic mind."

901. ZIMMER, Heinrich. *The King and the Corpse: Tales of the Soul's Conquest of Evil*. Ed. Joseph Campbell. New York: Pantheon, 1948. 316 pp.

This volume gives us a scholar's "creative reactions" to a number of popular stories that range from Arabia through Irish paganism, medieval Christianity and the Arthur cycle to the myths of Hinduism, all sharing the theme of man's attempt to face the problem of evil. Zimmer's method is not an "anatomization, systematization and classification," but an imaginative retelling of the stories interspersed with commentary that draws on Jungian psychology and Zimmer's own studies of Indian philosophy and religion. Four Arthurian heroes are evoked in retellings of medieval Welsh, French and English tales: Gawain, Owain, Merlin and Lancelot ("the most interesting and inspiring animus-figure of the Western tradition"). In the discussion of the Middle English *Sir Gawain and the Green Knight* parallels with Buddhist legend and pagan myths emphasize the testing of the solar hero by the forces of life and death, which in Zimmer's view has been "watered down" by the theme of chivalric honour. Yet the narrative preserves in striking detail the archetypal theme of "birth, death and rebirth in unending cycle."

Critics have argued (see Moorman) that this archetypal interpretation of *Sir Gawain and the Green Knight* cannot do justice to the artistic qualities and the individual handling of the old themes by the Gawain poet, yet Zimmer's imaginative reading clarifies the story's symbolism.

902. *ZONAILO, Carolyn. "*The Beast in the Jungle*: The Observer's Art." *Dragonflies* 2:2 (1980) 163-188.

In the later fiction of Henry James "his narrative method" takes on the "dynamics of the psycho-analytic process." In his *Prefaces* James describes the artist as an observer who "watches" life in order to catch its finer "vibrations" and create the "illusion of life" in the psychological reality of his characters. Through subtle manipulations of point of view and narrative voice James makes his principal characters themselves into artist-observers who watch external events and their own reactions, so that the subject of his stories becomes the "process of consciousness becoming conscious of itself." In the end it is the imaginative quality, the "resonance" of his metaphoric images, that creates the psychic perception of James's fiction. Not only is the writer an image-maker, "his characters also make images, and through his techniques James is able to create, as well as describe, consciousness." To illustrate these general points about James's fictional techniques we are given an in-depth interpretive reading of the novella *The Beast in the Jungle* (1903) that unravels the multiple "imaginal" meanings in the story's key metaphor of the beast crouching in the jungle, watching for its prey. The image embodies much more than the protagonist's fear of the "animalistic, primitive, sexual part" of his psyche. The beast is also "that part of the mind, the psyche, that watches and reflects on consciousness." It suggests and symbolizes the subconscious awareness of his own egotism and insensitivity that will finally spring on him with the full force of nature's revenge, when the woman he failed to marry has died.

A most perceptive analysis that brings out the subtle shades of moral ambiguity and psychological finesse in one of James's finest stories. The relation between the artist-observer and the image of the beast in the jungle is penetratingly explored. The author acknowledges her indebtedness to Gaston Bachelard's phenomenology of the literary image and especially to James Hillman's research into dream imagery in his book *The Dream and the Underworld* (1979).

AUTHOR INDEX

Numbers refer to entries in the bibliography.
Stars (*) indicate good or excellent criticism.

SUBJECT INDEX

Specific archetypes have been indexed, though of many key words only the most important occurrences are given. General Jungian notions recurring throughout the bibliography, such as individuation, transformation, wholeness, and collective unconscious, have not been indexed.

Numbers refer to entries in the bibliography.

Jos van Meurs is a Dutchman, born in Indonesia and educated in the Netherlands. He studied English in the University of Amsterdam and is Senior Lecturer in English and American literature in the University of Groningen. Communications will reach him through the English Department, Faculty of Letters, University of Groningen, The Netherlands.